W9-BCZ-371

The Government and
Politics of the PRC

In memory of Ivan D. London

The Government and Politics of the PRC: A Time of Transition

Jürgen Domes

Westview Press / Boulder and London

Wingate College Library

The paper used in this publication meets the minimum requirements of the American National Standard for Permanence of Paper for Printed Library Materials Z39.48-1984.

All rights reserved. No part of this publication may be reproduced or transmitted in any form or by any means, electronic or mechanical, including photocopy, recording, or any information storage and retrieval system, without permission in writing from the publisher.

Copyright © 1985 by Westview Press, Inc.

Published in 1985 in the United States of America by Westview Press, Inc., 5500 Central Avenue, Boulder, Colorado 80301; Frederick A. Praeger, Publisher

Library of Congress Cataloging in Publication Data
Domes, Jürgen.
    The government and politics of the PRC.
    Bibliography: p.
    Includes index.
    1. China—Politics and government—1949–
I. Title.
DS777.75.D66 1985   951.05   84-29939
ISBN 0-86531-565-5
ISBN 0-86531-566-3 (pbk.)

Printed and bound in the United States of America

10   9   8   7   6   5   4   3   2

"Chairman Hua is worthy of being called Chairman Mao's good student and successor, the wise leader of our Party and people, and the brilliant supreme commander of our army."

> —Yeh Chien-ying, in his report on the revision of the CCP Party statute at the Eleventh Party Congress, August 13, 1977

"During the last four years, comrade Hua Kuo-feng has also done some successful work, but it is extremely clear that he lacks the political and organizational ability to be the chairman of the Party. That he should never have been appointed chairman of the Military Commission, everybody knows."

> —Decision of the Politburo of the CCP, December 5, 1980

Contents

Tables and Figures

Figures

Preface

This book tries to look at China as one country among many, singular in a number of ways but also with many similarities to others. It is inhabited by a people that is as special as any other people in the world, but one that shares, too, with all other peoples the same joys and the same pains, elated and hurt by the same happiness and the same tribulations.

The political development of China is an international concern, and the study of Chinese politics is an international endeavor. This study has, therefore, immensely profited from a constant exchange of opinions with a considerable number of China scholars in many different countries. For encouragement, critical comments, disputes, and, last but by no means least, friendship and personal kindness over many years, I particularly wish to thank Marie-Claire Bergère, Lucien Bianco, Chang Chen-pang, Ch'en Ting-chung, Lowell Dittmer, Jean-Luc Domenach, June Teufel Dreyer, Dennis Duncanson, Fan Chih-yüan, Roland Felber, B. William Frolic, Thomas Gold, Merle Goldman, David S.G. Goodman, Harry Harding, Harold Hinton, Ellis Joffe, Gottfried-Karl Kindermann, Willy Kraus, P. Ladislao La Dany, Li T'ien-min, James T. Meyers, Ramon Myers, Jan Prybyla, Lucian W. Pye, Robert Scalapino, Benjamin Schwartz, Richard Thornton, Horst F. Vetter, Ezra Vogel, and Lynn White.

In the Research Unit on Chinese and East Asian Politics of the Saar University, Barbara Krug has provided me with important sources on economics. Susanne Stroop has read the manuscript, prepared many of the suggested readings, and helped with her inquisitiveness. For the latter part of the study, support was rendered by Eberhard Sandschneider, who made many linguistic suggestions and whose contributions showed a high degree of dedication. Ch'in Ching-ying helped find many source materials and asked questions that helped clarify several points. Maria-Theresia Trabandt not only typed the whole manuscript with great dedication and care, but she virtually screened it, coming up with a number of very valuable opinions and suggestions. While expressing my gratitude to these people, I also wish to say that I am proud to work with such excellent and pleasant people.

At Westview Press, Barbara Ellington shepherded the manuscript in its formative stages; I appreciate her diligence and dedication. Megan L. Schoeck was confronted with the hideous task of editing a manuscript by an author whose English is of a very moderate standard at best. She solved this task with understanding, empathy, and cheerfulness.

My wife, Marie-Luise Näth, endured the time of writing with great patience, and she also, working in the same profession, helped with a large number of suggestions.

To all of these people, I again express my deep gratitude. It goes without saying that I alone am responsible for this study and in particular for its shortcomings and mistakes.

The book is dedicated to the memory of Ivan D. London, professor of political psychology at Brooklyn College, New York. For almost nineteen years, he and his wife, Miriam, with great methodological care and an admirable research spirit, attempted to understand the basic realities of life in China under Communist rule by interviewing refugees and Chinese living abroad. For a long time, many China scholars neglected their findings, but since 1977, the results of Ivan London's research have been fully corroborated by the official media of the Chinese Communist Party. What some of us already knew has become obvious: he was right, and his many critics among the eulogizers of Chinese communism were wrong. He died on April 12, 1983, long before he could finish his great contributions to the study of China. My grief is mellowed only by my pride in having known him and in having been accepted by him as a colleague. I hope that had he lived, he would not have been too annoyed by this study.

Jürgen Domes

A Note on Romanization

All systems of romanization for the Chinese language are anything but ideal. In this book, except for a few geographic names, the romanization system of Wade and Giles is used to transcribe Chinese names and terms. Until January 1979, this system was generally used in Western academic works on China. Since then, many studies have changed to the *Han-yü p'in-yin* (Hanyu pinyin) system, which was officially introduced by the authorities of the People's Republic of China. I did not use this system, because I consider it even less ideal than that of Wade and Giles. For the benefit of readers more used to the *Han-yü p'in-yin* system, however, those spellings are provided in the end matter of this book.

Introduction

Home to almost 22 percent of mankind in 1982,[1] China is the most populated country on earth, and it is third largest in territory, ranking behind only the Soviet Union and Canada. The country's continental dimensions alone should give it the status of a major world power. When Mao Tse-tung, chairman of the Chinese Communist Party (CCP), proclaimed victory in the civil war against his Nationalist opponents and the establishment of the People's Republic of China (PRC) on October 1, 1949, the country entered a new period in its history of 3,500 to 4,000 years—an era in which its fate was to be decided by an elite dedicated to the implementation of Marxist-Leninist philosophical and political prescriptions.

These prescriptions include the development of a modern socialist great power, the establishment of a socialist society first and a Communist society later, as well as the promotion of "world revolution," which means the spreading of Marxist-Leninist oriented political systems everywhere on earth. Ideological zeal, therefore, should add to the quantitative potential of China to give it world power status. And indeed, the size of the country and the enormous social and political experiments that seem to have been unfolding there since 1949 have caught the imagination of innumerable observers all over the world, particularly in countries with developed industrial mass societies like the United States, Japan, and the nations of Western Europe.

Yet the PRC, with the largest population and the third largest territory, ranked only 139 out of 175 countries in 1982 when it came to per capita gross national product (GNP). This discrepancy between size and economic achievement determines the political position of the PRC in the world: It is indeed the largest underdeveloped country, a nation that must be reckoned with in international politics, but for the time being it is at most a major regional power in East Asia. Although it may become one of the most important powers in the world sometime

1

in the future, its political and strategic capabilities today are rather limited.

With the death of Mao Tse-tung on September 9, 1976, and the ensuing purge of the cultural revolutionary radical left of the CCP in a military coup d'etat on October 6 of the same year, politics in the PRC moved into a new stage, into a time of transition. This book attempts to provide an introduction to the political system of the PRC during this time of transition. To put the discussion of political developments since 1975, the last year of the era of Mao Tse-tung, into context and perspective,[2] I begin with a brief description of the basic geographic, economic, and social conditions that influence political decision making, including a very general survey of the history of China. Then, the institutional framework in which Chinese politics operate today is introduced, with special emphasis on the historical development of the relevant institutions and their political interactions. Given this background, I then present a more detailed account of political developments between 1975 and 1983 and attempt to discuss the fate of the Chinese economy since 1975, the changes occurring in the Chinese society, as well as the role of the PRC in world affairs after the death of Mao.

In order to understand the recent past of and the present situation in China, and in order to be able to develop tentative projections for the future of that country's political system, we have to ask a number of questions.

- How does the geographic setting in which the political system of the PRC operates present itself?
- What are the basic economic conditions of the country, how have they developed since 1949, and how can the economic performance under Marxist-Leninist leadership be evaluated?
- Which are the basic structures of the Chinese society, and what changes have taken place in the cities and villages of China under CCP rule?
- How does the institutional framework in which political decision making is conducted present itself? In particular, how did and how do the relations between the CCP organization, the administrative machine, and the armed forces function?
- What are the major loci of decision making, and what are the patterns of political group formation?
- How have such patterns developed since 1975 and with what results?
- Are there clearly recognizable periods into which the development of Chinese politics since the mid-1970s can be divided?

- What is the current lineup of forces within the CCP leadership, and which type of group formation does it represent?
- Where does the PRC go from here, i.e., what are the future perspectives of the political system in terms of alternative projections?
- Can the experience of China since the death of Mao provide clues for a typology of transition in Communist-ruled countries?

But which methods should be used in order to arrive at viable answers to such questions? Since the early 1960s, the study of Chinese politics has suffered, not so much from a lack of data and source materials as people who are not working in this field usually assume, but from faulty analysis and interpretation. When the official Chinese news media in 1977 started to reveal the true facts about the political and social realities in the PRC under the leadership of Mao,[3] and also to publish more candid accounts of present developments, a number of Western images of China became suspect.

1. *China, the emerging world power.* According to this image, hundreds of millions of Chinese, motivated and led by competent leaders, were engaging in a tremendous effort to make their country finally rich and strong (*fu-ch'iang*), as Chinese statesmen had previously done in the nineteenth century. In order to understand this country better, and to prepare for cooperation with this awakening world power, westerners were urged to listen to the self-presentation of "the Chinese"—but that meant the ruling elite, not the people.
2. *China, the populist microcosm.* In this image, a new model of popular participation in political decisions was in the making. Liberated from the shackles of social repression, the common people had a share in deciding their own fate, and that gave them, unlike "the masses" in most developing countries, a fervent hope, a new vista of life.
3. *China, the socialist system that works.* According to this image, a socialist society had developed that was not blurred by the weaknesses of other socialist systems, in particular that of the USSR. The cadres were dedicated and incorruptible, political dissidents were treated with leniency and "reeducated" rather than physically liquidated. The bureaucracy was supervised by the masses, and the elite did not enjoy special privileges.
4. *China, the development model.* According to this image, measures had been taken that could serve as a shining example for other developing countries, because these measures had enabled the PRC to solve "the problem of feeding the people, the problem of

employment, the problem of basic education for all, the problem of sufficient health services and hygiene."[4]

Today, these four images of China have been proved to be incorrect, even though most of the people who promoted them were sincere in their endeavors.

Although these people have been forced into reappraising their interpretations by the avalanche of information that has come out of China since 1977, another group of social scientists—in fact, a slight majority of China scholars in the United States and a considerable number in Europe and Japan—has not had to do so.[5] In general, these social scientists, whose interpretations of China have been more often right than wrong, have abided by at least five ground rules.

1. They use, in a comprehensive manner, the official CCP media as their sources, but they broaden the base of their data by interviews with refugees from the PRC, with overseas Chinese visitors to the PRC, and people other than officials inside China (where and whenever this is possible) and by taking into account information from Hongkong and T'aiwan, which has very often been proved to be accurate.
2. When working with official CCP sources, they use them consistently and constantly compare their contents over long periods of time.
3. In their work with official sources, they not only test their reliability and try to filter out their factual contents, but they also attempt to decode the messages of political communication that these sources often contain. This means that they obey the rules of textual criticism developed more than 150 years ago.
4. They combine such textual criticism with detailed knowledge of personnel and the fact that even ceremonial texts and name lists may have political significance.
5. They constantly keep a critical distance from the object of their studies. Hence, although they may "love China," they are aware of the fact that professionally, China specialists must be detached scholars.

In the last issue of his bulletin *China News Analysis*, which has presented some of the most reliable information about the PRC for almost thirty years, the dean of the observers of Chinese politics, Father Ladislao La Dany, summed up his experiences in working with official CCP sources in "ten commandments," which are quoted here because they explain the analytical approach better than anything else.

1. Remember that no one living in a free society ever has a full understanding of life in a regimented society.
2. Look at China through Chinese glasses, not through foreign glasses, not therefore trying to sort out Chinese events in terms of our own problems.
3. Learn something about other communist countries and
4. about the basic tenets of Marxism.
5. Keep in mind that words and terms have not the same meaning in a Marxist society and elsewhere.
6. Keep your common sense: the Chinese may be characteristically Chinese, but they are human beings, with the normal reactions of human beings.
7. Persons are not less but probably more important than issues. A group may adopt the programme of those who oppose them, in order to retain power. . . .
8. Do not believe that you know all the answers. China poses more questions than it provides answers.
9. Do not lose your sense of humour. A regimented press is too serious to be taken very seriously.
10. Above all, read the small print.[6]

Although I personally would somewhat qualify the seventh point of La Dany's "commandments"—issues should be taken very seriously, too, in my view—I have attempted to follow his directives as well as the five ground rules for social scientists in this book.

This work draws upon a number of sources, which have to be listed in a clear-cut priority catalog of their validity, a scale of importance that can be presented here as the result of more than twenty years of "China-watching."

1. Most important are internal CCP documents, which are often published in T'aiwan or Hongkong but are not regularly available and, hence, cannot offer a complete picture.
2. Provincial radio broadcasts, which are monitored outside the PRC, and reports from the provincial CCP press.
3. The central media, mainly the newspapers *Jen-min jih-pao* (People's daily [*JMJP*]), *Kuang-ming jih-pao* (The Light daily [*KMJP*]), *Chieh-fang-chün pao* (Liberation Army daily [*CFCP*])—which, however, is not very often available—and *Kung-jen jih-pao* (Workers' daily [*KJJP*]); the two CCP theoretical monthlies, *Hung-ch'i* (Red flag [*HC*]) and *Liao-wang* (Outlook [*LW*]); a number of other journals; and the broadcasts of the Central People's Broadcasting Station in Peking.

4. Interviews with refugees from the PRC.
5. Reports and journals put out by the PRC authorities in foreign languages.
6. Reports from foreign news media correspondents in Peking.
7. Reports from foreign travelers to China.
8. Reports from some—though not all—Western embassies in Peking.[7]

When studying the PRC, the observer in general and the social scientist in particular should at every moment be aware of the fact that the political system of that country is in many respects entirely different from that which we find in countries with a pluralistic representative system. In the PRC, there exists a totalistic single-party system of Communist persuasion. This type of a political system is characterized by the facts that

1. the Marxist-Leninist cadre- and career-party members believe they are an elite that is promoting a predestined course of history and, therefore, claim a political monopoly;
2. the Party claims this monopoly as the vanguard of the proletariat, and its rule is consequently defined as being a "dictatorship of the proletariat";
3. legal political interest articulation develops only within the elite and not between different competing elites;
4. political decision making thus evolves in a process of *intra*elite rather than *inter*elite conflict;
5. the government is organized according to the principle of concentration rather than of separation of the powers;
6. however, elements of power differentiation and power diversification *may* develop from the competition among intra-Party groups and functional subsystems, but this situation is not the same as pluralism in democratic societies.

How does such a political system fare, and how does it work in a time of transition? I shall try to present some very tentative and initial answers to these questions, answers that may or may not stand the test of what historians will have to say about the PRC a number of decades from now.

PART 1

The Material and Historical Framework

CHAPTER 1

The Geographical Setting

Area and Boundaries

With an area of approximately 3,691,430 square miles, the PRC is not only the third largest country in the world, it is larger than the smallest of the continents, Australia; only insignificantly smaller than Europe in geographic terms (i.e., from the Atlantic Ocean to the Ural Mountains); and about 2.1 percent larger than the United States. A compact land mass, the PRC extends almost 2,500 miles from north to south and almost 3,000 miles from east to west.[1]

Most of the country is situated in the zone of moderate climate, yet it stretches from the southeastern fringe of the Siberian frost region into the tropics. Hence, the average temperatures vary between 20°–25°C in southern China and −5°–0°C in the high Northeast. Differences in climate are greater during the winter than during the summer. In January, the average temperature ranges from 10°–15°C on the island of Hainan in the south to 30° below zero in the northernmost province of Heilungkiang, a difference of more than 40 degrees. In July, however, average temperatures stand at 30°C in the south and 10°C in the northeast, a difference of only 20 degrees.

Precipitation shows even a larger variance than temperature. In the southeastern provinces of Kuangtung and Fukien, the average annual precipitation is 60–120 inches, but the desert areas of Ninghsia, western Kansu, and Sinkiang in the northwest receive only about 2 inches of rainfall per year.

Large parts of the country are mountainous: 68 percent of the territory is higher than 3,300 feet, 18 percent reaches from 1,650 to 3,300 feet, and only 14 percent lies lower than 1,650 feet. The PRC shares with Nepal the highest mountain on earth, Chomolungma (Mt. Everest), which has an altitude of 29,028 feet. The second lowest region on earth, the Turfan Depression in Sinkiang at 928 feet below sea level, is also a part of China. There are nine mountains higher than 19,500 feet and seventeen between 6,500 and 19,500 feet.

However, barely one-third of this vast land can be used for agriculture or forestry. Pastures occupy about 10 percent of the area and forests, approximately 12 to 13 percent, most of them in Northeast China—the former Manchuria. In 1982, agriculturally cultivated land comprised almost 240 million acres, or 10.1 percent of the whole territory.[2] New cultivation remains limited to pastureland of average to poor quality, and the cultivation of new arable land would infringe upon animal husbandry. Nevertheless, the PRC newly cultivated 42.7 million acres of land during the twenty-five years from 1957 to 1982. In the same period, however, almost 72.4 million acres were lost to settlements, transport establishments, and—last but not least—erosion for a net loss of 29.7 million acres.[3] That means that between 1957 and 1982, the arable land per capita decreased from 0.42 acres to less than 0.24 acres. In other words, the PRC has to feed almost 22 percent of the world's population from barely 7 percent of the world's arable land.

A vast land empire, the PRC borders eleven countries: North Korea, the USSR, Outer Mongolia, Afghanistan (only 46.6 miles), Pakistan, India, Bhutan, Nepal, Burma, Laos, and Vietnam. Yet only the boundaries with Afghanistan, Pakistan, Nepal, Burma, and Outer Mongolia are guaranteed by treaties that China recognizes as valid. Territorial claims and border conflicts are a burden on the PRC's relations with the USSR, India, Vietnam, and because China claims islands and a shelf in the South China Sea, there are similar problems with the Philippines and Malaysia, too. Furthermore, the island of T'aiwan, the P'enghu (Pescadores) Archipelago, the island groups of Chinmen (Quemoy), Matsu, Tungyin, Wuchiu, Tungsha (Pratas), and parts of Nansha (Spratlys) are controlled by the Chinese Nationalist government in T'aipei, which has, until now, no more renounced its claim of being the "only legitimate government of China" than the government of the PRC has given up its goal to "liberate T'aiwan" with the use of military force. Since 1950, the PRC has been involved in border wars six times: with Nationalist China in the T'aiwan Strait (1954, 1958), with India (1959, 1962), with the USSR (1969), and with Vietnam (1979).

Economic Regions

Within China's borders, the population and the economic regions are unequally distributed. If one draws a line from the easternmost tip of Outer Mongolia to the China-Burma-Laos triangle, approximately 78 percent of the inhabitants of the PRC would live east of that line, on 32 percent of the territory. All but one of the more important economic regions—the province of Ssuch'uan with more than 100 million people and the Red Basin of Ch'engtu, a very rich agricultural region—are also situated east of the line. The vast wheat-growing areas of the Northern Chinese Plain are in this area, as are the extremely fertile rice- and vegetable-growing regions of Chekiang Province and of the lower Yangtzu Valley up to Wuhan. In this eastern third of the country, there are also the fertile basins of central Hunan, central Hupei, and the Pearl River Delta around the South China metropolis of Canton. With the possible exception of the Northern Chinese Plain in dry years, these regions have been—for more than 2,000 years—and still are the agricultural surplus areas of China.

Centers of heavy industry, in particular of coal mining and steel production, are in the southern portion of Northeast China (the gigantic Anshan-Fushun-Penhsi combine), Inner Mongolia (the steel complex of Paot'ou), Wuhan, Peking, Chungking, and, to a lesser extent, Ch'angsha (the Hsiangt'an steel mill), Shanghai, and Nanking (the Moanshan steel mill). Machine building and most of the light and consumer goods industries are concentrated in Shanghai, Canton, T'ienchin, Ch'ingtao, and Hangchou, to which have been added, since 1949, the new western Chinese industrial centers of Sian and Lanchou.

Oilfields have been developed almost entirely since the establishment of the PRC, and they are mainly in the northern and northwestern regions: Tach'ing in Heilungkiang, Yümen in Kansu, the Tsaidam Basin in Ch'inghai, and Karamai in northwestern Sinkiang, rather close to the Soviet border. Since 1972, new oilfields have been established at Nanchung in Ssuch'uan (on the fringe of the Red Basin) and at Shengli, close to the Shantung coastline. Offshore drilling along the North and East China coasts appears promising.

Natural Resources

The PRC can indeed qualify as being rather rich in natural resources. The country's deposits of coal, iron ore, and most nonferrous metals are the largest on earth. Coal can be found mainly in Northeast China (the former Manchuria) and in the provinces of Shansi, Shensi, Inner Mongolia, Hopei, Shantung, Ssuch'uan, Kueichou, and Yünnan. There are also a number of deposits, but much smaller and of poorer quality, in some areas of Central-South China.

Iron ore is also concentrated in the Northeast where so far, up to two-thirds of the PRC's steel production has occurred. But there are also large amounts of iron ore deposits in Hopei, Inner Mongolia, the Central mountain areas, and on the island of Hainan. In South China, there are huge deposits of tin (mostly in Kiangsi, Hunan, Kuangtung, and Kuangsi). Tungsten is mainly found in Kiangsi, Hunan, Sinkiang, and many areas of southwestern China, where there are also large amounts of copper. Hunan, Kuangtung, and Yünnan have antimony; Kuangsi and Kuangtung, lead, zinc, and mercury. In Sinkiang, one finds large deposits of uranium and also of most major nonferrous metals. Another of China's assets is an abounding wealth of waterpower, particularly in the southern and southwestern parts of the country.

However, the use of all these natural resources is hampered by insufficient transport and communication lines. Related centers of steel production have been developed close to the most important coal and iron ore mines—as in southern Manchuria, Hopei, and Inner Mongolia— but most other raw materials for the industry must be transported over vast distances. China has, indeed, a large number of rivers, among which the longest are the Yangtzu (3,437 miles); the Huanghe, or Yellow River (2,904 miles); the Amur, or Heilungkiang (2,345 miles inside the PRC); and the Chukiang or Pearl River (1,217 miles). But of these, only the Yangtzu from Chungking to the East China Sea, the Chukiang up to Canton, and parts of the Heilungkiang are navigable for oceangoing vessels. Most of the other rivers descend too steeply or, on the plains, are too shallow for major navigation. Domestic transport, therefore, has to rely on railroads and highways, and both of these types of communication lines are still extremely underdeveloped.[4] Hence, China's potential to become a modern industrial power is very promising, but the realization of this potential appears to be difficult and extremely costly and will most probably come about fully only after a long period of time.

Population

In terms of national development, the population of the PRC may be more of a liability than an asset. There are still no entirely reliable data on the number of Chinese. The overall result of the last census— conducted with a great deal of manpower support from United Nations agencies and with the help of quite sophisticated data processing facilities—was a population figure of 1,008,175,288 as of midnight, June 30, 1982. Earlier, there had been a not very reliable census in 1953, which had resulted in a figure of 582.6 million inhabitants. The annual population growth rate from 1957—when the official figure of 646.5 million was given—until 1978 has been estimated at 2 percent annually by a number of Western observers.

The PRC leadership itself did not publish any population figures until 1979, i.e., for twenty-two years, but since then, the following official figures have been given—always for the end of the respective year:

1978	958.09 million
1979	970.92 million, a growth of 1.34 percent
1980	982.60 million, a growth of 1.20 percent
1981	997.36 million, a growth of 1.50 percent

If the official figures for 1980 and 1981 are correct, they would mean a growth rate of 1,552 people per hour, almost 26 per minute, which would be equivalent to one person every 2.3 seconds.

Since 1978, the CCP leadership has engaged in a large-scale campaign to promote family planning and birth control, in the course of which the number of children for each family was first limited to two and then, in 1981, to one. Strict controls, the withholding of welfare payments, forced sterilization, and even severe fines have been utilized in order to push this campaign. It appears to have been quite successful in the cities, but in the villages, where about four-fifths of the people live, successes so far have been very limited.

Generally, it is advisable to be extremely cautious with all officially published data from the PRC. When they are used in this book, it is with such caution—and, in fact, only to indicate trends. The figure given as the result of the 1982 census—more detailed results of which will be published piecemeal until 1985—would set the population of the PRC at 21.96 percent of that of the whole world. China's share of the world's population would, then, have been greatly reduced from 300 years ago, when it stood at about one-third to 35 percent. Nevertheless, the country has experienced a population explosion since the early 1950s, which renders all developmental efforts rather difficult. If one follows the official data, the population of the PRC grew from 1953 to 1982 by more than 425 million, or 73.05 percent—i.e., by almost three-quarters.

In 1982, according to officially published data, the population was distributed over the twenty-nine administrative units and the six regions of China as shown in Table 1.1. According to the same data, 48.65 percent of the people live in what the Chinese usually call "the North" (Pei-fang), and 51.35 percent in "the South" (Nan-fang). Coastal provinces contain 40.21 percent of the people; inland provinces, 59.79 percent.

About 86 percent of all inhabitants of the PRC live in villages or small country towns with fewer than 20,000 people; the remaining 14 percent live in urban settlements with more than 20,000 people, more than half of whom—or approximately 8 percent—live in cities with more than 500,000 inhabitants. In 1979, Shanghai, as an administrative unit, had 11.4 million inhabitants (Shanghai proper, about 6–6.5 million); Peking, as an administrative unit, almost 8.8 million (Peking proper, between 4 and 4.5 million); and T'ienchin, as an administrative unit,

Table 1.1. Population of administrative units of the PRC, 1982
(in millions)[5]

Administrative Unit	Population	Administrative Unit	Population
Northeast China (Tungpei)	90.94	Central-South China (Chung-nan)	271.88
Heilungkiang	32.66	Honan	74.42
Kirin	22.56	Hupei	47.80
Liaoning	35.72	Hunan	54.01
		Kuangtung	59.23
North China (Huapei)	114.56	Kuangsi	36.42
Hopei	53.01	Northwest China (Hsipei)	69.35
Shansi	25.29		
Inner Mongolia	19.27	Shensi	28.90
Peking	9.23	Ninghsia	3.90
T'ienchin	7.76	Kansu	19.57
		Ch'inghai	3.90
East China (Huatung)	294.40	Sinkiang	13.08
Shantung	74.42	Southwest China (Hsinan)	162.70
Kiangsu	60.52		
Chekiang	38.88	Ssuch'uan	99.71
Anhui	49.67	Kueichou	28.55
Kiangsi	33.18	Yünnan	32.55
Fukien	25.87	Tibet	1.89
Shanghai	11.86		

over 7.5 million (T'ienchin proper, 4 million). Other cities with more than 1 million inhabitants are Chungking, Shenyang, Wuhan, Canton, Harbin, Nanking, Ch'engtu, Talien, Sian, Ch'ingtao, T'aiyüan, Fushun, Ch'angch'un, Chengchou, and Lanchou.

The age structure differs widely from that in most developed industrial societies. Although we do not have detailed official figures, it appears reasonable to assume that 35 percent of all inhabitants of the PRC are below fifteen years of age; another 30 percent between fifteen and thirty; about 28–30 percent or so, between thirty and sixty; and between 5 and 6 percent, older than sixty.

Such figures indicate a heavy stress on the educational system, and this stress is further aggravated by the fact that during the Great Proletarian Cultural Revolution, beginning in the summer of 1966, elementary schools were closed for at least one year; secondary schools, for three to four years; and the institutions of higher learning, for periods ranging from five to nine years. After 1976, secondary schools, and even more so the colleges and universities, were therefore jammed with applicants who had had their education delayed, while students who had just graduated from the lower levels pressured for entrance, too. In 1980, about 11 million applicants registered for the preliminary examinations, of whom 3.3 million qualified for the final college entrance examination. That examination was successfully passed only by 285,000, or 8.64 percent—2.6 percent of those who had originally registered.[6] In 1981 and 1982, this figure seems to have increased to about 7 percent of the original registrants.

After the Cultural Revolution, the period for elementary schooling was set at five years, to be followed by two years each for junior and senior secondary schools. Since 1981, however, the time has been extended to six years for elementary and three years each for junior and senior secondary schooling in most of the administrative units of the PRC. According to official data released in 1982, there were supposed to be 143.33 million pupils in the elementary schools, or between 90 and 95 percent of the relevant age bracket.[7] Yet this figure provokes skepticism because, in late 1982, the plan projection for 1985 was set at only 130 million pupils in the elementary schools, which would mean about 77 percent of the relevant age bracket.[8] One may come closer to reality if one assumes that by 1983, about 75 percent of all elementary-school-age children were really going to school.

Skepticism should also be applied to the figure of 60.24 million students in the secondary and vocational schools given in 1980, because the plan figures for 1985, which were revealed in 1982 (a total of 4.2 million for the senior branches of both types of schools per year), would only allow an overall figure of about 50 million, or 30–35 percent of that age bracket—and, indeed, a figure of 50.15 million was given for 1983. The information that there were 1,279,500 students in colleges and universities in the academic year of 1982/1983[9] appears to be reliable, but that number would be only about 0.5 percent of the relevant age bracket, too small for a developing country.

In 1949, about 75 percent of the populace was illiterate. In 1982, this figure was down to 34 percent, a decrease of 54.6 percent, which constitutes a remarkable developmental achievement.[10] The most pressing shortages of qualified manpower are in the fields of technicians and technological and natural science personnel. Here, the PRC is short millions of trained people. The current leadership is obviously aware of this problem and has made considerable efforts to alleviate it, but it will take at least two more decades before the country may have enough qualified personnel for the huge tasks of modernizing the economy and the society.

The ground is even more unsafe in regard to religion in the PRC. Not only are there no reliable official data—because the CCP leadership, with its principally antireligious ideology, does not offer them—but religion has traditionally not played a very important part in Chinese life.

The overwhelming majority of the Chinese pay occasional reverence to different noninstitutionalized forms of nature and ancestral worship. Taoism and Buddhism are regarded by many Chinese as easily compatible with these older forms of worship. Before 1949, there were about 2 to 3 million Taoist and approximately 5 million Buddhist nuns and monks in China. Since the establishment of the PRC, and particularly during the Cultural Revolution, these people have been severely persecuted. Most of their temples have been closed and their scriptures outlawed. Since 1978, however, a number of temples and monasteries, especially in areas visited by foreign tourists, have been reopened, and there are some indications that Taoist and Buddhist religious activities are intensifying to some degree.

Islam was the largest of the revelational world religions in China before 1949, when there were between 50 million and 65 million Muslims, most of them living in Kansu, Ch'inghai, Ninghsia, and the Turanian areas of Sinkiang. In this case, too, there were severe persecutions immediately after the takeover by the CCP, yet the Party has been unable to destroy Islam, particularly in Sinkiang. When the first slight modifications in the CCP's policies toward the Muslims were indicated during the winter of 1979/1980, a very strong wave of identification with the old religion occurred among the Turanian people, for whom Islam has highly nationalist overtones.

Before 1949, the Christian churches rallied about 3.5 million Catholics and about 600,000 Protestants. Although exposed to even more thoroughgoing persecution than the Muslims, most Christian communities continued to exist underground, and the attitude of the CCP toward the Christian religious organizations has also been cautiously loosened since 1978. About 250–300 churches of different Christian denominations have been reopened; a limited number of Bibles can be published and sold; and in many cities, Christian denominations, the leaders of which cooperate with the CCP, can hold public services again. It seems that the Christian churches, in particular the Catholic church, not only survived almost thirty years of severe persecution but even added several millions to their flocks during the era of suppression, which, in a somewhat more sophisticated manner, still continues.

These recent developments, however, do not—and will not—change the fact that Islam and Christianity only appeal to a minority, less than 6–8 percent, of the population. They have never been a decisive factor in Chinese society.

National Minorities

If only quantities are considered and the country looked at as a whole, the same situation holds true in regard to China's national minorities. Although the PRC is officially defined as a multinational state, between 92 and 94 percent of the people regard themselves as Han, or Chinese, in the narrower ethnic sense. Only 6–8 percent belong to a minority group, and most of them live in Northeast, Northwest, and Southwest China.[11] Articles 112–122 of the constitution of the PRC, which was promulgated on December 4, 1982,[12] guarantee cultural autonomy to and the establishment of autonomous administrative units for the national minorities, of which fifty-four are officially recognized. The most important national minorities are

- the Thai group, to which the almost completely Sinicized Chuang as well as the Thai, Miao, and Yao belong
- the Tibetans and some other Tibeto-Burmese tribes
- the Turanians, which comprise the Uighur, Kazakh, Uzbek, Tatar, Turkmen, and Kirghiz nations
- the Mongols
- the Chinese Muslim group, which is called the Hui people
- the ethnically Iranian Tadzhiks
- the Manchus and Koreans in Northeast China

The autonomy of these national minorities is in fact limited to bilingual schooling in Chinese and the particular minority language; to the promotion of folklore, especially for purposes of tourism; and to bilingual street signs and posters in minority areas. At the same time, a continuous process of penetration and assimilation has developed, which, since the mid-1950s, has been consistently promoted by the CCP through systematic Han settlement in the minority areas.

The proportion of Uighurs in the population of Sinkiang has thus dropped from 70 percent in 1949 to barely 50 percent today, and that of the Kazakhs, Uzbeks, Tatars, Kirghizs, Turkmens, Tadzhiks, and Mongols combined has dropped from 15 to 10 percent, while the Han proportion has more than doubled from 15 to over 40 percent. In Inner Mongolia today, only 5–8 percent of the people are Mongols, but almost 90 percent are Han. Even in Tibet, the proportion of Han, who were virtually nonexistent there in 1949, has increased to more than 20 percent.

Yet, in spite of this Han penetration of the minority areas, problems for the leadership may develop in the future. Many Tibetans, in particular, have not yet resigned themselves to Chinese colonial rule. When a delegation sent by the Dalai Lama—the spiritual head of the Tibetans who lives in exile in India—visited Tibet in June 1980, mass demonstrations of loyalty to the Dalai Lama and opposition to Chinese rule occurred in the capital, Lhasa.

Since late 1979, the effects of the worldwide Islamic renaissance, combined with a gradually rising influence of Pan-Turanian ideas, have begun to make themselves felt in Sinkiang, and occasionally they have resulted in explosive situations. In September 1980, for instance, one could find, on the streets of Ürümchi and Turfan, handwritten slogans saying Long live the independence of East Turkestan! or This is not Sinkiang, it's Uighuristan![13]

Such indications of increasing unrest among the minorities, however, do not mean that China may fall apart. For such a development, the 92–94 percent Han population is just too compact a block. The cultural unity of the Han is based on a strong historical continuity; hence history also has to be regarded as a very important part of the framework for politics in China.

CHAPTER 2

The Historical Background

Origins of the Han

Official Chinese texts of any political persuasion—such as textbooks, public relation handouts, and government-sponsored historical pamphlets—tend to speak about China as a country with "5,000 years of history." In light of modern historical research, however, this statement appears to be an exaggeration. Until now, no written sources on the history of China have been found that date back later than about 1300 B.C., and the first traces of any meaningful political organization that later developed into a unit of statelike proportions seem to stem from the period between 1700 and 1500 B.C. The history of China thus ranges over somewhat more than 3,500 years—or at the most, 3,800 to 4,000 years—with approximately 3,300 years of written documentation. But where did the people who are now usually called the Han come from?[14]

Within the regions that are now populated by the Han, at least eight primitive cultures developed in prehistoric times. By migration, assimilation, and conquest, these cultures contributed elements to the organized village-type societies of the Yang-shao and Lung-shan cultures, which occupied what is now Central China and parts of the lower Huanghe Basin between about 2500 and 2000 B.C. Yet it took centuries more of migrations and invasions, together with the appearance of bronze as the major material for weapons and ornaments, until the first small states—or rather village federations—were established by the people who settled in the Huanghe area between 1800 and 1500 B.C. These people may be considered as the ancestors of the Han of today.

A product of amalgamation rather than a tribe of distinct ethnic origin, these people combined proto-Mongoloid, Mongoloid, and probably Tibeto-Burmese and Ural-Altaic elements. From the outset, their identity was more cultural than racial. They developed definite forms of style and buildings and, above all, sophisticated systems of irrigation that demanded a political organization larger than that of the individual village. Such a political organization is first reliably documented for the state of Shang, which lasted from about 1500 to about 1050 B.C. It had military and administrative networks that were bound to the ruler by presents of land and human subjects as remuneration for services rendered by the army and civilian government, a system of early feudalism. With its center in the central Huanghe Valley, its territory covered the area that is now the province of Honan and parts of Hopei, Shansi, and Shantung. It was here, and during the Shang period, that the ideographic script was developed, and about 3,000 of today's Chinese characters date back to this period.

By about 1028 B.C., however, the state of Chou, originally a feudal fief of the Shang, conquered the Shang area and established a system of "mature feudalism,"[15] with intricate organizational networks that relied on lord-vassal relations. Gradually, the approximately 5 million Shang people merged with the Chou subjects. This merger can be considered the beginning of an advanced state administrative organization, and of a distinctive "Chinese" culture.

China: Nation or Concept?

From 771 B.C. until about 500 B.C., the feudal fiefdoms gradually increased their strength and autonomy in relation to the central ruler, whose powers became more and more ceremonial. As a result of this development, the country split into a number of feudal states, which still had to formally obey the center during the period of Spring and Autumn (*Ch'un-ch'iu*, 771–481 B.C.) but were almost entirely independent during the period of the Warring States (*Chan-kuo*, 480–221 B.C.). The more than 500 years of these two periods were therefore an era of division, but they were also the time when classical Chinese philosophy emerged from the teachings of K'ung-tzu, or Confucius (551–479 B.C.); Lao-tzu (fourth century B.C. according to recent research); Mo-tzu (479–438 B.C.); and Meng K'e, or Mencius (372–289 B.C.).[16] Furthermore, in this era, the Chinese civilization spread along most of the Huanghe, to include Shensi and parts of Kansu; into the Yangtzu Valley; and southward to what is now Hunan, Kuangtung, and parts of Kuangsi. During the fourth century B.C., large parts of Ssuch'uan were included in the realm of Chinese civilization, and when Yünnan and Kueichou followed suit during the fourteenth and fifteenth centuries A.D., the area of Han settlement had almost reached its current scope.

This spread of culture, however, does not mean that an integral "Chinese nation" conquered its realm: What we now call the Chinese, or even the Han, can hardly be considered a nation. There is no common ethnic origin, and there has been, throughout all of Chinese classical history and right into the twentieth century, no consciousness of being a nation among nations.

Although the Central State (*Chung-kuo*)—derived from the central location of the territory under direct administration by the ruler in the Chou period—is one of the names the Chinese have given their realm for more than 3,000 years,[17] it is just one among many names. It is still not the only one today, since both Chinese states, the PRC and the Republic of China (*RoC*) on T'aiwan, use the term "central splendor" (*Chung-hua*) in their official names. The word "China" seems to originate from the first dynasty of the united country, the Ch'in, but it is used only in foreign languages. The Chinese have, over long periods, called themselves after the ruling dynasty. They were—and are now in terms of the dominating cultural group in the country—Han people (*Han-jen*), they were also—and still are as overseas Chinese in Southeast Asia—T'ang people (*T'ang-jen*), and from the seventeenth century right into our century they were, Ch'ing people (*Ch'ing-jen*). It was only about 100 years ago that the name Central State people (*Chung-kuo-jen*) gradually became the most widely used. In the usual Chinese perception, however, this last term indicates a citizen of China regardless of his or her ethnic origin. It is not a term that denominates the member of a nation in the generally accepted sense of the word: determined by the unity of territory, ethnic origin, and language.

Such terminological confusion is the result of the traditional Chinese world view.[18] In this view, there was neither creation nor creator, but there was a determining cosmological principle, the nonpersonified heaven (*T'ien*). The dominating will of heaven was represented on earth by the Son of Heaven (*T'ien-tzu*), which was the title of the Chinese emperor. It was he who carried the Mandate of Heaven (*T'ien-ming*), which, however, could be taken away from him by the Change of Mandate (*Ke-ming*)—still used today as the Chinese word for revolution. In principle, the Mandate of Heaven legitimized the rule of the Son of Heaven over everything under the heaven (*T'ien-hsia*). The term *T'ien-hsia* has a double meaning in Chinese: It can mean the whole earth, but it can also—and did for many centuries—stand for the area under the emperor's control, i.e., for China, not in the sense of a territorial state, but in the sense of a civilization. This civilization was, in the traditional Chinese world view, characterized by culture, refinement, good manners, and behavior according to the ethical standards formulated by traditional Chinese philosophy. The closer one was geographically located to the seat of the emperor, the more one partook of civilization. Hence, *T'ien-hsia* must be considered as a system of concentric circles of declining civilizing intensity: The "barbarians" who lived the furthest

from the emperor—e.g., the people in Europe, Africa, or the Americas—
were the most uncivilized.

But the Chinese realm had a double identification. Besides the moral
idea of the world, the *T'ien-hsia*, there was the effectively organized
territorial state under the emperor, the State (*Kuo*). In principle, *Kuo*
and *T'ien-hsia* could one day become one and the same, but in fact,
they did not. They were rather different expressions of "Chineseness,"
and *T'ien-hsia* was considered to be more substantial than *Kuo*. As
Joseph Levenson has stated:

> There is destruction of *kuo* and destruction of *t'ien-hsia*. Between destruction
> of *kuo* and destruction of *t'ien-hsia* what distinction should be made?
> "Change the surname, alter the style"—this is a description of the de-
> struction of *kuo*. The widespread dominion of benevolence and righteousness
> (*jen* and *i*) decayed into the rule of beast-eat-man, men, leaders eating
> each other—this is a description of the destruction of *t'ien-hsia*. . . . Culture
> and morality, then, the whole world of values, belong to *t'ien-hsia*. If men
> have a stake in *kuo* at all, it is only a political stake. . . . But civilized
> man as man, by the very fiber of his human being, must be committed
> to *t'ien-hsia*. . . . *The civilization, not the nation, has a moral claim on man's
> allegiance.*[19]

Viewed from the *T'ien-hsia* concept, to be "Chinese" is therefore not
a national, and even less so a racial, distinction; it is a civilizing concept.
That means that every foreigner (*Wai-kuo-jen*) is potentially a Chinese.
If one just accepts Chinese civilizing values, and, as a symbol of that
acceptance, speaks and writes Chinese, one can become a Chinese as
well. It appears almost impossible to build a nation on such a concept,
and indeed, loyalty to the state has traditionally been loyalty to the
rulers—as long as they carry the Mandate of Heaven, i.e., as long as
they are considered benevolent and adhering to the spirit of *T'ien-hsia*.
In such a view, China has been—and for many Chinese, may still be
today—a concept of life rather than of a nation. In more than 2,000
years of history as an empire, the country has seen many rulers, many
Kuo, but there has also been a strong social and cultural continuity. We
shall now look briefly at this continuity of *T'ien-hsia* in changing *Kuo*,
but before we do so, it seems appropriate to point out that with *T'ien-
hsia* being the substantial object of loyalty, the idea of a nation in
general, and of nationalism in particular, is alien to China. That idea
was imported from the West in the late nineteenth century, and one
may doubt whether it will really take root.

Historical Cycles and Basic Aspects
of the Traditional Society

Although the mainstream of Chinese ethical and political thought, as it had developed about 550 B.C. and after, emphasized the benevolence of the ruler, rule by example rather than by law, and the relative autonomy of lineages or clans, which were regulated through traditions of behavior, one of the independent feudal states, the state of Ch'in, in the early part of the third century B.C., adopted the ideas of a new philosophical school as official ideology. This was the School of the Legalists (*Fa-chia*), and their ideas were most succinctly condensed by Han Fei (280–233 B.C.). The legalists believed in rule by law, by definite written regulations, which provided for clear—and mostly rather cruel—punishments as well as rewards for negative or positive behavior. Theirs was the idea of a centralized state with a bureaucracy obedient to the ruler, which made the reliance on the loyalty of feudal vassals obsolete.[20]

With such an ideology, King Cheng of Ch'in, about 230 B.C., set out to conquer the other feudal states of China, and he accomplished the unification of the country within nine years. In 221 B.C., he proclaimed himself the First August Supreme Ruler (*Shih huang-ti*). From then until the abdication of the last emperor of the Ch'ing dynasty on February 12, 1912, i.e. for 2,132 years, the title of the emperor of China remained August Supreme Ruler (*Huang-ti*), and this era is usually considered by historians as the time of the Chinese Empire.

Ch'in Cheng, or *Shih huang-ti*, with extreme efficiency but with even more extreme ruthlessness, set out to create a unified state. The feudal fiefdoms were abolished, a centralized administrative organization with a bureaucracy dependent only upon the emperor was established, weights and measurements were unified, and a large standing army was kept in order to defend the state against enemies from within and without. A system of free purchase and sale of land ended the era of feudalism, although some feudal remnants, such as the corvée, continued to exist. But if the usual definition for the phenomenon of feudalism is applied— a system of exchange of fiefdoms and servants for military and administrative services rendered by vassals to the lord—the Chinese society ceased to be a feudal one around 200 B.C.

The Ch'in dynasty was the first in a series of thirty-four dynasties. During the imperial era of 2,132 years, the country was divided for over 600 years, or 31 percent of the time. Table 2.1 gives an overview of the imperial dynasties.

As a rule, a dynasty was established either by the leader of a peasant rebellion from within the country—usually a general or a leading official—or by foreign invaders, who always intruded from the north

Table 2.1.   Dynasties ruling the Chinese Empire, 221 B.C.-A.D. 1912

Dynasty or Historical Period	Dates	Capital	Origin
Ch'in	221-206 B.C.	Hsienyang (near Hsian)	Chinese
Western Han	206 B.C.-A.D. 8	Ch'angan (Hsian)	Chinese
Hsin	A.D. 9-25	Ch'angan	Chinese
Eastern Han	25-220	Loyang	Chinese
Three Kingdoms (San kuo) Shu, Wei, and Wu	220-265	Loyang, Ch'engtu, Nanking	Chinese
Western Chin	265-317	Loyang	Chinese
North-South Division	317-589	Various	Hun,
North: Six Dynasties	329-580		Proto-Mongol, Tibetan, Turkhoid
South: Five Dynasties	317-589	Nanking	Chinese
Sui	589-618	Ch'angan, Loyang, Yangchou	Chinese
T'ang	618-906	Ch'angan, Loyang	Chinese
North-South Division	907-1289		
North: Three Dynasties	937-1234	Various	Tartar (Turkish)
South: Five Dynasties	907-960	Loyang K'aifeng	Chinese
Northern Sung	960-1127	K'aifeng	Chinese
Southern Sung	1127-1289	Hangchou	Chinese
Yüan	1234 (1289)-1368	Peking	Mongol
Ming	1368-1644	Nanking, Peking (since 1403)	Chinese
Ch'ing	1644-1912	Peking	Manchu

and were of Ural-Altaic, Finno-Ugrian, Mongol, or Tibetan origin. In one case, that of the Ming dynasty, the founder was a Buddhist monk, Chu Yüan-chang, who led an uprising that came close to being a national revolution against the Mongolian Yüan dynasty.

The first, or the first two or three, emperors of a dynasty would usually unify the country with very repressive and cruel methods and emphasize military values as well as a centralized administration. Then would follow a series of intellectually capable rulers who would develop the economy and promote the arts. As the time went by, corruption would become rampant, and the court would indulge in refined entertainment, sexual permissiveness, and intraelite conflicts. Such a decay would result in a neglect of irrigation and river protection, which, in turn, would exacerbate floods or drought and always resulted in famine. As a result, the peasants would become unruly, banditry would spread over vast areas, and the economy would decline rapidly. Such a situation would be considered, by scholars as well as by many common people, an indication that the ruling dynasty had lost the Mandate of Heaven. The emperor would be overthrown by rebellion or an invasion of hordes from the northern barbarian tribes, and the historical cycle would start all over again.

Yet, although the dynasties changed, and one after the other cycle went its course, the major aspects of the traditional Chinese society, which developed from the Ch'in period to the T'ang period, remained basically unchanged, at least until the middle of the nineteenth century. Varying *Kuo* followed each other in the same *T'ien-hsia* society.

This society was, as has already been pointed out, by no means feudal. Instead of using that term, the society should be called instead patrimonialist, modified by an early type of agrarian capitalism. The traditional Chinese society was characterized by five basic aspects.

1. It was an agrarian society. More than four-fifths of the Chinese people lived in villages and derived their income from agriculture, either as landlords and owner-farmers or as tenants and rural workers.
2. It was basically self-sufficient. China's production of agricultural goods and handicrafts mostly satisfied the demand. If not, there were shortages and famines, but hardly any attempt would be made to alleviate the deficit with imports. Foreign trade was limited to "tributes" sent to the emperor by foreign monarchs and to the "gifts" he presented to them in return, which were often more valuable than what had been presented to him.
3. It had, as we have seen, a high degree of continuity from the Han period until the last century.
4. Its main structure was that of the autonomous unit of the lineage, or clan. The clan, led by the oldest male member, served as the basic judicial unit and as the major welfare organization. This arrangement did not necessarily mean that the clan also constituted an institution of communal living. The masses of the people lived mostly in smaller family units, but they were under clan jurisdiction.

5. Its supralocal and interregional coherence was guaranteed by a centralized administration with a highly bureaucratic character, which limited the autonomy of clans and self-administering associations and groups to the local level.

The bureaucrats were recruited from the group that enjoyed the highest social prestige in traditional China, the literati, or *shih*. This group consisted of those people who had passed—or sometimes had bought their passing marks—the three-level examinations administered by the government.[21] Only about 5 percent of this group, which made up 1–2 percent of the total population, belonged to the imperial bureaucracy. The central administration was mainly concerned with public works (dikes, canals, irrigation systems, and defense fortifications) and with the levying of taxes, which was often leased out to nonofficial members of the *shih*. By the mid-nineteenth century, there were barely 30,000 imperial officials in China, i.e., one for every 15,000–17,000 inhabitants.[22]

As a rule, the imperial administration—the state—ended on the level of the county (*hsien*) government. Below that level, the *shih*, peasants (*nung*), artisans (*kung*), and businessmen (*shang*)—in that order of social prestige—regulated their own affairs. Hence, the central authority had no direct access to the individual. Between the people and the bureaucracy there had developed an intricate system of local self-administrating bodies in charge of schooling, welfare, health services, and local security. Only after 1,000 years of continuity was this society affected by influences that came from abroad, not through invaders from the north, but overseas from the south.

The Impact of the West

In the sixteenth and seventeenth centuries, Portuguese and Dutch ships had landed in southern China, and a trickle of trade had developed between their countries and the Chinese Empire. In 1557, the Portuguese had even secured a settlement concerning Macau, mainly because the Chinese authorities did not want them to spread their influence over more of Kuangtung. All through the eighteenth century, the Manchu dynasty had regarded the Europeans as being almost entirely uncivilized barbarians. Although the emperors were willing to accept tributes from the Europeans, they could never consider them equal to the Chinese. In light of the classical Chinese world view,[23] the attack by Western invaders in 1839 was a traumatic shock for the country's elites.

When this attack started, the ruling Manchu dynasty had already entered the declining part of the historical cycle. Poorly trained and equipped, the Chinese armies were no match for the British invaders who forced the opening of China to foreign trade and foreign missions through the Opium War (1839–1842) and, together with the French, the Lorcha, or Arrow, War (1857–1860). With these and other military as well as diplomatic actions, the European powers, the United States, and—after 1894—Japan pressured the Manchu court into humiliating treaty arrangements.

Great Britain secured the island of Hongkong and the Kowloon Peninsula as a colony and forced China to lease the New Territories north of Hongkong and Weihaiwei in Shantung. France extorted a lease of Kuangchouwan in Kuangtung; Germany occupied Ch'ingtao; and Russia secured Lüshun and Talienwan in southern Manchuria, which it had to cede to Japan in 1905. In addition, areas of foreign settlement with extraterritorial administration were established in Shanghai, T'ienchin, Hank'ou, Chiuchiang, Amoy, and the island of Shamien (opposite Canton). Extraterritoriality was also extended to foreign residential areas—so-called concessions—in twenty-one other Chinese cities. The country had to accept the principle of extrajurisdiction, which meant that foreigners could not be tried by Chinese courts.[24] In order to secure easy access to foreign imports, China was forced to agree to the establishment of a Chinese Maritime Customs Administration under foreign control, which set very low import tax rates for European, U.S., and Japanese industrial goods.

From the fact that early in the twentieth century, Chinese intellectuals began to call the agreements extorted from China by the foreign powers unequal treaties (*Pu-p'ing-teng t'iao-yüeh*), one is able to sense the shock the Western invasion had on Chinese self-consciousness. In China's traditional world view, the barbarians, by definition, were unequal in the sense of being inferior to the inhabitants of the Central State. Now China had to strive for equality with the barbarians, who had achieved de facto superiority over the country's citizens.

Indeed, the country had been an easy prey for the modern techniques of power application used by the Western invaders, which China could not match either militarily or economically. Under the impact of this experience, the traditional political system of China broke down, and the traditional society, at least along the East China coast and in the lower Yangtzu Valley, started to disintegrate. In intellectual and social terms, the major results of this process of disintegration were

- the questioning of the traditional Confucian values by thousands of young intellectuals who had gone to the West for academic studies
- the emerging of a new upper class of businessmen in the cities who traded with Western countries

- the gradual establishment of national Chinese light industries, which more and more replaced the work of artisans
- the decay of the lineage system in the cities, where the modern urban family increasingly became the prevailing social unit
- the emergence of a new literature in the colloquial language rather than the classical literary one

These developments, however, did not reach most of the Chinese countryside. After almost 100 years of Western influence, Chinese society by the mid-1930s was therefore characterized by a dichotomy between the increasingly modernizing cities in the eastern and central parts of the country on the one hand and the villages, which remained socially and economically backward and undynamic, on the other.

Hundred Years of Turmoil

The Ch'ing dynasty elite had succeeded in suppressing a popular revolt in southern China—the T'aip'ing Rebellion, which devastated large parts of the country between 1850 and 1864. After that, Chinese reactions to the Western invasion unfolded in three consecutive stages. At first, a number of traditionally educated civilian and military leaders of Han origin—the most prominent being Tseng Kuo-fan, Chang Chih-tung, and Li Hung-chang—attempted to remedy China's problems by combining the restoration of Confucian values with the material modernization, mainly through the acceptance of Western military and communication technologies. But the total defeat of the modernized Chinese military forces by the much smaller neighbor Japan in 1894–1895 indicated that this approach was not sufficient. In fact, one cannot have Western technology without Western science or Western science without Western logic. Western logic, in turn, is a product of Western thought and Western world views in general.

After China's defeat in the First Sino-Japanese War, a number of younger scholars realized the interdependence between technology, academic knowledge, thought, and the political system. Two of them in particular, K'ang Yu-wei and Liang Ch'i-ch'ao, were impressed by the rapid modernization of Japan and initiated the second step of the Chinese reaction: a thoroughgoing reform of the administrative and educational system centering around replacing the traditional examination rules with modern, Western-oriented education. In early 1898, they convinced the young Emperor Kuang-hsü that, as in Japan, forceful action from the throne could turn the country around. For 100 days, China was bombarded with an avalanche of reform regulations signed by the emperor. But then, ultraconservative court circles around the Empress Dowager Tz'u

Hsi carried out a coup d'etat, put Kuang-hsü under house arrest, and abolished all his modernizing edicts. Reform had failed, too.

In the eyes of a young Cantonese physician, Dr. Sun Yat-sen, and many other foreign-trained young intellectuals, only one last way was left to remedy the country's ills, revolution. Between 1894 and 1907, Sun designed a platform that he hoped could save China from decay and humiliation. Its major planks were the overthrow of the Manchu dynasty and the establishment of a modern, pluralistic representative system in a Chinese republic (*Chung-hua min-kuo*); the abolition of the unequal treaties through negotiations with foreign powers; the nationalization of basic industries and banks; the gradual development of a social welfare system; and the equal distribution of the arable land among owner-farmers. With this program as a base, Sun founded, in 1905, the Revolutionary League (*T'ung-meng-hui*)—later renamed the National People's party (*Kuo-min-tang* [KMT]) as the major revolutionary force. After a number of abortive attempts to stage an uprising of the Han against the alien Manchu dynasty, Sun and his associates finally succeeded in forging a powerful coalition of their league; southern Chinese secret societies; regional interest groups in Hunan, Hupei, Kuangtung, and Ssuch'uan; and some of the modern crack military units.

On October 10, 1911, this coalition rose in revolt at Wuhan, and less than three months, almost all of South and Central China fell to the revolutionary forces. On January 1, 1912, in the old Ming dynasty capital of Nanking, the Republic of China was proclaimed, and Sun was appointed its first president. But in the north, a general loyal to the dynasty, Yüan Shih-k'ai, assumed control. In order to avoid civil war, Sun entered into an agreement with Yüan. The latter forced the last Manchu emperor to abdicate and accepted the establishment of a republic, and Sun ceded to him the office of the president. Yüan, however, only planned to start another historical cycle with himself as the first emperor of a new dynasty. Thus, a conflict developed between the KMT and the president.

In 1914–1915, Yüan managed to suppress a rebellion of the KMT against him and had himself proclaimed emperor. Only a few months later, however, he had to step back into the position of president of the republic under mounting pressure from regional military leaders, the warlords (*Chün-fa*). He died on June 6, 1916, and soon after, China fell apart. For more than thirty years, China was divided into different regions—varying in number from seven to thirteen—and these regions were dominated by warlords who fought each other, in ever varying coalitions, as they vied for the control of taxable areas. The official government of this First Republic (1912–1928) mostly controlled only the area around the capital, Peking.

Beginning in 1917, Sun Yat-sen tried, through coalitions with various southern warlords, to establish a KMT government with control over the whole of China, but his efforts were in vain. Only after the KMT, still under his leadership, had accepted organizational and political help from the young Soviet Union and joined in a coalition with the CCP, which had been founded in 1921, were the prerequisites for the conquest of China created: a revolutionary base in Kuangtung, a revolutionary cadre organization for the KMT, and a Party army under direct control of the KMT leadership. After the death of Sun on March 12, 1925, the commander of that Party army, Chiang Kai-shek, emerged as the major KMT leader. In 1926–1927, he led the army to the conquest of most of South China, broke with the CCP and the Soviet Union in 1927, and finally, in 1928, marched his troops into Peking, and established the Second Republic (1928–1949) with its capital at Nanking.

This establishment of a new republic, however, did not yet mean the real unification of China. From 1929 to 1936, Chiang had to fight several civil wars against a number of warlords. By the summer of 1936, the warlord system—except for a few remnants in Ssuch'uan, Shansi, Yünnan, and Sinkiang—had broken down, and Chiang's KMT government was in full control of about one-fourth of the territory and almost two-thirds of the populace. Yet, by 1927, a more formidable enemy had emerged for the KMT: the CCP, among whose leaders Mao Tse-tung became increasingly important and had achieved almost total control of the Party by early 1935. The CCP guerrilla forces fought the KMT until the Japanese invasion on July 7, 1937, when the two groups joined into a united front for a second time, this time against a foreign aggressor.

The new civil war had been conducted by the Communists with varying successes and failures, but they had at least managed to survive, and they had still had an army of almost 100,000 men at their disposal when the Second Sino-Japanese War (July 7, 1937–September 3, 1945) broke out.

In the eastern and central parts of China, the KMT-dominated national government had staged a considerable developmental effort between 1928 and 1937. With the passing of a civil and criminal code, and laws governing trademarks, shipping, insurance, and banking, the legal system had been brought up to the international standards of the twentieth century. These laws, however, could only be enforced in the cities and their surrounding areas in East and Central China; they never really reached the countryside.

Furthermore, there was remarkable progress in education, public finance, and communication. The literacy rate rose from 10 to 25 percent; the school attendance rate, from less than 20 to 35.4 percent; and the number of students, from 8 million to 22.6 million. In 1937, there were three times as many university graduates as in 1928, though the number was still too small, 75,000—only 1 for every 6,000 inhabitants.[25] In 1935, a new currency was introduced, and it remained stable until the outbreak of the war in 1937. Despite great rearmament efforts in the wake of the expected Japanese aggression, the state budget was, for the first time since 1911, fully balanced only in fiscal year 1936/1937. During the same period, 4,097 miles of new railroads were built[26] and almost 53,000 miles of new roads, including about 21,000 miles with macadam cover.[27]

The KMT regime was also quite successful in achieving international equality for China. Starting with the abolition of foreign control over the customs services on January 1, 1931, the KMT diplomats, in long negotiations with the world powers, finally succeeded in obtaining the cancellation of the last of the special privileges that had been granted by the unequal treaties on October 10, 1943. After the Japanese surrender on September 3, 1945 and the acceptance of the RoC as a standing member of the United Nations Security Council, the unequal treaties had been totally abolished.

Yet the KMT failed to provide solutions for the problems of poverty and backwardness in the Chinese countryside, where more than 80 percent of the population still lived. Furthermore, many of the government's early developmental achievements had been destroyed during the second Sino-Japanese War. The war had brought runaway inflation to China and with it, corruption, blackmarketeering, and an increasing deterioration of the social and economic conditions in the cities. Under the impact of these developments, the KMT also failed in its poorly coordinated efforts to stage a recovery after the war.

This was the hour of the CCP. Motivated and dedicated to a new stage of revolution, the Party's army resumed the civil war and, after 1946, succeeded in defeating one KMT unit after the other. By early 1950, the CCP had conquered all of the Chinese mainland. Chiang Kai-shek and the KMT elite, together with almost 1.5 million Nationalist soldiers and civilians, fled to T'aiwan.

The then undisputed leader of the victorious CCP, Mao Tse-tung, proclaimed the establishment of the PRC on October 1, 1949, while his troops were still fighting KMT remnants in southwestern China. A new stage had begun in the ongoing Chinese revolution, which, in fact, appears to be nothing else than the protracted and painful process of the Central State's entry into the modern world. In this new stage, Marxist-Leninists have tried to promote this process by using the prescriptions that socialism offers. We shall have to examine their performance until 1975 before we can describe and analyze their politics in the time of transition after the death of the revolutionary leader.

CHAPTER 3

Basic Economic Conditions

Transport and Communications

For a territory as vast as the PRC, accessibility in terms of communication lines is indeed vital in order to transport not only people but, even more so, raw materials to the industrial locations as well as food grains from agricultural surplus areas to deficit areas. The CCP, therefore, immediately after taking power, began making a considerable effort to improve the transport situation. Yet there are still grave shortages in this field.

The weakest point seems to be civil aviation. Although domestic air routes have expanded from 7,080 miles, operated with 12 aircraft, in 1949 to about 52,330 miles, operated with 193 aircraft, in 1975 and to more than 119,000 miles, operated with 240 aircraft, in 1980,[28] the equipment is used on the average for only three hours per day, which is much less than in most countries of the world. This low amount of use is owing to a shortage of runways and night-flight equipment, which would have to be greatly increased to make full use of the fleet.

More important than aviation is transport by sea and the few really navigable rivers. The PRC has more than twenty-five harbors that can accommodate ocean-going vessels, the largest being Shanghai, Canton, Ch'ingtao, Talienwan, Lüshun, T'ienchin, Amoy, Fuchou, and Nanking, Chenchiang, and Wuhan on the Yangtzu River. But by 1982, these harbors had a total of only 330 berths available, of which 147 could handle ships of more than 10,000 tons,[29] and container facilities have been established only since 1980. It will take a tremendous effort to expand the handling capabilities, which are not sufficient for the requirements of an accelerated economic development program. Although the ocean-going merchant marine grew from 454 ships and 990,331 tons in 1949 to 466 ships and 2,828,290 tons in 1975, and from there to 943 ships and 7,291,489 tons in 1981,[30] it is still not sufficient, so considerable parts of the country's international trade have to be handled by foreign vessels, which means losses in foreign exchange.

For domestic transport, roads are increasingly important. Yet, although 42.5 percent of the transport volume was moved on roads in 1981, there is still no national network of paved highways. Out of a total of 544,000 miles of all kinds of roadways, 420,000 miles, or 77.2 percent, were supposed to have some kind of surface by 1981, but only 8,080 miles of those roads could be considered as first- or second-class highways.[31] Mostly, paved highways end a few miles outside the cities and continue as dirt roads. The major modern thoroughfares are the highways connecting Tibet with Ssuch'uan and Ch'inghai and Sinkiang with Kansu and Shansi, but there is still no paved, all-weather north-south or east-west highway connection.

Communication therefore relies mainly on the railways, which move more than 55 percent of the transport volume. In the field of railway development, the PRC has made remarkable advances since 1949. In 1981, there were 31,181 miles of railroad in operation,[32] which means that 15,087 miles of new railway lines had been constructed in thirty-two years, an average of a little over 471 miles per year. This figure contrasts with the average annual railway construction of 410 miles under the KMT government from 1928 to 1938, indeed impressive progress.

In order to arrive at a realistic picture of the problems that the PRC still faces in regard to its railroad network, a comparison with India is useful. In 1981, the PRC had 1 mile of railroad per 118.4 square miles of territory; India, 1 mile per 34.2 square miles. Although the PRC railway system transported 912 million people in 1980, the Indian railways carried 3,650 million. Only 1,038 miles of railways, or 3.3 percent of the system, were electrified in the PRC; in India, the figure was 2,920 miles, or 7.7 percent.[33] About 84 percent of the Chinese network is still single track, and this fact hampers the transportation of the bulk goods moved in raw material transfers.[34] To give just one example: In May 1982, 20 million to 30 million tons of coal waited for transportation for more than three months in the coal-mining areas of Honan, Shansi, Shensi, Inner Mongolia, and Ninghsia when they were urgently needed elsewhere.[35]

The situation in the fields of transport and communication therefore serves as a major constraint for the development of the country's industries, although considerable progress was made in this regard between 1949 and 1975, the year before the death of Mao Tse-tung.

Industries and Industrial Performance, 1949–1975

When the CCP took over power on the mainland of China, the goal of the Party was twofold. On the one hand, it set out to create a "socialist society," which was supposed to move later into the process of "transition to communism"; on the other hand, it also started an effort to develop the Chinese economy from a backward agrarian one into a modern industrial one. Yet before such a development could start, it was first necessary to reconstruct the existing industries, which had been damaged or at least their production had been greatly reduced, during eight years of foreign and four years of civil war. For the task of reconstruction, the Party cooperated with private enterprise, in particular in the areas of light and consumer goods industries. Even in 1952, 17.1 percent of the industrial production still came from private enterprises, 21.9 percent originated from "mixed" private-state operations, and 61 percent came from entirely state-owned factories.[36]

Within only three years, from 1949 to the end of 1952, the runaway inflation was vanquished. Destroyed and damaged plants were rebuilt or repaired, and the full existing capacity of the industries was utilized. By late 1952, the figures of the last year before the war, 1936, had again been reached in almost all areas of production, and in some cases even surpassed. This reconstruction feat may be considered as one of the greatest achievements of CCP rule in China.

After reconstruction had been completed, the further development of the economy could be started. Guidelines for this development were set by the First Five-Year Plan, which was in effect from 1953 to 1957 but was only published in 1955. This plan was modeled after the example of the Soviet Union under Stalin. It emphasized the speedy expansion of basic and heavy industries, and it was strongly supported by Soviet loans, as well as by Soviet specialists and advisers. With this aid, 166 new industrial complexes were established between 1953 and 1957, and they formed the core of the industrial development in the 1950s. By 1957, these new complexes were providing 30 percent of the PRC's cast iron production, 39 percent of the steel production, 91 percent of the new tractors, 80 percent of the trucks, and 25 percent of the production of electric energy. Besides the establishment of these 166 complexes, the PRC received 24,000 blocks of technological data from the Soviet Union, including 1,400 blueprints for whole plants. More than 10,000 Chinese engineers and technicians were trained in the Soviet Union, and almost 11,000 Soviet technical advisers worked in China.[37]

Yet by 1957, a contradiction had evolved: The fast expanding heavy industry contrasted with underdeveloped light and consumer goods industries and a still backward agriculture. The income differentials between the cities and the villages had widened, and the supply of light industrial goods had begun to deteriorate. In order to solve these problems, Mao himself, during the winter of 1957/1958, introduced a new development platform that called for the promotion of both heavy industry and agriculture and the simultaneous use of modern technologies and traditional production methods in both sectors of the economy. For industry, this plan meant the so-called Great Leap Forward (*Ta yao-chin*), in which the PRC was supposed, with the help of small backyard furnaces and the deployment of "workers' armies" in "production battles," to reach and overtake the per capita production of Great Britain in steel and coal within fifteen years, i.e., by 1972. At first, from 1958 until 1960, heavy industry expanded almost unbelievably, but then, organizational chaos and the misallocation of resources pushed the country into a very grave economic crisis. Some sectors of industry broke down, and it took the enactment of drastic revisions in the developmental concept by a majority of the CCP leaders to stage a gradual recovery between 1962 and 1965. By the end of 1965, this recovery had been completed, and the industry was expanding again, this time, however, more in the older industrial centers—Shanghai, T'ienchin, Canton, Wuhan, and southern Liaoning—than in the new industrial regions that had been developed in the 1950s in Northwest China and parts of South China. The boom that began in 1965 was soon—between 1966 and 1968—interrupted by the turmoil of the Cultural Revolution. This violent conflict affected the cities more than the countryside, and production was hurt by strikes, demonstrations, and factional infights in the factories that verged on civil war. Again, 1969 to 1971 were years of recovery—and limited expansion—but between 1972 and 1975, a balanced development of heavy and light industries, albeit with slight recessional features in 1974, began to unfold. Overall, the basic and heavy industries did comparatively well during the twenty-six years from 1949 to 1975, as the figures in Table 3.1 show. Although also expanding, the light and consumer goods industries experienced a slightly less dramatic growth, as Table 3.2 indicates.

Quantitatively speaking, China's industrial performance between 1949 and 1975 was indeed remarkable. In these twenty-six years, the value of the heavy industrial production, in constant prices, rose almost sixty-eight times and that of light industrial production, fifteen times. Even if we exclude the years of reconstruction, when, at least to a significant degree, existing capacities were again mobilized, and look only at the twenty-three years from the beginning of the First Five-Year Plan in 1953 until 1975, the production value of heavy industry increased eleven times and that of light industry, six and a half times. There were, however, great variations in industrial growth, as the figures in Table 3.3 suggest rather clearly.

From 1953 through 1975, the average annual growth rate of all industrial production stood, according to these data, at 13.3 percent, which indicates a rather forceful development in spite of all variations. During the same period, the industrial production of the RoC on T'aiwan

Table 3.1. Production of basic and heavy industries in selected years between 1949 and 1975[38]

Item [a]	1949	1952	1957	1960	1962	1969	1971	1975
Coal	32.4	66.5	130.7	280.0	185.0	281.6	353.6	482.0
Steel	0.16	1.35	5.35	18.7	8.0	16.0	21.0	23.9
Crude oil	0.12	0.44	1.46	5.10	5.75	20.38	36.70	77.06
Electricity (billion kwh)	4.31	7.26	19.34	41.0	45.0	99.0	123.0	195.8
Cement	0.66	2.86	6.86	12.0	6.9	22.5	30.9	46.26
Tractors (1,000 units)					9.52	5.24	17.28	47.0	78.4
Machine tools (1,000 units)	1.58	13.73	28.3	30.0	34.0	127.0	145.8	174.9

[a]If not otherwise stated, in million tons.

Table 3.2. Production of light and consumer goods industries in selected years between 1949 and 1975[39]

Item	1949	1952	1957	1960	1962	1969	1971	1975
Cotton cloth (billion m)	1.89	3.83	5.05	4.9	3.5	6.6	7.2	9.4
Sugar (million t)	0.20	0.45	0.86	0.92	0.48	1.35	1.50	1.74
Paper (million t)	0.11	0.37	0.91	1.12	1.07	1.95	2.58	3.41
Radio receivers (1,000 units)	4.0	17.0	352.0	n.a.[a]	n.a.	2,500.0	6,000.0	9,356.0
TV sets (1,000 units)				1.0	3.0	5.0	18.0	178.0
Bicycles (1,000 units)	14.0	80.0	806.0	1,840.0	1,000.0	3,026.0	4,030.0	6,232.0

[a]n.a.=not available.

Table 3.3. Average annual growth rates of industrial production (in percent)[40]

	Heavy Industry	Light Industry	Overall Industrial Production
1949–1952	48.9	30.0	34.8
1953–1957	25.8	· 13.3	18.4
1958–1960	51.1	15.3	34.0
1961–1962	-34.7	-15.0	-27.4
1963–1968	7.9	11.7	9.4
1969–1971	36.0	16.6	26.6
1972–1975	7.6	8.1	7.9

grew at an annual average of 14.2 percent, an almost comparable pace of development.

Agriculture and Agricultural Performance, 1949–1975

The same summary cannot be made in regard to agriculture. Although large arable regions had suffered from the impact of the civil war, the food grain production of the Chinese mainland was comparatively high in 1949, a year with a very good harvest. Productivity, however, increased remarkably, when the CCP enacted a sweeping land reform between 1950 and 1953, confiscating the arable land owned by landlords and part of the land owned by rich farmers for distribution among poor farmers, tenants, and landless village workers. More than 40 percent of the agriculturally used land of China, 115 million acres, changed ownership, and after the land reform, there were almost 120 million owner-farmers with approximately equal holdings in the country.

Yet, according to the program of the CCP, this was only a transitional situation. In 1953, the Party started to push ahead with the "socialist transformation of agriculture," which meant the collectivization of the villages. First, so-called lower-level agricultural production cooperatives were formed, in which the peasants still had the deed to their land but farmed collectively, sharing the profit according to the land and the implements they had brought into the cooperative.

In 1955, Mao pressured the Party elite into an acceleration of the drive toward the collectivization of agriculture. Now, in a second step, so-called advanced socialist agricultural cooperatives were established, which followed the model of the Soviet *kolkhoz*. In these units, the deeds for the land were transferred to the collective, and the peasants received remuneration according to the amount of work done by each of them, computed in terms of work points. Only their houses and small patches of private plots remained in their own hands. By late 1957, except for some national minority areas, the whole Chinese countryside had been collectivized.

But soon, the level of collectivization was still further raised. In 1958, Mao initiated the system of people's communes (*Jen-min kung-she*) with the aim of collectivizing not only production but the whole life of the peasant. Although the first and second stages of collectivization had not, or at most only marginally, affected the growth of agricultural production, this third step did so very definitely. Between 1958 and 1960, the output of food grains—the Chinese *liang-shih*, which includes rice, wheat, barley, sorghum, corn, soybeans, potatoes, and sweet potatoes—dropped by more than 28 percent, and until 1962, China

Table 3.4.   Development of agricultural production, 1949-1975[43]

Year	Food Grain Production (in million t)	Population (in millions)	Per capita Production (in kg)	Per capita Production Comparison (in percent) with 1931-1937	1949
1931-1937 average	171.0	485.0	352.6		
1949	150.0	540.0	277.8	-21.2	
1951	143.7	557.0	258.0	-26.8	- 7.1
1957	195.05	646.5	301.7	-14.4	+ 8.6
1958	200.0	659.0	303.5	-13.9	+ 9.3
1960	143.5	689.0	208.3	-40.9	-25.0
1962	160.0	690.0	231.9	34.2	-16.5
1965	194.5	737.0	264.0	-25.1	- 5.0
1971	246.0	835.0	294.6	-16.4	+ 6.0
1975	285.0	919.7	309.9	-12.1	+11.5

experienced its greatest famine since 1879. At least 20 million people died,[41] probably even more than 25 million, but either figure is more than the number of people who died from famine in India in the thirty years from 1950 to 1980.

Under the impact of this grave food crisis, the CCP leadership— probably against Mao's will and at least without his active participation— decided to "readjust" the communes so that they functioned almost solely as administrative units after 1961/1962. The ownership of land was transferred to the production teams (*Sheng-ch'an-tui*), units of 15– 40 peasant families instead of the average 4,500-family communes of 1958. The teams organized farmwork and distributed the remuneration, but the individual peasant could again cultivate private plots—which, by 1975, consisted of 6.4 percent of all arable land but produced 30 percent of the agricultural output[42]—engage in private sideline occupations, raise some pigs and fowl, and sell their own products in free village markets. These measures resulted in a recovery of agricultural production, which, by 1965, had again almost reached the absolute figures of 1957.

During the Cultural Revolution, and also during its immediate aftermath between 1969 and 1971, several attempts were made by the leftist forces in the PRC leadership, most notably by Marshal Lin Piao— Mao's designated successor until Piao's death on September 12, 1971— to raise the levels of collectivization again in order to stage a return to the commune concept of 1958, but all of these attempts failed. The readjustments of 1961/1962 prevailed, although they were heavily disputed.

Under these circumstances, the agricultural production continued to recover, but even in 1975 it was not yet sufficient to feed the population, and the per capita food grain output was still 12.1 percent less than the annual average for 1931 to 1937. The quantitative performance of PRC agriculture until 1975 can be found in Table 3.4, which shows

Table 3.5. China's GNP and per capita GNP average annual growth rates,
1949-1975 (in percent)[46]

Period	Average Annual GNP Growth	Average Annual per capita GNP Growth
1949-1952	18.9	16.6
1953-1957	5.5[47]	4.1
1958-1960	3.8	1.9
1961/62	- 6.0	- 7.1
1963-1968	7.9	5.9
1969-1971	11.3	8.6
1972-1975	7.0	4.5

that between 1949 and 1975, the per capita food grain production of
the PRC never reached the level of the 1930s, i.e., before the second
Sino-Japanese War. In 1960, it was one-fourth less than in 1949, and
after 1960, it surpassed the 1949 level again only in 1971, and the 1957
level only in 1975.

In order to alleviate the shortcomings of agricultural production, the
PRC turned to importing large amounts of grain in 1961. In the fifteen
years from 1961 to 1975, the country imported a total of 78,103,000
tons of food grains, while it exported, during the same period, 23,051,000
tons for a net deficit of 55,052,000 tons, or an annual average of almost
3.7 million tons.[44]

Development of the GNP, 1949–1975

Since the industrial production growth rate wavered greatly between
different periods during the time from 1949 to 1975, and so did the
growth rate of agricultural production, the GNP rate also showed uneven,
though still remarkable, growth. It is not easy to establish reliable figures
for GNP growth in China since the official data are hardly trustworthy
for much of that time. Even the assessments of the overall economic
situation by foreign scholars show considerable variation. Subramaniam
Swamy calculated, for the period beteen 1952 and 1972, an average
annual GNP growth rate of 3.5 percent; the late Alexander Eckstein
offered a figure of about 4–4.5 percent for the same period. Arthur
Ashbrook, Jr., however, came up with 5.9 percent for the period from
1952 until 1971; the T'aiwan economist Wei Wou, with 6.4 percent for
1953 to 1974; and the British economist Werner Klatt, 6.4 percent for
1950 to 1972.[45] The average of these assessments would stand at 5.05
percent, which may be rather close to the truth. The data in Table 3.5
are from the work of Willy Kraus.

If one includes the period of reconstruction after the civil war, the
figures in the table suggest an overall average annual GNP growth rate,
for the twenty-six years until 1975, of 7.4 percent and a growth rate
of the per capita GNP of 5.5 percent. Yet if one starts the overview

with the first year of the First Five-Year Plan, 1953, the average annual GNP growth rate for the twenty-three years would stand at 5.9 percent, and that of the per capita GNP at 4.1 percent. For those twenty-three years (1953–1975), comparative figures for the RoC on T'aiwan are available: They show an average annual GNP growth rate of 8.7 percent and an average per capita GNP growth rate of 5.8 percent.[48]

It is, however, important to realize that these growth rates were uneven. It seems that the economy of the PRC, in the period from its establishment until shortly before the death of Mao, went through clearly recognizable economic cycles, which may have been influenced by the successive implementation of rather different developmental concepts.

Economic Cycles and Concepts of Development

If we accept the estimates presented in Table 3.5, although they may be somewhat too high, and assume that the average annual GNP growth rate in the PRC between 1953 and 1975 was indeed 5.9 percent, we may establish a median fluctuation of 1.5 percentage points in both directions as comparatively normal. Stabilized sustained growth, then, would mean growth rates varying between 4.4 and 7.4 percent. However, a review of the figures presented by Kraus shows that growth remained within this variance in only six of the twenty-three years; in seventeen of the years, it was either much higher or much lower, with the extremes of 18.8 percent increase (1958) and 21.1 percent decline (1961).[49] From 1953 to 1957, i.e., during the period of the First Five-Year Plan—the only one of five that was really implemented until 1980—the PRC experienced a remarkable expansion of industrial production and a modest but distinct growth of agricultural production. After exploding agricultural increases in 1958, and until 1960 in industry, an extremely severe depression resulted from the policies of the Great Leap Forward, which were aggravated by severe natural calamities in 1959, 1960, and 1961. These three bitter years (*San k'u-nien*)—as the people in China called them at that time and the CCP media has called them since 1977—threw the country back five years in industry and at least twelve years in agriculture, or seven to eight years in overall economic performance.

Recovery started slowly in 1962, accelerated in 1963, and was fully accomplished by 1965 when the level of 1957/1958 was reached again. There was a brisk expansion in 1966, but it was soon interrupted by the politically produced recession of the Cultural Revolution in 1967/1968. Since then, 1969/1970, 1972/1973, and 1975 were years of booming development, while—again chiefly for political reasons—there was a slowdown in 1971 and almost stagnation in 1974.

We can thus observe between six and eight changes in the economic cycle in the PRC from 1953 to 1975. Such shifts may be—at least partially—attributed to the fact that during this period, three rather different concepts of development were followed in the PRC.

The first of these concepts, the one that dominated during the period of the First Five-Year Plan, may be called Stalinist. It was characterized by centralized planning and management of production, supply, and consumption. The first developmental priority was given to the sector of basic and heavy industries; agriculture ranked second; and light and consumer goods industries, a rather poor third. Material incentives, which resulted in distinct wage differentials, were considered the major motivating force for economic development.

The second concept did not follow Soviet prescriptions as the first one had. It was indeed genuinely Chinese, and we may call it Maoist. It was implemented in 1958/1959. The forces of the CCP Left around Mao Tse-tung and his close associates tried to revive it from 1968 to 1971, albeit with rather limited success. This concept was characterized by a decentralization of planning and management in agriculture as well as in light industries on the level of the people's commune—i.e., the township—combined with a continuing centralization of heavy industry, for which all major decision making remained on the national level. The first developmental priority was now equally allocated to agriculture and heavy industry, while light industry continued to range behind those two sectors. Nonmaterial incentives were considered the major motivating force. Mao and his close aides believed that such nonmaterial incentives could be generated by a system of mass mobilization and development through enthusiastic austerity.

But as we have already seen, the implementation of the Maoist concept of development ended in dismal failure. From the ensuing economic crisis, by improvisation rather than by deliberate design, a third concept emerged and it was promoted by the majority of the civilian CCP leaders. It can be called the concept of readjustment and was characterized by attempts to decentralize planning and management in *all* economic sectors on the provincial and regional levels. Agriculture received the first developmental priority, and second priority was allocated to agricultural auxiliary industries—e.g., fertilizer and agricultural tools and machinery. Heavy industry ranked only third, and light and consumer goods industries were still ranked last. Again, as in the Stalinist concept, material incentives were considered the major motivating force for economic development. The concept of readjustment was implemented from 1959/1960 to 1966 and also, with slight variations, from 1972 to 1975.

But by 1975, strong forces within the CCP elite were working for a return to the Maoist prescriptions of 1958. Should the PRC follow a path of economic and social development dominated by traditional categories of growth and technological advance, or should it rely on mass movements, mobilization, and class struggle? During the last year of Mao's life, this question was still by no means definitely answered.

CHAPTER 4

Social Stratification

Structures and Developments in Rural Society

In 1981, official PRC sources indicated that 75.4 percent of the country's total work force was employed in agriculture,[50] approximately the same share as in 1975 when the figure given was 74 percent.[51] The rural population, at the same time, was said to compose 86.1 percent of the total populace, only slightly lower than the 89.4 percent estimated for 1949.[52] Given the usual unreliability of statistical data published by institutions in the PRC, these figures may not be very exact, but it appears reasonably certain that about three-fourths of the gainfully employed earn their living from agriculture and that at least four out of every five people live in the more than 7 million hamlets, villages, and small towns that form the Chinese countryside.

Hence, social developments in the villages immensely affect the overall development of China, and they are therefore a very important part of the framework for political decision making. Before 1949, approximately one-half of the rural people were owner-farmers; one-fifth each, part-tenants and full tenants; and one-tenth, landless farmhands. Landlords and rich peasants owned probably about 40 percent of the arable land, but they represented only 10–15 percent of all peasants, and the 85–90 percent middle and poor peasants owned only about 60 percent of the land.

Farmhand wages were very low, and the cost of land rents varied between 45 and 70 percent of the main crop in South China and 35 and 50 percent in North China.[53] Yet it was not only the lack of arable land and the resulting tenancy system that distressed the peasants. Since the second decade of the twentieth century, the tax burden, which hit the owner-farmers most, had been steadily increasing, and consequently large portions of the rural population were running up ever larger debts.

The land reform that the CCP implemented from 1950 to 1953—although carried out with significant terror with at least five million executions[54]—alleviated many problems. The land reform program divided the rural population—according to standards that varied widely from place to place—into five categories: landlords, rich peasants, middle peasants, poor peasants, and landless farmhands. All landlord property was confiscated, the rich peasants had to cede part of their land, the middle peasants were mostly left untouched (only the part-tenants could now own the previously rented farmland), and the seized property was divided equally among poor peasants and farmhands.

By the summer of 1953, the traditional rural ruling class either had been physically annihilated or had at least forfeited its property, and frequently its prestige. The CCP had managed to transfer the lowest level of state and Party organization from the county (*hsien*) to the township (*hsiang*), which meant that the location of government moved from only about 2,500 to more than 200,000 places in the countryside. At the same time, property was equalized, and the income groups in the villages became more balanced. Average data from different regions indicate that middle peasants now accounted for 80 percent of the rural population, whereas the poor peasants made up 15 and the rich peasants about 5 percent. According to these data, the average size of a middle peasant's farm was about 2.3 acres, the poor peasants cultivated an average of 2.1 acres, and the rich peasants owned 3 acres.[55]

The middle peasants in particular profited from the changes the land reform brought to the villages. The schools were opened, often for the first time, to their offspring, and modest improvements in their economic conditions made it possible for them to buy simple consumer goods, which they had rarely been able to afford since 1937. Those rich peasants whose property was not essentially reduced by the land reform also experienced some improvement in their living conditions. The poor peasants could not participate in the social improvements to the same extent since, in most cases, they first had to learn the principles of independent farm management. Yet they found comfort in the improvement in their social prestige, for now they were known as "progressive elements" and the rural Party and administrative cadres were mostly recruited from their ranks. Those former landlords who had survived the terror of the land reform became the new social pariahs. They were granted neither civil rights nor the right to vote; they had lost their property; and only a few of them were given, subject to revocation, some patches of unirrigated or stony land.

Thus, the land reform brought about a reversal of the power and property structures, and the collectivization campaign of 1953/1955–1957 reduced social and economic differences in the villages even more. But it, too, could not reduce the gap between wealthier and poorer villages, or between the agricultural surplus and deficit areas.

By late 1957, almost all the Chinese peasants had been organized into 762,000 advanced socialist agricultural cooperatives, each with an average of 150–160 peasant households. All arable land, draft animals, cattle, and larger agricultural implements had now been transformed into collective property, although individual peasants kept small pieces of land as private plots (*Tzu-liu-ti*), which could be cultivated for the support of the family and for the sale of surpluses. Most of the fowl, rabbits, domestic animals, homes and the ground on which they stood, and small implements remained private property, but the peasants were now remunerated solely according to their labor, and had thus, in fact, become farmhands.

Whatever little the peasants still owned after the collectivization was taken away from them in the people's commune movement between May and November 1958, when 99 percent of the peasants were organized into 26,578 communes with an average of 4,637 households.[56] In these new communes, the whole life was to be collectivized, but the grave economic crisis of 1959–1961, together with the vehement resistance against the new collectives on the part of a large majority of the peasants, forced the CCP elite to enact drastic revisions in the commune concept. By 1962, the structures in the communes bore little resemblance to the model of 1958, and despite great efforts of the leftist forces around Mao and Lin Piao to raise the levels of collectivization again in 1969–1970, and to restrict the activities of the peasants, these structures prevailed toward the end of the era of Mao Tse-tung.

By 1975, there were therefore three levels of agricultural collective units: 52,000 people's communes, averaging about 2,600 households each; 700,000 production brigades (*Sheng-ch'an ta-tui*), each comprising an average of about 190–195 households (mostly a village or a cluster of hamlets); and 5,150,000 production teams (*Sheng-ch'an-tui*), of about 25–30 households each (mostly part of a village or one hamlet).[57] The commune was the lowest unit of public administration. It managed the hospitals, secondary schools, and a number of workshops as well as other enterprises. In many cases, it also owned the means of transportation. The coordinating functions of the commune included the responsibility of recruiting manpower from the brigades and teams for public works that transcended the scope of the brigade.

The brigades were responsible for the management of primary schools and, in many cases, kindergartens and day nurseries. They usually controlled those workshops that were not under commune management, all the heavy and medium-sized machinery—if available—and frequently the irrigation facilities. As a rule, the brigades were also in charge of all public works within their realm, and they coordinated the agricultural production of the teams.

The teams owned all arable land, large livestock, draft animals, and most agricultural tools. As the basic accounting unit, the team was responsible for guaranteeing a fixed amount of production (*Pao-ch'an*) for delivery to the state procurement organization. The *pao-ch'an* system gave the team responsibility for the planning and direction of all collective agricultural production, and the team therefore also had the power to distribute all remunerations in cash and kind to the peasants.

The peasant households could work on small private plots, which composed between 5 and 7 percent of the arable land, and engage in some private sideline occupations, including the raising of a limited number of fowl and pigs. But the team remained the unit of employment, and also the major working unit for the collective fields, which composed at least 93–95 percent of the farmland.

Hence, between 1949 and 1975, remarkable developments took place in the structures of the rural society. The middle peasants—since the mid-1960s divided into upper middle peasants (former owner-farmers) and lower middle peasants (former part-tenants)—became the new economical leaders in the villages, and the poor peasants (former tenants and farmhands) became the new political leaders. The former landlords and rich peasants, between 5 and 10 percent of the rural population, were still the pariahs without any substantial rights.

In some village areas, considerable progress was made in the development of a rural health service, albeit a primitive one, and of basic educational opportunities. Yet school fees still had to be paid, and compulsory education was mostly not enforced, so that only about half of the school-age children really went to school. Other rural developments included the facts that the use of chemical fertilizer slowly started to spread and the mobility of the rural population seemed to increase to a limited extent.

On the other hand, new social differences developed in the countryside after the early 1960s. The dividing line now was not only between comparatively rich and poor villages but within the villages, between those families who were able to reap modest profits from the cultivation of private plots and family sideline occupations and a strong minority of families that either had too little manpower in the household or were too lazy to make such profits. This latter group provided potential support for any attempt by the elite to raise the level of collectivization again.

Structures and Developments in Urban Society

The CCP already controlled considerable parts of the countryside when, between March 1948 (Loyang) and December 1949 (Ch'engtu), the Party's military arm, the People's Liberation Army (*Jen-min chieh-fang-chün* [PLA]), conquered the cities of China. In the cities, the upper class consisted of industrialists, large merchants, bankers, and high KMT officials who were knit into a comparatively close network. Academics, intellectuals in the humanities, technicians, and most administrative personnel formed an upper middle class, and artisans, small-shop owners, primary-school teachers, and also foremen and other highly skilled workers could be considered as parts of a lower middle class. The lower class was made up of industrial workers, unskilled laborers, and many beggars, mostly refugees from the countryside, and its share in the urban society ranged from 25 to 30 percent.

In order to overcome the devastating results of twelve years of war and to speed up the recovery of the urban economy, the CCP was first forced to cooperate with the upper and middle classes. Industrialists, businessmen, and even artisans had feared that the Communists, once victorious, would seize their property, but they were just asked to join in the efforts at recovery, and the majority of them were at first left unharmed by the victors of the civil war. In fact, they profited from the order and stability that the CCP managed to bring to the cities within a few months after its victory. Most of the intellectuals, who had suffered from the repressive features of KMT rule, also supported the Communists because they hoped for wider perimeters of cultural and academic freedom and because the Party appealed to the often fervently nationalist sentiments of the intelligentsia.

As the economic recovery unfolded, the CCP started to turn against the entrepreneurs and urban businessmen. In early 1952, a mass campaign was launched against tax evasion, fraud, bribery, industrial espionage, and theft of state property—the so-called Five-Anti-Campaign (*Wu-fan yün-tung*)—and "shock forces" from the Communist Youth League and the Party's labor unions attacked members of the bourgeoisie and pressured them into admitting such "crimes." Approximately 500 businessmen were executed, 34,000 were put into prison, and more than 2,000 committed suicide.[58] By the end of 1953, the business community had been thus thoroughly disciplined, so it did not offer much resistance when, within eleven weeks during the winter of 1955/1956, almost all industrialists, bankers, and large-shop owners "voluntarily" presented their property to the state for a compensation of 5 percent of the profit to be paid for twenty years.[59]

In late 1956, the nationalization of industries, banks, department stores, hotels, and restaurants was completed. At the same time, almost 6 million, or over 90 percent, of the artisans in the cities and more than 3.5 million of the small-shop owners were organized into cooperatives, in which, starting in 1958, they no longer shared in the profits but received regular wages. For industrial workers, wages were regulated by a decree in June 1956, and since then, all regularly employed Chinese workers have been divided into eight wage grades, with the difference between (the lowest) grade 1 and (the highest) grade 8 varying between 1 to 3.35 in heavy industry and 1 to 2.61 in the food industries.[60]

Thus, the CCP, in less than eight years, had succeeded in effecting the transformation of industry, handicrafts, and commerce into state or collective property. In terms of ownership, the cities of the PRC had become part of a socialist society by the end of 1957. Yet social contradictions continued to exist.

These contradictions became manifest first between intellectuals and the Party. From December 1954 to the end of 1955, a Campaign to Purge Counterrevolutionaries (*Su-fan yün-tung*) had already been directed against the non-Communist intelligentsia. In the course of this campaign, 81,000 intellectuals had been "unmasked and punished," and more than 300,000 had lost their civil rights because of "political unreliability."[61] Only when terror and uncertainty had brought academic teaching and research almost to a standstill, had the Party initiated relaxations in January 1956.

From these relaxations, there developed the Hundred Flowers Campaign (*Pai hua yün-tung*), in the course of which, in May and June 1957, exhorted by Mao Tse-tung himself, many intellectuals aired their misgivings about the policies of the CCP in public. Soon, this movement went out of control. Beginning with criticism of individual abuses and lower-level Party cadres, it grew into an all-out attack on the CCP, its leadership, the Marxist-Leninist ideology, and the political system. In June 1957, the Party struck back. Between July and November of that year, about 400 critics were executed, and according to the contemporary PRC media, between 300,000 and 550,000 were sent to concentration camps for "reform through labor" (*Lao-tung kai-tsao*).[62] Yet when most of those who had thus been treated were rehabilitated after twenty-one or twenty-two years of forced labor, in 1978/1979, figures totaling 946,000 rehabilitations were cited by the PRC media.[63]

With such measures, the CCP was able to silence the critical intellectuals, but it could hardly win back their support. On the contrary, when a second, and much less extensive, period of relaxation started in 1960/1961, criticism spread to the ranks of CCP intellectuals as well. The opposition was sharpened by the great famine that hit not only the villages but also the cities in 1961/1962. During that winter, food rations in most cities averaged between 3.8 and 12 ounces of unhusked rice—or the flour equivalent—and 0.1–0.2 ounces of edible oil per day, to which, once a month, 3.5–7 ounces of sugar and meat were added.[64]

Although the situation improved in 1963, and the food supply was at least stabilized in the cities by the fall of 1964, the economic crisis had intensified three major contradictions in the urban society.

- between the privileged Party cadres and the other groups of the populace
- between high school and university students, who became restive about the decreasing chances of employment, and many of their teachers
- between the workers in wage grades 1–4 and those in wage grades 5–8, as well as between all regularly employed workers—about 65–70 percent of the industrial labor force—and the 30–35 percent of the industrial laborers who worked only as contract or "temporary" workers (*Lin-shih kung-jen*), without any job security and without sharing any social benefits.

These contradictions exploded between May and August 1966 when the so-called Great Proletarian Cultural Revolution started. This grave political crisis culminated in 1967, and it ended only during the winter of 1968/1969. The left wing of the CCP around Mao, Lin Piao, and some of their closest associates mobilized high school and college students, apprentices, and contract workers as well as workers in the lowest wage grades against civilian Party cadres, intellectuals, and the earners of higher wages. Terror reigned in most Chinese cities, resulting in between 2 and 3 million deaths and the persecution of large segments of the urban society. Only when the movement went out of control and civil strife reached warlike proportions, did the PLA intervene to dissolve and suppress the cultural revolutionary mass organizations.

Students in large numbers were sent down to the countryside (*Hsia-fang*), where, as a disciplinary measure, they had to stay in the villages for an unspecified length of time. Until late 1975, more than 12 million high school and college students worked in the villages,[65] but many of them returned illegally to the cities, where they were soon to create new social problems.[66] Yet in spite of such contradictions and crises, there can be no doubt that social changes were much more effective in the urban society of the PRC than in the rural society. Toward the end of Mao Tse-tung's life, about 75 percent of the urban population was literate, and more than 80 percent of the school-age children in the cities went to school.

In 1981, official Chinese data—which appear to reflect a situation that did not change much in six years, so that these figures can generally be also applied to 1975—gave a number of 99.67 million people in the nonagricultural labor force. Of these people, 55.8 percent worked in industry and construction; 21.2 percent, in the services, including commerce and trade; 18.8 percent were cadres or belonged to the military; and 4.2 percent worked in the public health or utilities sectors.[67]

The social stratification of the urban population had undergone significant change, although the income and standard of living differentials between the classes had not decreased much. The old upper class had lost not only its economic power and political influence but also large parts of its material basis for life.

Cadres and military officers in the higher ranks, scientists, technical specialists, and artists and writers who demonstrated absolute loyalty to the politics of the CCP formed a new upper class, with relatively high incomes and important personal privileges. The new upper middle class consisted of engineers, workers in the wage grades 5–8, and the majority of the cadres in the Party and administrative machines. In this group, many of the former independent artisans could also be found.

Workers in wage grades 1–4, most employees in the services, and the few still existing owners of small mobile shops formed a new lower middle class, with at least some reasonable hope for future upward mobility. The new lower class comprised contract workers, the unemployed, and after the late 1960s, the great number of students who had returned illegally from the *Hsia-fang*. By 1975, this class's share in the urban population had grown to between 30 and 35 percent, i.e., slightly more than the old lower class of unskilled labor, contract workers, unemployed, and beggars in the cities before 1949. It was this new lower class that had the major potential for social unrest and, hence, was a concern for the elite, which, in changing composition, ruled the PRC.

Elite Structures and Elite Composition

So far, we have concentrated on the social structures and developments between the establishment of the PRC in 1949 and 1975, the year that preceded the death of Mao Tse-tung. When we turn to a discussion of the elites, however, we can include developments until 1983 because, on the one hand, a number of data are only available for the period since 1980, and, on the other hand, the structures of the political society in the PRC, except during the Cultural Revolution and its immediate aftermath between 1966 and 1972, have not much changed since the mid-1950s. This political society is a system of seven concentric circles with first gradually and later abruptly increasing degrees of participation in the political process.

The outermost seventh circle comprises the whole adult population, which is only the object of political decision making and which, in

1982, consisted of approximately 560 million people over eighteen years of age.[68] The next, the sixth, circle includes the members of the mass organizations, who are used as elements of mobilization in order to carry through the policies decided on by the central policymaking bodies. The major mass organizations are the All-China Federation of Labor Unions, the Chinese Communist Youth League, the All-China Youth Federation, the All-China Students' Federation, the National Women's Federation, the All-China Federation of Industry and Commerce, the Chinese Federation of Literacy and Art Circles, and the federations of poor and lower middle peasants, which are organized in most, though not all, administrative units. For most of these organizations, no membership figures have been given since 1965, but it appears safe to assume that by 1982, they had a total of between 140 million and 150 million members, or between 25 and 27 percent of the adult population.

In the fifth circle, there are the members of the CCP, who were said to have numbered 39,657,212 at the beginning of 1982,[69] or about 7 percent of the adult population. This share compares with 9.7 percent in the Soviet Union and almost 16 percent in East Germany. The organizational density of the CCP is therefore lower than that of other ruling Communist parties, but it has also entered the process of transforming from a revolutionary cadre party to a career-oriented mass party. Hence, the Party members, although serving as examples of affirmative attitudinal response to elite stimuli for the masses and as a reserve pool for political recruitment, are, as a whole, not able to influence political decisions even marginally. Yet from their midst, there arises the structure of the four inner circles, of which the fourth through the second can be considered as layers of a service hierarchy; only the first represents a decision-making hierarchy, which, in itself, is also structured.

The fourth circle is made up of those people who are officially called cadres (*Kan-pu*), and their number is given as about 14.5 million if one excludes the military,[70] which means 2.6 percent of the adult population and 36.5 percent of the Party members. These people are responsible for executing the directives of the leadership at the base. In the process, they may be able to change the thrust of the directives in some detail, but they, too, have no influence on the formulation of policy.

In the third circle, there are the recipients of internal Party documents— e.g., the serialized *Documents for Study* (*Hsüeh-hsi wen-chien*) or the circulars of the Party center (*Chung-yang fa-pu,* abbreviated, *Chung-fa*)—which seems to include between 700,000 and 1 million people,[71] or 0.125–0.178 percent of the adult population, respectively, and 1.8 to 2.5 percent of the Party members. This circle, in times of intraelite conflict, is occasionally addressed by the contending groups and factions, but its members are still not directly involved in such conflicts, although they may become their victims.

The second circle consists of the leading cadres (*Ling-tao kan-pu*). It includes about 80,000 persons, that is, 1 for every 7,000 adults, or 1 for almost every 500 Party members, and it comprises all leadership personnel down to the level of deputy bureau chiefs, deputy regimental commanders, and *hsien* magistrates or Party secretaries.[72] This group has close connections with the political elite, and in times of intraelite conflict, the contending groups and factions recruit followers from its members. Yet its members still are not involved in political decision making. That is the domain of the first and innermost circle, the political elite. This group decides the allocation of leadership positions, and it has a say in political formulation. It is in this circle of 1 person for every 700,000 adults or 50,000 Party members that intraelite groups form and power and policy conflicts are mainly decided. This political elite includes all leadership personnel down to the level of ministers, governors, provincial party secretaries and alternate secretaries, military district commanders and political commissars. It consisted of 581 people in October 1965, 506 in August 1970, 550 in October 1973, and 803 in April 1983. Within this political elite, three additional concentric circles can be detected:[73]

1. The executive heads, i.e., those persons who occupy the one leading position in all major Party, state, and military organs down to the level of the administrative units. They numbered 195 people in 1965, 130 in 1970, 112 in 1973, and 184 in 1983.
2. A decision combine, which includes all political leaders who are, at a given period, directly involved in the preparation of major policy decisions and who participate in the inner councils of policymaking. I would suggest that in 1983, this group comprised the members and alternates of the Politburo and the Secretariat of the CCP, the members of the Buro of the Party's Central Disciplinary Investigation Commission, and the members of the Presidium of the Central Advisory Commission. The decision combine, in my view, consisted of 32 members in both 1965 and 1970, 38 members in 1973, and 40 members in 1983.
3. The leadership core, which represents the very heart of rule formulation and which is identical with the Standing Committee of the Politburo. It numbered seven people in 1965, five in 1970, nine in 1973, and six in 1983.

Those de facto structures of the political elite, however, are superseded by the official structures, and it appears appropriate to use official

Table 4.1. Age structure of the CCs since 1956 (in percent)[74]

Age Group	Eighth CC (1956)	Ninth CC (1969)	Tenth CC (1973)	Eleventh CC (1977)	Twelfth CC (1982)
Under 40 years		2.5	3.6	3.2	
40-49 years	7.5	3.9	4.4	5.4	5.3
50-59 years	68.0	34.3	16.0	7.5	16.9
60-69 years	9.3	42.4	54.7	55.9	49.7
Over 70 years	5.2	16.9	21.1	28.0	28.1
60 years and older	14.5	59.3	75.8	83.9	77.8
Average age in year of appointment	53.9	61.4	62.1	64.6	64.4

structures as the basis for discussion when we turn to the issue of leadership composition. The following quantitative analysis therefore concentrates on the full members of the Central Committee of the CCP (*Chung-kung chung-yang wei-yüan-hui* [CC]).

Since 1949, five CCs have been appointed in the PRC: the Eighth in 1956, the Ninth at the end of the Cultural Revolution in 1969, the Tenth in 1973, the Eleventh in 1977, and the Twelfth in 1982. The number of full members has been steadily increasing, from 97 in the Eighth CC to 170 in the Ninth, 195 in the Tenth, 201 in the Eleventh, and 210 in the Twelfth. Fluctuation has been considerable, ranging from 63 percent of the members of the Eighth CC not being reappointed to the Ninth to 28.2 percent of the Ninth not being reappointed to the Tenth.

Yet, if we examine the age structure, geographic origin, education, Party seniority, organizational origin, and apparat positions of the five CCs, a number of common features can be detected in each area. For instance, the age structure shows the average age of the CC members has been increasing since the 1950s, as is indicated in Table 4.1. In terms of geographic origin, all five of the CCs have been heavily biased toward southern China—in the Chinese definition of *Nan-fang*, i.e., south of the Yangtzu but including all of Ssuch'uan and Hupei—and also toward the inland provinces as opposed to the coastal regions. Hence, the majority of the CC personnel represent a southern and inland elite, as Table 4.2 shows. Of the twenty-nine administrative units of the PRC, only two—Yünnan and Ninghsia—have never had any of their natives on a CC. Provincial representation in terms of birthplace expanded gradually from seventeen provinces in 1956 to twenty-two in 1969 to twenty-six in 1973, and it has since remained at that number.

The data on the educational background and study abroad of the CC members indicate that although the proportion of members with some higher education remained stable and high from 1956 until 1973, albeit

Table 4.2. Geographic origin of CC members since 1956 (in percent)[75]

Province	Eighth CC (1956)	Ninth CC (1969)	Tenth CC (1973)	Eleventh CC (1977)	Twelfth CC (1982)
Hunan	23.3	19.9	17.7	16.6	13.0
Hupei	10.9	17.2	10.1	12.1	8.9
Kiangsi	7.6	7.9	6.5	9.4	8.3
Ssuch'uan	10.9	7.3	7.7	9.9	10.7
Total for inland bloc: 23.7% of the population	52.7	52.3	42.0	48.0	40.9
Anhui	2.2	0.7	2.9	2.7	3.6
Chekiang	1.1	2.0	1.8	1.6	1.2
Ch'inghai				0.6	
Fukien	5.4	4.6	2.9	5.0	4.1
Heilungkiang	1.1	0.7	0.6	0.6	1.2
Honan	4.3	4.0	4.7	1.6	4.1
Hopei	4.3	6.0	4.7	5.0	5.3
Inner Mongolia	1.1	1.3	1.8	1.1	1.2
Kansu		0.7	1.2	0.6	0.6
Kiangsu	4.3	3.3	4.1	2.7	5.3
Kirin		0.7	0.6		0.6
Kuangsi		1.4	2.4	2.2	1.2
Kuangtung	6.5	6.0	4.1	2.2	1.2
Kueichou			0.6	0.6	0.6
Liaoning	1.1	2.6	2.4	1.1	2.9
Ninghsia					
Peking			1.2	1.1	3.6
Shanghai		1.3	4.7	2.2	3.6
Shansi	5.4	4.6	5.9	6.6	5.9
Shantung	3.3	5.3	3.5	3.9	5.9
Shensi	6.5	2.0	4.1	6.1	2.4
Sinkiang		0.7	1.3	1.1	1.8
Tibet			0.6	0.6	1.2
T'ienchin			1.2	1.6	0.6
Yünnan					
South China (51.35% of the population)	70.6	72.8	67.5	65.7	59.8
North China (48.65% of the population)	29.4	27.2	32.5	34.3	40.2
Inland provinces (59.79% of the population)	70.6	68.9	68.0	71.3	69.8
Coastal provinces (40.21% of the population)	29.4	31.1	32.0	28.7	30.2

Note: Numbers do not add to 100% because of rounding.

with significant variations between colleges and military academies from 1956 to 1969, it has since declined remarkably. The proportion of CC members who have studied abroad has significantly decreased ever since 1969, and especially since 1977, as Table 4.3 shows. At first glance, it seems astonishing that the ratio of higher education and primary education graduates should vary between 7:1 and almost 4:1 in the leadership of a Party that calls itself "proletarian." This trend seems to have been broken from 1973 to 1977, but in 1982, with a relationship of 4.7:1, it reappeared.

The Party seniority of the CC members, measured by the duration of membership in the CCP, changed remarkably between 1956 and 1982, mainly because of biological coercion. A comparison between those people who joined the CCP before the Long March in 1934/1935 and those who joined between 1935 and 1949, as well as the newcomers after 1949, is given in Table 4.4. Although the proportion of those revolutionary veterans who joined the CCP before 1935 dropped from 99 percent to a little less than half between 1956 and 1982, it is still significant that nearly half of all members of the Twelfth CC had been CCP members for periods between forty-seven and sixty-one years by 1982. In 1973, it seemed that the new generation—those who had joined after 1949—was coming up. This trend, however, was reversed in 1977, and in 1982 the proportion of those who had entered the CCP after the establishment of the PRC decreased once more, thus indicating that a major generational change has not yet occurred.

In terms of organizational origin, the variation between civilian cadres and military men has been remarkably strong, and so has the variation in the representation of mass organizations between 1969 and 1982. These variations are shown in Table 4.5. Organizational origin, however, does not necessarily mean apparat position, i.e., the position a CC member held at the time of appointment to a CC. In this regard, the major position is counted only in terms of central or regional, military or civilian machines. For example, a first provincial party secretary who concurrently holds the position of first political commissar of a military district is counted only as regional civilian, not as part of a regional military machine. With the Cultural Revolution, a tendency toward militarization and regionalization of the CC elite started. The trend toward militarization was broken with the demise of Lin Piao in 1971, but the trend toward regionalization continued until 1977, as Table 4.6 indicates.

This survey leads to the conclusion that in spite of remarkable changes in some areas, significant elements of continuity have, since the mid-1950s, characterized the political elite in the PRC, as represented here by the full members of the Party's CCs. This political elite was and,

Table 4.3. Educational background of CC members since 1956 (in percent)[76]

Last Type of School Attended	Eighth CC (1956)	Ninth CC (1969)	Tenth CC (1973)	Eleventh CC (1977)	Twelfth CC (1982)
Colleges and universities	44.3	23.8	26.8	25.7	29.7
Military academies	15.5	35.7	36.8	30.1	24.2
Normal schools	13.4	16.7	9.7	8.6	6.0
Total higher education	73.2	76.2	73.3	64.4	55.9
Secondary schools	7.3	10.3	8.9	18.4	27.3
Primary schools	6.2	11.9	8.3	10.4	10.1
No formal education	4.1	1.6	7.7	6.7	2.7
Total primary education	10.3	13.5	16.0	17.1	12.8
Studies abroad	46.4	32.5	20.9	10.4	10.5

Note: Some totals do not add to 100% because of rounding; data for Eighth CC incomplete.

Table 4.4. Party seniority of CC members since 1956 (in percent)[77]

Period of Joining CCP	Eighth CC (1956)	Ninth CC (1969)	Tenth CC (1973)	Eleventh CC (1977)	Twelfth CC (1982)
1921-1935	99.0	80.4	63.2	67.2	49.2
1935-1949	1.0	11.9	15.4	16.9	37.0
Before 1949	100.0	92.3	78.6	84.1	86.2
After 1949		7.7	21.4	15.9	13.8

Table 4.5. Organizational origin of CC members since 1956 (in percent)[78]

Group	Eighth CC (1956)	Ninth CC (1969)	Tenth CC (1973)	Eleventh CC (1977)	Twelfth CC (1982)
Civilian cadres	69.0	31.0	44.6	55.4	66.3
PLA commanders	19.6	35.3	25.9	21.2	16.2
PLA polit-commissars	11.4	14.7	11.6	11.2	9.0
Total PLA	31.0	50.0	37.5	32.4	25.2
Mass organizations		17.7	17.9	11.2	7.1

Note: Not all totals add to 100% because of rounding or incomplete data.

Table 4.6. Apparat position of CC members since 1956 (in percent)[79]

Machines	Eighth CC (1956)	Ninth CC (1969)	Tenth CC (1973)	Eleventh CC (1977)	Twelfth CC (1982)
Central civilian	46.1	20.4	22.7	25.4	38.2
Central military	23.1	21.0	13.8	16.4	10.8
Regional civilian	28.6	32.0	40.2	41.3	38.2
Regional military	2.2	26.6	23.3	16.4	12.8
Central machines	69.2	41.4	36.5	41.8	49.0
Regional machines	30.8	58.6	63.5	57.7	51.0
Civilian machines	74.7	52.4	62.9	66.7	76.4
Military machines	25.3	47.6	37.1	32.8	23.6

Note: Totals for Eleventh CC do not add to 100% because of incomplete data.

despite a tendency toward decrease because of biological reasons, still is dominated by aging veteran revolutionaries, and the southern and inland parts of the country are clearly overrepresented. Tendencies toward a stronger representation of persons who have joined the Party since 1949 and of spokesmen of the mass organizations, which appeared during and after the Cultural Revolution, have been thwarted, as has the tendency toward a militarization of the elite. Ever since the establishment of the PRC, the elite has been faced with the task of forging and sustaining support from society. It has done so with varying success at best.

Social Coalitions and Their Development Until 1975

Even if participation in the political process in the PRC is limited to a group that consists of 1 person per 700,000 adults, or 1 person per almost 50,000 CCP members—with recruitment of active followers extending only to 1 person per 7,000 adults or 500 Party members—this situation does not mean that policymaking never reflects developments in the society at large. In the 1950s, some of the more primitive ideas that arose from the theory of totalitarianism tended to create the impression that in what was called "totalitarian states," an extremely efficient elite imposed its will upon a totally silent populace. With the benefit of hindsight over more than sixty-five years of Marxist-Leninist regimes, and thirty-four years of PRC history, we are able to take a somewhat more differentiated approach to the explanation of interactions between elite and society in totalistic single-party systems, in China as elsewhere.

It is suggested that the seizure of power by totalistically oriented elites, and the stability of political systems dominated by such elites, depend upon the forging and sustaining of social coalitions (this necessity does not mean that the elites consider themselves as faithful executives of such coalitions). Within all strata of any given society, specific hopes, expectations, and requests are inherent. Elites can only seize power if they manage to respond to them, and in order to stay in power, elites have to renew such responsiveness, at least occasionally. A social coalition is defined here as a loose alliance that accumulates the demands of different social strata, demands that are usually, though not always, inherent rather than openly pronounced.

The CCP elite was able to defeat the KMT in the civil war and to seize power in China in 1949 because it managed to secure the support of a formidable social coalition that consisted of a sizable majority of five strata of Chinese society.

- its own basic-level cadres
- industrial workers
- intellectuals
- secondary school and college students
- landless farmhands, poor peasants, and large portions of the middle peasantry

Until the mid-1950s, the ruling elite was able to hold this social coalition together. It offered the basic-level cadres career channels and also a number of quite agreeable privileges. The living conditions of the industrial workers improved, and as "proletarians," they ranked high in the new prestige scale of the urban society. Until the end of the Korean War, the Party's propaganda appealed to the nationalist sentiments of many intellectuals, who also hoped that the new regime would offer them a larger share of participation in the political process and more freedom of expression. The students experienced an increase in the chances for education and upward mobility, and the land hunger of large segments of the Chinese peasantry was satisfied by the land reform movement. Because the early years of Communist rule had brought peace and stability after twelve years of continuous war, even many members of the urban upper and upper middle classes were positively inclined toward the new ruling elite, at least until they were hit by the persecutions of the Five-Anti Campaign in 1952/1953.

Yet in the mid-1950s, this social coalition started to erode. It was first deserted by the non-Communist intellectuals and a large number

of students who were then in school. The repressive policies of 1955—
the purge campaign among intellectuals—did not, as the elite had hoped,
result in the reeducation of these groups, but rather in their fervent
opposition, which became articulated during the Hundred Flowers
Campaign in the spring of 1957. Although the CCP finally succeeded
in disciplining the non-Communist intelligentsia with harsh suppression,
it was not able to win back the support of that group until the death
of Mao. As a result of the establishment of the people's communes and
the ensuing economic debacle in the villages, most peasants were the
next to turn their backs on the Party by the fall of 1958. Whenever the
ruling elite, since then, has attempted to raise the level of collectivization,
passive and occasionally even active resistance has arisen in the villages.
Such negative attitudinal responses from the peasants forced the leadership to engage in the readjustment of the communes, and it led to
the breakdown of the attempt to return to the prescriptions of 1958
between 1969 and 1971. Continuous and regionally or nationally coordinated opposition has not developed in the countryside, but the peasants
also have not returned to full-fledged support of the elite's policies.

The basic-level cadres started to develop a feeling of insecurity when
the central authorities tried to make them the scapegoats for the economic
crisis that followed the Great Leap Forward in 1959/1960. In many
places, these cadres joined the peasants in passive resistance,[80] or at
least tried to strike a balance between the conflicting demands of the
elite and the peasantry. The persecutions carried out by the Maoist
mass organizations during the Cultural Revolution and the frequency
of shifts in the political line between 1969 and 1975 increased the
insecurity of the basic-level cadres and wore out their motivation to
respond favorably to elite stimuli. The permanently employed industrial
workers, particularly those in grades 5–8 of the wage scale, left the
social coalition when their privileges were attacked during the Cultural
Revolution. In early 1967, they spearheaded the urban resistance against
the activities of the Maoist mass organizations.

Hence, Mao Tse-tung, Lin Piao, and their close associates in the
cultural revolutionary Left had to rely on a quite different coalition of
social forces that at the outset, in 1966–1967, comprised a majority of
urban students, workers in the lowest wage grades, contract workers,
and some segments of the lowest income group among the peasants.
This was, although reasonably organized and highly motivated, a minority
social coalition. And it was, in turn, left by most students when the
PLA cracked down on their mass organizations and sent millions of
them to the countryside.

Between 1971 and 1975, many students returned illegally from the
villages to their home cities.[81] Since they could receive neither working

permits nor food or textile rations there, they provided a potential for criminal activities, and crime, prostitution, and black marketeering increased dramatically in the early 1970s.[82] Furthermore, the number of young people who fled to Hongkong rose sharply after 1969: In the summer of 1975, more than 52,000 youngsters who had arrived as refugees since 1969 were living in the British colony.[83]

Attempts by followers of the cultural revolutionary Left to prepare for a return to the Maoist policies in the countryside, which conflicted with attempts of their rivals in the elite to sustain the results of the readjustment in the people's communes, tended to further destabilize the situation in the villages between 1973 and 1975. In order to fend off such a new collectivist offensive, many production teams reported low harvest figures so they could distribute more food grains among the peasant households. Other teams gave collective land to peasants for individual production and used the transport facilities of the collective to move the products of private sideline occupations to free markets. Many peasants worked on their private plots when the weather was favorable and reserved the periods of bad weather for working the collective fields, or they delegated the weaker members of their families for collective work while the more able-bodied tilled the private plots.[84]

By 1975, the policies that were promoted by the cultural revolutionary Left—i.e., the equalization of wages, higher levels of collectivization, priority of political indoctrination over factual knowledge in education, and the Maoist concept of development through enthusiastic austerity—could muster support only from a social coalition of contract and low-wage-grade workers, cadres who had advanced during the Cultural Revolution, the lowest strata of village society, and those students who had not been sent to the countryside because of elite connections.

Most other social strata opposed the Left, although for many different reasons and still not in a coordinated manner. The time for a new, anti-Maoist coalition had arrived, and such a coalition would develop rapidly during the last year and a half of the aging and ailing Party leader's life.

Before following the events that shaped PRC policies in early 1975, we should first look at the development and current state of the political institutions, which provide a frame for the political process.

PART 2

Political Institutions

CHAPTER 5

The Chinese Communist Party

A Note on the Role of Institutions

It would be misleading if one described the political institution of the PRC without first calling attention to the fact that since 1949, the ruling CCP elite has only acted within the limits of Party and state law as long as the law has not been perceived to be an impediment for the implementation of political goals. Hence, the country's constitution and the Party statutes have been—and probably still are—of only limited importance for political decision making.

One of the main characteristics of the political system in the PRC is its institutional instability, or its institutional dynamics. For thirty-four years, the country has had the provisional constitution of 1949 and the four permanent constitutions of 1954, 1975, 1978, and 1982. In the same period, five different Party statutes were enacted: September 26, 1956; April 14, 1969; August 28, 1973; August 18, 1977; and September 6, 1982.[1] With the exception of the years from 1954 to 1957 and since 1978, i.e., for twenty-six out of thirty-four years, formal organization played only a minor role in the political process. From 1956 to 1977, no Party congress served its statutory term of five years, nor did the CCs appointed by the Party congresses: The Eighth CC exceeded its term by almost eight years, the Ninth served only four years and four months, and the Tenth served four years.

The National People's Congress did not convene in thirteen of the thirty years in which it formally officiated: 1961, 1964, 1966 to 1974, 1976, and 1977. One former chief of state—the chairman of the PRC—Liu Shao-ch'i, whose term ended officially in January 1969, was deposed in October 1968 and not by the organ that alone had the constitutional right to do so, the National People's Congress, but by a plenary of the Party's CC, which had not even rallied the statutory quorum. In April 1976, a prime minister was appointed, and a deputy premier deposed, by a decision of the Party's Politburo without even an attempt to seek constitutional legitimization. One should keep these facts in mind while looking at the structure of the political institutions, of which the CCP is today obviously the most important.

Basic Trends in Party History

The Party was founded as an organization of revolutionary intellectual youth, with strong Soviet support, in late June 1921,[2] when the twelve delegates of the First Party Congress represented a total of fifty-seven members. At that time, some of the delegates intended to postpone organizational activities and to continue concentrating on academic studies of Marxism, but the majority decided to start a centralized organization under the leadership of Ch'en Tu-hsiu, a well-known scholar, as secretary general. Until the summer of 1923, the CCP tried to organize an autonomous labor movement, and it perceived that the KMT was its major rival and severely criticized the policies of Sun Yat-sen's Nationalist party. But soon after the Soviet Union and the Communist International (Comintern), on the one hand, and the KMT, on the other, had concluded an alliance, the CCP was pressured by the Comintern to form a united front with the KMT in the form of a bloc from within (*Tang-nei he-tso*), which meant that the CCP members would join the KMT but also retain their own special Party organization. The alliance with the KMT and a broad nationalist, anti-Western urban movement in the summer of 1925 brought the Chinese Communists their first major success: Within a few months, CCP membership increased from almost 1,000 to more than 10,000.[3]

The Party was able to further broaden its influence within the KMT during the struggle for succession among Nationalist leaders after the death of Sun in March 1925. By early 1926, Communists dominated the organization, propaganda, and peasant-work and labor-work departments of the KMT's central party headquarters, as well as considerable parts of the political commissars' machine within the KMT army in and around Canton. But the commander of that army, General Chiang Kai-shek, became increasingly irritated by the Communist influence and struck a first blow against the CCP on March 20, 1926, by arresting several leading Communists and disbanding the workers' militia, which was led by the Party. As a result, a number of CCP leaders demanded that the Communists withdraw from the "bloc from within," yet Stalin and, under his influence, the Comintern forced the CCP to continue the alliance. This decision of the authorities in Moscow proved to be justified for the moment.

When Chiang led his army against the warlords in July 1926, the Communists were able to strengthen their influence tremendously in the rear of the KMT army, particularly among the impoverished peasants of Hunan. In the spring of 1927, when the Nationalist forces had reached the Yangtzu, conquering Shanghai and Nanking, CCP membership had already increased to 58,000, Communists occupied the ministries of agriculture and labor in the national government of the KMT, which had moved to Wuhan. The labor unions led by the CCP numbered 2.8 million members, and 2 million peasants had joined the peasant associations that Mao Tse-tung was rallying in Hunan.[4]

It appeared as if the time was ripe to remove the bourgeoisie from the united front and, after a stage of dictatorship by a bloc of petty bourgeoisie, peasants, and workers—i.e., cooperation of the CCP with the left wing of the KMT—to establish the dictatorship of the proletariat in China, meaning the rule of the CCP. This goal was what Stalin hoped to achieve by his insistence on the united front strategy, but the right wing and the center of the KMT waged a preemptive strike. On April 12, 1927, under the leadership of Chiang, these groups broke with the Communists and destroyed the CCP organization by massive repression and terror, first in Shanghai and soon after in most of southern China. In July 1927, the left wing of the KMT, with headquarters in Wuhan, also broke with the CCP. The united front strategy had failed. Ch'en Tu-hsiu was made the scapegoat and removed from the leadership of the Party, which now seemed as though it would be paralyzed for a long time.

But Mao Tse-tung led an abortive rebellion of soldiers, miners, and farmhands in some areas of Hunan in September 1927 and escaped with the remnants of his followers to the Chingkang Mountains near the border between Hunan and Kiangsi. There, he joined forces with the remnants of another CCP-influenced military unit under General Chu Te, and the two established a revolutionary base, a Soviet area (*Su-wei-ai ch'ü*), from which they gradually expanded their influence. The official CCP leadership, meanwhile, convened a Sixth Party Congress in Moscow in the summer of 1928. After that congress, the official leaders turned to subversive organizational work in the cities along the East China coastline, particularly Shanghai. But by 1932, they had worn themselves out by factional infighting, so the actual center of Communist activities in China shifted more and more to the Soviet areas led by Mao.

From 1928 to 1931, the Soviet areas were growing in South China and, by guerrilla tactics, succeeded in fending off three major offensives launched by Chiang Kai-shek's KMT army. Through extensive land reforms, the CCP guerrilla army secured the support of tenants and landless peasants and, by 1933, had brought almost 60 million inhabitants under the control of its approximately 200,000 soldiers. A fourth KMT offensive was partially withstood, too.

But in the spring of 1934, the national government mobilized 550,000 troops for a fifth offensive under the personal command of Chiang. The official CCP leadership, which had fled to the Soviet area in southern Kiangsi in 1932/1933, managed to push Mao aside and decided to confront the enemy with a stationary trench instead of mobile guerrilla warfare. The results of this decision were devastating. In October 1934, the Nationalist forces had encircled 100,000 CCP troops in a small area of southernmost Kiangsi, and the Red Army was threatened with complete destruction. At this moment, the CCP leaders decided to attempt a breakout, and on October 16, 1934, about 90,000 guerrillas pushed through the encirclement and escaped eastward to southern Hunan.

Thus began the heroic phase in the history of the CCP known as the Long March (*Ch'ang-cheng*). The Red Army, continuously fighting troops of the national government, provincial military units, and native tribes, marched almost 7,000 miles, crossing Hunan, Kueichou, Ssuch'uan, eastern Tibet, the Gobi Desert, and Kansu. After more than a year, about 15,000–20,000 Communists reached the area around Paoan in northern Shensi where they established their new base—a tight elite of motivated revolutionaries, hardened by a long period of suffering. During this time, an enlarged conference of the Politburo at Tsunyi in Kueichou had appointed Mao chairman of the Military Commission of the CC in January 1935, and since the Party at that time was basically identical with the Red Army, Mao had actually become the leader of the Communist movement in China. In mid-1937, he and his forces, numbering now about 80,000, controlled an area of 4 million inhabitants in Shensi. But this area was remote and extremely poor, and the KMT army—despite some moves toward a KMT/CCP rapprochement after the temporary arrest of Chiang Kai-shek by warlord troops in Sian in December 1936—made plans for a sixth and probably final offensive against the Communists. The CCP urgently needed a respite in order to survive.

This respite was gained when Japan attacked China on July 7, 1937, and the Communists could conclude a second united front with their enemies in the KMT to resist the Japanese aggression together. This time, however, the Communists retained their territorial base, their administrative autonomy, and their own troops in a formal coalition, a bloc from without (*Tang-wai he-tso*).

From 1937–1944/1945, the KMT army fought desperate defensive battles against the major part of the invading Japanese troops, and with very heavy sacrifices it succeeded in holding most of West China until the end of the war. Meanwhile, the Communists soon turned to guerrilla activities and established new administrative areas behind the Japanese

Table 5.1.   Development of CCP membership, 1949-1977[6]

Year	Party Members	Year	Party Members
1949	4,500,000	1961	17,000,000
1953	6,000,000	1969	21,000,000
1956	10,734,384	1973	28,000,000
1959	13,960,000	1977	35,000,000

lines in northern China and Tungpei (Manchuria). Their guerrilla warfare never constituted a serious strategic threat to the Japanese forces, but it immensely strengthened the position of the CCP. Within the Party, Mao and his supporters had managed to purge the remnants of the old official leadership, which was loyal to Stalin and the Comintern, by 1938/1939. Thus, Mao became the undisputed Party leader, a development that was finally confirmed at the Seventh Party Congress, in May 1945, when he was chosen chairman of the CC.

By then, the Party consisted of more than 1 million members. It controlled areas of about 95 million inhabitants and had 910,000 regular soldiers and 2.2 million local militiamen at its disposal.[5] Most of the rural areas in northern China and the north and center of Tungpei were already in its hands. From this base, and after a peaceful settlement of the postwar organization of China could not be achieved with the KMT, the CCP set out to conquer the country in 1946, a task that it accomplished in less than four years. The fighting Party had thus, and mainly through its own efforts though not without Soviet support, turned into a ruling Party, which grew fast in membership numbers, as Table 5.1 indicates.

Since 1949, the history of the CCP has been identical with the history of the PRC. There were the triumphs of successful economic recovery after the war, of the heavy-handed suppression of remaining KMT resistance, and of the land reform as well as the successes in economic development during the First Five-Year Plan, in agricultural collectivization, and in the socialist transformation of the urban society. These achievements were celebrated at the Eighth Party Congress in September 1956, which seemed to introduce a period of full institutionalization of Communist rule.

Yet with Mao's collectivist offensive in the Great Leap Forward of 1958, its almost total failure, and the ensuing economic crisis, The Chairman's charisma started to erode. From 1962 to 1965, intraparty conflict developed between Mao, Lin Piao, and their close associates on the one hand and the majority of the civilian Party leadership around Liu Shao-ch'i and Teng Hsiao-p'ing on the other. By late 1965, this conflict had reached the stage of an open rift, which culminated in the Cultural Revolution (1966–1969), a crisis that became a traumatic experience for the whole Party. When the crisis subsided, the Maoist left wing had succeeded in purging almost half of the members and alternates of the Politburo, 55.7 percent of the full CC members, nine out of thirteen members and alternates of the Secretariat, and twenty-three out of twenty-eight provincial Party leaders. Many thousands of Mao's adversaries within the CCP had been killed, died in prison, sent to concentration camps, or sent to the countryside for manual labor. But the Cultural Revolution had also resulted in a total breakdown of Party organization. The reconstruction of the civilian Party machine, mostly under the supervision of the PLA, started with the reestablishment of the central decision-making organs at the Ninth Party Congress in April 1969, when Lin Piao became the only deputy and designated successor of Mao. The reconstruction continued with the reestablishment of the provincial Party organizations, which took place between November 1970 and August 1971. At the same time, the Party organization was reestablished in about 17 percent of the *hsien* and in about one-third of the basic-level units.

Yet the reconstruction of the CCP organization coincided with a new intraparty conflict, the Lin Piao crisis, which culminated in the purge and death of Mao's designated successor on September 12, 1971. In 1972 and 1973, the first cadres to have been purged during the Cultural Revolution came back to the fore, among them Teng Hsiao-p'ing, who returned to the CC at the Tenth Party Congress in August 1973 and a few months later to the Politburo and its Standing Committee. While the Party machine evolved anew everywhere in the country, the elite remained split between the Maoists of the cultural revolutionary Left and the increasingly strong forces that supported the policy prescriptions of the early 1960s. A new conflict was in the making, which shall be reviewed later. Now, however, a description and an analysis of the CCP as an institution in 1983 are presented.

Membership and Organizational Structure

With almost 40 million members in the fall of 1982, the CCP is the largest Communist Party in the world. The tasks and the organization of the Party are currently regulated by a Party statute that was promulgated at the Twelfth Party Congress on September 6, 1982.[7] Like its predecessors of 1956, 1969, 1973, and 1977, the statute proclaims the maxim of "democratic centralism" as the Party's organizational principle: "The individual Party member obeys the Party organization, the minority obeys the majority, the organizations of the lower levels obey those of the upper levels, and all organizations as well as all members of the whole Party obey the Party Congress and the CC."[8]

Under democratic centralism, the idea of democracy is formally safeguarded by the provision that all leading organs are to be elected. The idea of centralism—in reality, more important than that of democracy—requires full attention to Party discipline and unconditional obedience. Every CCP member is considered a "vanguard fighter of the workers' class," who must "conscientiously study Marxism/Leninism and the Thought of Mao Tse-tung"—the latter now defined as the crystallization of the collective wisdom of the CCP." He or she must be "loyal and devout to the Party" and has to "actively fulfil all Party tasks."[9] In particular, the members are urged to maintain the "unity of the Party": The formation of factions is absolutely prohibited.[10]

The ruling elite considers the CCP members to be the major mobilizing and developmental cadres in the country. On all levels and in all areas of political and social activities, they are responsible for the implementation of the policies that have been decided upon by the leadership. In principle, every "Chinese worker, peasant, soldier, intellectual, and other revolutionary element" above the age of eighteen can join the CCP.[11] The application for membership must be supported by two guarantors, and the applicant has to serve between one and two years as a "candidate member." After that, and with the approval of the next higher level of the leadership, he or she can be accepted as a full member of the Party.[12] In practice, however, applicants for membership are usually accepted only after an invitation to apply, and the overwhelming majority of new members is recruited from the Communist Youth League (*Kung-ch'an-chu-yi ch'ing-nien t'uan* [CYL]), from among nonpartisan cadres in the mass organizations, and—since 1978—from scientific circles.

Since 1961, no data have been published on the social origin of the CCP members. At that time, 69 percent were peasants; 14 percent, workers; and 11 percent, intellectuals. Women provided 10 percent of the membership; national minorities, barely 1 percent.[13] It appears that these figures have not changed much since 1961, although the proportion of women may have significantly increased. There are no data available to support this assumption, which, nonetheless, seems to be correct.

The organizational structure of the CCP is very similar to that of any ruling Communist Party (see Figure 5.1). It has the form of a pyramid, on the base of which there are the Party branches (*Tang-te chih-pu*) or, in case of a larger membership in the respective units, general branches (*Tsung-chih-pu*) and basic organizations (*Chi-ts'eng tsu-chih*). The basic organizations hold annual members' congresses and are led by a committee and a secretary (*Shu-chi*). In the cities, the basic organizations are usually established according to the functional principle, i.e., in "factories, shops, schools, offices . . . , PLA companies, and

70

Figure 5.1.   ORGANIZATIONAL STRUCTURE OF THE CHINESE COMMUNIST PARTY

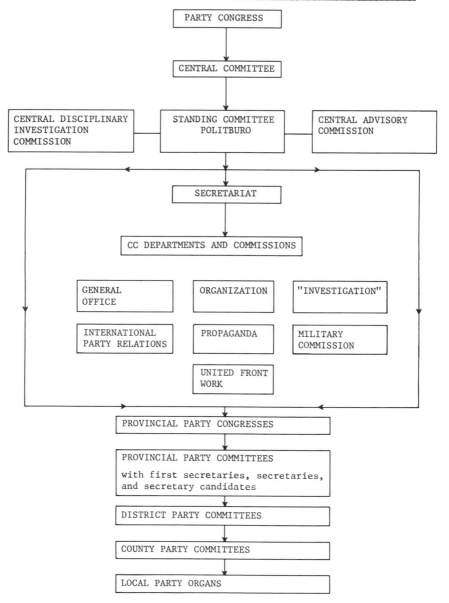

other basic units," yet there are also organizations established according to the territorial principle, with Party branches on a "street basis."[14] In the countryside, both principles are combined, with basic organizations in people's communes (wherever they still exist), cooperatives, state farms, and villages. Here, of course, residence and place of work are mostly identical.

In 1959, there were a total of 1,050,000 Party branches with an average membership of thirteen. In the fall of 1982, there were supposed to be about 1,460,000 basic organizations and branches with an average membership of twenty-seven.[15] On the higher levels, the civilian Party machine is organized strictly according to the territorial principle. All levels have their Party congresses, elected by the Party congress of the respective lower level, which, in turn, elect party committees. The committees then appoint a Secretariat under the leadership of a first secretary (*Ti-i shu-chi*), a Disciplinary Investigation Commission (*Chi-lü chien-ch'a wei-yüan-hui*), and—on the provincial level only—an Advisory Commission (*Ku-wen wei-yüan-hui*). Party congresses on the county level are held every three years; on the provincial level, every five.[16]

The next level consists of the Party organizations in the townships (*hsiang*). Then follow the organizations in the 2,772 *hsien* (counties), autonomous hsien, banners (*ch'i*), and municipalities (*shih*), which are in turn directed by the organizations in the 208 districts (*Ti-ch'ü*), autonomous districts, and leagues (*meng*).[17] The second highest level consists of the CCP organizations in the twenty-one provinces, five autonomous regions, and the three directly administered cities of Peking, Shanghai, and T'ienchin.

There is, however, one exception to the principle of territorial rather than functional organization on the higher levels: The PLA has its own pyramid of Party organizations, rising from the "base" in the companies through the battalions, regiments, divisions, and corps up to the eleven military areas. It is only on the central level that the civilian and the military Party machines are finally combined.

The provincial Party committees (PPCs), and particularly their executive organs, the provincial secretariats with their first secretaries, are rather important parts of the ruling elite with a considerable amount of autonomy. This autonomy was particularly strong in the aftermath of the Cultural Revolution, between 1971 and 1979/1980, but even after that period, their support is still considered to be of great value for the central leadership, especially during periods of acute intraelite conflict. On the eve of the Cultural Revolution, in October 1965, there were 267 secretaries and alternate secretaries of the PPC. After the reconstruction of the PPCs, by August 1971, their number had decreased to 158.

However, by August 1982, on the eve of the Twelfth Party Congress, the number had risen again to 283, including 234 full and 49 alternate secretaries. At the same time, the standing committees of the PPC had a total of 705 members.

Then, a restructuring of the PPC took place in the spring of 1983 in all twenty-nine administrative units, and the number of secretaries was greatly reduced as well as the membership of the standing committees, starting in Ssuch'uan on February 6 and ending in Shensi on April 18. Since this reform the total number of members on the standing committees is 334, ranging from 9 to 15 per province. There are now only 100 secretaries and 47 alternate secretaries left, the lowest figure since the early 1950s. Fifty-seven members of this group belong to the CC, and four belong to the Central Advisory Commmission (CAC).

A group of special political importance among the regional leadership is formed by the first secretaries of the twenty-nine administrative units on the provincial level of CCP organization, although since the restructuring in the spring of 1983, this title has not yet been conferred on the new leaders of the PPC in nine of the provinces. Of this group of twenty-nine, twenty-three are full members of the CC, and four are members of the CAC. A list of their names reflects clearly the political developments in the period after the death of Mao. Of the twenty-nine first secretaries appointed between the Cultural Revolution and the demise of Lin Piao, not a single one is still in office, nor are any of those appointed between 1971 and Mao's death.

Of the current group, five were appointed in 1977 and 1978; thirteen, between early 1979 and the Twelfth Party Congress; and eleven, since September 1982. In terms of their experience during the Cultural Revolution, twenty-two, or almost 76 percent were purged; five, or 17 percent, survived substantially unharmed; and for two, the record is not clear. Yet by September 1, 1983, no cadre whose career had been advanced by the Cultural Revolution was still in office as provincial first secretary. The average age of those twenty-seven members of the group for whom age data are available was 65.0 years at the end of 1983. A list of the group is given in Table 5.2.

The Party congresses of the administrative units on the provincial level—as well as those of the eleven military areas—are also the electorates for the National Party Congress (*Ch'üan-kuo tai-piao ta-hui*), which was officially designated by the Party statutes of 1956, 1969, 1973, 1977, and 1982 as the highest leading organ of the CCP. In fact, however, only the 1,026 delegates of the Eighth Congress and the 1,545 delegates of the Twelfth Congress were, at least formally, elected by the representative organs on the provincial level, and there is no available information whatsoever on the procedure of choosing the 1,512 delegates

Table 5.2. Provincial first secretaries of the CCP, September 1, 1983

Province	Name	Born	Appointed	Cultural Revolution Status	Member of
Yünnan	An P'ing-sheng	1912	Feb. 1977	survived	CC
Kuangsi	Ch'iao Hsiao-kuang	1917	Feb. 1977	survived	CC
Hunan	Mao Chih-yung	?	June 1977	survived	CC
Inner Mongolia	Chou Hui	1917	Sept. 1978	purged	CC
T'ienchin	Ch'en Wei-ta	?	Oct. 1978	purged	CC
Shensi	Ma Wen-jui	1909	Jan. 1979	purged	CC
Ninghsia	Li Hsüeh-chih	1922	April 1979	purged	CC
Shanghai	Ch'en Kuo-tung	1911	Feb. 1980	purged	CC
Kueichou	Ch'ih Pi-ch'ing	1921	June 1980	purged	CC
Kuangtung	Gen. Jen Chung-yi	1913	Nov. 1980	purged	CC
Liaoning	Kuo Feng	1914	Nov. 1980	purged	CAC
Peking	Tuan Chün-yi	1913	Jan. 1981	survived	CAC
Tibet	Gen. Yin Fa-t'ang	1922	Jan. 1981	survived	CC
Honan	Liu Chieh	1913	Jan. 1981	purged	CAC
Sinkiang	Gen. Wang En-mao	1913	Oct. 1981	purged	CC
Kirin	Ch'iang Hsiao-ch'u	1918	Nov. 1981	purged	CC
Fukien	Hsiang Nan	1916	Feb. 1982	purged	CC
Hopei	Kao Yang	1913	July 1982	purged	CAC
Kiangsi	Pai Tung-ts'ai	1908	Sept. 1982	purged	CC
Shantung	Su Yi-jan	1914	Dec. 1982	purged	CC
Ssuch'uan	Yang Ju-tai	1924	Feb. 1983	purged	CC
Heilungkiang	Li Li-an	1919	Feb. 1983	purged	CC
Shansi	Li Li-kung	1928	March 1983	purged	CC
Hupei	Kuan Kuang-fu	1931	March 1983	?	
Chekiang	Gen. Wang Fang	1920	March 1983	purged	CC
Kansu	Li Tzu-ch'i	1929	March 1983	purged	CC
Anhui	Huang Huang	1934	March 1983	?	
Kiangsu	Han P'ei-hsin	1922	April 1983	purged	CC
Ch'inghai	Chao Hai-feng	1915	April 1983	purged	CC

of the Ninth Congress, the 1,249 delegates of the Tenth Congress, or the 1,510 delegates of the Eleventh Congress. Most probably, they were simply appointed by the respective central leaders. According to the current Party statute—similar provisions existed before, too—the congress is convened by the CC every five years. It receives and discusses the reports of the CC, the CAC, and the Central Disciplinary Investigation Commission (*Chung-yang chi-lü chien-ch'a wei-yüan-hui* [CDIC]); revises the Party statute; and elects the CC, the CAC, and the CDIC.[18]

Yet in reality, the congress has never been more than a rubber-stamp body. So far, its meetings have been only for the purposes of demonstration and acclamation of the victors in intraelite conflicts, after the solution of which they have usually been convened. Even the election of the CC has always been held according to nominations by the Congress Presidium, which has been, at least two-thirds of the time, identical with the body thus "elected." Hence, the congress is hardly a part of the central decision-making organs of the CCP, to which we can now turn our attention.

Central Decision-Making Institutions

Other than the congress, the CC has had some decision-making powers at certain periods—particularly from 1956 to 1959, from 1977 to early 1980, and probably again since September 1982. The Party statute determines that the CC is elected by the congress for a term of five years and that the CC is supposed to be the highest leadership organ of the CCP between congresses.

Since the Eighth Congress in September 1956, five CCs have officiated:

- the Eighth CC with 97 full and 73 alternate members, to whom there were added, in May 1959, three full and 25 alternate members; officially from September 1956 to April 1969, but in practice until the summer of 1966
- the Ninth CC with 170 full and 109 alternate members; officially from April 1969 to August 1973, but in practice until September 1971
- the Tenth CC with 195 full and 124 alternate members; from August 1973 to August 1977
- the Eleventh CC with 201 full and 132 alternate members; from August 1977 to September 1982
- the Twelfth CC with 210 full and 138 alternate members; since September 10, 1982.[19]

Of the 210 full members of the current Twelfth CC, 11, or 5.2 percent, are women, and fourteen, or 6.7 percent, belong to national minorities. Two of the members had been appointed to the Sixth CC in 1928, having served now for fifty-five years; 13 had been appointed to the Seventh CC in 1945 (6 of them, however, did not belong to the Ninth, and 3 were not members of the Tenth); and 38 had been appointed to the Eighth CC (of whom 25 did not belong to the Ninth, and 19 were not members of the Tenth).

According to the statute, the alternate members shall substitute for full members who leave the CC, and one would assume that the alternates would be the natural reserve for the full members of the next CC. Since the Cultural Revolution, however, such has not been the case. Of the 109 alternates of the Ninth CC, only 16, or 14.7 percent, became full members of the Tenth, and of the 124 alternates of the Tenth, only 19, or 15.3 percent, became full members of the Eleventh CC. This figure decreased to 15 alternates of the Eleventh CC (11.4 percent) who are now full members of the Twelfth.

Plenary sessions, or plenums, of the CC have been held at rather varying intervals. After the establishment of the PRC in September

1949, there were twenty-nine CC plenums in thirty-four years, for an average interval of fourteen months between them. Yet this average does not present a meaningful picture. As far as the activities of the CC as a body are concerned, there have, in fact, been five distinct periods since 1949.

- from September 1949 to September 1956, with an average interval between two plenary sessions of twenty-one months
- from September 1956 to August 1959, average interval, 4.6 months
- from August 1959 to October 1968, more than twenty-seven months
- from April 1969 to July 1977, about twenty-four months
- since August 1977, so far eight months

The irregularity of plenary meetings indicates that the CC's importance in the policymaking process is indeed quite limited. Hence, the members of the CC derive their often significant political influence, not from their position in this body, but from other leading positions that they occupy in the Party, state, or PLA machines.

A much more important institution in the central Party leadership is the Secretariat (*Shu-chi ch'u*), which, from its establishment in 1956 until late 1966, directed the daily work of the civilian Party machine. Abolished during the Cultural Revolution, it started to operate again during the second half of 1979 and was officially reinaugurated, under the leadership of Hu Yao-pang as secretary general (*Tsung-shu-chi*), in late February 1980.[20] Since the Twelfth Congress, the secretary general has also been entrusted with the tasks of convening and chairing the sessions of the CC and of convening the meetings of the Politburo, as well as of its Standing Committee.[21] The Secretariat, which meets at least once a week, coordinates all administrative work of the Party machine, and it prepares the meetings of the Politburo as well as those of the Politburo's Standing Committee. A list of the secretaries of the Secretariat in 1983 is given on Table 5.3.

At the end of 1983, the average age of the secretaries was 66.5 years or, if the two alternates are included, 64.1 years. Under the direction of the Secretariat, the daily work of the Party center is conducted by the General Office (*Chung-yang pan-kung-t'ing*)—which is in charge of personnel affairs as well as of supplies for the central Party organs and their security[23]—and by the five departments (*Pu*) for propaganda, organization, united front work, international Party relations, and investigation (which means secret services and security).[24] The central Party machine also includes a number of other offices and institutions, including the editorial boards of *JMJP* and *HC*; the Central Party School; a Buro for the Translation of the Works of Marx, Engels, Lenin, and

Table 5.3.   Secretaries of the Secretariat of the CC, September 1, 1983[22]

Name	Year of Birth	Party Position	State Position
Secretary General			
Hu Yao-pang	1915	Secretary General; Member, Politburo	
Secretaries			
Ch'en P'i-hsien	1914	Member, CC	Vice-Chairman, National People's Congress
Hsi Chung-hsün	1913	Member, Politburo	
Hu Ch'i-li	1929	Member, CC	
Ku Mu	1914	Member, CC	State Councillor
Teng Li-ch'ün	1920	Member, CC; Director, CC Propaganda Dept.	
Wan Li	1912	Member, Politburo	First Vice-Premier
Yao Yi-lin	1917	Alternate, Politburo	Vice-Premier
Gen. Yü Ch'iu-li	1914	Member, Politburo	Director, General Political Dept., PLA
Alternate Secretaries			
Ch'iao Shih	1924	Member, CC; Director, CC General Office	
Mme. Hao Chien-hsiu	1936	Member, CC	

Stalin; a Committee for the Edition of Mao's Works; and a Party History Research Center.

Before the Cultural Revolution, the highest supervisory organ of the CCP was the Central Control Commission, which was mainly responsible for maintaining Party discipline, but it was abolished in the fall of 1966. Then, on December 22, 1979, the third plenum of the Eleventh CC decided to establish the CDIC,[25] which has since taken over the tasks of the former Central Control Commission. On September 11, 1982, the Twelfth Congress elected 132 members of the CDIC, the daily work of which is conducted by a Standing Committee of 11 under the leadership of Ch'en Yün as first secretary, General Huang K'ê-ch'eng as second secretary, and Wang Hê-shou as permanent secretary with the assistance of five other secretaries.[26]

In order to encourage old Party leaders to comply with semiretirement, the Twelfth Congress added yet another organ to the fold of central Party institutions, the CAC. The members of this body must have been members of the CCP for at least forty years. They can suggest policies to the Politburo and the CC and are supposed to "propagate within and outside the Party the directives and policies of the Party."[27] The CAC has 172 members and chooses from its own midst a Standing Committee of 24. It is currently led by Teng Hsiao-p'ing (its only member also belonging to the CC) as chairman (*Chu-jen*), who, in turn, is assisted by four vice-chairmen: General Hsü Shih-yu, Li Wei-han, Po I-po, and T'an Chen-lin.

In spite of this host of institutions, of which the Secretariat is indeed very strong politically, the real central decision-making body of the CCP, and hence, of the PRC, is the Party's Politburo (*Cheng-chih-chü*). According to the Party statute, the Politburo executes all leadership functions of the CC, as long as the CC is not in session, and it decides the policies of the Party. During the 1950s and the early 1960s, from April 1969 to March 1971, from August 1973 to May 1976, and again since September 1977—i.e., in almost twenty-eight out of thirty-four years of PRC history—the Politburo has indeed been the most important institution of political leadership.

In September 1956, seventeen full members and six alternates of the Politburo were elected by the Eighth CC, including all thirteen incumbents from the preceding Politburo. In May 1959, three more members were added. Of these twenty-six leaders, three died before 1966, and eleven of the remaining twenty-three were purged during the Cultural Revolution.

The Ninth CC, in April 1969, elected twenty-one members and four alternates to the Politburo, of whom three died and six were purged in the context of the Lin Piao crisis. Of the twenty-two members and four alternates of the Tenth CC's Politburo, five died, one was purged and rehabilitated,[28] and four were arrested on October 6, 1976. The Politburo of the Eleventh CC started out with twenty-three members and three alternates. Before 1980, one member died, four members and one alternate were purged, and six were added to the group, which, on the eve of the Twelfth Congress, therefore consisted of twenty-four members and two alternates.

On September 12, 1982, the Twelfth CC elected twenty-five members and three alternates to the current Politburo. Table 5.4 provides a list of these leaders as of September 1983 (by which time, one member, Liao Ch'eng-chih, had died.

At the end of 1983, the average age of these Politburo members was 74.9 years, or, if one includes the alternates, 73.0 years. Of the whole group of twenty-seven, nineteen, or 70.4 percent, are 70 years or older. Twenty-one, or 77.8 percent, joined the CCP before the Long March, and only one joined after 1949. The average Party membership term is 53 years. One member and one alternate are women, and two members

Table 5.4. Members of the CCP Politburo, September 1, 1983[29]

Name	Date of Birth	CCP Member Since	Politburo Member Since	Cultural Revolution Status
Standing Committee				
Hu Yao-pang	1915	1933	1978	purged
Marshal Yeh Chien-ying	1897	1925	1966	survived
Teng Hsiao-p'ing	1904	1921	1956-1967, 1974-1976, since 1977	purged
Chao Tzu-yang	1919	1938	1979; alternate, 1977-1979	purged
Li Hsien-nien	1905	1927	1956	survived
Ch'en Yün	1905	1925	1945-1967, since 1978	purged
Other Members				
Gen. Chang T'ing-fa	1914	1932	1977	purged
Fang Yi	1912	1931	1977	survived
Hsi Chung-hsün	1913	1929	1982	purged
Marshal Hsü Hsiang-ch'ien	1902	1925	1966-1967, since 1977	survived
Hu Ch'iao-mu	1908	1936	1982	purged
Gen. Li Te-sheng	1916	1933	1973; alternate, 1969-1973	advanced
Ni Chih-fu	1932	1958	1977; alternate, 1973-1977	advanced
Marshal Nieh Jung-chen	1899	1921	1966-1967, since 1977	survived
P'eng Chen	1902	1922	1945-1966, since 1979	purged
Sung Jen-chi'ung	1909	1926	1982	purged
Mme. Teng Ying-ch'ao	1904	1921	1978	survived
Ulanfu	1906	1926	1977; alternate, 1956-1967	purged
Wan Li	1912	1936	1982	purged
Gen. Wang Chen	1908	1927	1978	survived
Gen. Wei Kuo-ch'ing	1906	1928	1973	survived
Yang Shang-k'un	1907	1925	1982	purged
Gen. Yang Te-chih	1910	1928	1982	survived
Gen. Yü Ch'iu-li	1914	1932	1977	survived
Alternates				
Mme. Ch'en Mu-hua	1921	1938	1977	survived
Gen. Ch'in Chi-wei	1912	1932	1982	purged
Yao Yi-lin	1917	1935	1982	purged

belong to national minorities.[30] Ten, or more than one-third, have a PLA background, and ten to eleven currently occupy leading positions in the PLA. Of these twenty-seven leaders, fourteen, or 51.8 percent, were purged during the Cultural Revolution; two advanced as a result of it; and eleven, or 40.7 percent, survived it in office.

In one respect, the CCP is different from other ruling Communist parties: Since 1956, it has had, in addition to the Politburo, an institutionalized innermost leadership core that holds the very highest decision-making power. That is the Standing Committee of the Politburo (*Cheng-chih-chü ch'ang-wu wei-yüan-hui*), which, except for periods of extremely acute intraelite conflict, usually meets once or twice a week and seems to try to agree on an issue before it goes to the Politburo for a decision.

Until the summer of 1966, the Standing Committee consisted of Mao as chairman of the CC, his five deputies, and the secretary general of the CC. In August 1966, this circle was enlarged to eleven members, of whom, however, five were purged in early 1967. In April 1969, the Standing Committee had five members. Two were purged in 1970 and 1971, but in August 1973, the group was enlarged to nine members, of whom, by late 1976, five had died, three had been purged, and one had been added, for a remaining group of two: Hua Kuo-feng and Yeh Chien-ying. The Eleventh CC appointed a Standing Committee of six, of whom, by the spring of 1980, one had been purged, and two had been added for a total of seven members. This number was reduced to the current six at the first plenum of the Twelfth CC in September 1982. In 1983, the average age of this group was 75.5 years, and none of its members had belonged to the Party for fewer than forty-five years.

Until the Twelfth Congress, the official Party leader was the chairman (*Chu-hsi*). This position was held by Mao Tse-tung from May 1945 until his death on September 9, 1976. In October 1976, Hua Kuo-feng took over the chairmanship, which he held in practice until December 1980 and officially until June 1981. After that, the last holder of this office was Hu Yao-pang, for approximately fourteen months before the Twelfth Congress abolished the post of chairman. Hu Yao-pang, as secretary general of the CC, currently holds a position that is—at least for the time being—considered to be merely executive, while the Standing Committee now officially functions as the collective Party leadership.

Yet of course, there is one who seems to be somewhat "more equal than the others." In the CCP, only one position is left with the title *Chu-hsi* ("chairman" in Chinese), the chairmanship of the CC's Military Commission. It is held by Teng Hsiao-p'ing. However, even the collectively led Party is by no means an entirely monolithic unit. Within the elite, there exist competing and contending groups, so we should pay some attention to the patterns of group formation that have evolved over the years.

Patterns of Intraelite Group Formation

In the course of the successive conflicts within the CCP since the late 1950s,[31] many observers of Chinese politics, particularly East Asian scholars and Western journalists, have adopted the use of the term "faction" in a poorly defined way, so when it comes to the patterns of intraelite group formation in the PRC, we are faced with confusing rather than illuminating terminology. There have been a "cultural revolutionary faction," a "moderate faction," "radical faction," "secret police faction," "military faction," "Lin Piao faction," "Chiang Ch'ing faction," "Teng faction," "Hua faction," "pragmatic faction," "Shanghai faction," "petroleum faction," "First Field Army faction," and so on and so forth.

In such usage, the term "faction" has sometimes stood for groups that, according to our understanding, shared the same view on certain individual issues. Occasionally, however, it has also been applied to groups that were operating from what seemed to be a common political platform covering a variety of problems. Moreover, the term has described personal bonds of loyalty or, in some cases, functional interests of different subsystems, no matter whether they were real or existed only in the eyes of the beholder. From this terminological hodgepodge, one can draw only two conclusions.

1. The political process in the PRC is even more dominated by the dynamics of group formation than it is in many other countries.
2. The injudicious use of the term "faction" does not contribute anything to the understanding of the patterns of group formation.

Exact distinctions and precise definitions are necessary, and I propose that we start to develop them from a discussion of the content of conflicts. East Asian observers of Chinese politics, Western journalists, and—in a much more sophisticated manner—proponents of the political culture approach in social science[32] have argued that the issue of conflict in the PRC has been primarily, if not exclusively, personal confrontation and power struggle. Many academic observers in the West, however, have suggested that, in fact, policy disputes have dominated the Chinese scene.

In my view, elements of power struggle, personal confrontation, and policy dispute are inseparably interwoven in intraelite conflicts. These elements are indeed combined with equal weight and equal intensity in political confrontations in which power positions as well as political platforms are at stake.

The patterns of group formation, too, are determined by both the personal *clientèle* and power networks, on the one hand, and the policy considerations and platforms, on the other. The former prevail in primary group formation, and appear to be more important in protosecondary group formation, while the latter prevail in secondary group formation.

Primary Group Formation

Primary group formation, so far, has usually taken place as an agglomeration of interpersonal relations that developed either from structural or from functional criteria.

Structural groups are primarily formed on the basis of common regional origin (*T'ung-hsiang*), common educational background (*T'ung-hsüeh*), or common organizational experience over many years (*T'ung-hang*). In the context of the sociopolitical analysis of the CC members, we have already observed the importance of provincial origin in terms of purged or ascending leaders. Concerning common educational background, the group of cadres who have studied in France particularly has to be considered. Besides Teng Hsiao-p'ing, three other members of the current Politburo[33] and the chairman of the State Planning Commission from 1954 to 1967, the late Li Fu-ch'un, should be mentioned in this regard, and last, but by no means least, Chou En-lai belonged to this group.

Concerning common experience and the cooperation in the same organizations over many years, we first have to point to the importance of the field-army groups, which are based on the five large units of the PLA in the final stage of the civil war. Their position and influence will be discussed when the political role of the military is discussed.[34] But in the civilian sphere, similar relations may be found as well. Thus, from 1977 to 1980, three former vice-ministers of General Yü Ch'iu-li—the former minister of petroleum industry and at that time, chairman of the Planning Commission—and one other leading former bureaucrat of that ministry were in charge of the State Economic Commission and of the ministries for metallurgical, chemical, and petroleum industries.[35] Hence, inside the PRC, people started to talk about the petroleum clique (*Shih-yu chi-t'uan*).

Functional groups can be defined as groups that, in the political decision-making process, tend to form their attitudes on the basis of the interests of different functional subsystems that conflict with each other. This type of primary group formation has, so far, not been very common in the PRC. Yet from 1972/1973 until 1978/1979, the secret police cadres and from 1967 until the late 1970s, the diplomatic machine

tended to act with a comparatively high degree of coherence, as did
the regional military machines between 1967 and 1973 and the scientific-
technological establishment from 1972 to 1978/1979. Yet these examples
were exceptions rather than the rule, and they will most probably remain
so as long as the political system of the PRC has not reached the stage
of full-fledged institutionalization.

Protosecondary Group Formation

Protosecondary group formation is still mainly power and position
oriented, although it transcends the elements of primary group formation.
Within the PRC elite, this type of formation has thus far produced one
major type of group, which came into existence in the aftermath of the
Cultural Revolution and which I call "experience groups." For the
biographical experience of a leading cadre, it makes a tremendous
difference whether he or she was purged during the Cultural Revolution,
whether he or she managed to survive in office during that major
political crisis, or whether his or her career advanced significantly as a
result of it. Table 5.5 provides information about the development of
the three experience groups of Cultural Revolution—purgees, survivors,
and advancers—as far as their representation on the four CCs since
1969 is concerned.

Secondary Group Formation

Secondary group formation means the formation of alliances as factors
of competition in intraelite conflicts. Since the late 1950s, such conflicts
have, as a rule, gone through a stage of differentiation, culminating in
or occasionally ending with precritical confrontations, and then through
a stage of conflict resolution, culminating in a critical confrontation.

During both stages of conflict, the primary groups, as a rule, have
not operated independently. Instead, they have tended to act as the
elements of alliances, which were in all cases both platform and power
oriented politically. The character of such alliances, however, has changed
in the different stages of conflict. Since 1970, the protosecondary experience groups have mostly served as a factor that facilitated the
formation of these alliances.

Secondary group formation, then, has developed in two distinctly
different ways.

1. latent and short-term opinion groups, which are formed during
   clearly defined disputes on practical issues or appointments and
   are based on individual or primary group decisions, which concern
   only the very issue or appointment at stake

Table 5.5. Cultural Revolution experience groups in the CCs since 1969

Experience Group	Ninth CC (1969)	Tenth CC (1973)	Eleventh CC (1977)	Twelfth CC (1982)
Purgees				
Number	3[36]	21	78	111
Percentage of CC	1.8	10.8	38.8	52.9
Percentage increase or decrease		+500.0	+259.0	+ 36.3
Survivors				
Number	86	103	87	62
Percentage of CC	50.6	52.8	43.3	29.5
Percentage increase or decrease		+ 4.3	- 18.0	- 31.9
Advancers				
Number	81	71	32	16
Percentage of CC	47.6	36.4	15.9	7.6
Percentage increase or decrease		- 23.5	- 56.3	- 52.2
Unknown status				
Number			4	21
Percentage of CC			2.0	10.0
Percentage increase or decrease				+400.0

2. intermediate- to long-term factions, i.e., coherent circles, which are based on alternative platforms and exclusive claims for political power and overall control

The different character of these two types of secondary intraelite group formation can be further specified if we introduce the term "coalition" again, here meaning political coalitions within the elite. Then we may define opinion groups as issue-based coalitions, which are, in principle, limited to short-term cooperation, whereas factions are program-based coalitions which principally are not limited in time.

Since the late 1950s, the condensation of opinion groups into factions has always indicated the escalation of an intraelite conflict from the stage of differentiation to the stage of conflict resolution in an overall crisis. But as long as opinion groups have characterized the secondary intraelite group formation, the consensus on issues may have been disrupted yet the consensus on procedures—i.e., the agreement between the opponents on the regulation of conflicts in the statutory decision-making bodies of the Party—still has prevailed. Once factions—in our precise definition of that term—emerge, the immediate result is a

Table 5.6. Patterns of intraelite conflicts in the PRC

Criteria	Stage of Differentiation	Stage of Conflict Resolution
Beginning of stage	Consensus on issues breaks down	Consensus on procedures breaks down
Type of secondary group formation	Opinion groups	Factions
Character of groups	Issue-based coalition	Program-based coalition
Duration of groups	Short term	Medium term
Capability of elite consensus	Low	Nonexistent
Type of confrontation	Precritical	Critical
Result of confrontation	Dismissals of individual leaders, compromise on issues, groups survive	Elimination of the defeated faction's leadership

breakdown of the consensus on procedures. Table 5.6 attempts to present a systematic overview of the patterns of intraelite conflict and the related patterns of group formation, which may help lead one to a better understanding of the developments in the PRC since the late 1950s, in general, and the political events since 1975, in particular.

CHAPTER 6

The State
Administrative Machine

Constitutional Development, 1949–1982

When the PRC was proclaimed on October 1, 1949, the construction of the new state began with the establishment of provisional organs of a state administrative machine by a united front, in which eight non-Communist united front parties participated under the leadership of the CCP.[37] The new government presented itself as a "coalition," thus camouflaging the developing system of single-party rule in the same way as in Eastern Europe between 1945 and 1953. This strategy conformed to the Marxist-Leninist doctrine of revolutionary development in its version devised by Mao Tse-tung, according to which the CCP should, in the initial stage of its rule, create a "new democracy." In this stage, the petty bourgeoisie and the national bourgeoisie were still considered revolutionary classes, which could be represented by political parties and participate in ruling the country.

The eight parties that were willing to cooperate with the CCP consisted of groups of former KMT members who had defected to the Communists during the last stage of the civil war; liberal intellectual circles, which were driven to side with the CCP by the repressive methods of the ancien régime; and those industrialists and businessmen who had stayed in China and were willing to work with the new rulers.

On May Day, 1950, these parties stated their submission to CCP leadership in a joint declaration: "We, the democratic parties [Min-chu tang-p'ai] of China, are totally united under the leadership of the great CCP and its Chairman Mao Tse-tung, to build up an independent, free, democratic, and happy China."[38] During the winter of 1950/1951, they were forced by the CCP to agree to limitations of their activities, which ensured that they could never compete with the Party. They are not allowed to merge, to establish their own youth or student organizations, or to recruit workers, peasants, soldiers, or cadres of the state administrative machine as new members. Thus, they were confined to so-called assigned masses (*So-lieh-hsi-te ch'ün-chung*), which altogether made up less than one-tenth of the populace.

When the stage of transition to socialism was proclaimed in the autumn of 1953, the united front parties had to accept the task of "educating" their members and those groups of the population from which they could recruit to become "useful parts of the socialist society." The Hundred Flowers Campaign in 1957 gave them a last chance to propose and propagate their own ideas about the future of China. But when they used this opportunity, they became the first and foremost victims of the purge against the critics of the Party in June 1957.

Since then, these united front parties have become totally marginal. From 1966 to 1978/1979, they disappeared entirely from the Chinese scene. Yet in October 1979, all of them could—for the first time since 1959/1960—convene party congresses. Their new chairmen, at that time, averaged seventy-eight years old. The parties were also again represented at the Fifth Political Consultative Conference, which convened before the Fifth National People's Congress (NPC) in February 1978, yet their activities have been limited to sporadic meetings and forums. In fact, they do not participate in any meaningful political decision making.

Since 1949, the following eight groups have made up the non-Communist united front parties.

- KMT Revolutionary Committee (*Chung-kuo kuo-min-tang ke-ming wei-yüan-hui* [KMTRC]), which rallies former KMT generals who defected to the Communists in 1948/1949, former members of the KMT bureaucracy, and defectors from T'aiwan. Its chairman is Wang K'un-lun (born in 1902).
- Democratic League (*Chung-kuo min-chu t'ung-meng* [DL]), which rallies scholars in the humanities, some technicians, people who are considered as belonging to the petty bourgeoisie, and some returned overseas Chinese. Its chairwoman is Mme. Shih Liang (born 1900).
- National Democratic Construction Association (*Ch'üan-kuo min-chu chien-kuo-hui* [NDCA]), which rallies former industrialists and businessmen, the so-called national bourgeoisie. Its chairman is Hu Chüeh-wen (born 1895).
- Association for the Promotion of Democracy (*Chung-kuo min-chu ts'u-chin-hui* [APD]), which rallies schoolteachers, academic staff below the professorial level, and older artists. Its chairman is Chou Chien-jen (born 1887), who is also a member of the CCP.

- Democratic Peasants' and Workers' Party (*Chung-kuo nung-kung min-chu tang* [DPWP]) which, despite its name, rallies engineers, technicians, medical doctors, and former small-shop owners. Its chairman is Chi Fang (born 1890), but it is now actually led by Chou Ku-ch'eng (born 1898).
- September 3 Society (*Chiu-san hsüeh-hui* [9-3]), which rallies natural scientists, mostly university professors. Its chairman is Hsü Te-heng (born 1890).
- *Chih-kung tang* (CKT), which rallies returned overseas Chinese, in competition with the DL, and is supposed to work in overseas Chinese settlements abroad. Its chairman is Huang Ting-ch'en (born 1901).
- League for the Democratic Self-Government of T'aiwan (*T'aiwan min-chu tzu-chih hui* [LDT]), which rallies people of T'aiwan origin who live in the PRC and is supposed to do underground work in T'aiwan itself. Its chairman is General Ts'ai Hsiao (born 1920), who is also a member of the CCP.

The leaders of these eight parties had an average age of almost 84.9 years at the end of 1983, three of them being older than 90.

From September 21 through 30, 1949, representatives of the CCP, the eight non-Communist united front parties, the PLA, different mass organizations, and a number of specially invited democratic personalities met in Peking for the first plenary meeting of the Chinese People's Political Consultative Conference (*Chung-kuo jen-min cheng-chih hsieh-shang hui-yi* [CPPCC]). On September 27, its 584 delegates passed a provisional constitutional document, according to which the temporary organs of state power were organized. The highest decision-making body, according to this provisional constitution, was supposed to be a Central People's Government Council. Of its sixty-three members when this council was established under the chairmanship of Mao Tse-tung, there were thirty-two Communists, twenty-two members of the non-Communist united front parties, and nine nonpartisans. A State Administrative Council, led by Chou En-lai as prime minister, took over the leadership of the state administrative machine. Of its thirty-one ministries and commissions, sixteen were headed by Communists, and fifteen by non-Communists.

Yet the CCP had secured the most important positions in the new government for its members. Moreover, it dominated, with twenty-one out of twenty-eight seats, the Revolutionary Military Council, which was also led by Mao himself and was, until 1954, the second most important decision-making body after the Politburo of the Party, particularly because, until 1954, the PLA was in charge of regional administration in most parts of the country. But by the summer of that year, a centralized administrative machine had been built up, and the time had come to substitute the provisional constitution and the temporary state leadership organs with more permanent arrangements and systems.

Until then, the CPPCC had acted somewhat like a parliamentary body. After 1954, however, it was converted into the leading organ of the united front, continued to exist until 1966, and again became viable after 1978. According to a new statute promulgated on December 11, 1982, the CPPCC is now a consultative organization with the task of propagating and participating "in the spreading of . . . the national policies for the unification of the motherland . . . , the national policies towards intellectuals . . . , national minorities . . . , the Overseas Chinese . . . , and the national foreign policy."[39] From 1954 until 1966, the CPPCC was headed by Chou En-lai, and from 1978 to 1982 by Teng Hsiao-p'ing. The current chairwoman is the widow of Chou, Mme. Teng Ying-ch'ao (a Politburo member born in 1904).

De jure for almost twenty-one years—but de facto for twelve of them—the structures and functions of the organs of state leadership were regulated by the constitution of the PRC promulgated by the First NPC on September 20, 1954.[40] According to its provisions, the NPC was to be the highest organ of state power and would delegate the powers of all other institutions of the state administrative machine. Indirectly elected by the people's congresses (PCs) of the provinces, autonomous regions, and directly administered cities for a term of four years, the NPC was to convene once a year for a plenary meeting. The NPC formally had all legislative powers, and it decided on the economic plans and the state budget.

It elected, also for four years, the individual chief of state, the chairman of the PRC (*Chung-hua jen-min kung-he-kuo chu-hsi*), who had the power to represent the country in foreign relations, bestow orders of merit, grant amnesties, and conclude treaties with the approval of the NPC's Standing Committee. He was also, in his concurrent capacity as chairman of the National Defense Council, commander in chief of the armed forces. Last but not least, he was chairman of the Supreme State Conference, a body that consisted, according to the constitution, of the chairman of the PRC, the vice-chairman of the PRC, the chairman of the NPC's Standing Committee, the prime minister, and other people the chairman of the PRC wished to invite to attend the meetings. This institution became, between 1956 and 1965, the most important switchboard between the Party and the state. From September 1954 to April 1959, Mao himself was chairman of the PRC, followed—de facto—from April 1959 to January 1967 and de jure until October 1968—by Liu

Shao-ch'i. From October 1968 to January 1975, the vice-chairman, Tung Pi-wu, officiated at ceremonial functions as chief of state.

Between the annual plenary sessions of the NPC, which usually lasted about ten days, its functions were taken over by the Standing Committee of the NPC (*Ch'üan-kuo jen-min tai-piao ta-hui ch'ang-wu wei-yüan-hui*), which also, with the consent of the chairman of the PRC, appointed and dismissed the ministers and chairmen of the commissions on the State Council. In 1954, the Standing Committee consisted of 79 members, including its chairman and 13 vice-chairmen. At the Second NPC, in 1959, this number remained unchanged, but there were 16 vice-chairmen. At the Third NPC, in 1965, the number of members increased to 115, including 18 vice-chairmen.

The 1954 constitution determined that the State Council (*Kuo-wu-yüan*) should lead the work of the state administrative machine as the major central executive institution. It was headed by the prime minister (*Kuo-wu-yüan tsung-li*)—from September 1954 to January 1976, Chou En-lai—who formed something like an inner cabinet with the vice-premiers (ten in 1954 and sixteen each in 1959 and 1965). The plenum of the State Council, which rarely met, consisted of the premier, the vice-premiers, the chairmen of commissions, and the ministers. In all, these numbered forty in 1954, forty-eight in 1959, fifty-five in 1965, and fifty-eight in early 1966 on the eve of the Cultural Revolution.

All legal courts in the PRC were under the leadership of the Supreme People's Court (*Tsui-kao jen-min fa-yüan*), the president and members of which were elected by the NPC upon the suggestion of its Standing Committee, while the tasks of prosecution, supervision of the courts, and also the supervision of the whole administrative machine were officially entrusted to a Supreme People's Procuratorate (*Tsui-kao jen-min chien-ch'a-yüan*) under a procurator general. Its members were appointed by the NPC's Standing Committee.

The First and the Second NPCs, indirectly elected in 1954 and during the winter of 1958/1959, each consisted of 1,226 delegates, of whom 986 represented the administrative units; 150, the national minorities; 60, the PLA; and 30, the overseas Chinese. But the membership of the Third NPC, elected in late 1964, more than doubled to 3,040 delegates: 2,587 from the administrative units, 300 from national minorities, 120 from the PLA, and again 30 from the overseas Chinese.

But this large body only held one plenary session, from December 20, 1964, to January 4, 1965. Then the Cultural Revolution began, and during its course, not only the Party machine but the state administrative machine collapsed. The last session of the NPC's Standing Committee convened on April 26, 1966;[41] after that date, this body was not mentioned again for almost nine years. The Supreme People's Court stopped operation in January 1967; the Procuratorate had already been abolished in December 1966. The State Council, too, ceased to function in early 1967, and for three and a half years, only eight of its fifty-eight members were still carrying out their duties. A new minister was finally appointed in November 1970,[42] but until early 1975, the State Council, which by then again had twenty-four members, remained a rump institution.

It was only in January 1975, ten years after the Third NPC, that the Fourth NPC could assemble for its one and only plenary session. The 2,885 delegates of this body were not even indirectly elected, just appointed by the Party center. On January 17, 1975, they passed the second constitution of the PRC, a very brief organizational statute of thirty articles providing for organs of state leadership that, even formally, were meant to be no more than executive instruments of the Party.[43] The NPC, according to this constitution, remained the highest organ of state power but was now under the leadership of the CCP. It was supposed to elect the prime minister and the members of the State Council according to the nomination by the CC of the CCP, and the chairman of the CC was officially designated as the supreme commander of the armed forces of the whole country. The new constitution abolished the position of an individual chief of state and substituted a collective chief of state, the NPC's Standing Committee, which, besides keeping its other functions granted by the 1954 constitution, took over the ceremonial functions of the former chairman of the PRC, being represented in this respect by its chairman.

The NPC's term of office was prolonged to five years, and its Standing Committee—now a body of 167 members, including the chairman and twenty-two vice-chairmen—again acted between its meetings. The State Council won importance as the major executive body, now also called the People's Government, and it was established with a prime minister, twelve vice-premiers, and twenty-six ministers, i.e., thirty-nine members. Also reestablished was the Supreme People's Court, but the Procuratorate and the National Defense Council did not reappear, nor did the Supreme State Conference.

In the three years after the new constitution went into effect, the Standing Committee met only four times, i.e., once every 9.4 months on the average, as opposed to once every two weeks between January 1965 and April 1966. In fact, only the State Council was again functioning regularly before the first session of the Fifth NPC convened in Peking on February 26, 1978. During the winter of 1977/1978, the twenty-nine people's congresses of the administrative units assembled to elect the delegates for the Fifth NPC, although it is now not known how these electoral bodies had been established. They chose 2,981 delegates, to which there were added 503 delegates from the PLA and 13 delegates from the PRC citizens of T'aiwan origin for an overall number of 3,497 delegates.

On March 5, 1978, the Fifth NPC promulgated the third constitution of the PRC, and it lasted for four years and nine months as opposed to three years and almost two months for the second.[44] This document took a middle position between the two earlier constitutions. With sixty articles, it was twice as long as the second but still much shorter than the first.

The position of an individual chief of state remained abolished, and so did the Supreme State Conference and the National Defense Council. But the powers of the chairman of the NPC's Standing Committee were now more clearly circumscribed, giving him explicitly the function of a ceremonial chief of state. The chairman of the Party's CC was to be the commander of the armed forces, the prime minister of the State Council was to be elected by the NPC according to nomination by the CC of the CCP, and the ministers were now to be nominated by the premier. The Procuratorate was also reestablished with the same functions as in the first constitution.

The Standing Committee of the NPC, now enlarged to 196 members including its chairman and twenty vice-chairmen, met about once every one and a half months in the almost five years until late 1982. The State Council functioned regularly, and even the plenary sessions of the NPC were held once a year. The fifth of these plenary sessions, on December 4, 1982, promulgated the fourth constitution of the PRC, which has been officially in force since January 1, 1983, and which was implemented, in terms of appointments to the organs of state leadership, at the first session of the Sixth NPC, which met from June 6 through June 21, 1983.[45]

In its preface, the new constitution accepts implicitly the Four Basic Principles of the CCP,[46] but it substitutes the term "proletarian dictatorship" for "people's democratic dictatorship," albeit with the following definition: "led by the working class, and based upon the alliance of workers and peasants, in its essence, therefore, the proletarian dictatorship." The PRC is then defined as "a socialist state under people's democratic dictatorship, led by the working class and based upon the alliance of workers and peasants" (Art. 1).

The constitution guarantees limited private property, and it mentions the rural people's communes only in passing, without giving explicit information about their tasks, while the administrative functions of these former collectives are transferred to township (*hsiang*) people's governments (Arts. 8, 95, and 105). For all practical purposes, this change means that the system of the people's communes has been abolished. In Articles 33 to 50, the constitution contains an impressive catalog of civil rights, including the equality of all citizens before the law; the "freedom of speech, publication, assembly, association, and demonstrations on the streets"; the freedom of religion; personal freedom; the statement that the "living quarters of the citizen cannot be violated"; the freedom of correspondence; and the freedom of academic research (albeit not of academic teaching), literature, and the arts. These provisions are, however, greatly limited by Article 51: "In executing their freedoms and rights, the citizens of the PRC are not allowed to violate the interests of the state, the society, the collective or the legitimate freedoms and rights of other citizens." The right to strike, which had been granted by the constitutions of 1975 and 1978—although to no real effect—is no longer mentioned.

In summary, the new constitution, with its 138 articles, is very close to that of 1954, which, in turn, was modeled in large part after the 1936 "Stalin constitution" of the USSR. It creates a viable framework for the institutionalization of rule, but this fact does not necessarily mean that such institutionalization will definitely develop during the period the constitution is in effect.

Central Organs of State Leadership

According to the constitution of December 4, 1982, the NPC—again without any qualification called the "highest organ of state power"— is still indirectly elected by the PCs of the twenty-nine administrative units and by the PLA. It also has delegates from the overseas Chinese and from the PRC citizens born on T'aiwan. Its functions are similar to those provided for in the 1954 constitution, and its term of office is five years.

The Sixth NPC, which convened in June 1983, numbered 2,978 delegates. Their electoral origin and social and political backgrounds— as given by the CCP media—are shown in Table 6.1, and they established a total of six committees.

- Nationalities Affairs Committee, chaired by the Tibetan Ngapo Ngawang Jigme (nonpartisan)
- Legal Affairs Committee, chaired by P'eng Ch'ung (CCP)
- Financial and Economic Committee, chaired by Wang Jen-chung (CCP)
- Committee on Education, Science, Culture, and Health, chaired by Chou Ku-ch'eng (DPWP)
- Foreign Affairs Committee, chaired by Keng Piao (CCP)
- Overseas Chinese Affairs Committee, chaired by Admiral Yeh Fei (CCP)[48]

Table 6.1. Delegates of the Sixth NPC, June 1983[47]

Group	Number	Percentage
Electoral origin		
Administrative units	2,649	88.95
PLA	276	9.27
Returned overseas Chinese	40	1.34
T'aiwanese	13	0.44
Special groups		
National minorities	403	13.53
Women	632	21.22
Social background		
Peasants and workers	791	26.56
Cadres	636	21.36
Intellectuals	701	23.54
Soldiers	276	9.27
Political affiliation		
CCP	1,862	62.53
Non-Communist parties	543	18.23
Nonpartisan	573	19.24

One of the major innovations of the new constitution is the reintroduction of an individual chief of state. The president of the PRC is elected by the NPC for five years, and he can serve two terms of office (Art. 79). His functions are mainly ceremonial: He proclaims the laws and officially appoints the members of the State Council, bestows honors, grants amnesties, and represents the stae in foreign relations, but he can also proclaim martial law and a state of emergency (Arts. 80 and 81). On June 18, 1983, the Sixth NPC elected Li Hsien-nien to that position (a member of the Politburo's Standing Committee, born 1905)[49] and the Mongol Ulanfu to the post of the vice-chairman of the PRC (a member of the Politburo, born 1906).

When the NPC is not in session, its powers are exercised by the Standing Committee of the NPC, as in the three earlier constitutions. The current Standing Committee consists of 154 members and a secretary general. The names of the chairman and the twenty vice-chairmen are given in Table 6.2.

At the end of 1983, the average age of the twenty-one members in the Presidium of the NPC's Standing Committee was 75 years. The group consists of eleven CCP members (ten are members of the CC, including two Politburo members and one secretary, and one is a member of the CAC), eight members of the non-Communist united front parties, and two Tibetan nonpartisans. Four of the group are members of national minorities; one is a woman. There are eleven survivors and ten purgees

Table 6.2.   Chairman and vice-chairmen of the Standing Committee of the
Sixth NPC, elected June 18, 1983

Name	Date of Birth	Party Affilia- tion	Cultural Revolution Status	Member of
Chairman				
P'eng Chen	1902	CCP	purged	PB
Vice-Chairmen				
Ch'en P'i-hsien	1914	CCP	purged	Secretary, CC
Gen. Wei Kuo-ch'ing	1906	CCP	survived	PB
Keng Piao	1909	CCP	survived	CAC
Hu Chüeh-wen	1895	NDCA	survived	
Hsü Te-heng	1890	9-3	survived	
P'eng Ch'ung	1915	CCP	purged	CC
Wang Jen-chung	1907	CCP	purged	CC
Mme. Shih Liang	1900	DL	survived	
Chu Hsüeh-fan	1905	KMTRC	purged	
Ngapo Ngawang Jigme	1911	non- partisan	survived	
Panchen Erdeni (the Panchen Lama)	1938	non- partisan	purged	
Ishak Bey Saifudin	1916	CCP	survived	CC
Chou Ku-ch'eng	1898	DPWP	purged	
Dr. Yen Chi-tz'u	1900	9-3	survived	
Hu Yü-chih	1896	DL	survived	
Jung Yi-jen	1916	NDCA	purged	
Adm. Yeh Fei	1914	CCP	purged	CC
Gen. Liao Han-sheng	1911	CCP	purged	CC
Gen. Han Hsien-ch'u	1912	CCP	survived	CC
Huang Hua	1913	CCP	survived	CC

of the Cultural Revolution. The high degree of representation of non-Communists in this body indicates that it is mainly ceremonial.

The same is certainly not the case with the State Council, which consists entirely of CCP members. This body is the leading institution of the state administrative machine, as Article 85 of the constitution states: "The State Council of the PRC, i.e. the Central People's Government, is the executive body of the highest organ of state power, it is the highest organ of state administration."

Since the Sixth NPC's first session, the State Council has had a total of fifty-two members, but they rarely meet as a whole. The new constitution has formalized the long-standing practice of the work being done by an inner cabinet by providing for a Standing Conference of the State Council (*Kuo-wu-yüan ch'ang-wu hui-yi*), which consists of fifteen members: the prime minister, four vice-premiers (one of whom is also secretary general of the council), and ten state councillors (*Kuo-wu wei-yüan*). Their names are given in Table 6.3. The fifteen members

Table 6.3. Members of the Standing Conference of the State Council, appointed June 19, 1983[50]

Name	Date of Birth	Cultural Revolution Status	Member of	Other Positions on State Council
Prime Minister				
Chao Tzu-yang	1919	purged	PB	Chairman, Comm. for Restructuring the Economic System
Vice-Premiers				
Wan Li	1912	purged	PB	
Yao Yi-lin	1917	purged	PB alt., CC Secr.	
Li P'eng	1928	purged	CC	
T'ien Chi-yün	1929	survived	CC	Secretary General
State Councillors				
Fang Yi	1912	survived	PB	Chairman, State Scientific and Technical Comm.
Ku Mu	1914	survived	CC Secr.	
K'ang Shih-en	1915	survived	CC	
Mme. Ch'en Mu-hua	1921	survived	PB alt.	Minister of Foreign Trade
Chi P'eng-fei	1910	survived	CC	
Chang Ching-fu	1914	purged	CC	Chairman, State Economic Comm.
Wu Hsüeh-ch'ien	1921	purged	CC	Min. of Foreign Affairs
Gen. Chang Ai-p'ing	1910	purged	CC	Min. of Defense
Wang Ping-ch'ien	1925	purged	CC	Min. of Finance
Sung P'ing	1917	purged	CC	Chairman, State Planning Comm.

of this group had an average age of 65.4 years at the end of 1983, and all are full members of the CC. Three belong to the Politburo, two are alternates, and two belong to the CC Secretariat. The group includes nine purgees and six survivors of the Cultural Revolution.

Under this leadership group, the State Council is divided into eight commissions and thirty-seven ministries and ministry-level institutions as shown in Figure 6.1. Thirteen of the thirty-seven ministries are responsible for special branches of industry. In some cases, they still have direct command of all factories of their respective branch, but in most others, their orders have to pass through the regional administrative organs until they reach the individual enterprises.

A new addition to the State Council in June 1983 was the establishment of the Ministry of State Security. While the old Ministry of Public

Figure 6.1.   ORGANIZATIONAL STRUCTURE OF THE STATE ADMINISTRATIVE MACHINE

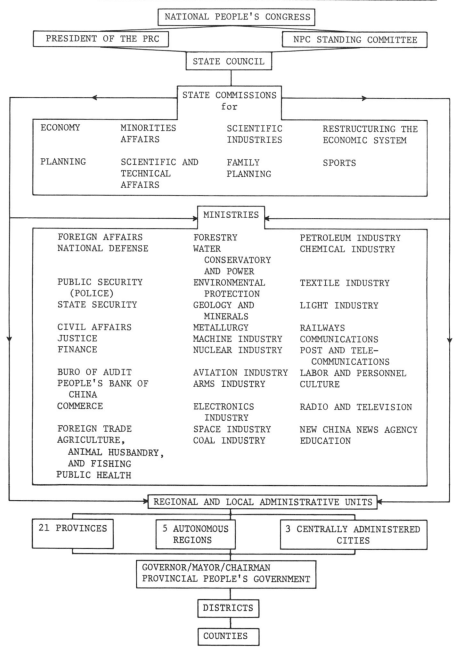

Security is now confined to regular police affairs and crime prevention, the new institution has been put in charge of political police, social supervision, and intelligence. At the same time, mobile state security forces have been placed under its control, for the first time since the existence of the PRC.

The fifty-two members of the State Council had an average age of 63.7 years at the end of 1983—in the context of the PRC, a rather young group. They are assisted by 156 vice-ministers and vice-chairmen of commissions, to whom there must be added 32,000 "leading cadres" in the offices in Peking, and more than 300,000 cadres in subordinate organizations of the state administrative machine.

Finally, the Supreme People's Court with its new president, Cheng T'ien-hsiang (a member of the CAC, born 1914), and the Supreme People's Procuratorate with its procurator general, Yang Yi-ch'en (a member of the CC, born 1914), were given the same functions that had been provided for by the 1954 constitution. The military leadership, however, went over to a newly created body, the Central Military Commission, which will be discussed in Chapter 7.

Regional and Local Administration

With the promulgation of the 1954 constitution, regularized organs of administration were formally established on all subcentral levels of government, too. Regional and local PCs (*Jen-min tai-paio ta-hui*), directly elected on the *hsiang* (township) and *ch'ü* (city district) levels—albeit at that time in open assemblies with usually only one candidate per seat— appointed the People's Government Council (*Jen-min cheng-fu wei-yüan-hui*) of their respective units and elected the delegates for the *hsien-* (county-) level PCs. These, in turn, appointed the People's Government Council of the *hsien* and elected the delegates to the PCs on the provincial level.

These structures, however, broke down during the Cultural Revolution. The provincial-level PCs were not reelected from 1964 to 1980/1981, and between January and April 1967, the People's Government Councils ceased to operate. A new type of "temporary power organ" came into being, the Revolutionary Committee (*Ke-ming wei-yüan-hui* [RC]). The first of these institutions was established in Heilungkiang on January 31, 1967, and the establishment of the RCs on the provincial level was completed on September 5, 1968. By early 1970, RCs had been formed for most units on all administrative levels.

At that time the RCs combined, on their respective levels, the leadership of the Party, the administration, and the economy. They were supposed to be organized according to the principle of revolutionary trinity (*Ke-*

ming san-chieh-he), uniting representatives of the Maoist mass organizations, revolutionary cadres (i.e., Party members who supported the cultural revolutionary Left), and representatives of the PLA. Yet in fact, the PLA dominated, at least at the outset: Almost half of the members of the provincial-level RCs were soldiers, twenty-one out of twenty-nine were headed by generals, and about 70 percent of the *hsien* RCs were also led by officers or political commissars of the PLA.

During the early 1970s, however, the RCs, in the course of a gradual restabilization of the political system, lost most of their original all-embracing functions. The reconstruction of the regional Party machine in 1970/1971 took from them the leadership of the Party organizations and placed them under the control of the PPCs; the reestablishment of the regular mass organizations in 1973/1974 removed these organizations from RC control. In the 1978 constitution, the functions of the RCs were actually defined in the same way those of the People's Government Councils had been in 1954, only the name RC remained in use for almost one and a half more years.

But in July 1979, the NPC passed a regional and local government law that renamed the RCs, now to be elected by the PCs of the respective level, as people's governments (*Jen-min cheng-fu*) and their chairmen as governors (*Sheng-chang*) in the case of the provinces, mayors (*Shih-chang*) in the case of the centrally administered cities, and chairman of the People's Government" (*Jen-min cheng-fu chu-hsi*) in the autonomous regions.[51] The new legal regulations became effective on January 1, 1980, thus liquidating the last vestiges of cultural revolutionary terminology in the realm of regional and local administration.

These provisions were reconfirmed by the 1982 constitution (Arts. 95–111), which lays down terms of office for the PCs of five years on the provincial level and three years on the *hsien* and *hsiang* levels. It has also advanced direct election of the congresses to the *hsien* level, providing for a vote by secret ballot. With very few exceptions, however, there is still only one united front–supported candidate for each seat, and the congresses on the provincial level continue to be indirectly elected by the *hsien*-level congresses.

The twenty-nine administrative units on the provincial level include twenty-one provinces (*sheng*); the three centrally administered cities (*chih-hsia-shih*) of Peking, Shanghai, and T'ienchin; and the following five autonomous regions (*tzu-chih-ch'ü*), which are officially designated as self-governing units for national minorities (1982 constitution, Arts. 112–121).

1. *Sinkiang Uighur Region:* Almost half of the population of this region consists of Uighurs; 10 percent is composed of Kazakhs, Uzbeks,

Kirghizs, Turkmens, Tatars, Tadzhiks, and Mongols; and 40 percent of the people are Han Chinese. The regional PC is headed by the Han general Wang En-mao; the regional government, by the Uighur Ismail Aymat.

2. *Tibet:* Although 75 percent of the population is still Tibetan, and only 22 percent Han—as opposed to less than 1 percent in 1950— the Han general Yin Fa-t'ang heads the regional PC while the regional government is led by the Tibetan Dorjie Tzaidan.

3. *Ninghsia Hui Region:* About one-third of the population is Hui— which means Chinese Muslims of mixed Han-Turkish-Mongolian origin—almost half is Han, and the less than 20 percent remaining belong to different small minorities. The Han Chinese Li Hsüeh-chih heads the regional PC; the Hui Hei Po-li, the regional government.

4. *Inner Mongolia:* Here, only 5–8 percent of the population is still Mongol, and more than 90 percent is Han. The regional PC is headed by the Han Chinese Chou Hui; the regional government, by the Mongol Buh'e.

5. *Kuangsi Chuang Region:* The Chuang are an almost entirely Sinicized people of Thai origin. They make up 27 percent of the population; other minorities, 6 percent; and 67 percent is Han. The Party leader, Ch'iao Hsiao-kuang, is a Chuang and so is the head of the regional government, Wei Ch'un-shu.

Thus, in four of five autonomous regions, the Party leaders are Han Chinese, and the regional state administrative organs in all five cases are led by members of the largest minority. The latter are, however, lower in rank in the PC than the Han regional first secretaries, two of whom belong to the PLA.

Between the provincial and the *hsien* levels—which means, between the regional and the local state administrative institutions—administrative entities without congresses have been established. These represent the provincial authorities and have to coordinate the work of the lower-level units. There are 208 of these units: 1 administrative area (*hsing-cheng-ch'ü*)—the island of Hainan in Kuangtung Province—8 leagues (*meng*) in Inner Mongolia, 29 autonomous areas (*tzu-chih-chou*), and 170 areas (*ti-ch'ü*).[52]

On the local administration level, there were, in late 1980, 2,772 units, which included 3 autonomous banners (*tzu-chih-ch'i*), 53 banners (*ch'i*), 71 autonomous *hsien* (*tzu-chih-hsien*), 431 city districts (*ch'ü*), 214 provincially or area-administered cities (*shih*), and 2,000 regular *hsien*.[53] On this level, as well as on the level of the *hsiang*, the coordination between Party and administrative machines is particularly tightly knit.

The *hsien* magistrates, *shih* mayors, and also the *hsiang* magistrates and village chiefs are, in almost all cases for which there are data available, members of the respective Party committee.

Below the *hsien* level, there are *hsiang* and county towns (*chen*). Their exact number is not known, but it should be between 55,000 and 60,000. The number of the lowest administrative units in the countryside, the administrative villages (*hsing-cheng-ts'un*), most probably ranges between 700,000 and 750,000.

How does this impressive large state adminstrative machine relate to the Party? This question must be addressed before the description of the organs of the state is concluded.

Party and State

Karl Marx's hypotheses about the future of human society assumed that in advanced industrial societies, the "proletariat" would compose the overwhelming majority of the populace, that this proletariat would organize itself to enact social changes under its dictatorship, and that this dictatorship would thus, in fact, be a spontaneously developed type of majority rule.

Lenin, however, devised the concept of the revolutionary cadre party and advanced the idea that in order to lead the proletarian-socialist revolution to success, the urban proletariat and the rural masses needed a tightly organized leadership core that would consist of the most advanced elements of the proletarian class, the Communist Party. The Party was to provide an elite of visionaries who knew about the predetermined development of society, and their task would be to promote this very development. Hence, this elite—the vanguard of the proletariat, which would act for the proletariat and in its name—would define the "real needs" of the masses, and it would create—by propaganda as well as coercion, if necessary—their "consciousness" so they might accept the elite's definition of their needs as their own. For a considerable period of time, proletarian dictatorship would therefore assume the form of a dictatorship by the proletarian Party.

That is the meaning of the term "leadership by the Party," which is regularly used by the ruling elite of the PRC. The term has its ideological basis in the axiomatic assumption of historical materialism that the economic and social forces provide the base for everything while beliefs, culture, law, and also the state belong to the superstructure. Marxists, therefore, can only perceive of the state as an instrument, a machine (apparat) in the hands of a class that belongs to the base. A state ruled by a Marxist party is consequently a machine, an instrument in the hands of the proletarian party: The Party proposes, the state disposes.

In this respect, the CCP has always closely followed Marxist-Leninist orthodoxy. This belief was also, as we have seen,[54] bluntly expressed in the texts of the 1975 and, somewhat more moderately, the 1978 constitutions. Yet, since the separation of state and Party leadership on the provincial level, which was formally implemented between the summer of 1979 and the spring of 1981, the patterns of Party leadership over the state administrative machine have become somewhat more subtle. Nevertheless, the CCP has made sure that its domination of the state remains unchallenged; and in doing so, the Party has mainly used three instuments.

1. *Explicit provisions in the state constitution and the Party statute.* In its preface, the 1982 constitution mentions "leadership by the CCP" four times, and its definition of "people's democratic dictatorship" as being "in its essence, proletarian dictatorship" makes unmistakably clear what is meant. Moreover, the 1982 Party statute, in its "General Program," defines the CCP as "the vanguard of the Chinese working class, the reliable representative of the interests of the people of all nationalities, and the leading core for the cause of socialism in China." Leadership by the Party means, according to the statute's "General Program," "The Party must guarantee that the legislative, judicial, and executive organs of the state, the economic and cultural organizations, and the mass organizations can work actively, independently, responsibly, and in a coordinated manner." With these provisions, the Party can stake a legal claim to its leadership over the state.

2. *The institution of the Party groups (tang-tsu).* Article 46 of the 1982 Party statute provides for the establishment of Party groups in the "leading bodies of all central, regional, and local state organs," which have to "ensure that the guidelines and policies of the Party are put into practice." The members of these Party groups are appointed by the Party committee on the respective level or organ (Art. 47), and they are responsible for the guidance of the work of all Party members in their organizational sector.

3. *The interlacing between Party organs and the personnel of institutions in the state administrative machine,* the most important of the three instruments. Although "only" 62.53 pecent of the NPC delegates are members of the CCP and only 52.4 percent of the Presidium of its Standing Committee belongs to the Party, the leading figures of all central state administrative organs are Communists: the chairman and vice-chairman of the PRC, the chairman of the NPC's Standing Committee, the prime minister of the State Council, and the chairman of the powerful Central Military Commission belong to the Politburo; the procurator general of the Supreme People's Procuratorate is a member

of the CC; and the president of the Supreme People's Court is a member of the CAC. All fifty-two members of the State Council are also CCP members, and thirty-nine of them have full membership on the CC, two are CC alternates, and one is a member of the CAC.

A similar situation occurs in the provincial, municipal, and regional governments of the twenty-nine administrative units of the country. All of the leaders in these units belong to the secretariat of the respective PPCs, twenty as secretaries and nine as alternate secretaries, although none of them heads the Party machine in their respective unit. In addition, eleven are members and four are alternates of the CC.

Interlacing between the organs of state leadership becomes even more clear if we look at it from the angle of the Party. The Politburo is the most important body, and among its twenty-seven members and alternates we find the chairman and the vice-chairman of the PRC, the chairman of the NPC's Standing Committee and one of its vice-chairmen, the prime minister, two vice-premiers, two state councillors, the chairman and all four vice-chairmen of the Central Military Commission, the chief of the General Staff, the commander in chief of the PLA Air Force, and the commanders in chief of the Shenyang and Peking Military Areas.

With such safeguarding provisions, the CCP, so far, has been able to prevent the evolution of a competing elite from the ranks of the state administrative machine, an elite that could develop its own policy concepts. The Party indeed commands the state. But "the Party" in the PRC does not mean the civilian Party machine alone; instead, this term stands for a combination of the civilian Party machine and the PLA, which has a share in all leadership organs of the CCP, particularly the most decisive ones. Unlike most Communist-ruled countries—now obviously with the exception of Poland—the armed forces in the PRC form a politically active subsystem of their own.

CHAPTER 7

The Armed Forces

An Outline of Chinese Communist Military History

The Chinese Communist armed forces, the PLA as they have been called since the last stage of the civil war, were born out of an amalgamation of units of the KMT National Revolutionary Army (*Kuomin ke-ming chün*) under the command of officers who belonged to the CCP, groups of workers' militia of peasant guerrillas, and a considerable number of bandits (i.e., impoverished peasants who had taken to robbery to make their living) when the KMT and the CCP split in 1927.[55] From the very beginning, and at least into the early 1950s, the PLA has been a fighting army and inseparably connected with the Party. In fact, from 1927 through about 1939/1940, the PLA was the most important part of the Party, and from 1934 until 1936/1937, Party and army were almost identical: The army was the Party in arms, consisting almost entirely of CCP members and accounting for approximately 90 percent of Party membership.

When the CCP started to strike back against the persecution of its members by the KMT in 1927, there were four major events from which the fighting forces of the Party originated.

1. *The Nanch'ang uprising of August 1, 1927.* Upon the orders of the CCP leadership, three KMT generals who had just joined the CCP during the period of KMT-CCP cooperation—Chu Te, Yeh T'ing, and Ho Lung—led their units—the KMT army's ninth, eleventh, and twentieth corps—in an attack on the capital of Kiangsi, Nanch'ang. The city was conquered on August 1, but it could only be held until August 5, when other units loyal to the KMT retook it and defeated the rebels. Chu Te managed to escape with about 1,000 soldiers into southern China. By early 1928, he had 3,000 men under his command and was desperately fighting KMT troops in the southern part of Hunan. In spite of its

failure, the Nanch'ang uprising is celebrated as the point of establishment of the CCP armed forces.[56]

2. *The autumn harvest uprising in September 1927.* An emergency conference of the Party's CC held on August 7, 1927, after the Nanch'ang failure, ordered Mao Tse-tung, who had been organizing peasant associations in his native province of Hunan since late 1926, to stage an uprising in Hunan during the time of the autumn harvest in September. Mao succeeded in rallying armed coal miners' militia units, some units of the peasant association's militia, and one regiment of KMT soldiers led by Communist officers for an attack on Ch'angsha, the capital of Hunan, on September 8. But again, the uprising failed. Nevertheless, Mao was able to escape with about 700 men, and he organized them into the first division of what was now called the Chinese Workers' and Peasants' Red Army (*Chung-kuo kung-nung hung-chün*). In January 1928, he withdrew with them to the Chingkang Mountains and there established a base for guerrilla warfare.[57]

3. *The establishment of the Oyüwan Soviet in late 1927.* Again, some KMT units led by Communist officers, peasant militia groups, and also a number of armed branches of traditional Chinese secret societies rallied in November 1927 in Huangan and Mach'eng *hsien*, Hupei, for an attack against the KMT army because of its persecution of CCP members in the province. This time, the uprising was, at the outset, more successful. Led by Hsü Hai-tung—who was later joined by Hsü Hsiang-ch'ien and Li Hsien-nien—the rebels in Hupei held their own for a couple of weeks. Yet finally, the pressure of the KMT army became too strong for them to stay on the plains. Hence, they withdrew to the Tapiehshan mountainous area along the borders of Hupei, Anhui, and Honan, where they established the Oyüwan Soviet District (called thus after the old names of the three provinces) at the end of 1927. By the spring of 1928, they had been able to consolidate their guerrilla base in these mountains.[58]

4. *The P'ingchiang uprising in July 1928.* A regimental commander of the KMT Hunan provincial troops, Colonel P'eng Te-huai, who had fought successfully against the autumn harvest uprising in September 1927, was persuaded by one of his battalion commanders to secretly join the CCP in April 1928. On July 22 of that year, P'eng led his troops in revolt against the KMT and succeeded in occupying P'ingchiang *hsien* in Hunan for a number of weeks. By September, however, he had been forced out of that area by the government's troops. He then engaged in mobile warfare and held his own until December 1928 in different parts of southern Hunan.[59]

During 1928 and 1929, the units that had originated from these events established a number of Soviet areas as guerrilla bases in southern

China. In May 1928, Chu Te's units joined Mao's troops in the Chingkang Mountains, and by December 1928, P'eng Te-huai had escaped to that area, too.

From this core group, there developed, throughout 1929 and 1930, the Central Soviet Area, which soon embraced the larger part of southern Kiangsi and the bordering regions of Hunan and Fukien. The Oyüwan Soviet, too, expanded its area of control into a number of *hsien* in Anhui, Hupei, and southeastern Honan. In addition, other guerrilla bases were established in Ssuch'uan, western Hupei, Kuangsi, and by 1932, northern Shensi.

The Red Army succeeded in defeating three consecutive "extermination attempts" by the KMT government troops, and by the spring of 1933, it numbered approximately 200,000 soldiers. A fourth extermination campaign, however, eliminated a number of guerrilla bases in Honan, Hupei, and Anhui and limited the Oyüwan Soviet to a small, unaccessible area in the Tapiehshan. On March 1, 1934, more than 300,000 KMT soldiers under the leadership of Chiang Kai-shek himself—who was advised by the German General Hans von Seeckt—started the fifth extermination campaign against the Central Soviet Area in southern Kiangsi. By October, the KMT forces, now numbering 550,000, had succeeded in encircling the remaining soldiers of the Red Army in the southernmost region of that province, but 90,000 of them finally broke through to begin the Long March which brought their remnants, about 15,000–20,000 of them, into the small Soviet area around Paoan in northern Shensi about a year later.[60]

The substance of the Red Army had been saved, but the Communist guerrillas were now in a much more threatened position than before. In the south, only a few small units had been left behind in the mountainous border areas between Kiangsi and Fukien and between Hupei and Anhui.

Until the summer of 1937, the new Soviet area in northern Shensi gradually expanded around its capital, Yenan, and when the second Sino-Japanese War broke out in July 1937, the hostilities between the KMT and the CCP came to an end. Under the second united front agreement between the two parties, the Army, now numbering 80,000 soldiers, was reorganized into the Eighth Route Army (*Pa-lu-chün*) of the Chinese Nationalist armed forces, albeit with full autonomy from the KMT. Chu Te became commander in chief, with P'eng Te-huai as deputy commander and Yeh Chien-ying as chief-of-staff. This army was divided into three divisions.

- the 115th division, mostly units that had originated from the Chingkang base, under the command of Lin Piao; in 1938, an

independent brigade under the command of Nieh Jung-chen was
separated from this division
- the 120th division, the old units of Ho Lung and P'eng Te-huai
  now under the command of Ho Lung
- the 129th division, mostly units that had originated from the Oyüwan
  Soviet under the command of Liu Po-ch'eng.

In addition, the Communist guerrilla forces that had been operating in
scattered areas of southern China, mostly in northern Anhui and western
Fukien, were united into the autonomous New Fourth Army (*Hsin-ssu-chün*), commanded by Yeh T'ing and his deputy Ch'en Yi.

All of these units remained under effective CCP control. In particular,
they retained the system of having political commissars, representatives
of the Party on all levels of military command, down to and including
the platoon, who were responsible for political, cultural, and recreational
activities among the troops and for ensuring that the military officers
obeyed Party orders. A large number of the political commissars had
gone from political schools of the Red Army into the units of the forces;
others were civilian Party cadres who served in this position concurrently,
or sometimes as full-time political commissars. But there had also always
been a considerable number of commissars who had been troop officers
first, and later returned to military command positions. In fact, the
interaction between the troop officer and the political commissar networks, in terms of personnel interchange between the two chains of
command, became increasingly common after the early 1940s.[61]

During the Second Sino-Japanese War, the CCP armed forces fought
mainly a guerrilla type of war against the Japanese, but until the autumn
of 1940, they were also occasionally engaged in conventional operations,
most notably the so-called hundred regiments campaign from August
20 to December 5, 1940.[62] But then, the southern Anhui incident occurred.
The New Fourth Army, against the orders of the KMT High Command,
had crossed the Yangtzu into the southern part of Anhui where it was
attacked by KMT troops on January 4, 1941, and its main force almost
annihilated. After this clash, the remnants of the unit reorganized in
the northern part of the province.

This incident, in fact, marked the real end of the second KMT-CCP
united front, although it officially continued to exist until early 1947.
From now on, both sides prepared for the showdown that each expected
after the war. After early 1941, the CCP troops only defended themselves
against occasional Japanese attacks—constantly expanding their area
behind the Japanese lines and in the so-called liberated regions in
northern China and increasing their military strength—while the Nationalist army bore the brunt of the war. The Communist-led forces had

increased the number of regular soldiers in their fold to 910,000 by the spring of 1945, so they were well prepared for the civil war that began in late 1945 and was openly fought as an all-out confrontation between the two parties after January 1947.

In July 1947, all armed forces under the leadership of the CCP were unified as the Chinese PLA, the name they still use today. Their units, already numbering more than 2.5 million men, underwent reorganization into five field armies (*Yeh-chan-chün* [FAs]).

• The Northwestern FA under the command of P'eng Te-huai with Hsi Chung-hsün as political commissar, which operated in Shansi, Shensi, and Ninghsia. In February 1949, it was renamed the First FA.

• The Central Plains FA under the command of Liu Po-ch'eng with Teng Hsiao-p'ing as political commissar, which operated in Honan, Hupei, and Anhui. In February 1949, it was renamed the Second FA.

• The East China FA under the command of Ch'en Yi with Jao Shu-shih as political commissar, which operated in Shantung, Kiangsu, and parts of Anhui. In February 1949, it was renamed the Third FA.

• The Northeast FA under the command of Lin Piao with Lo Jung-huan as political commissar, which operated in Tungpei. In February 1949, it was renamed the Fourth FA.

• The North China FA under the command of Nieh Jung-chen with Li Ching-ch'üan as political commissar most of the time, which operated in Hopei, Inner Mongolia, and parts of Shansi. In February 1949, it was the only one of the five large PLA units to keep its name.

Chu Te became the commander in chief of the PLA, and Yeh Chien-ying served as his chief of staff. In this battle order, the Chinese Communist armed forces braced for victory in the last stage of the civil war. Between February and late November 1948, Lin Piao conquered all of Manchuria and then moved his troops south, first to aid Nieh Jung-chen in the capture of Peking and T'ienchin in January 1949 and afterward to proceed through Honan to the Yangtzu in Hupei. After very severe fighting all through the spring and summer of 1948, the troops under Liu Po-ch'eng and Ch'en Yi defeated the main force of the Nationalist army in the Hsüchou-Huaihai battle, which raged from November 6, 1948, to January 10, 1949, and resulted in more than 400,000 deaths for the KMT army and almost 300,000 for the PLA. After this battle, the backbone of the Nationalist troops had been broken.

Between April and December 1949, the First FA, in very costly and difficult battles, conquered Shensi, Kansu, and Sinkiang. The Second FA captured Wuhan and then turned toward the southwest, conquering Ssuch'uan, Kueichou, and Yünnan; the Third FA captured Shanghai and conquered Kiangsu, Chekiang, Kiangsi, and Fukien; and the Fourth FA swept south through Hunan and Kuangtung, conquering Canton in October 1949 and finally Hainan Island in early May 1950. However, the Third FA's attempt to capture the island group of Chinmen (Quemoy) as a stepping-stone to the seizure of T'aiwan failed with the devastating defeat of its amphibious forces in the battle of Kuningt'ou on October 25, 1949.

By early 1950, all of the Chinese mainland had thus been conquered by the PLA, which was now entrusted with the tasks of building up the regional and local administrations and of overseeing the great campaigns for social and political change in the country. For this purpose, the PRC was divided, until the early part of 1954, into six administrative areas: the Northeast (Tungpei), garrisoned by units of the Fourth FA but under a civilian government; North China, under the direct control of the central government and garrisoned by the North China FA; East China, under the control of the Third FA; Central-South China, under the control of the Fourth FA; Southwest China, under the control of the Second FA; and Northwest China, under the control of the First FA.

When the PRC decided to attack the U.S. and United Nations forces in Korea in October 1950, all FAs had to send troops into the new war. The combat experience during the Korean War, from 1950 until July 1953, had ambiguous results for the PLA. On the one hand, the armed forces of the PRC could pride themselves on having successfully stopped the offensive of a world power, and their equipment had been thoroughly modernized with Soviet help during the course of the war. On the other hand, the PLA had lost 900,000 men—110,000–130,000 of whom were killed in action—a loss that showed that this revolutionary army would have to modernize its structures, its chains of command, and even more so, its tactics.

These tasks were given to P'eng Te-huai, who was appointed minister of national defense, and thus entrusted with the actual command of the PLA, in September 1954. With P'eng's assumption of office, a period of professionalization began for the army. Its personnel in the regional and local administrative machines was either discharged from the military or recalled to the ranks. In 1955, new uniforms similar to those of the USSR, military ranks, and insignia were introduced, with ten major leaders receiving the rank of marshal: Chu Te, P'eng Te-huai, Liu Po-ch'eng, Ch'en Yi, Lin Piao, Nieh Jung-chen, Hsü Hsiang-ch'ien, Yeh

Chien-ying, Ho Lung, and Lo Jung-huan. Activities were concentrated on professional military training, and the number of soldiers was gradually reduced from 5,500,000 to about 3,600,000. Yet in spite of this drive toward a more professional military, the PLA— in particular, its air force and artillery—suffered a defeat in the Quemoy crisis from August to October 1958. This fact weakened P'eng Te-huai's position, and when he attacked Mao's policies of the Great Leap and the people's communes in summer of 1959, he was purged. Lin Piao succeeded him as minister of national defense.

The new PLA leader could credit himself with the smashing victory won by the troops of General Ting Sheng in the Sino-Indian Border War of October–November 1962, but Lin Piao's main interest was directed toward a new drive for the political indoctrination of the troops.[63] From 1960 to 1965, a large-scale campaign attempted to imbue the PLA members with Maoist doctrines, and in this context, military ranks and insignia were abolished in May 1965.[64]

The campaign prepared the PLA for the Cultural Revolution, in the high tide of which, between January and August 1967, it took over the regional political leadership and became the most powerful factor in Chinese politics. With Lin Piao as the officially designated successor of Mao, it appeared for some time that the PRC was heading toward military rule. But an active role of the military in politics often also means that politics enter the military, and this tendency held true for the PLA, too. In the Lin Piao crisis of 1970/1971, the majority of regional military leaders turned against the minister of national defense, who lost his position, and also his life, in September 1971. Since then, the PLA has gradually turned toward professionalization again, although its role in politics still appears formidable. The PLA also conducted a not very successful campaign, which could almost be called a defeat, during the Sino-Vietnamese Border War of February/March 1979, and this experience has obviously strengthened those forces in the army that call for more professionalization and a thoroughgoing modernization of the army's organizational structures as well as of its equipment. On August 1, 1983, the PLA received new uniforms, again modeled after USSR examples, and it was announced that ranks and insignia would be reintroduced in 1985.[65]

During the whole history of the PLA, primary group formation of the *t'ung-hang* type, on the basis of the traditional units that finally condensed into the five FAs, has been a very important aspect of Chinese military politics. Officially, the FAs were dissolved into the military area commands (MACs) and into corps in early 1954, but the old FA networks have mostly remained intact into the present. It would certainly be incorrect to reduce the analysis of intra-PLA group formation and conflicts

Table 7.1.   FA affiliations of PLA leaders, 1965–1983 (in percent)[66]

Year	First	Second	Third	Fourth	North China	Unknown
1965	17.2	20.2	19.5	25.5	9.2	8.4
1970	9.3	13.2	21.2	34.0	7.8	14.5
1977	11.4	16.7	26.5	19.3	13.6	12.5
1983	13.6	18.2	18.2	22.0	14.8	13.2

solely to the level of the existence of these loyalty groups or networks of the old FA, but they have played an important part in all differentiation processes within the PRC armed forces, and they will most probably continue to do so until the generation that joined the Red Army before the end of the Long March, or possibly even that which joined before the Korean War, has left the scene.

In order to illustrate this point, it should be noted that during the Cultural Revolution, the number of members of the Fourth FA loyalty group in the active PLA elite around Lin Piao increased dramatically while that of the First FA, which had been commanded by P'eng Te-huai, was drastically reduced. After the demise of Lin Piao, the proportion of the Fourth FA members dropped in turn, while those of the Second and Third FAs increased remarkably. Since 1977, a tendency toward a balance between these groups can be detected—a balance that was previously visible before the Cultural Revolution, in 1965. Table 7.1 presents data on the FA affiliation of major PLA leaders at four different periods from 1965 to 1983. The PLA is obviously a military establishment with very close relations to the Party, but what about its numerical strength?

Strength and Deployment

With 4,238,210 soldiers in June 1982,[67] the armed forces of the PRC are numerically the largest in the world. This statement, however, requires substantial qualifications when one moves into a detailed analysis.

The ground forces consist of the equivalent of 305 divisions with a total of 3,471,000 men, and they have approximately 10,000 tanks, 3,500 armored personnel carriers (APCs), 20,000 heavy and medium guns, and 18,000 mortars and light artillery pieces at their disposal. In their organization, a distinction is made between the combat forces (*Yeh-chan pu-tui*) and the territorial forces (*Ti-fang pu-tui*), which are responsible for internal security, border defense, and the garrisoning of the provinces.

The combat forces account for about two-thirds of the ground forces, with 2,281,000 soldiers in 179 divisions—105 of which are organized into thirty-four army corps and one airborne corps—and fifty-seven independent regiments (three independent cavalry, nine armor, ten field artillery, twenty-nine heavy artillery, and six antiaircraft regiments). But less than 25 percent of the combat forces is partly or fully mechanized. The most modern artillery systems used are those of the mid-1960s, and the most modern tanks, so far, are copies of Soviet models of the late 1950s. The heavy weaponry of the PLA field forces therefore consists of weapon systems developed between 1950 and 1965. Light weapons, too, are not newer than 1970 in terms of basic design.

The territorial forces mainly consist of forty-two divisions of state security troops (*Kuo-chia an-ch'üan pu-tui*), four border defense divisions, and fifty-one independent border defense regiments. The total manpower of these units is about 725,000 soldiers, some of whom were placed under the control of the new Ministry of State Security in June 1983 in order to have something similar to the mobile KGB units in the USSR. In addition, there are thirty-one divisions and twenty-six independent regiments of territorial defense forces (*Shou-pei pu-tui*) with approximately 465,000 men, which are of rather limited combat value.

The PLA air force consists of 415,000 men, of whom 120,000 are responsible for the defense of the air bases and logistics. The air force's major problem is that its equipment, too, appears outdated. There are approximately 5,500 planes available, including 4,750 jet fighters, but the most modern of these planes are constructed according to models that were developed about 1963, and the bulk of the air force equipment still hails from the late 1950s.

The PLA navy consists of 350,000 men, of whom 30,000 serve with naval air-force units and 38,000 with the marines. The navy can deploy 116 submarines, of which 30 have been constructed since 1970 (among them 5 nuclear-powered and ten missile-launching boats), and 81 were built in the USSR or according to Soviet models in the period 1955–1965. There are fourteen newer Chinese guided-missile destroyers, commissioned between 1970 and 1980, and three former Soviet ones launched between 1938 and 1940. To these can be added twenty-four frigates (fifteen commissioned between 1973 and 1980 and eight between 1956 and 1965), ten corvettes, and twenty-three large minesweepers. Besides the submarines, the real strength of the navy lies in 476 smaller coastal defense ships and 245 fast patrol boats with rocket launchers that can deploy rapidly, but mostly only close to the coast and to upstream naval bases. The navy, which has a total of about 1,640 ships available (including landing craft and auxiliary vessels),[68] is therefore primarily a defense arm of the armed forces with the tasks of coastal defense and safeguarding public security.

The most modern part of the PLA is the so-called Second Artillery, which stands for the nuclear and missile forces. By mid-1984, the PRC's

Table 7.2. PLA military areas and deployment of forces, 1984[70]

Military Area	Provinces	Share of Combat Forces (percent)	Share of Air Force (percent)
Shenyang	Heilungkiang, Kirin, Liaoning	14.8	14.9
Peking	Peking, T'ienchin, Hopei, Shansi, Inner Mongolia	21.0	13.4
Chinan	Shantung	7.2	10.4
Nanking	Shanghai, Kiangsu, Chekiang, Anhui	8.8	17.9
Fuchou	Fukien, Kiangsi	8.2	4.5
Canton	Hunan, Kuangsi, Kuangtung	9.3	14.9
K'unming	Yünnan, Kueichou	4.7	1.5
Ch'engtu	Ssuch'uan, Tibet	5.5	3.1
Lanchou	Kansu, Shensi, Ch'inghai, Ninghsia	7.9	7.5
Ürümchi	Sinkiang	4.8	1.5
Wuhan	Hupei, Honan	7.9	10.4

stockpile of nuclear weapons was believed to include several hundred fission and fusion devices. In terms of launchers, there were about eighty medium-range ballistic missiles (MRBMs), eighty to ninety intermediate-range ballistic missiles (IRBMs) and perhaps eight to ten intercontinental ballistic missiles (ICBMs) with a limited range of 4,000–4,500 miles. In 1980, a longer-range (8,000-mile) ICBM was successfully tested, but ICBM development seems still to be impeded by a lack of precision-targeting technology.

To recruit manpower for these armed forces, the PRC has introduced a draft system, which officially extends to all male citizens above the age of eighteen. In June 1984, the terms of duty were set at three years for the ground forces; four years for the air force, technical units, and naval auxiliary units; and five years for the navy and the marines.[69] Since 1980, it appears that the PLA has run into recruiting difficulties and that it is no longer easy to get soldiers to enlist for professional military service, a term that is now set at twenty years.

As far as force deployment is concerned, the navy is divided into three major units—the North Sea, East Sea and South Sea fleets—in a relation of 1:1.8:1.2, and the territorial forces are stationed all over the country in numbers that do not differ widely from province to province. The combat troops and the air force, however, are divided among the eleven major command units, the military area commands (MACs), in a quite uneven way as Table 7.2 indicates.

This deployment reflects a threat perception that still allocates the highest priority to a perceived threat from the Soviet Union. The four

MACs along the borders of the USSR and Outer Mongolia (Shenyang, Peking, Lanchou, and Ürümchi) compose 48.5 percent of the field army strength and 37.3 percent of the air force, although these shares have already been reduced, respectively, from 50.7 and 50.5 percent in 1982. If the tensions between the PRC and the USSR should relax, the deployment of the PLA forces would probably undergo significant changes in the future. But who decides this deployment and who commands the troops? In other words, What is the command structure of the armed forces?

Command Structure

The PLA command structure is comparatively complicated. Officially, the chairman of the PRC was the supreme commander of all armed forces under the 1954 constitution, which means between 1954 and early 1967. Under the constitutions of 1975 and 1978, however, this position was reserved for the chairman of the Party's CC, and the minister of national defense acted as commander in chief of the PLA, although he did not use this title. But in fact, the PLA, at least until June 1983, had always been led by the Military Commission of the CC of the CCP (*Chung-kung chung-yang chün-shih wei-yüan-hui*, abbreviation, *Chung-yang chün-wei*). From January 1935 until his death in September 1976, this body was chaired by Mao Tse-tung himself, and from October 1976 to December 1980, by Hua Kuo-feng. The minister of national defense has usually assumed the position of a first vice-chairman, and for considerable periods in the 1950s and 1960s, acting chairman. De facto since December 5, 1980, and de jure since June 29, 1981, the chairmanship of the Military Commission has been separated from the chairmanship of the CC, and Teng Hsiao-p'ing has been chairman of the Military Commission.

Information about the composition of the Military Commission is very limited. A list of its members has never been published, not even their number. Yet between January 1980 and June 1983, membership was confirmed by the CCP media for twenty-three people, most of whom, with very few exceptions, were military leaders. Among them, an inner circle of nine became visible after the Twelfth Party Congress in September 1982: the chairman, Teng Hsiao-p'ing; three vice-chairmen, the Marshals Yeh Chien-ying, Hsü Hsiang-ch'ien, and Nieh Jung-chen; a standing vice-chairman and secretary general, Yang Shang-k'un; and four deputy secretary generals, the generals Yü Ch'iu-li, Yang Te-chih, Chang Ai-p'ing, and Hung Hsüeh-chih.

The constitution of the PRC promulgated on December 4, 1982, established a new organ with very strong statutory powers in the

Table 7.3. Members of the CMC, June 20, 1983[73]

Name	Date of Birth	FA Background	Cultural Revolution Status	Member of
Chairman				
Teng Hsiao-p'ing	1904	Second	purged	PB
Vice-Chairmen				
Yeh Chien-ying	1897	Fourth	survived	PB
Hsü Hsiang-ch'ien	1902		survived	PB
Nieh Jung-chen	1899	North China	survived	PB
Yang Shang-k'un	1907		purged	PB
Members				
Yü Ch'iu-li	1914	First	survived	PB
Yang Te-chih	1910	North China	survived	PB
Chang Ai-p'ing	1910	Third	purged	CC
Hung Hsüeh-chih	1913	Fourth	purged	CC

framework of the state administrative machine: the Central Military Commission (*Chung-yang chün-shih wei-yüan-hui* [CMC]). This body, according to the constitution, "leads [*ling-tao*] the armed forces of the whole country."[71] Its chairman is elected by the NPC, without prior nomination by the chairman of the PRC, and its members are elected by the NPC after nomination by the chairman of the CMC.[72] When the first CMC was placed in office by the Sixth NPC on June 20, 1983, it turned out to be a very small and obviously highly powerful group of nine members, entirely identical with the leading circle of the Party's Military Commission. A list of them is presented in Table 7.3.

At the end of 1983, this group had an average age of 76.8 years, eight of its nine members being 70 or older. These nine people have an average CCP membership duration of 56.2 years, and they all participated in the Long March. Five of them are survivors and four purgees of the Cultural Revolution. The group includes seven full members of the Politburo and two other CC members. It is easily the most senior of all political bodies in the PRC, and probably the most influential after the Politburo itself.

Under the guidance of the Party's Military Commission, and since June 1983 under the official direction of the CMC, the Ministry of National Defense takes charge of the regular leadership work. From its establishment in September 1954 until October 1982, its minister was a member of the Politburo, but the same is not true of the current minister, General Chang Ai-p'ing, who is only a regular CC member. In his work, he is currently assisted by two vice-ministers.[74] Officially, the ministry is part of the State Council, but in fact, it reports to the

Party's Military Commission, and now probably to the CMC. Moreover, the ministry also serves as the General Headquarters of the PLA, and it oversees all organs of the central military machine.

Under the Ministry of National Defense, three departments are the major institutions of central military leadership (see Figure 7.1).

1. *The General Staff.* This department is responsible for the drafting of strategic plans, for decisions on troop deployment, and for all staff work usually done by similar organs in other countries. But since there is no general headquarters for the PLA ground forces, they are also under direct command of the General Staff. The current chief of the General Staff, General Yang Te-chih (member of the Politburo), is assisted by eight deputies, of whom three are members of the CC, one is an alternate member of the CC, and two are members of the CAC.[75]

2. *The General Political Department* (GPD). The GPD is in charge of all political work of the PLA, including the cultural and recreational activities of the troops. With political departments in all units down to the regimental level, and political commissars down to the platoon level, the GPD heads a formidable chain of command of its own. It is headed by the director of the GPD, currently General Yü Ch'iu-li (member of the Politburo), who has eight deputies, two of them members of the CC and two of the CAC.[76]

3. *The General Rear Services Department* (GRSD). The GRSD's responsibilities include control over the whole area of logistics, weapons and ammunition supplies, transport facilities, and the military medical service. There is a direct chain of command down to the rear services departments on the division level, but the political importance of this network appears to be rather limited. The GRSD is headed by a director, General Hung Hsüeh-chih (member of the CC), who is aided by eleven deputies, two of them members of the CAC.[77]

As already pointed out, there is no central command for the PLA ground forces, but under the General Staff, central headquarters have been established for two types of services.

1. *The service arms* (*Chün-chung*), i.e., the PLA navy and the PLA air force. The PLA navy general headquarters, currently with Admiral Liu Hua-ch'ing (member of the CC) as commander in chief, has direct command over all naval forces at all times in peace or war. The PLA air-force general headquarters, currently with General Chang T'ing-fa (member of the Politburo) as commander in chief, however, assumes direct command over all air-force units only in times of mobilization, emergency, or war. In times of peace, the air-force units respond to the

Figure 7.1. ORGANIZATIONAL STRUCTURE OF THE ARMED FORCES

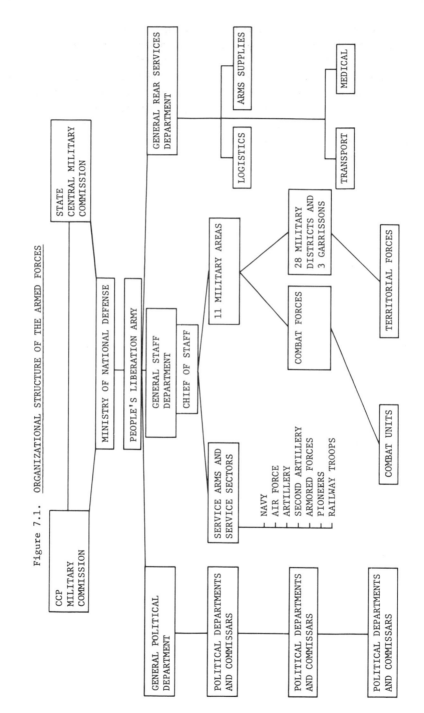

MACs, and the central headquarters of the air force oversees recruitment, training, general air strategy, the choice of weapon systems, and supplies.

2. *The service sectors* (*Ping-chung*), of which there are five: Artillery, Second Artillery, Armored Forces, Pioneers (Engineers), and Railway Troops. The central headquarters of these sectors have no direct command over troops at any time. They are responsible only for recruitment, training, the choice of weapon systems, supplies, and general administration. Of their five commanders, three are members of the CC, and one is a member of the CAC.[78]

In the absence of a general headquarters for the PLA ground forces, the commanders in chief of the eleven MACs report directly to the General Staff. The MACs were formed after the end of the Korean War, at the time of the formal dissolution of the FAs in the spring of 1954. They are in direct command of the combat forces and in times of peace, of the air forces stationed in their respective realms as well. Moreover, they supervise the territorial forces, which are directly commanded by the provincial or regional military district, and the city garrison commands.

For the combat forces, the MAC commanders in chief suggest people for appointment as corps commander, nominate the division commanders, and directly appoint the commanders of regiments and battalions for all units under their command. Until the early 1970s, the commanders in chief usually served for long periods: Between 1954 and 1973, their average term of duty in one area was 8.7 years, with one each having served for nineteen, fourteen, and thirteen years. Transfers in December 1973, during the winter of 1979/1980, and again during the winter of 1982/1983, however, have changed this situation drastically, so that the eleven MAC commanders in chief who were serving in September 1983 had served an average term of barely three years. Information on this group of military leaders is provided in Table 7.4.

The average age of the eleven MAC commanders in chief was 67.9 at the end of 1983, and with only two of them older than 70, this is, for the current situation of PLA leadership, a comparatively young group. Only two of them joined the CCP and its armed forces after 1935, so nine belong to the Long March generation. It should also be noted that all of them took part in the Korean War. In the group, there are nine full members of the CC, which is indicative of the importance of the MACs. FA affiliation is rather uneven: Five came from the Second FA network, three from the Fourth FA, two from the North China FA, one from the Third FA, and none of them from the First FA. In this context, we should remember that Teng Hsiao-p'ing was political com-

Table 7.4.   Commanders in chief of the MACs, September 1, 1983

MAC	Name	Date of Birth	FA Back-ground	Cultural Revolu-tion Status	Member of
Shenyang	Li Te-sheng	1916	Second	advanced	PB
Peking	Ch'in Chi-wei	1912	Second	purged	PB alt.
Chinan	Jao Shou-k'un	1915	Third	survived	
Nanking	Hsiang Shou-chih	1914	Second	purged	CC
Fuchou	Chiang Yung-hui	1916	Fourth	survived	CC
Canton	Yu T'ai-chung	1909	Second	survived	CC
K'unming	Chang Chih-hsiu	1921	North China	purged	CC
Ch'engtu	Wang Ch'eng-han	1914	Second	survived	CC
Wuhan	Chou Shih-chung	1921	Fourth	survived	CC
Lanchou	Cheng Wei-shan	1914	North China	purged	
Ürümchi	Hsiao Ch'üab-fu	1914	Fourth	survived	CC

missar of the Second FA, and that the chief of the General Staff, General Yang Te-chih, served with the North China FA.

The Military in Politics

In the CCP, it has never been doubted that "the Party" is in command of the armed forces. Yet such a general statement does not indicate the relations between the civilian Party machine and the military as a political entity *within* the CCP. These relations have undergone several changes since 1949.

For the first four years after the establishment of the PRC, civilian Party leadership and military leadership could be clearly distinguished only on the central level. On the regional level, there had not yet evolved distinctly different chains of command of civilian Party, army, and state administrative subsystems; instead, civilian and military cadres shared in the regional administration as well as in the regional Party machines, which were still in the stage of construction. At the beginning of 1953, there were, among the 345 members of the leading organs in the six "great regions," 104 military men, a share of 30.1 percent. If one only counts the CCP members in these organs, the share of the PLA was 36.4 percent.

This situation changed drastically in 1954 when the great regions were abolished and the first constitution was promulgated. Within less than two years, by early 1956, two clearly distinguishable subsystems had evolved: a civilian Party machine with its own chains of command and the PLA, which, under the leadership of P'eng Te-huai, turned more and more toward professionalization. Moreover, since 1958/1959, the civilian Party leadership, strongly influenced by Liu Shao-ch'i and Teng Hsiao-p'ing, has succeeded in establishing and strengthening its own position within the PLA by way of the political commissar network.

Although most of the political commissars of the troop units had a military background, 77.3 percent of the commissars of the territorial organizations, the MACs and the military district commands in 1965 had gained their experience in the civilian Party machine. At the same time, only 28, or 10.5 percent, of the 267 PPC secretaries were military men. These figures indicate that in the mid-1960s, the civilian Party machine definitely dominated civilian-military relations within the CCP.

But soon, a drastic change occurred. When the civilian Party and the state administrative machines collapsed during the high tide of the Cultural Revolution, the PLA remained the only relatively intact major institutional subsystem. Using the slogan, Three-Support, Two-Military Work (*San-chih liang-chün kung-tso*)—which stood for the support of the workers, the peasants, and the Left and for management and training by the military—the PLA, between January and August 1967, took over the leadership of the administration, economy, and political work of almost all provinces of the PRC. At the Ninth Party Congress in April 1969, 85 out of 170 full members of the CC were military men, and so were twelve out of twenty-one full members of the new Politburo.

Between December 1969 and August 1971, the PLA supervised, and in many cases fully controlled, the reestablishment of the regional and local Party machines. The results of these political activities of the military were obvious: Of the 158 secretaries and alternate secretaries of the twenty-nine reestablished PPCs, 98, or 62 percent, belonged to the PLA. Generals and political commissars with military backgrounds held twenty-one of the twenty-nine positions of PPC first secretaries, and concurrently, those of the RC chairmen. In six provinces, MAC commanders in chief assumed the leadership of Party and government, five provinces were led by their respective provincial military district commanders, and ten were guided by PLA commissars. The other four active MAC commanders in chief and twenty-two military district commanders became secretaries of the new PPC. The PRC seemed to approach the status of a military regime, and the situation was indeed accurately described by Ralph Powell in 1970 when he stated that "the generals control the Party which commands the gun."[79]

But with Lin Piao's fall from power and death on September 12, 1971, the balance started to change again. Although most of the military leaders kept their positions in the provinces until the thoroughgoing transfer of MAC commanders in chief in December 1973, the majority of new appointments to regional and central government and Party positions were made from the ranks of the civilian Party machine. This development has accelerated since 1977, so that in the summer of 1983, only four of the twenty-nine PPCs were still led by representatives of the PLA, three of them career political commissars. A similar development

Table 7.5. PLA representation on leading organs of the CCP and the PRC, 1965–1983 (in percent)

Organ	1965	1971	1975	1978	1983
NPC Standing Committee	17.4	a	14.4	17.3	10.4
State Council	25.4	a	33.3	16.3	5.7
PPC secretariats	10.5	62.0	35.2	22.9	6.2
PPC first secretaries	10.7	72.4	48.3	17.2	13.8
CC (full members)	34.0	50.0	37.5	32.4	25.2
Politburo (total)	25.0	56.0	34.6	40.0	40.7
Politburo (full members)	33.3	57.1	36.4	42.8	41.7

[a]Nonexistent or practically nonexistent.

can be observed among the membership of the CC, and also in the leading organs of the state administrative machine, as is illustrated by the data presented in Table 7.5.

These data indicate clearly the retreat of the military from the civilian executive organs on the central and provincial levels since the overthrow of Lin Piao, but they also show that this retreat has not been a retreat from politics, as can be concluded from the data concerning the military's Politburo representation, which, in 1983, was still significantly higher than in 1965. No other ruling Communist Party has so many generals in the Politburo. Moreover, the PLA, so far, has prevented the packing of the political commissar positions in its territorial organizations by members of the civilian Party machine, as happened between 1958/ 1959 and 1965. In the summer of 1983, only 43, or 28.1 percent, of the 153 political commissars on the MAC or military district levels were civilian cadres.

One last aspect of great importance should be discussed. The importance of the PLA in political crises distinguishes its position from that of the armed forces in other Communist, single-party systems. The reason for this singular political position of the Chinese Communist military can be found in its long history of a close connection, and over some periods even identity, with the Party. As long as the Long March generation still controls the most important power positions, this historical experience continues to produce aftereffects, which gives the Chinese PLA a distinctly political character. We shall observe this fact again as we now turn to an account of the political developments that have shaped the current patterns of the political institutions since early 1975.

PART 3

The Politics of a Transitional Crisis System

CHAPTER 8

Conflict over Personal Succession, 1975/1976

The Fourth NPC and Mao's Reaction, January–April 1975

One may argue that the Cultural Revolution from 1966 to 1969 marked the end of Mao Tse-tung's dominating influence on the Chinese political scene and that the purge and death of his once-designated successor, Marshal Lin Piao in September 1971 made the retreat of The Chairman into the position of a mere legitimizer of decisions taken by other CCP leaders even more obvious.[1] Yet even if one insists that Mao still played the most important role in PRC politics until and including the Tenth Party Congress in 1973, there can be hardly any doubt that by the autumn of 1974, the ruling elite had started to brace itself for The Chairman's final departure. Mao was eighty-one, and his health appeared to be deteriorating gradually. Moreover, Prime Minister Chou En-lai, who held the second position in the pecking order of the leadership core, was suffering from cancer and entered a hospital on May 9, 1974, from which he only occasionally and briefly emerged—for the last time on September 7, 1975.[2] Hence, the problem of succession became imminent, and it had to be solved by an elite that was neither united nor easily willing to arrive at compromise solutions.

Nevertheless, such a compromise solution had been achieved at the Tenth Party Congress in August 1973, as far as the composition of the CCP leadership was concerned.[3] Within this leadership, a number of intraelite groups became visible, emerging from a mixture of primary and protosecondary group formation patterns. Some of these groups were based on common opinions; others, on common experience; yet others, on functional subsystems, and the last type, in particular, displayed a rather high degree of fluctuation. But with a number of qualifications, at least seven such groups could be detected.

1. the veteran civilian cadres who had survived the Cultural Revolution in office
2. the veteran civilian cadres who had been rehabilitated after having been purged during the Cultural Revolution
3. the cultural revolutionary Left, which formed the hard core of the leftist forces within the CC
4. the mass organization Left, a group of cadres who rose to prominence after the Cultural Revolution, mostly from the basic levels of the Party, or from "model peasant" and "labor hero" designations
5. the secret police Left, i.e., cadres closely connected with the security establishment of the early 1970s
6. the central military machine
7. the regional military leaders (the most fluctuating of all the groups)

The major issue that determined the coalitions and confrontations among these groups after 1973/1974, and increasingly so after early 1975, was the question of who would succeed Mao Tse-tung as leader of the CCP and, hence, the country. Should it be Chou En-lai—and after he had fallen ill, the man Chou had considered as his trusted lieutenant in 1973 and 1974, Teng Hsiao-p'ing? Or should it be one of the leaders of the Maoist Left? Further disagreements developed between the cultural revolutionary Left and the mass organization Left, on the one hand, and the two military groups, on the other, over the question of whether the newly formed urban militia should be an independent force or be supervised by the PLA, and also between all three leftist groups and the two groups of veteran cadres over the problem of promotion of younger cadres from the basic and middle to the upper levels of Party organization.

In addition to these power political disagreements, policy disputes emerged among the intraelite groups, starting a process of elite differentiation almost immediately after the Tenth Party Congress. There were five major problem areas.

1. *Science and technology.* The Left emphasized Chinese self-reliance; the veteran cadres and a large number of the military leaders argued that massive technology imports from Western countries were necessary.
2. *Education.* The Left fought for the priority of political indoctrination and combined work-study curricula as well as open admission to secondary and tertiary institutions; the rehabilitated veteran cadres stressed factual knowledge, regularized instruction, and entrance examinations.

3. *Culture.* The Left attempted to uphold the cultural revolutionary monopoly of Chiang Ch'ing's "revolutionary romanticism"; both groups of veteran cadres, supported by some, though not all, of the regional military leaders, tended toward a broadening of the parameters of competition between different styles and approaches, including a more positive attitude toward China's cultural heritage.

4. *Industrial wages.* The Left argued for equalization and against stressing material incentives; the veteran cadres, in particular, wanted to continue—and possibly to expand—a highly differentiated, incentive-oriented wage system.

5. *Rural societal policies.* The Left wanted once again to raise the level of agricultural collectivization by giving more power to the brigades and communes at the expense of the teams, by reducing the size of private plots, and by restricting the peasants' private sideline occupations. Most of the regional military leaders, supported by a number of veteran cadres, wanted preservation or even expansion of private plots, private animal husbandry, and other individual activities of the peasants.

All of these different disputes, in the final analysis, came down to the same fundamental question that had dominated the crisis of the Cultural Revolution: Should class struggle, development through mobilization, and "permanent revolution" or organizational stabilization, growth-oriented development, and modernization through technology have priority in the future of the PRC? In other words, Should China follow the Great Leap and cultural revolutionary prescripts of Maoist persuasion, or should China strive for future great-power status by adhering to the policies devised as a result of Liu Shao-ch'i and Teng Hsiao-p'ing's concept of readjustment, which had been resumed by Chou En-lai and his supporters after the demise of Lin Piao in 1971?

At the beginning of 1975, the alliances within the Party in support of one or the other of these alternatives had started to stabilize. The leftist forces, i.e., the Maoists, including The Chairman himself, could rally ten or eleven members of the Politburo; those groups that opposed the leftist positions were represented by eight or nine Politburo members; and one or two members were wavering. But in the CC, only one-third of the full members supported the Left, with about one-half opposing it, and on the provincial level, the Left was comparatively weak, controlling only the leadership of six or seven out of the twenty-nine administrative units.[4]

The first major round of this intraelite conflict went against the Left. In order to ratify the stabilization of the state administrative machine, the Fourth NPC convened in Peking from January 13–17, 1975,[5] the first meeting of an NPC in ten years. The decisions of this meeting had been prepared at the second plenum of the CCP's Tenth CC, which had been held in the capital from January 8 to January 10, and these decisions appeared to be mainly dominated by the growth-oriented policies of the veteran cadres and the majority of the military leaders.

The new constitution of the PRC made the production teams the basic rural accounting units, and it also guaranteed the ownership of private plots by the peasants as well as private sideline occupations.[6] At the NPC meeting, Chou En-lai, in his report on the work of the government, which was read to the congress in his absence, proclaimed a new goal for the country: "In this century, we must accomplish the all-out *modernization of agriculture, industry, national defense, and science and technology,* so that our country's national economy proceeds into the front-row of the world!"[7] This goal was soon to be known as the four modernizations (*Ssu-ke hsien-tai-hua*), and, as such, it became the slogan of the antileftists among the elite.

Hence, the policy decisions of the second plenum and the NPC meeting reflected the positions of the forces that opposed Maoist pre-scriptions. The personnel decisions, on the other hand, were the results of a compromise. Although Teng Hsiao-p'ing was appointed first vice-premier, the leftist leader Chang Ch'un-ch'iao became second in line among the twelve vice-premiers, six of whom represented the different groups of the Left.[8] Of the thirty-nine members of the State Council, there were three representatives each from the cultural revolutionary Left, the mass organization Left, and the secret police Left. But veteran cadres and military representatives accounted for three-quarters of the State Council membership, and ten of the new ministers had been purged or at least severely criticized during the Cultural Revolution.

Compromise dictated the appointments to the top positions in the PLA also. The Fourth NPC confirmed Marshal Yeh Chien-ying, then seventy-seven, as minister of national defense, Teng became chief of the General Staff, and Chang Ch'un-ch'iao became director of the PLA's General Political Department.[9]

These developments, particularly the policy decisions, apparently irritated Mao Tse-tung. Not only did he not participate in the second plenum or the NPC meeting, but it was reported that he sent no message to either of the two conferences.[10] Moreover, less than a month later, the CCP media published an important directive (*Chung-yao chih-shih*) from The Chairman in which he argued that money as a means of exchange, and in particular the eight-grade wage system in industry, were "capitalist characteristics which survive in the socialist society." Hence, the current socialist society was not so much different from the old society, and—so Mao held—it was now the time to engage in a campaign for the "restriction of bourgeois rights."[11]

This proclamation by the Party leader, which directly contradicted the decisions of the Fourth NPC, was further elaborated in two articles by the leftist leaders Yao Wen-yüan and Chang Ch'un-ch'iao in the March and April editions of the Party's theoretical journal, *Hung-ch'i* ("Red flag").[12] Both articles developed an almost comprehensive platform, calling in particular for an equalization of wages, the restriction of private activities by the peasants, and a gradual transmission of power from the production teams to the brigades and the communes. From a speech by a young female delegate from Hunan to a major agricultural conference in December 1976, Mme. Lung Yü-lan, we know that Hua Kuo-feng had promoted almost exactly the same ideas in rural societal policies during 1974 and 1975.[13]

The two articles by Yao and Chang sounded the clarion call for a new campaign to study the theory of proletarian dictatorship, in the course of which the central CCP media continued to exude cultural revolutionary doctrines. Yet in fact, economic and social policies still followed the approaches of the concept of readjustment, which had been revitalized by Chou En-lai and his associates in 1971. Thus, the contradictions between central propaganda and the political reality, particularly on the provincial level, became increasingly visible, and so became the contradictions between Maoist policy prescriptions and the wishes of considerable parts of the populace.

The Strike Wave and the Rightist Storm, June–September 1975

As early as late 1974, reports that indicated social contradictions and popular discontent began to filter out of the PRC. Returning Hongkong visitors and refugees from South China brought out stories of rusticated youths returning illegally to their home cities, of farmers spending more time on their private plots for sideline earnings than in collective production, and of workers going slowly in the factories. In November 1974, three former Red Guards put up a huge wall poster in the very center of Canton, using the pseudonym Li I-che, to publish their call for a system of social justice and freedom of speech.[14]

By early 1975, sabotage activities had led to the disruption of railway communication in a number of cases, which prompted the Party center to issue a circular concerning problems of transport security on March 27.[15] But these incidents were only the beginning of a larger movement in the spring and summer of 1975 when industrial workers, mainly those in wage grades 6–8, started to openly oppose the policies of the

Left. In early March, the equalization of industrial wages became one of the major slogans of the leftist forces, which provoked the resistance of parts of industrial labor. From June through September 1975, a veritable wave of large-scale strikes and labor unrest hit a number of cities in Central and South China, particularly Hangchou, Wuhsi, and Wuhan.[16]

At the same time, the provincial media were full of reports of undesirable activities in the countryside. These reports indicated that the peasants in the communes—in particular in Chekiang, Kiangsu, Kiangsi, Kansu, and Liaoning—had begun to engage in the "restoration of capitalism." They "speculated," "started small production," and "corrupted the cadres and Party members." They "left agriculture to engage in commerce," and in this way, "the individuals made money, while the collective fields were neglected and became barren land."[17] In the context of these developments in society, Teng Hsiao-p'ing, who was now in charge of the state administrative machine as the deputy of the ailing Chou En-lai, tried, beginning in July 1975, to overcome the contradictions between propaganda and reality by an all-out return to pre–cultural revolutionary policies.

Beginning in late May, the media again stressed the importance of material incentives and economic growth, and occasionally, there were even statements legitimizing the peasants' sideline occupations in the rural communes. During a visit to Shanghai in mid-June, Teng Hsiao-p'ing, while inspecting the construction site of a new petrochemical complex in Chinshan *hsien*, proclaimed that "practical things should take command."[18] This statement was diametrically opposed to the positions taken by the cultural revolutionary Left. Moreover, during the spring and summer of 1975, the return to pre–cultural revolutionary policies was combined with an attempt to bring back pre–cultural revolutionary personnel.[19] More than sixty prominent purgees of the Cultural Revolution were appointed to leading positions, particularly on the provincial level.

In July, Teng began to prepare for an official acceptance of the policies of readjustment. On July 18, two recently rehabilitated leading cadres, Hu Yao-pang (former first secretary of the CYL) and Hu Ch'iao-mu (former deputy director of the CC's Propaganda Department), were appointed to the Academy of Sciences. In their new positions, they drafted, upon Teng's request, a "Report Outline on the Work of the Academy of Sciences" in which it was suggested that "one should not talk about class struggle in science and technology."[20] That document was followed in August by another document of twenty articles entitled "On Some Problems of the Extension and Acceleration of Industrial Growth," this time signed by Teng himself.[21] In this programmatic statement, Teng and his associates argued that the four modernizations must be the guidelines for all economic work, and they stressed material incentives, an emphasis on productivity and growth, and the necessity of importing foreign technology.

This stress on growth-oriented policies was soon ideologically justified by the propagation of the three directives (*San hsiang chih-shih*) of Chairman Mao, which Teng—and the PRC media until early November 1975—proclaimed to be the link (*kang*) of all activities:

Study the theory of proletarian dictatorship!
Keep order and unite!
Let the national economy forge ahead![22]

Basing his actions on these slogans, Teng, who was acting for the ailing Premier Chou En-lai and running the daily affairs of the state administrative machine throughout most of 1975, aimed at a return to the policies of readjustment even in the areas of education and science, which the cultural revolutionary Left had regarded as its own bailiwick.

In the face of these changes, the three leftist elite groups started to prepare for a counterattack against what they now started to call the "rightist storm of reversal of [cultural revolutionary] verdicts" (*Yu-ch'ing fan-an feng*). By October 1975, the process of crystallization of these three groups into a united Left faction had begun.

Yet before this process was completed, a national agricultural conference attended by more than 3,700 leading cadres, the First National Conference on Learning from Tachai in Agriculture, was convened in the northern Chinese model brigade of Tachai and in Peking from mid-September to mid-October. This conference became the scene for controversies that were still characterized by differences within the Left but even more so between the Left and the moderate forces around Teng.[23] The conference began on September 15 with addresses by Teng Hsiao-p'ing and Chiang Ch'ing, Mao's wife, and it was concluded on October 15, in the Capital, with a speech by Hua Kuo-feng, vice-premier and minister of public security. The PRC press has published only Hua's speech, but from attacks against Teng that appeared in the media during the spring of 1976,[24] it is possible to reconstruct the major thrust of his argument, and the text of Chiang Ch'ing's address was published in T'aiwan in December 1975,[25] and later large parts of it were confirmed by PRC sources.

Three different concepts of rural societal policy were proposed at the conference, and they can be identified as follows.

1. Teng Hsiao-p'ing called for a confirmation of the concessions that had been granted for the private initiative of the peasants in 1961/1962 and—wherever necessary to promote the growth of production—even for their expansion.

2. Chiang Ch'ing argued for a gradual return to the original organizational concept of the communes, as they had been developed in 1958, by means of an anticapitalist mobilization of the poor and lower-middle peasants to wage class struggle in the villages. She also ventured a snide cut at Hua Kuo-feng by hinting that the socialism in the countryside was threatened not only by "capitalist-roaders" still in power but also by the timidity of nice gentlemen of Malenkov's ilk (*Ma-lien-k'e-fu-i-shih-te hao-hao hsien-sheng*).

3. Hua Kuo-feng, possibly supported by Ch'en Yung-kuei and other leading agricultural cadres, also advocated a restoration of the original concept of the communes, but through mechanization of agriculture and through strengthening the communes and brigades at the expense of the teams rather than through permanent revolutionization.

Hence, Hua and the cultural revolutionary leftists agreed on the goals but not the methods of rural societal policies. Yet in spite of this difference, the leftist groups coalesced into a faction soon after the Tachai conference, and thus, the conflict over personal succession gradually developed into open confrontation.

The Leftist Counterattack and the Second Purge of Teng Hsiao-p'ing

The succession problem became acute as a result of a series of deaths, since in the short period of seventeen months, from April 1975 to September 1976, five out of nine members of the innermost leadership core, the Politburo's Standing Committee, left the political scene: Tung Pi-wu (aged eighty-nine) died on April 2, 1975; K'ang Sheng (seventy-four), on December 7, 1975; Chou En-lai (seventy-seven), on January 8, 1976; Marshal Chu Te (ninety), on July 6, 1976; and finally, Mao Tse-tung himself (eighty-two), on September 9, 1976. The last three deaths, in particular, provided the framework for a crisis that shook the very foundations of the PRC's political system in 1976.

This crisis commenced with a joint drive on the part of the united Left faction. This drive was soon to be called the "counterattack against the rightist storm of reversal of verdicts" (*Fan-chi yu-ch'ing fan-an feng*), and its first major target was Teng Hsiao-p'ing.

In early November, a close associate of Chiang Ch'ing, Mme. Hsieh Cheng-yi (member of the CC), organized the opposition against Teng among the faculty and students of the old cultural revolutionary strongholds in the capital, Peking University and Ch'inghua University. Until mid-December, the leftist campaign was confined to wall posters and scattered meetings of students, but after that, the media also began to call for the criticism of still unidentified opponents of the Cultural Revolution, mainly in the fields of education and culture. On January 1, 1976, the joint New Year's editorial of *JMJP*, *HC*, and *CFCP* quoted a "newest directive of Chairman Mao" that proclaimed that "unity and stability" did "not mean to give up class struggle, which is the only key link [*kang*]."[26]

The death of Chou En-lai on January 8 precipitated the attempts of the Left to overthrow Teng. On January 15, it was still Teng who delivered the eulogy for the deceased premier, stating, in a desperate attempt to fend off the attacks against him: "Let us turn grief into strength, unite under the leadership of the party center headed by Chairman Mao, and, *taking class struggle as the link*, earnestly study the theory of proletarian dictatorship!"[27] This appearance, however, was to be Teng's last public one until July 1977. Against all expectations of almost every foreign observer of Chinese politics, the PRC press, on February 7, 1976, suddenly identified Hua Kuo-feng as "acting premier of the State Council." In mid-February, the official press started to attack Teng—albeit still without mentioning his name—as "that unrepentant capitalist-roader within the Party" who had tried to "reverse the verdicts."[28] He had obviously lost his battle against the united Left and was about to be purged once again. But how could he lose—the vice-chairman of the CC, first vice-premier, and chief of the General Staff? In fact, his defeat did not occur as inexplicably as many observers thought.

After the death of Chou, the united Left—and Mao, its legitimizer—rallied at least nine out of nineteen full members and two out of four alternates of the Politburo,[29] while three full members and one alternate increasingly veered toward the Left.[30] Against this majority, Teng could at best rally seven full members and one alternate,[31] and of that number, old Marshal Liu Po-ch'eng, ailing and feeble, no longer participated in the meetings, and the two leaders of the Third FA loyalty group, Hsü Shih-yu and Wei Kuo-ch'ing, mostly remained in Canton. Of the leaders who regularly attended Politburo meetings in Peking, therefore, between eleven and fifteen were against and only five were for Teng and his positions.

Thus, Teng's fate was decided, at least for the time being. On February 27, he was first criticized by name on wallposters on the Peking University campus,[32] and on March 10 and 28, unsigned editorials in the *JMJP* finally indicated that the Party center now gave full support to the campaign against him. Although his name was still not mentioned, Teng could easily be identified as the man to whom the two "newest directives" of Mao referred.

> While making socialist revolution, we still do not know where the bourgeoisie really is—it sits right in the Communist Party—the bourgeois are the power-holders within the Party who take the capitalist road![33]

> This man does not understand Marxism-Leninism, he represents the capitalist class. . . . He said he will "never reverse verdicts," yet this cannot be trusted. What does that mean, "Three directives as the link"?— class struggle is the link, everything else hinges on it![34]

At 7:47 P.M. on April 7, 1976, the world finally learned from the official PRC news agency, NCNA, about the second purge of Teng: "In the news item released at 2:10 P.M., the words 'that unrepentant capitalist-roader in power in the Party' are superseded by the words 'the unrepentant' capitalist-roader in power in the Party, Teng Hsiao-p'ing!'" Only a few minutes later, Radio Peking broadcast the news that the Politburo of the CCP, "upon the suggestion of our great leader, Chairman Mao," had unanimously decided to appoint Hua Kuo-feng as first vice-chairman of the CC and prime minister. The resolution of the Politburo continued:

> The Politburo of the CC of the CCP discussed the counterrevolutionary incident which has occurred on the T'ienanmen Square, as well as Teng Hsiao-p'ing's behavior during the recent period. It holds the opinion, that the problem of Teng Hsiao-p'ing has assumed the character of an antagonistic contradiction. Upon the suggestion of our great leader, Chairman Mao, the Politburo unanimously decided to remove Teng Hsiao-p'ing from all his positions inside and outside the party. He retains his Party membership pending on a later review.[35]

These decisions immediately received regional ratification through the still well-oiled ritual of mass rallies and affirmative messages from all twenty-nine PPCs.

On the very afternoon of April 7, however, while the Politburo was still in session, soldiers commanded by officers of the former Third FA took Teng from his Peking residence to a military airport, and from there via Nanking to Canton. There, he was protected from all possible attacks by Hsü Shih-yu and Wei Kuo-ch'ing and lived in the resort of Ts'unghua for almost a year.[36] The minister of education, Chou Jung-hsin, was less fortunate. On May 5, 1976, Reuters reported his death from a brain hemorrhage, information that was not at that time confirmed by the PRC press. In August 1977, the PRC media finally revealed that

Chou had died on April 13, 1976, "persecuted to death by the 'gang-of-four.'"[37]

Yet Teng Hsiao-p'ing's second purge was by no means the only event that shook the Chinese political scene in April 1976. It was preceded—and followed—by events in which the Chinese masses, so often called the "real heroes" by Mao and his close associates, started to intervene directly in the intraelite conflict, but in an entirely different way from what Mao had hoped. The antileftist social coalition started to move to the fore.

T'ienanmen and the Anti-Maoist Mass Movement

Beginning on March 29, 1976, a continually swelling crowd staged demonstrations against the Maoist Left on T'ienanmen Square, in the very center of Peking.[38] The demonstrators paid homage to the memory of the late Premier Chou, who was rapidly becoming an antisymbol to Mao, by laying down wreaths with banners praising Chou at the memorial for the revolutionary martyrs in the middle of the square. These activities were staged with the obvious aim of making the forthcoming *Ch'ing-ming* festival—the traditional Chinese Memorial Day—on April 4 a day of anti-Maoist manifestations.

The slogans used during the demonstrations gave a clear indication of the movement's thrust: "Down with the Empress Dowager! Down with Indira Gandhi!" (directed against Chiang Ch'ing); "Down with Ch'in Shih-huang! The time of Ch'in Shih-huang has gone already!" (directed against Mao); "The current antirightist campaign is the campaign of a small handful of ambitionists to reverse verdicts!"; "Long live the four modernizations!"; "Teng Hsiao-p'ing shall direct the work of the Party center!"; and "We want real Marxism-Leninism, not false Marxism-Leninism!" On April 3, the first clashes between the demonstrators on the one hand and workers' militia, police, and later PLA garrison troops on the other hand occurred on the square. The clashes escalated on April 4, when more than a million people gathered, and reached the level of widespread violence on April 5, when from 100,000 people, according to contemporary official sources, to 2 million people, according to later reports by the PRC media,[39] rioted for the whole day. The demonstrators included secondary school and college students, workers, young women, intellectuals, and even a considerable number of lower-level cadres. The security and PLA forces had more than a hundred men wounded, seventeen of them badly, and the PRC media, at a much later date, revealed that more than 100 demonstrators had been killed, and almost 4,000 arrested.[40]

Related, and often similar, incidents were officially reported in the spring of 1976 from Chengchou (Honan), Amoy (Fukien), Nanch'ang (Kiangsi), the Chaowuta League (Liaoning), Haik'ou (Hainan Island), and K'unming (Yünnan).[41] But the T'ienanmen and related demonstrations—which the CCP leadership at that time branded as counterrevolutionary incidents waged by a small handful of class enemies, bad elements, insurgents, gangsters, and monsters and freaks—were only the tip of an iceberg. Even after their suppression, popular unrest continued in several parts of the country throughout most of the summer and autumn of 1976. On April 29, a suicide commando group of youngsters threw a bomb at the entrance of the Soviet embassy in Peking, killing two PLA soldiers who were on guard there.[42] Rumors of foul play in elite politics mushroomed, and forged documents, the most prominent of which were several versions of a supposed testament by Chou En-lai, were circulated.[43] Leaflets insinuated that the late premier had been murdered by the cultural revolutionary Left.

After May, not only the cities but also the countryside became unruly. According to a report by Vice-Premier Ch'en Yung-Kuei to the Second National Conference on Learning from Tachai in Agriculture in December 1976, the peasants in a number of communes began "to operate black markets, and the collective economy disintegrated."[44]

The power establishment of the united Left in the Party center blamed this wave of popular dissent on Teng Hsiao-p'ing and his followers, who wanted to stay in office, but this explanation seems too simplistic. All the information that is now available about the large-scale unrest in 1976 suggests that the major forces behind the dissent were rusticated youths—in particular those who had illegally returned to their cities—industrial workers, intellectuals, and parts of the peasantry. This was indeed a forceful social coalition, which had now openly turned against Mao Tse-tung and his leftist associates and which had started to influence intraelite politics by encouraging the enemies of the united Left to continue the struggle against the cultural revolutionaries for an other-than-Maoist future for the country.

Prelude to a Showdown: May–September 1976

With the removal of Teng Hsiao-p'ing from office on April 7, 1976, the conflict over personal succession had gone through its precritical confrontation, severely aggravated by the manifestations of the anti-Maoist mass movement. The immediate result was a strengthening of the united Left's position in the center. The central media, controlled by Yao Wen-yüan and other representatives of the cultural revolutionary

Left, called vehemently for an expansion of the purge to Teng's former followers, in particular, the recently rehabilitated cadres in the provinces.

On April 18, the *JMJP* set the tune, quoting Mao's remarks that "the bourgeoisie is right inside the Communist Party" and stating that the "struggle between two lines" was a "life-and-death showdown." While the T'ienanmen demonstrations were compared with the Hungarian revolution of 1956, Teng himself was now called "the Nagy Imre of China."[45] Beginning in early May, the attacks on Teng's policies escalated. He was blamed for having put practical things—rather than class struggle and politics—"in command." His attempts to import more Western technology now became "a slave-like adoration of foreign things," and praise was heaped upon those basic-level cadres who had opposed his policies during the high tide of the rightist storm in 1975.[46] The policies of the cultural revolutionary Left were also reflected by a new upsurge in the rustication of intellectual youth—of whom it was reported that 12 million were staying in the countryside—by hymnic praise for work-study schools and workers' universities, and in continuing attacks on "capitalist tendencies within the people's communes."[47]

Yet, on the other side of the coin, increasing evidence indicated that the conflict was continuing. Under the impact of the leftist attack, veteran cadres who had survived the Cultural Revolution, as well as those who had been purged and rehabilitated, and a large number of military leaders, first in the provinces and then in the enter, closed ranks and began to form an antileftist faction, which can be called "the military-bureaucratic complex." By mid-July, it had become evident that the campaign against the revisionist policies of 1975 was being somewhat played down in the provinces, where the emphasis was placed on discipline and unity rather than on class struggle and revolution. More-over, most of the provincial leaders who had been appointed in 1974 and 1975, during Teng's tenure, remained in office, although some of them decided to cut down their public appearances for awhile. The generals and bureaucrats in the provinces apparently regarded the new leftist drive as a passing phenomenon.

And indeed, the provincial leaders had preoccupations other than class struggle, as they were forced to deal with natural calamities that exceeded those of most preceding years. A number of provinces, particularly Shensi, Anhui, Hopei, and Heilungkiang, reported severe droughts that did great damage to the crops,[48] but the most devastating blows of nature were yet to come. On May 29, two major earthquakes victimized considerable areas in the western part of Yünnan,[49] and almost exactly two months later, on July 28, one of the worst earthquakes in history, the T'angshan quake, hit eastern Hopei. According to an internal circular of the Hopei PPC that was published in Hongkong in early 1977, the

T'angshan quake left 655,237 people dead and probably more than a million homeless, and thus it assumed the dimensions of a national catastrophe.[50]

The impact of that earthquake on intraelite politics was strong, if not crucial. It enhanced the position of the military-bureaucratic complex, which took charge of the relief work, most of which was done by military aid teams from all over China. Moreover, the T'angshan disaster and the other natural calamities nourished traditional superstitions among the people, who began to talk about an impending "change of the heavenly mandate." Even more important was the fact that while everybody else was preoccupied with struggling against the effects of the disaster, the group around Chiang Ch'ing had nothing more urgent to do than to issue, in the name of the Party center, a cable exhorting the victimized people in the T'angshan region to "study earnestly Chairman Mao's important directives, to deepen and broaden, with class struggle as the link, the criticism of Teng Hsiao-p'ing's counter-revolutionary revisionist line, and the great struggle against the rightist storm of reversal of verdicts."[51]

After early August, the leftist propaganda drive for a comprehensive purge of rehabilitated veteran cadres and other members of the military-bureaucratic complex intensified. Yet opposition to the Left also increased. From the end of July on, almost all provincial media—with the exception of those in Shanghai, Liaoning, Kirin, and Anhui—intensified their calls for unity, monistic (*I-yüan-hua*) leadership by the Party committee, and the promotion of production—distinctive slogans of the military-bureaucratic complex, which now occasionally found their way into the central media as well.[52]

Thus, the intraelite conflict entered the stage of impending resolution. The showdown was accelerated because, now, the problem of personal succession had to be solved. On July 6, Marshal Chu Te had died, and Chairman Mao's health was beginning to deteriorate rapidly. On June 15, a spokesman for the Ministry of Foreign Affairs had notified diplomats that Mao, for reasons of health, would no longer receive foreign guests. While the country was still reeling under the impact of the T'angshan quake and other natural calamities, Mao died on September 9, 1976, in an atmosphere of unrest and uncertainty. His lying in state seemed to give a short breathing space, but the memorial service in T'ienanmen Square on September 18 was the last occasion at which all active Party leaders gathered in a not-too-convincing show of unity.

In fact, the factions within the leadership underwent a rearrangement during September 1976 in preparation for the critical confrontation. After the deaths of Chu Te and Mao Tse-tung, the military-bureaucratic complex could rally six full members and one alternate of the Politburo, the united Left could call on eight full members and two alternates, and one or two full members and one alternate vacillated. At some point between early August and late September, however, the united Left ceased to be united as Hua Kuo-feng and the two other representatives of the secret police Left on the Politburo, Wang Tung-hsing and Chi Teng-k'uei, changed sides and joined the military-bureaucratic complex in a new coalition.[53]

With a background in the security establishment and the lower and middle echelons of the civilian Party machine, Hua had basically always been an opportunist with a sober sense of the gravitations of power and a considerable degree of flexibility on principles. The reluctance of the provincial Party and regional military leaders (who were increasingly impressed by the clout the anti-Maoist mass movement had generated) to join the new antirightist campaign in the spring and summer of 1976 obviously indicated to Hua that there was no longer a favorable climate for development through mobilization in the country.

Experiences during and after the T'angshan disaster may finally have convinced Hua that the chances of running the PRC without military and provincial backing were poor indeed. Soon, he started to demonstratively seek the company of military men and veteran cadres[54] and to stress unity and obedience to the CCP in his public statements. These and other indications suggest the hypothesis that Hua paid the price that the military-bureaucratic complex—at some point during the second half of September—had quoted for its support of his candidacy for Party leadership: a purge of the cultural revolutionary Left and a gradual retreat from Mao's program of permanent mobilization.

The Peking Coup d'Etat of October 6, 1976

Barely four weeks after the death of Mao, events in the PRC took another dramatic turn. Beginning in late September, communication among the members of the leadership core broke down, the cultural revolutionary Left continued to call for a new purge of rightists, and using a doubtful "last will" of Mao that stated that one should "act according to the established directives,"[55] Chiang Ch'ing and her associates tried to bind Hua and other leaders to radical Maoist concepts. On October 4, writers in the Chiang Ch'ing group declared in the *KMJP* that capitalist-roaders wanted to "split the Party" and that " all supporters of Chairman Mao's proletarian revolutionary line" should "heighten their vigilance."

That, however, was to be the last public statement of the cultural revolutionary Left. On the evening of October 6, 1976, soldiers of the Central Guard Division (then usually called Unit 8341) and of the State

Council's guard unit, under the leadership of Marshal Yeh Chien-ying and General Wang Tung-hsing, arrested the whole leadership core of the cultural revolutionaries: Chiang Ch'ing, Wang Hung-wen, Chang Ch'un-ch'iao, and Yao Wen-yüan—from now on to be attacked by the CCP media with the pejorative epithet, "the gang of four" (*Ssu-jen-pang*). The Peking workers' militia, except for a few skirmishes on the part of some of its units with PLA troops in the suburbs, did nothing to help the four, because its leader, Ni Chih-fu, had joined the winning side. In Shenyang, Mao's nephew, Mao Yüan-hsin, was arrested, and for two days, a critical situation developed in Shanghai, the most important leftist stronghold. In the first days of October, General Hsü Shih-yu had come up from Canton and had temporarily taken over the command of the Nanking Military Area troops, a position he had previously held from 1954 to 1973. Nanking troops then entered Shanghai on October 6, and during the following two days, they disarmed the Shanghai workers' militia with considerable bloodshed, arresting most members of the Shanghai Municipal PC.

The leaders of the coup d'etat had won a swift and resounding success, but it was still more than two weeks until its results were officially made known to the Chinese people. On October 8, the NCNA published only the facts that the Politburo had decided to build a mausoleum for Mao and to prepare for the publication of a fifth volume of his selected works as well as of an edition of his collected works. All three tasks were assigned to Hua Kuo-feng, who was now, for the first time, called the "leader of the CC of the CCP." News about the arrest of the so-called gang of four appeared for the first time in Hongkong papers on October 11,[56] and it was not until October 23 that the appointment of Hua as chairman of the CC and of the CC's Military Commission was announced at a mass rally in T'ienanmen Square in Peking, in which all remaining members of the Politburo, with the exception of the ailing Marshal Liu Po-ch'eng, participated. More than half of the rally participants were soldiers, and Hua himself appeared in military uniform, thus indicating that the PLA had been the decisive factor in the critical confrontation. The major address was given by the first secretary of the Peking Municipal PC, Wu Te, and while attacking the cultural revolutionary Left with very strong words, Wu also promised, "We shall continue to criticize Teng!" (*Wo-men shi-hsü p'i Teng!*).[57]

Of the ten members of the Politburo's Standing Committee who had officiated since early 1975, only two were now left in office: Hua Kuo-feng, the new official leader, and Marshal Yeh Chien-ying. Among the politicians who now started to move the PRC into the post-Mao era, Li Hsien-nien, a civilian cadre who had survived the Cultural Revolution in office, gained increasing importance. Including these three Party leaders, only twelve out of the twenty-two full members of the Politburo remained in their positions. Seven of them could be considered representatives of the military-bureaucratic complex, and five had previously belonged to or veered toward the old united Left, the core group of which was now removed from the Chinese political scene. Also temporarily removed from this scene was Teng Hsiao-p'ing, who waited for further developments in the vicinity of Canton. It was this fact that made some observers in the fall of 1976 already doubt whether the elevation of the lackluster security cadre Hua Kuo-feng had indeed been the final word in the conflict over the personal succession to Mao.

CHAPTER 9

The Era of
Hua Kuo-feng, 1976–1978

Unrest and Stabilization Efforts, 1976/1977

The swift and effective way in which the military-bureaucratic complex overthrew the leadership core of the cultural revolutionary Left on October 6, 1976, in Peking and almost simultaneously in Shanghai and Shenyang, had eliminated the organizational strongholds of the leftists. However, it could not yet ensure the new leadership—centered around Hua Kuo-feng, Yeh Chien-ying, and Li Hsien-nien—undisputed control over the whole country.

Although the ruling elite had been riddled by power and policy conflict, the Party's chains of command had been weakened since the end of 1974, and increasingly so since the April crisis of 1976. Work discipline slackened, and an increasing number of people became restive against orders given by cadres, who, in turn, were insecure about future policy developments and therefore tried to please "the masses" by sluggishly executing orders from the upper levels. Strikes, labor unrest, and sabotage activities continued and even increased during the last quarter of 1976 and the first three months of 1977.

According to seventy-eight newscasts and commentaries collected between November 1976 and May 1977, the PRC media reported that sabotage of production caused severe damage in twenty-one out of the twenty-nine administrative units of the country.

Severe damage certainly affected railway traffic. I collected forty-six newscasts and commentaries broadcast on provincial and central media between December 1976 and April 1977 in which sabotage, disorders, disruption, and strikes were reported from twenty-three of the administrative units. The situation became particularly serious in Kueichou, Honan, Yünnan, and Chekiang, where railroad traffic was restored in some areas only by mid-March 1977, and in Kansu, where the transportation plan could not be fulfilled for nineteen consecutive months and extremely severe damage and sabotage were reported for several weeks in November and December 1976. In Honan, Anhui, and Sinkiang, PLA units had to be moved in to get the trains running again. On February 21, 1977, the *JMJP* took note of the damage stating that it would "take three to five years to repair fully the sabotage inflicted to the railway network."

In some areas, oppositional activities were not confined to strikes, labor unrest, and sabotage of transport facilities. Between November 1976 and June 1977, I collected sixty-six newscasts and commentaries from the PRC media that reported factional fights developing into armed struggle and open attacks on CCP offices and PLA installations, as well as the appearance of organized resistance in seventeen administrative units. In 1980, a leading CCP cadre estimated that the number of lives lost nationwide during the disturbances in the winter of 1976/1977 was 45,000–50,000.[58]

Some of these media reports, however, may have been exaggerated in order to make the new leadership's attempts to restore public order appear more successful. Yet combined with a considerable amount of information from overseas Chinese visitors to the PRC between the fall of 1976 and late spring 1977, the reports indicate that there was widespread unrest and great insecurity at least for a number of months.

In order to counteract such difficulties and to stabilize its hold over the country, the new leadership in Peking replaced Mao's cultural revolutionary dictum that great disorder (*ta luan*) was necessary in the quest for great order (*Ta chih*). In the drive for a new tightening of control structures, the ruling elite relied mainly on the PLA and the security establishment and resorted to increasingly stern measures. Beginning in March 1977, public executions of criminals and saboteurs were seen by overseas Chinese visitors on wall posters in Shanghai, Hangchou, K'unming, and later in the capital itself. An Amnesty International report released in August 1978 documented thirty-eight executions of counterrevolutionaries and bad elements between November 1976 and February 1978.[59]

Such an uncompromising repression of unrest began to produce results. During the first quarter of 1977, the situation improved remarkably, and by early summer, public order had been restored in most of the country. But the repression was not sufficient to overcome unrest. The stabilization efforts also had to be extended into the realm of personnel decisions in order to ensure that the military-bureaucratic complex established safe control over the state administrative, military, and Party machines. In the State Council, two vice-premiers and four ministers were purged in late 1976 and ten new ministers appointed, seven of whom had been purgees during the Cultural Revolution.

Still more important was the reshuffle of provincial Party leaders, which had begun with the reorganization of the Shanghai PPC under Admiral Su Chen-hua in late October 1976. Between that date and July 1977, thirteen of the twenty-nine administrative units received new PPC first secretaries. Of those thirteen newly appointed provincial Party leaders, nine were rehabilitated cultural revolutionary purgees, and four had survived the Cultural Revolution in office. The whole group of former purgees was at the same time strengthened by a number of new appointments to the central PLA organs.

However, attempts to restore public order and to stabilize rule, generally successful as they may have been during the first half of 1977, continued to meet with popular opposition, albeit on a considerably smaller scale, even in the summer of that year. Scattered local unrest, sabotage by the class enemy, and security problems in the railway system persisted according to twenty-four newscasts and commentaries broadcast in fourteen administrative units between April and September 1977.

The authorities usually blamed such problems on followers of the gang of four, yet in fact, opposition seemed to come from much larger segments of the society. In a moment of rare candidness in June 1977, the commander of the Kiangsi Provincial Military District, General Hsin Chün-chieh, attempted to analyze the composition of what he called "the class enemy": "A large number of new and old counter-revolutionaries; beaters, smashers, and looters; corrupt elements; monsters, freaks; treacherous so-called old cadres; treacherous *hommes-des-lettres*; speculators; hooligans; and loafers, the scum of society."[60] Translated into less pejorative language, this analysis meant large segments of the young generation, intellectuals, peasants who were working for a better living through private initiative, basic-level cadres who helped them, and workers who tried to earn some extra money through moonlighting. It appears that another forceful social coalition was being formed and that it was beginning to pressure for more thoroughgoing policy changes than those enacted by the Hua-Yeh-Li triumvirate, which had toppled the cultural revolutionary Left but did not do much to revise a number of major planks in the Maoist platform.

Maoism Without Mao

In the immediate aftermath of the October 6, 1976, coup d'etat, there were indications in the CCP media that with the purge of the cultural revolutionary Left, far-reaching revisions of Maoist policies were to be expected. Yet in fact, such revisions remained rather limited during the first one and a half years after the death of The Chairman. In the area of wage policies, the egalitarian impetus of Mao's doctrines disappeared, and the highly differentiated pay scale was definitely reconfirmed as official policy. In education, final examinations for colleges and secondary schools were reintroduced, and during the summer of 1977, the country was prepared for a return to a rather strict system of entrance examinations for colleges and universities, the regulations for which were finally published in October of that year.[61] In the field of culture, Chiang Ch'ing's revolutionary model operas and revolutionary romantic piano concertos were no longer performed, but similar ones were substituted for them. Some particularly praised the memory of Chou En-lai, and others elevated Hua Kuo-feng, who was now called the wise leader (*Ying-ming ling-hsiu*), and his pictures were now being spread all over the country and hung beside those of Mao. On the other hand, classical puppet theater and traditional dialect operas started to be performed again in December 1976, although the classical Peking court opera was still missing from the cultural scene all through 1977. Beethoven, Mozart, and Bach, however, were "rehabilitated" in February 1977, and by the summer of that year, translations of nineteenth-century Russian and Western literature—considered decadent only a year before—could again be bought in bookstores in the larger cities. All of these changes indicated that the parameters of cultural activities were slowly widening.

However, Hua Kuo-feng and his major supporters from the public security and the mass organization Left were determined to save as much of Mao Tse-tung's heritage as possible. In this attempt, they were partially supported by Marshal Yeh Chien-ying and Li Hsien-nien, who were afraid that any more far-reaching liberalization, or even a thoroughgoing revision of Maoist policies, would destabilize the political system.

For Hua himself, an ardent proponent of collectivist approaches, the continuation of Maoism was also necessary because continued reverence of Mao and his doctrines provided the only basis for Hua's legitimation as Party leader. As early as October 1976, his aides in the propaganda machine of the CCP had started to spread the story that on April 28 of that year, Mao had told Hua, "With you in charge, I am at ease!" (*Ni pan shih, wo fang hsin!*). Soon, the PRC was flooded with "socialist realistic" oil paintings of Hua sitting beside Mao, who, supposedly uttering that legitimizing statement, had his hand on Hua's arm in a gesture of benediction.

Hua's fight to preserve as much as possible of Mao's concepts began in the area of agricultural and rural societal policies, where he could claim a certain amount of expertise. In late November, the central media carried a major article from the National Buro of Supply and Trade

Cooperatives in which adherents of the policies of readjustment were obviously trying to commit the Party to these policies. The article quoted again the very moderate Rural Economic Policy promulgated by the Politburo in March 1971: "Under the conditions that the collective economy is active, and well-conducted, its development is not hampered, and it is given absolute priority, one must induce and encourage the commune members to develop legitimate family sideline occupations . . . and promote the rural markets."[62]

In striking contrast to this policy, however, an entirely different version of the new CCP leadership's program for the villages was presented at the Second National Conference on Learning from Tachai in Agriculture, for which more than 5,000 delegates from rural people's communes convened in Peking in December 1976. This conference closed on December 25 with a speech by Hua Kuo-feng, and since this speech was his first major policy statement since October 6, it assumed the dimensions of a "state-of-the-nation address." The new Party leader emphasized his call for the mechanization of agriculture, but at the same time, he reiterated his desire to raise the levels of collectivization. Hua insisted on increasing the powers of the communes and brigades at the expense of the teams as a means to "prepare, step by step, the transition to communism." As the most important instrument for the strengthening of the higher level production units, he recommended the expansion of these enterprises that were owned by the brigades and communes.[63] In the field of rural societal policies, therefore, Hua and his associates stuck to the concepts of Mao, although they differed with the ideas of Lin Piao and the cultural revolutionary Left in terms of the instruments that should be used to accomplish the Maoist goals.

During the first quarter of 1977, the drive to preserve the doctrines of Mao intensified. In early February, the late Chairman's 1956 speech "On the Ten Great Relationships" was published for the first time in the PRC (it had, however, been published in T'aiwan in 1968), and on March 1, the fifth volume of the Selected Works of Mao Tse-tung appeared in bookstores all over the country. On the occasion of its publication, the CCP media, in unison, celebrated again the great theory of continuing the revolution under the proletarian dictatorship, which Mao supposedly had founded by systematically summing up the experience of revolutionary history.

A few weeks earlier, the group around Hua had already stated its position that Mao's prescripts were to be followed meticulously even though he had left China's political scene. A joint editorial in JMJP, CFCP, and HC in early February—ironically, precisely a year after Hua had been promoted to the position of acting prime minister—proclaimed that "whatever policies Chairman Mao formulated we shall all resolutely defend, whatever instructions Chairman Mao gave we shall all steadfastly abide by!" (*Fan-shih Mao chu-hsi tso-ch'u-te chüeh-ts'e, wo-men tou chien-chüeh wei-hu. Fan-shih Mao chu-hsi-te chih-shih, wo-men tou shih-chung-pu-yü-ti tsun-hsün!*).[64] This statement was to provide, about one year later, the pejorative name for the group around Hua Kuo-feng in the intraelite conflict that began to unfold then. From the summer of 1978 on, this group was increasingly referred to as "the whatever faction" (*Fan-shih p'ai*). Maoism without Mao was going to come under increased criticism, and on December 5, 1980, the Politburo of the CCP declared in a resolution: "The 'two whatevers' which comrade Hua Kuo-feng has coined, have, for a time, upheld this opinion, which goes totally against Marxism. When he coined the 'two whatevers,' he wanted in reality to continue the wrong 'leftist' line of comrade Mao Tse-tung's late years."[65]

Sic transit gloria mundi! goes the old Latin saying. By the spring of 1977, the engineer of the impending further transition in the PRC, Teng Hsiao-p'ing, was about to make his second political comeback.

Teng Hsiao-p'ing Comes Back Again

The proclamation of Wu Te at the October 23, 1976, T'ienanmen rally that "we shall continue to criticize Teng" was occasionally repeated in the PRC media during the six weeks that followed that event. In late November, the Party newspaper in Canton, while lavishing praise upon the new leader, Hua Kuo-feng, even insisted, "Since the winter of last year and this year's spring, Chairman Mao . . . led the people of the whole country to wage the struggle of criticizing Teng and counterattacking against the rightist storm of reversal of verdicts."[66] Yet soon, admonitions to criticize Teng (*p'i Teng*) began to disappear from public usage, appearing for the last time in a broadcast from Hua's bailiwick, the province of Hunan, in early January 1977.[67]

On December 26, 1976, the *Nan-fang jih-pao* [Southern daily *(NFJP)*] in Canton, for all practical purposes, posthumously rehabilitated Marshal Ho Lung, a former Politburo member who had been put to death in prison in June 1969, by calling him "comrade" (*T'ung-chih*). His official rehabilitation occurred finally on the anniversary of his death, June 12, 1977, when the CCP *hsien* committee of his birthplace staged a memorial service for Ho.[68] But a much more important rehabilitation was about to take place: the second one of Teng Hsiao-p'ing.

On the first anniversary of Chou En-lai's death, January 8, 1977, wall posters in the capital attacked the Politburo members General Ch'en Hsi-lien and Wu Te, blaming them for slavishly following the gang of four in the suppression of the T'ienanmen mass movement and calling for the return of Teng to the political scene. Yet Hua Kuo-feng and others members of the Politburo, who had been advanced in their careers by the Cultural Revolution, put up stiff resistance to a second rehabilitation of Teng. However, the forces of the anti-Maoist social coalition, which had formed in the spring and summer of 1976, intensified their pressure on the elite, and in late February and early March 1977, the trees along the major thoroughfares in Peking were time and again lined with small bottles. The Chinese term for "small bottle" is *hsiaop'ing*, pronounced the same way and in the same tone as Teng's personal name, Hsiao-p'ing—hence, the message of these demonstrations was clear to everybody in the capital who knew Chinese.

Soon, pressure also came from leading Party members and CCP organizations. In a dramatic gesture of support for Teng's comeback, two Politburo members— Hsü Shih-yu and Wei Kuo-ch'ing, in the name of their units, the Party Committee of the Canton MAC and the Kuangtung PPC—sent a joint letter to the Party center and to Hua himself on February 1, 1977, in which they criticized the policies enacted since the overthrow of the cultural revolutionary Left.[69] After praising Hua for having proclaimed his great call, "Grasp the link, put the country in order" (*Chua-kang Chih-kuo!*), and repeating the routine statement that "the situation is excellent," Hsü and Wei added: "Yet the morale of the Party, the army, and the people is by no means free from problems. The thoughts of our revolutionary masses, our revolutionary cadres, and our revolutionary army are burdened by several severe problems and questions."

The first of these questions was identified as the evaluation of Chairman Mao.

> The eyes of the people are as bright as snow. Everybody has, in his heart, taken account of all merits and mistakes of Chairman Mao. If the Party center continues to hush up his shortcomings and mistakes, . . . the authority of the Party among the masses must suffer.

The second question, the two southern Chinese leaders went on, concerned the propaganda about Chairman Hua, whose appointment by the Politburo instead of at least by a CC plenary meeting was called an "emergency situation."

> We do not need to emphasize that the basis for comrade Hua Kuo-feng's appointment as chairman of the CC are the words written by Chairman Mao: "With you in charge, I am at ease!" No matter how golden these words may shine, they can only represent Chairman Mao's personal opinion, and they cannot express the will of the Party, the army, and the people.

Addressing the third question, the "review of some great mistakes since the establishment of the country," the letter came to its major point.

> During his lifetime, Chairman Mao branded all comrades in the Party, who dared to air opinions disagreeing with him, as class enemies . . . of course, this was correct in most cases. But we cannot deny that there have been cases where such an evaluation was incorrect . . . , and this category includes the problems of comrade P'eng Te-huai and comrade Teng Hsiao-p'ing.

The message of the Canton letter was clear: If Teng were not speedily rehabilitated, the southern leaders would challenge the legitimation of Hua himself.

During February and early March, at least seven or eight other provincial leadership groups are said to have communicated similar opinions to the Party center,[70] which was therefore faced with the possibility of an open rift if nothing was done to rehabilitate Teng. At an enlarged Politburo meeting, which convened in the capital from March 10–23, the pressures on Hua became insurmountable so he finally agreed in principle to a rehabilitation of Teng. Right after that meeting, Teng left his southern hideaway and returned to Peking.

One problem, however, had still to be solved. Hua and his close associates insisted that Teng had to write a statement of self-criticism before he could be liberated (*Chieh-fang*)—the formula used thus far for the return of cadres who had been purged during or after the Cultural Revolution. Teng, however, was not willing to make such a statement. In a Politburo meeting in May, a compromise solution was finally reached: Teng agreed to write a letter to the CC in which he recognized Hua as the Party leader without mentioning any self-criticism and after that, he would be rehabilitated (*Hui-fu*), i.e., "restored to his positions."

This decision was finally announced in a communiqué from the third plenum of the Tenth CC, which convened in Peking on July 16—21, 1977. This communiqué informed the country and the world that the man who neither understands Marxism-Leninism nor comprehends class struggle, and against whom Chairman Mao had "led the people of the whole country," was back in the center of political decision making.

> The plenary meeting unanimously decided to *restore* comrade Teng Hsiao-p'ing to his positions as member of the CC of the CCP, member of the CC's Politburo, member of the Standing Committee of the Politburo, vice-chairman of the CC, vice-chairman of the CC's Military Commission, vice-premier of the State Council, and chief of General Staff.[71]

Only a few days later, on July 31, the new triumvirate appeared at a large reception on the eve of the PRC Army Day.

> The Chairman of the CC of the CCP, chairman of the CC's Military Commission, and premier of the State Council, comrade Hua Kuo-feng, presided.
> The vice-chairman of the CC, vice-chairman of the CC's Military Commission, and minister of national defense, comrade Yeh Chien-ying, gave an important speech.
> The vice-chairman of the CC, vice-chairman of the CC's Military Commission, vice-premier of the State Council, and PLA chief of staff, comrade Teng Hsiao-p'ing, attended the reception. Also attending were. . . .[72]

After the rehabilitation of Teng, members of the military-bureaucratic complex finally felt secure enough to proceed toward the ratification of the October 6, 1976, coup d'etat and the formal confirmation of the new leadership arrangement at the Eleventh Party Congress of the CCP.

The Eleventh Party Congress, August 1977

The Eleventh Party Congress, which the CCP media mentioned only after its conclusion, convened with 1,510 delegates from August 12 through August 18, 1977. Together with Hua and Marshal Yeh, Teng Hsiao-p'ing dominated the event, and his return thus assumed triumphant proportions, although he was third in the official pecking order.

The congress started with a seven-hour speech by Hua Kuo-feng, at the beginning of which he indulged in hymnic praise for his predecessor.

> For more than half a century, Chairman Mao led our Party, our army and the people of all nationalities in our country to complete victory in the New Democratic Revolution . . . and then to our great victories in the socialist revolution and socialist construction . . . and through the Great Proletarian Revolution. Chairman Mao founded and nurtured the great, glorious and correct CCP, he created and tempered the heroic PLA, and founded and built the socialist New China with its proletarian dictatorship. . . . Chairman Mao was the greatest Marxist of our time. Integrating the universal truth of Marxism-Leninism with the concrete practice of the Chinese revolution and the world revolution, he inherited, defended and developed Marxism-Leninism in the realms of philosophy, political economy and scientific socialism. . . . Chairman Mao's monumental contributions to the theory and practice of revolution, made for the benefit of the Chinese people and the proletariat and revolutionary people of the whole world, are indeed immortal![73]

Hua, mentioning the name of Mao 178 times, confirmed all major policies of the new leadership and then declared, "With the smashing of the 'gang-of-four' as a symbol, our country's first Great Proletarian Revolution, which lasted for eleven years, is herewith pronounced as victoriously completed!"[74]

Even for those observers who had become used to twists and turns in PRC politics, the thought that the Cultural Revolution had finally arrived at its "victorious completion" with the arrest of Mao's widow, who had once been the vice-chairman of the CC's cultural revolutionary group, and with the triumphant return of Teng Hsiao-p'ing, previously the "second capitalist-roader in power," assumed the dimensions of irony. It requires some familiarity with Communist dialectics to understand what Hua's proclamation really meant: Not the Cultural Revolution, but the military-bureaucratic complex of veteran Party cadres, central and regional military leaders, and the security establishment had won a resounding victory immediately after the death of Mao, who had personally created and led the Great Proletarian Cultural Revolution. Moreover, it is noteworthy that Hua did not mention the T'ienanmen demonstrations of April 1976 at all.

On the second day of the congress, August 13, Marshal Yeh Chienying, then eighty years of age, introduced a new Party statute that eliminated most vestiges of the Cultural Revolution, and he used his speech to legitimize again the appointment of Hua as Party leader.

> Comrade Hua Kuo-feng was chosen by Chairman Mao himself as his successor. . . . Chairman Hua is worthy of being called Chairman Mao's good student and successor, the wise leader of our Party and people and the brilliant supreme commander of our army. Chairman Hua can certainly continue to carry forward our proletarian revolutionary cause pioneered by Chairman Mao and lead our Party, our army, and the people of all nationalities triumphantly into the twenty-first century![75]

The congress ended on August 18 with an eight-minute concluding address by Teng Hsiao-p'ing, who, with down-to-earth and brief sentences, set a tone that was different from that of the two other members of the triumvirate: "Deed and word must match. Theory and practice must be closely integrated. We must reject sweet generalities and every kind of boasting. There must be less empty talk, and more hard work. We must be steadfast and dedicated. . . . Our case is just. Our line is correct. Our goal must be attained. Our goal can be attained!"[76] On the last day of its meeting, the Party congress appointed the Eleventh CC, which, in turn, at its first plenum on August 19, appointed the new Politburo of the CCP.

The triumph of the military-bureaucratic complex is evident from the composition of the Eleventh CC's 201 full members. Among these, 110, or 54.7 percent, were reappointed from the full members of the Tenth CC; 20, or 10 percent, were promoted from alternate to full member status; and 71, or 35.3 percent, were new members. Of the 178 full members of the Tenth CC who were still alive at the time of the Eleventh Congress, 110, or 61.8 percent, were reappointed to the Eleventh CC; 5, or 2.8 percent, were demoted to the position of alternate members; and 63 or 35.4 percent, did not reappear. This figure of more than one-third of the outgoing Tenth CC included 17.8 percent of its civilian cadres, 29.6 percent of its military men, and 76.5 percent of its mass organization representatives.

In terms of Party seniority, 19.1 percent of those members of the Tenth CC who had joined the Party before 1935 and 39.3 percent of those who had joined the Party between 1936 and 1949 did not reappear, as opposed to 71.8 percent of those who had joined the Party after 1949. Representation of members who had joined the Party after the establishment of the PRC was down from 21.4 percent on the Tenth CC to 15.9 percent on the Eleventh, i.e., reduced by almost 30 percent, and the share of mass organization representatives decreased from 17.9 percent to 11.2 percent, 37.4 percent. Hence, the purge of the cultural revolutionary Left mainly affected the CC members with low Party seniority and the representatives of mass organizations.

The new CC was thus more cadre oriented and had a more veteran leadership group than its predecessor. The same held true for the newly appointed leadership core, the Politburo. Five members of the Politburo's Standing Committee were to lead the PRC, for the time being, in the transition from the era of Mao to the future: Hua Kuo-feng (then fifty-six years of age), representing those cadres who had supported Mao during the Cultural Revolution; Marshal Yeh Chien-ying (eighty), representing the central military machine; Teng Hsiao-p'ing (seventy-three), representing the rehabilitated cadres; Li Hsien-nien (seventy-two), representing the cadres who had survived the Cultural Revolution; and General Wang Tung-hsing (sixty-one), representing the security establishment.

Of twenty-three full members and three alternates of the new Politburo, twelve full members and two alternates had survived the Cultural Revolution in office. Six full members had been advanced in their careers as a result of the Cultural Revolution; and five members and one alternate belonged to the protosecondary group of purgees. Twenty of the full members had joined the CCP between 1921 and 1935; two, between 1936 and 1949; and only one, after 1949. Twelve of these twenty-three men had a military career background, and ten still held PLA positions.

In spite of his return to the political scene, Teng Hsiao-p'ing, in the immediate aftermath of the Eleventh Party Congress, could firmly rely on only nine votes on the Politburo, including his own, while Hua Kuo-feng had the definite support of seven members, including himself. The balance was held by the seven Politburo members who tended to follow the lead of Yeh and Li Hsien-nien. As long as Yeh and Li supported Hua, therefore, the era of Hua Kuo-feng could continue. Teng was still a long way from a possible victory over the Party leader.

The Fifth NPC and the Four Modernizations: Attempts at a New Great Leap

Although the Eleventh Party Congress had ratified the results of the overthrow of the cultural revolutionary Left and reestablished the Party's central leadership organs for the first years of the post-Mao era, the country still had to wait half a year until the leading organs of the state administrative machine could be put in order. This was to happen at the first session of the Fifth NPC. The election of delegates to the NPC proceeded between early November 1977 and early February 1978 in meetings of provincial and regional people's congresses, yet there are no indications of when and by whom these would-be parliamentary bodies had been elected. In order to prepare for the NPC, the second plenum of the Eleventh CC convened in Peking February 18–23, 1978, and made all major decisions for the forthcoming congress so the congress itself had only to ratify them.

The meetings of the NPC session itself began on February 26, and they lasted until March 5. A total of 3,497 delegates assembled in the capital: 503, or 14.4 percent, of them were nominated from the PLA—including Teng and his wife, Cho Lin—and 2,994, including 13 delegates chosen by PRC citizens of T'aiwan origin, represented the twenty-nine administrative units.[77] There were large variations in the number of people each delegate was supposed to represent. For the three centrally administered cities, the figures varied from 37,000 for T'ienchin to 65,000 for Shanghai; for the five autonomous regions, between 56,000 for Tibet and 288,000 for Inner Mongolia; and for the twenty-one provinces, between 143,000 for Ch'inghai and 413,000 for Shantung. Yet this situation was no different than those of the four earlier NPCs in 1954, 1959, 1964, and 1975. In order to account for the leading position of the "workers' class," cities and industrial regions have always been highly overrepresented in the NPC.

On March 5, the congress promulgated a new constitution of the PRC,[78] the third one in twenty-four years. It was more explicit than that of 1975, particularly in the area of institutional provisions, so it contained sixty articles instead of the thirty of its predecessor. Here, too, almost all vestiges of the Cultural Revolution were now extinguished, with one exception: The new constitution included the provisions of Articles 13 and 28 of the 1975 one into one Article 45, which read, in part, "Citizens enjoy . . . the freedom to strike, and have the right to 'speak out freely, air their views fully, hold great debates and write wall-posters' " (*Ta ming, ta fang, ta pien-lun, ta-tzu-pao*).

On the last day of the session, the NPC also appointed, on the recommendation of the Party's CC, the personnel for the leading organs of the state administrative machine. Marshal Yeh Chien-ying relinquished the Ministry of National Defense, which was taken over by Marshal Hsü Hsiang-ch'ien (then seventy-six years of age), and assumed the position of chairman of the NPC Standing Committee, which included the functions of a ceremonial chief of state. The Standing Committee now consisted of 196 members, of whom 20 served as vice-chairman; 154, or 78.6 percent, of them were members of the CCP; 25 belonged to seven small non-Communist united front parties; and 17 were nonpartisans.

Chiang Hua, a rehabilitated civilian cadre, was reconfirmed as president of the Supreme People's Court, a position that he had held since the Fourth NPC in January 1975. The new constitution reestablished the Supreme People's Procuratorate (*Tsui-kao jen-min chien-ch'a-yüan*),[79] which had been abolished during the Cultural Revolution, and Huang Huo-ch'ing, another civilian cadre who had been rehabilitated only in October 1977, after the Eleventh Party Congress, became its first president.

The most important personnel decisions, however, concerned the composition of the State Council. Hua Kuo-feng was confirmed as prime minister, to be aided by thirteen vice-premiers. Teng Hsiao-p'ing remained in his position as first vice-premier, and the fourteen members of the inner cabinet now included three whose careers had been advanced by the Cultural Revolution, seven who had survived it in office, and four who were former purgees.

Of the forty-five members of the whole State Council, however, all of them members of the CCP, the situation was different. Twenty-one were newly appointed, and the group consisted of twenty-three former purgees, eighteen cadres who had survived the Cultural Revolution, and only four whose careers had been advanced by it. Of these forty-five State Council members, Teng could rely on twenty-two to twenty-four, i.e., about half of the membership; Yeh and Li Hsien-nien, seventeen to nineteen; and Hua, only four.

One of the most important events of the NPC session was the delivery of the report on the work of the PRC government by Hua Kuo-feng, which lasted for more than six hours on February 26, 1978.[80] The title of the report set its tone: "Unite and strive to build a modern, powerful socialist country!" Under this motto, Hua made the four modernizations the central subject of his speech, and he called for an immense effort to change the economic and social situations in the country. By the year 2000, so he promised, the PRC would have been developed into a "modern, socialist industrial great power," which could compete with the most modern industrial nations of the day.

In order to achieve the thoroughgoing modernization of agriculture, industry, national defense, and science and technology, a particularly intense production drive was scheduled for the time until 1985.

> The ten years from 1976 to 1985 are crucial for accomplishing these gigantic tasks. In the summer of 1975, the State Council held a meeting to exchange views on a perspective long-range plan. . . . According to the plan, in the space of ten years we are to lay a solid foundation for agriculture, achieve at least an 85 percent mechanization in all major processes of farmwork. . . . Construction of an advanced heavy industry is envisaged, with the metallurgical, fuel, power and machine-building industries to be further developed . . . with iron and steel, coal, crude oil and electricity in the world's front ranks in terms of output, and with much more developed petrochemical, electronics and other new industries.[81]

For the years from 1978 to 1985, Hua called for an annual growth of agricultural production of 4–5 percent and of industrial production of more than 10 percent, which would mean annual GNP growth rates of at least 8 percent. Thus, the production goals for 1985 were set at 400 million tons of grain and 60 million tons of steel. Two major examples were set for emulation in the whole country: For agriculture, the example was the old Maoist model of the Tachai production brigade in Shansi, and for industry, the Tach'ing oilfield. By 1980, so Hua hoped, one-third of all industrial enterprises would have become Tach'ing-type enterprises, and one-third of the country's *hsien*, Tachai-type *hsien*.

In agriculture, the production of food grains should have first priority under the slogan, Taking grain as the key link (*Yi liang wei kang!*). Heavy industry, however, was to be the major area for development under the slogan, Taking steel as the link (*Yi kang wei kang!*). At the heart of this plan, heavy industry and the infrastructure were supposed to profit from the completion of "120 large-scale projects, which include ten iron-and-steel complexes, nine complexes for non-ferrous metals, eight coal mines, ten oil and natural gas fields, thirty power complexes, six new railroad lines, and five new key harbours."[82]

Hua Kuo-feng used a Maoist slogan of the 1958 Great Leap Forward when he stated that the new Ten-Year Plan should be completed successively with greater, faster, better, and more economical results. In fact, the new Party leader had called for a new Great Leap, but this time, it was to be based on opening the country to large technology imports from the West, i.e., from Japan, the United States, and Western Europe.

This policy was strongly supported by Li Hsien-nien, who became ever more influential in the realm of economic planning during the winter of 1977/1978, and the execution of the policy was, for about one and a half years to come, to be in the hands of the so-called petroleum clique, headed by the minister of petroleum industry from 1958 to 1967, General Yü Ch'iu-li, chairman of the State Planning Commission since 1975. Three of Yü's former vice-ministers and one engineer from his old ministry—K'ang Shih-en, T'ang K'e, Sun Ching-wen, and Sung Cheng-ming—were now in charge of the State Economic Commission and of the ministries for metallurgical, chemical, and petroleum industries, thus controlling the central areas of development earmarked by Hua in his Ten-Year Plan.

With the Eleventh Party Congress and the first session of the Fifth NPC, the basic features of Hua Kuo-feng's political platform had become clearly visible. The new official Party leader persisted in trying to save as much of Mao Tse-tung's ideological heritage as possible. Although Hua and his associates had rescinded the idea of class struggle as the motivating force of social development as well as the emphasis on development through mass movements and the priority of immaterial and emotional over material incentives, they continued to consider Mao's doctrines as the unchangeable guidelines in all other aspects of politics.

With these doctrines as a general principle, Hua and his group—in many respects supported by the survival cadres around Marshal Yeh and Li Hsien-nien—promoted five major policies.

1. In economic development, a new, concerted effort was to be made that aimed at the transformation of the PRC into a major modernized industrial power by the end of the twentieth century, centering on the expansion of heavy industry as the first developmental priority.
2. Material incentives and a highly differentiated wage system should be promoted, but under centralized planning and with a strong emphasis on collective ownership and production in the urban economy.
3. In rural societal policies, a raising of the levels of collectivization should remain on the agenda, and strict limits should be put on the individual initiatives of the peasants.

4. In education, Marxist-Leninist indoctrination should continue and possibly be strengthened, but priority should be given to factual knowledge and classroom performance.
5. In the realm of culture, the parameters of competition should be cautiously widened, but "socialist realism" should continue to be intensively promoted, and by no means was any cultural or even less so any political expression of dissidence to be tolerated.

The new stage in PRC politics after the death of Mao, in the eyes of his successor, was thus designed so that the late Chairman's ideas and prescriptions would continue to direct the Party's line but with a number of revisions that followed the patterns of policies enacted in the Soviet Union under Stalin in the 1930s and, in emulation of that model, in the PRC during the early and mid-1950s.

Teng Hsiao-p'ing and many other cadres, on the other hand, wanted to push much further with revisions of the PRC's basic domestic policies. Three major questions thus emerged, for which the political decision-making elite would have to provide answers during the years to come.

1. Should the revisions of Mao's policies be intensified and extended into a new, critical evaluation of his person and his central doctrines?
2. Should the levels of collectivization in the countryside be further lowered, more freedom be given to individual initiatives by the peasants, and thus, the collective agrarian economy exposed to thoroughgoing revisions?
3. Should the parameters of cultural competition be energetically expanded and possibly even political rights and freedoms, though to a limited extent, granted to the citizens?

To all these three questions, the answers of Hua and his supporters, and to a lesser extent those of Yeh and Li, would be negative, while Teng Hsiao-p'ing's answers would be mostly affirmative. Thus, the stage was already set for the next intraelite conflict, for which Teng started to brace himself in the spring of 1978.

CHAPTER 10

Teng Hsiao-p'ing's Offensive, 1978–1980

The Norm of Truth Debate

From April 27 through June 6, 1978, a National Army Political Work Conference (*Ch'üan-chün cheng-chih kung-tso hui-yi*) was held in Peking, rallying several thousand political commissars from all levels of the PLA hierarchy.[83] The director of the GPD, General Wei Kuo-ch'ing, opened the meeting with a call to unfold the good traditions of political work in the army, and it seemed at first that this conference would become a demonstration of leadership consensus along the lines set by the Eleventh Party Congress nine months before. But while the conference was proceeding, it became obvious that it was developing into a forum for the expression of differences among the ruling elite. Teng Hsiao-p'ing and his associates used the conference to issue a clarion call for an all-out ideological and political offensive against the forces around Hua Kuo-feng.

The meeting was still going on when the *KMJP*, in mid-May, published an article by a "specially invited correspondent"—most probably Hu Ch'iao-mu—which proclaimed the central slogan of Teng's drive: "Practice is the only norm of truth!" (*Shih-chien shih chien-yen chen-li-te wei-i piao-chun!*), arguing that all ideological guidelines always had to stand the test of whether they correspond to political, economic, and social realities.[84]

In late May and early June, the conflicting positions of Hua and Yeh Chien-ying, on the one hand, and Teng, on the other, were openly stated at the PLA Political Work Conference. On May 29, Hua and Yeh addressed the meeting.[85] Neither of them referred to Teng's newly established "norm of truth," and Hua exhorted the political commissars to "keep steadfastly and unfold the good tradition of political work." In his speech at the meeting on June 2, however, Teng called on them to "restore and unfold the good tradition of political work" and used Mao's formula to seek truth from the facts (*Shih-shih ch'iu shih*) to launch his attack on Maoist orthodoxy.[86] One of the major differences that had now surfaced was reflected by the two terms used: "keep steadfastly" (*chien-ch'ih*) and "restore" (*hui-fu*)—whether one should keep steadfastly or restore good traditions implied fundamental contradictions in the evaluation of the Cultural Revolution in particular and the whole period of Mao's late years in general.

During the four months that followed the PLA conference, the dispute over the norm of truth dominated the Chinese political scene. At the outset, Teng was accused of having opposed Mao continuously and of having tried to "cut down the banner of the Thought of Mao Tse-tung,"[87] but soon the central media started to take his side. On June 24, the Party's central organ reprinted a long article by a "specially invited correspondent" of the army paper, the *CFCP*, which argued extensively that "revising the Thought of Mao Tse-tung according to reality" was by no means "revisionism" but a correct Marxist procedure. If one "sought the truth from the facts," if one took "reality as the only norm of truth," one might have to revise (*hsiu-cheng*) "also some of the directives of Chairman Mao, yet this is not revisionism" (*hsiu-cheng chu-yi*)![88]

And indeed, Teng's offensive progressed successfully. On August 1, an editorial in the *CFCP* commemorating the fifty-first anniversary of the Nanch'ang uprising in 1927 fully endorsed Teng's line. This *CFCP* editorial, reprinted in the *JMJP* the following day, opened the gates for a sweep of the norm of truth idea through the provinces. One after another, the provincial leadership groups started to accept Teng's dictum. By mid-September, conferences held in Kuangsi, Heilungkiang, Anhui, Yünnan, Sinkiang, Honan, Hupei, Inner Mongolia, Fukien, and Kuangtung had taken up the Teng's line,[89] and by early October, the whole country was echoing it. About the same time, even Hua, whose forces were obviously losing this first battle, started to talk about *restoring* the Party's good, traditional work style.

By aiming his initial thrust at the doctrines of Mao, Teng had thus eroded the legitimacy of Hua and his supporters. The norm of truth debate was more than a scholastic exercise, it established that the future of the PRC would be directed, not by Maoism without Mao, but by a more flexible application of ideological prescriptions, which could pave the way for an all-out revision of Maoist concepts. Yet the debate only set the tune for much more thoroughgoing changes that were about to develop. During the summer and early autumn of 1978, the anti-Maoist social coalition of 1976 rallied again in the cities, and soon also in some villages. Rusticated and illegally returned young intellectuals, workers, and large portions of the urban youth started to move toward a quest for more liberalization, and Teng and his allies initially encouraged such a move in order to put even more pressure for policy changes on their adversaries in the decision-making bodies of the Party.

The Human Rights Movement, Winter 1978/1979

As early as the second anniversary of the T'ienanmen uprising of April 5, 1976, scattered wall posters in Peking had demanded a rehabilitation of that movement, which was still officially considered a counterrevolutionary incident. Such a rehabilitation, however, would have grave political implications: Wu Te, the chairman of the Peking Municipal RC and Party leader in the capital, one of the staunchest supporters of Hua Kuo-feng on the Politburo, had ordered troops and security forces to suppress the demonstrations in April 1976, and Hua himself, in his capacity as minister of public security, had been in charge of the ensuing persecution of the dissidents. Thus, a new evaluation of the "April 5 movement" would weaken their position, and consequently strengthen that of Teng. For this reason, Teng and his associates were indeed interested in such a new approach to the 1976 events.

On the other hand, rehabilitating the demonstrations of 1976 would mean legitimizing the intervention of social forces into intraelite conflicts, and perhaps, therefore, also endangering the current leadership. In this dilemma, Teng, rallying a slight majority of the central leadership, obviously decided to take the risk in order to promote his quest for major policy changes. He opted for a cautious and controlled widening of the parameters of political competition, for a limited liberalization, probably hoping that it would be possible to hold the forces that would thus be released at bay without gravely endangering the political system.

In early October 1978, Wu Te was removed from his posts in the capital and so was the commander in chief of the Peking MAC, General Ch'en Hsi-lien, although both kept their positions on the Politburo. With the former T'ienchin Party leader Lin Hu-chia substituting for Wu, and General Ch'in Chi-wei for Ch'en, two purgees of the Cultural Revolution took over the control of the capital.[90] They soon turned to a reevaluation of the T'ienanmen events of 1976. On November 15, the NCNA published a resolution of an enlarged meeting of the Peking Municipal PC's Standing Committee, which solemnly proclaimed the rehabilitation of the protesters of 1976: "That the broad masses remembered with grief the beloved Premier Chou, and that they fervently criticized the 'gang-of-four,' *these were entirely revolutionary activities*. All who have suffered persecution because they opposed the 'gang-of-four' are herewith acquitted according to the law, and their good name is restored."[91]

Immediately after this resolution had been passed, a book of poems and slogans of the April 5 movement was published, the title ironically being printed in the handwriting of Hua Kuo-feng,[92] and during the days that followed the publication of the resolution, the central media were busily rewriting the story of the 1976 demonstrations, now a great people's movement instead of a sinister counterrevolutionary plot of freaks and monsters.

Parts of the population of Peking perceived these developments as a signal. On November 18, wall posters, mostly attacking Wu Te, were posted in Peking, especially on a wall along one of the city's major thoroughfares, which was soon to be called "the democracy wall" (*Min-chu ch'iang*). During the following days, the public security forces stopped interfering with the placement of wall posters, and Teng himself gave cautious praise for the democracy wall in talks with foreign correspondents. Between late November 1978 and late March 1979, the movement spread and increased in strength. People started to call it "the spring in winter" and more and more the Human Rights movement (*Jen-ch'üan yün-tung*), the Democracy movement (*Min-chu yün-tung*), or the Human Rights and Democracy movement. Meetings were held, organizations and circles formed. Beginning in December, a number of unofficial, or underground, publications appeared, some as individual copies, some even as journals. The most important among them were *T'an-suo* [Exploration], *Ssu-wu lun-t'an* [April 5 tribune], *Jen-min chih sheng* [People's voice], *Ch'ün-chung ts'an-k'ao hsiao-hsi* [Masses' reference news], *Chung-kuo jen-ch'üan* [Chinese human rights], *Shih-tai* [Our age], *Min-chu yü shih-tai* [Democracy and our age], *Peking chih ch'un* [The spring of Peking], *Sheng-huo* [Life], *Ch'iu-shih-pao* [Seeking truth], *Chin-t'ien* [Today], *Huo-hua* [Burning flowers], *Ssu-hua lun-t'an* [Four Modernizations tribune], *K'e-hsüeh min-chu fa-chih* [Science, democracy, and law], and *Wu-t'u* [Fertile soil].[93]

Although the criticism of the movement initially had been directed at Wu Te and other leaders involved in the suppression of the 1976 demonstrations, its scope and intensity increased at a rapid pace after mid-December 1978. The movement now comprised quite different political persuasions, from reform-oriented Communists to democratic socialists and radicals to liberals, in the European sense of that term. Critical statements called for a new evaluation of Mao and his mistakes and crimes, and as the movement spread to other cities, vitriolic attacks on the current chairman of the Party began. A wall poster in Shanghai in December 1978 addressed Hua with the following remarks:

> You are an even greater coward than Mao Tse-tung. Your childish obedience is much more efficient than that of the gang-of-four. Small wonder, that

Mao Tse-tung saw in you his orthodox successor. Nobody elected you. . . .
You won the respect of Mao by murdering the martyrs of T'ienanmen
Square. With such a "fighting Experience," you then advanced with express
speed![94]

One of several major leaders of the movement, Wei Ching-sheng,
soon began a more general political discussion, calling for the democ-
ratization of the PRC's political system as a necessary "fifth modernization," without which the other four could not be achieved, and he
criticized Marxism directly.

Thus, a hundred years later, we can see that Marxist economics—"scientific
socialism"—has led to nothing! All the social systems set up according
to Marxist principles—i.e., the present communist countries—almost without exception neither acknowledge nor protect the equal human rights of
all the members of their societies. Even if these countries repeatedly and
smugly proclaim themselves to be "truly democratic" societies, on what
basis can they say that the people are their own masters if universal equal
human rights are absent? The living reality is that the basis of these "true
democracies" is the "proletariate," that is the vanguard of the proletariate,
the communist parties, the parties' monolithic leadership. To put it simply,
we are talking about dictatorship. What an absurd "truth" this is![95]

In March 1979, one of the most radical organizations of what was now
increasingly becoming a dissident movement, the Thaw Society, even
demanded a guarantee of civil rights; free discussion of conflicting
ideologies; freedom of assembly, information, and association; and an
open electoral competition between the CCP and the KMT in the whole
country.[96]

Wall posters and unofficial journals, however, were not the only
manifestations of the dissent as they sparked large-scale demonstrations.
In early January 1979, more than 10,000 destitute peasants from four
provinces, led by a young female intellectual and worker, Fu Yüeh-hua,
demonstrated in Peking and demanded better living conditions in the
villages. Rusticated intellectual youths who had returned illegally to
their cities started to call for their legalization and for work permits.
On February 5 and 6, about 25,000 of them demonstrated in Shanghai,
occupying the railway station for twelve hours and blocking street traffic
until they were driven away by security forces.[97]

Like the Hundred Flowers Campaign in the spring of 1957, the Human
Rights and Democracy movement had also surpassed the limits set by
the ruling elite and gone beyond the leaders' control. And also as in
June 1957, the elite started to strike back. On January 18, 1979, Fu
Yüeh-hua was arrested in Peking, and on March 27, the *JMJP* reported

that people had "accumulated" in several cities, "attacking government offices, beating cadres," and "sabotaging working discipline, production, and the society . . . from now on, such actions will be rigorously suppressed!"

Two days later, on March 29, the Peking Municipal RC issued a proclamation that stated that "from now on, meetings and demonstrations have to obey the orders of the people's police. . . . It is strictly forbidden to attack the organs of the Party, the government or the army!" Posters and leaflets were no longer to be placed "outside the designated areas." The most important aspect of this proclamation, however, was that it mentioned, for the first time, general limits for all political activities in the form of what was soon to be called the Four Basic Principles (*Ssu-hsiang chi-pen yüan-tse*): "All activities against *socialism*, against *proletarian dictatorship*, against the *leadership by the Party*, against *Marxism-Leninism and the Thought of Mao Tse-tung* . . . are prohibited according to the law and will be persecuted.[98]

In early April, a number of dissident leaders, most prominent among them Wei Ching-sheng and Jen Wan-ting, were arrested in the capital, more arrests followed in other cities, and by the fall of 1979, the repressive features of the political system in the PRC were in full sway. On October 16, Wei Ching-sheng was sentenced to fifteen years in prison,[99] in late November, the democracy wall was "closed" and transferred to a quiet suburban area;[100] and the sentencing of Fu Yüeh-hua to two years of imprisonment soon followed.[101] In the summer of 1980, as a final stroke to the movement, the constitutional right to post wall posters was officially abolished. The remnants of the Human Rights and Democracy movement went underground and formed active resistance groups, which seemed to be continuing their work even in 1983.

Once more, a large-scale attempt to introduce civil liberties and pluralistic forms of debate had been thwarted. The critics of 1978 had become dissidents, and many of them actively opposed the elite. They were now convinced that they had been betrayed by Teng, as the former Red Guards of the Cultural Revolution had believed that they had been betrayed by Mao in 1967/1968. But for Teng himself, the movement had served the purpose of pushing ahead his offensive toward the seizure of power and the implementation of those policies that he deemed necessary for the PRC.

Teng's First Victory: The Third Plenum, December 1978

This account of political developments in the PRC has moved far ahead, and I now have to return to the situation in late autumn of

1978, when, from November 11 through December 15, a Central Work Conference of the CC was held in the capital to prepare major policy decisions. While the high tide of the early stages of the Human Rights and Democracy Movement was sweeping through Peking, the central decision-making organs of the Party debated major problems of rural societal policies, the rehabilitation of leaders purged during the Cultural Revolution, a reevaluation of the role of Mao for the PRC, and changes in leadership personnel. During the sessions of the Central Work Conference, social pressures for reform increased and so did pressures from some sections of the Party and the PLA to speed up the rehabilitation of several major enemies of Mao who were still officially in disgrace.

The thoroughgoing policy changes enacted by the conference were confirmed by the third plenum of the Eleventh CC, for which 169 full members and 112 alternates convened on December 18. The plenum lasted until December 22, when a communiqué was passed that summed up the group's decisions. It marked a resounding victory for Teng and the forces around him.[102] The communiqué stated that "the plenum has highly evaluated the discussion of whether reality is the only norm of truth, which has given the Party a new, lively guideline." As far as Mao was concerned, the CC had now arrived at an evaluation of his personality that differed distinctly from that proposed by Hua at the Eleventh Party Congress [comments in brackets added by me]:

> The great merits which comrade [no longer "Chairman"] Mao Tse-tung has established in long years of revolutionary struggle cannot be extinguished. He was indeed a great [no longer "the greatest"] Marxist. . . . However, to expect a revolutionary leader to be without faults and mistakes would not be genuinely Marxist.

The CC plenum further decided upon sweeping changes in the area of rural societal policies, to which I shall turn later,[103] and it stipulated that "in order to prevent any development of a personality cult," Party leaders should no longer be given ceremonial epithets, nor should they be called by their titles, but only "comrade," and that the pronouncements of individuals should not be presented as "directives" or "orders." These stipulations meant that what, until the autumn of 1978, used to be the "latest directive of the wise leader, Chairman Hua" would now be quoted as just "Comrade Hua Kuo-feng has said. . . ." Not a single word of the communiqué mentioned Hua's Ten-Year Plan of early 1978. The plenum also decided to posthumously rehabilitate P'eng Te-huai and T'ao Chu, but even more important were the personnel changes enacted by the plenum. Nine purgees of the Cultural Revolution were co-opted as new full members of the CC, including the generals Huang

K'e-ch'eng and Ch'en Tsai-tao, Hu Ch'iao-mu, and Sung Jen-ch'iung. The plenum added one new vice-chairman to the Standing Committee of the Politburo: Ch'en Yün (then seventy-three years old), who also became the first secretary of the newly formed CDIC, a body of 100 members. Furthermore, Mme. Teng Ying-ch'ao—the widow of Chou En-lai—Hu Yao-pang, and General Wang Chen became new members of the Politburo, which had thus increased to twenty-seven members. Among them at least twelve could be called adherents of the group around Teng, eight took a more or less neutral stand, and seven supported the policies of Hua. In the inner leadership core, there were now two purgees, two cadres who had survived the Cultural Revolution, and two who had advanced during it.

Moreover, the group around Teng had secured its control over the CC switchboard—the General Office—and over the organization, propaganda, and united front work establishments in the central civilian Party machine. With such strength, it soon started to move toward the reestablishment of the CC's Secretariat, which was rebuilt during the summer of 1979 under the leadership of Hu Yao-pang.

Although Teng still had to compromise on the continuance of Wang Tung-hsing and Wu Te on the Politburo—leading figures of what was increasingly being called "the whatever faction"—Teng had succeeded in drastically changing the leading bodies of the Party. Policies changed again, too, first and foremost in the area that concerns four-fifths of the Chinese in their daily lives, the realm of rural societal policies.

A New Line in Rural Societal Policies

Following the Second National Conference on Learning from Tachai in Agriculture in December 1976—at which, as we have seen, Hua Kuo-feng, with the support of Ch'en Yung-kuei (then in charge of agriculture), had advocated raising the level of collectivization and curbing the private initiative of the peasants—it appeared throughout all of 1977 and well into the spring of 1978 that traditional Maoist rural policies would prevail in post-Mao China. The March 5, 1978, constitution of the PRC, while reconfirming the division of ownership and agricultural production for the three levels of communes, brigades, and teams and the position of the team as the basic accounting unit, opened the gate for a further radicalization of rural societal policies by stating that "the production brigade may become the basic accounting unit whenever the conditions are ripe."[104]

Yet the winds of change had started to blow. In May 1978, Teng Hsiao-p'ing and his associates began to initiate dramatic changes that involved all three major areas of rural policies: the levels of collectivization, the parameters for markets and sideline occupations, and the allocation of private plots. They started with fending off attempts to disenfranchise the teams. Only two days after the specially invited correspondent had proclaimed the new norm of truth in the *KMJP* on May 13, the *JMJP* indicated an incipient reversal of rural policies by issuing a call to "strengthen the first frontline of agricultural production, the production team" and introduced the provocative term "the sovereignty of the team" (*Sheng-ch'an-tui-te tzu-chu-ch'üan*).

Soon, the *KMJP* formulated, for the first time, one of the major arguments that was, from then on, to be used to attack the rural policies of Hua and Ch'en Yung-kuei and to support reforms in the communes: Maoist rural policies had not succeeded in providing enough food for the Chinese people. The *KMJP* declared that "the problem of feeding hundreds of millions of people has by no means been solved,"[105] and another *JMJP* editorial, on June 20, 1978, confirmed for the first time in years the legitimacy of the free village markets—officially called "rural collective markets" (*Nung-ts'un chi-t'i shih-ch'ang*, abbreviated, *Nung-ts'un chi-shih*)—within the socialist system. In these markets, which had come into existence in 1961/1962 in the context of the revision of Mao Tse-tung's original commune concept, the peasants were allowed to sell surplus products from their private plots and sideline occupations, usually once or twice a week. The prices were fixed by supply and demand, although the authorities frequently attempted to enforce fixed prices. In the autumn of 1978, Teng's associates intensified their attacks on the rural policies promoted by Hua. Hu Ch'iao-mu argued in a *JMJP* article on October 6 that the "sovereignty of the production team" should "not only be sustained, but expanded."

After such preparation, the third plenum, in its communiqué passed on December 22, settled the dispute over the division of power in the communes as well as other controversial issues of rural policy by unmistakably proclaiming that

> the commune members' private plots, family sideline occupations, and the trade in rural collective markets are necessary supplements of the socialist economy. Nobody is allowed to interfere with them at will. In the people's communes, the system of three-level ownership—commune, brigade, and team—with the production team as the basic unit, must be resolutely enforced. This system needs to be stabilized, it must not be changed.[106]

Moreover, the plenum members approved two other decisions on rural policy, including a draft of new Working Regulations for Rural People's Communes,[107] which opened the possibility of even further subdividing the teams into small working groups (*Tso-yeh-tsu*) of three to five families. These groups could contract for collective land, seed grains, and tools for cultivation on an annual, biannual, or triannual basis provided they gave a fixed production guarantee (*pao-ch'an*) to the State Procurement Organization through an agreement with the production team. This arrangement was not as drastic as Teng Hsiao-p'ing's proposal in 1962 to transfer the *pao-ch'an* to the individual peasant household (*Pao-ch'an tao hu*)—which, at that time, had been rejected by the CC because it meant the de facto liquidation of collective production—but it came rather close to it, particularly because, in the social context of the Chinese countryside, it is usually easy to organize such groups of three to five families from the same lineage for a system of *pao-ch'an* to the group (*Pao-ch'an tao tsu*).

One of Teng's staunchest supporters, Chao Tzu-yang, at that time first secretary of the CCP's Ssuch'uan PPC, began to pioneer structural reforms in the communes of his province immediately after the third plenum. In two major policy speeches to rural cadres during January 1979, he stated that sufficient supplies of grain, edible oil, and cotton were more important than anything else and that any method that would increase agricultural production was legitimate. Peasants should be given a breathing space (*Hsiu-yang sheng-hsi*) from exaggerated requests on the part of the collective. In particular, Chao recommended the formation of working groups, and he even used the term "basic accounting unit" for these units instead of the teams.[108]

During the early months of 1979, such groups were formed in Ssuch'uan, and soon also in Anhui (under the leadership of another follower of Teng, Wan Li), and the *pao-ch'an* was transferred from the teams to these groups. A number of other provinces in southern China followed suit, but in some locations, the peasants misunderstood the new line. In March 1979, reports from Hunan, Kiangsi, and Kueichou indicated that many of the peasants had applied for permission to leave the communes altogether and to get their land and tools back for individual production.[109] At that time, such a move was still considered incorrect. Even Chao Tzu-yang declared that the *pao-ch'an* should not go to the individual household and that any application of the Yugoslav or Polish policies, which had allowed peasants to quit the collectives, was entirely out of the question.[110]

By the spring of 1980, working groups existed in most provinces of the country, and, as could be expected, they were often organized within the framework of a lineage. Most communes and brigades retained only vague coordinating functions, and wherever the groups had been established, even the sovereignty of the production team became increasingly fictitious.

In regard to the free village markets, no further interference with them has been reported since the end of 1978, and they have begun to flourish again almost everywhere in the Chinese countryside. Even more important is the fact that in the spring of 1979, the peasants living in suburban areas were allowed to set up so-called agricultural supplementary goods' markets (*Nung-fu-p'in shih-ch'ang*) right in the cities for the first time since late 1958. The first province to establish these city markets was Yünnan in February 1979, and the last, Peking City, reintroduced these markets at the end of April.[111] Market regulations, however, varied widely in 1979. Peasants could sell products from their private plots—mostly fruits, vegetables, and eggs—and sometimes handicraft products, but seldom meat or fowl, all day long everywhere in the city in Canton and Kueilin. In Shanghai, markets were limited to the afternoons and evenings, but there were few restrictions on localities; in Hangchou, peasants could trade everywhere, but only after 4:00 P.M.; in Ch'angsha, the city markets were limited to the time between 3:00 and 6:00 P.M. and to fourteen locations, all of them small side alleys.[112]

As far as family sideline occupations were concerned, the major problem area was the private raising of animals. Here, too, sweeping changes occurred immediately after the third plenum. In January 1979, Ssuch'uan abolished all restrictions on the number of fowl that could be privately raised by each household,[113] and all other provinces followed suit with the exception of Hunan, the last being Peking City in April 1980. In regard to private hog raising, a controversy had raged since the early 1960s as to whether the principle of "one family, one pig" (*I chia i chu*) or "one person, one pig" (*I jen i chu*) should be applied, i.e., whether every household should be allowed to raise one pig per year or one pig per person per year—a matter of fundamental importance in the daily life of the peasants. Between January and May 1979, the principle of "one person, one pig" was adopted in all provinces, again with the exception of Hunan, and by February 1980, twenty-one out of the twenty-nine administrative units had abolished all limitations on private hog raising.[114] This change led, however, to an oversupply of pork in the summer of 1980, a considerable amount of which spoiled because of the lack of cold-storage facilities.

Of at least equal importance as the changes concerning the level of collectivization, markets, and family sideline occupations were those concerning the size of private plots. Since 1961, when these private plots were introduced, their share of the arable land had been limited to between 5 and 7 percent; in some areas, it had barely exceeded 1 percent. Yet after the third plenum had legitimized the existence of private plots, it was again Chao Tzu-yang, who, in early 1979, pioneered an increase in the size of these plots by expanding their share of the arable land in Ssuch'uan to 10–12 percent. Even this amount, however, did not satisfy Chao. In a speech to rural cadres in Ch'engtu on September 16, 1979—probably one of his last activities in Ssuch'uan before his transfer to the center in Peking—he introduced a new slogan, One-two is not enough, it must at least be one-five! (*I-erh pu kou, i-wu tsui shao!*), meaning that a share of 12 percent was not sufficient, it should be at least 15 percent of the arable land.[115]

The Ssuch'uan leadership soon followed Chao's advice, and in late 1979, a ceiling of 15 percent for the share of private plots in the overall amount of arable land was introduced.[116] The same ceiling of 15 percent was established in Kueichou in the spring of 1980, and Kansu set a limit of 13 percent.[117] The share in Hupei, however, remained at between 6 and 12 percent, and Hunan continued to limit private plots to 5–7 percent of the arable land.[118]

Other limits on the use of private plots also continue to exist. The official ownership remains with the production teams, although the plots are now allocated to the families for an unlimited period of time and can even be inherited. No title deeds are given, and the leasing or selling of plots is considered illegal.

All of these drastic departures from Hua Kuo-feng's platform for rural societal policies were symbolized by the dismantling of the Tachai model, which was the basis of the highly undeserved fame of Ch'en Yung-kuei, Tachai's former CCP secretary. The critics of Tachai first became vocal in Peking, right after the fourth plenum of the Eleventh CC, which, in September 1979, confirmed the decisions of the third plenum on rural policies. On October 6, the *JMJP* suddenly found that "grave mistakes in distribution" had been committed in Tachai due to "ultra-leftist adventurism." A few days later, the Shansi provincial leadership, even more outspoken, called Tachai "an abyss of corruption and exploitation."[119] In December 1980, it was finally officially announced that the Tachai brigade had achieved its model success, not by self-reliance—as the CCP and its Western admirers had previously claimed—but by a disproportionately high investment of state funds; that the brigade had "constantly forged production figures"; and that the people of Tachai had "suffered from leftist mistakes and were brutally suppressed."[120] Ch'en Yung-kuei himself had already been replaced as the leader of China's agricultural program in February 1979 by Wang Jen-chung—who, in turn, was replaced by Wan Li when Wang became director of the Propaganda Department of the CC in the spring of 1980. In September 1980, Ch'en was also removed from his position as vice-premier. To add insult to injury, he was made to run for a delegate's position to the Twelfth Party Congress from Shansi in 1982, but the Shansi Provincial Party Congress did not elect him.

Thus, from 1978 to 1980, rural societal policies were once again one of the major conflict areas in the PRC, as they had been between 1958 and 1962, in 1970/1971, and in 1975/1976, this time as part of the confrontation between the forces around Teng and those who supported Hua. In early 1980, opponents of the new line in rural societal policies argued that it constituted a retreat, but this opinion was answered by its proponents with the following statement.

> The people who argue that our policy in the villages constitutes a retreat are persons who think that the bigger the organization, the better. This is an error. The primitive society had public ownership, but it was a backward society. In modern times, public ownership of land in Tsarist Russia and India impeded the development of capitalism, and hence, social progress. . . . We should, therefore, not be frightened by people who say that our present policy is a retreat.[121]

These were daring words indeed. They indicated that Hua Kuo-feng had lost out in one of the major conflict areas and that a further triumph of Teng was in the making.

Teng's Second Victory: The Fifth Plenum, February 1980

Teng's first triumph at the third plenum had resulted not only in sweeping changes of rural policies, and in an escalation of the Human Rights and Democracy movement, but also in the beginning of a new evaluation of Mao Tse-tung and his role in Chinese history. In March 1978, the daily quotes from Mao's writings and sayings disappeared from the front page of the *JMJP*, and beginning in late April, they were no longer printed in boldface in the CCP publications. After the third plenum had stated in its communiqué that Mao, as every revolutionary leader, had not only great merits, but also "faults and mistakes," and after it had dramatically rehabilitated the first major CCP politician who had openly opposed The Chairman since 1940, Marshal P'eng Te-huai, criticism about the late Party leader increasingly appeared.

Attacks on the memory of Mao, however, sparked increasing resistance to the speed with which Teng Hsiao-p'ing and his supporters had started to revise the policies of the CCP. Teng's adversaries had two rather strong arguments going for their counterattack during the month of March 1979.

1. The Human Rights and Democracy movement had increasingly gone beyond Party control and had developed its own momentum, which started to pose a threat to the ruling elite as a whole.

2. The PRC assault on Vietnam in February–March, which had mainly been promoted by Teng himself, had not proceeded smoothly but had revealed grave weaknesses in the PLA, as even the army paper admitted, although in a veiled manner.[122]

Strengthened in their position by these developments, a number of leading cadres started to criticize Teng and his policies severely. They argued that the third plenum had "taken a negative attitude towards Chairman Mao" and had "cut down the banner of the Thought of Mao Tse-tung."[123]

In order to thwart this attack, Teng was forced to compromise. In an unpublished speech at an enlarged Politburo meeting on March 16, he agreed to curb the Human Rights and Democracy movement, setting the Four Basic Principles as the limits for all political and economic activities in the country. Thus, Teng succeeded in securing the continuing support of a number of military leaders, including the generals Li Te-sheng and Liao Han-sheng. By May, the counterattack of the forces of Maoist orthodoxy had failed, and as a signal of this failure, the *JMJP* reprinted a *CFCP* commentary that exhorted the PLA to "resolutely support and implement the policies decided by the Third Plenum."[124]

In late June, the second plenary session of the Fifth NPC confirmed that Teng's offensive had gotten off the ground again. P'eng Chen, just rehabilitated, was appointed a vice-chairman of the NPC's Standing Committee and chairman of the newly established Commission on Legislative Affairs of the NPC. Three other veteran purgee cadres who belonged to the coalition that rallied around Teng—Ch'en Yün, Po I-po, and Yao Yi-lin—were appointed as additional vice-premiers, thus increasing the number of former purgees in the inner cabinet from four out of fourteen to seven out of seventeen,[125] from 28.6 to 41 percent.

Even more important were the decisions made by the fourth plenum of the Eleventh CC, which assembled in Peking September 25–28, 1979. Not only did this plenum reconfirm the revision of rural policies initiated by the third plenum, but it also added twelve more members to the CC, all of them former purgees who had only recently been rehabilitated. One of them, P'eng Chen, was at the same time elevated to the Politburo as a full member, and so was Chao Tzu-yang, who had so far been only an alternate.[126]

As a result, the coalition of forces around Teng had thirteen to fourteen votes on the Politburo, the supporters of Hua accounted for seven, and seven to eight members could be counted in the middle group around Yeh Chien-ying and Li Hsien-nien. Finally, the plenum pushed the reevaluation of Mao and the history of the PRC into a new stage as it started to criticize the Cultural Revolution.

In an address on the eve of the thirtieth anniversary of the PRC's establishment, on September 29, it was Yeh Chien-ying, the ceremonial chief of state because of his position as chairman of the NPC's Standing Committee, who took the initiative. Yeh ventured a new and somewhat astonishing interpretation of the term "Thought of Mao Tse-tung": "What we call the Thought of Mao Tse-tung . . . is not the product of comrade Mao Tse-tung's wisdom alone; it is actually the wisdom of comrade Mao and his comrades-in-arms, it is indeed *the crystallization of the collective wisdom of the CCP.*" He then proceeded to voice the first official condemnation of the Cultural Revolution—which, only two years earlier, was still praised by Hua Kuo-feng as "personally initiated and directed by Chairman Mao"—by stating that that movement had "brought to the country a whole decade of *suppression, tyranny,* and *bloodshed.*"[127]

All through late 1979, the CCP media scathingly criticized the cruelties and "crimes" committed during the period of the Cultural Revolution. These attacks were to prepare the country for the ultimate, although posthumous, rehabilitation: that of Mao's main enemy during the 1960s, Liu Shao-ch'i, who had died in prison in 1969. Liu's widow, Wang Kuang-mei, had already reappeared after the third plenum, and on February 16, 1979, the *JMJP* had published an article by a journalist named Wu Chiang that had insinuated that Liu's line should no longer be called "counterrevolutionary." A full rehabilitation of Liu, however, would mean a further step in the criticism of Mao, and hence, the process met with stiff resistance, not only from the opinion group that was now increasingly called "the whatever faction" around Hua Kuo-feng, but also by some major veteran PLA leaders, first and foremost Yeh Chien-ying, who continued to rank ahead of Teng in the official pecking order of the Politburo.

Yet when the fifth plenum of the eleventh CC convened in Peking on February 23, 1980, for a meeting that lasted until February 29, such resistance had been overcome. The communiqué of this plenum fully rehabilitated Liu Shao-ch'i, the "renegade, traitor, and scab" of yore who had been expelled "forever" from the CCP in October 1968 but who was now officially proclaimed by the CCP leadership as a "great Marxist" and a "valiant revolutionary fighter."[128]

Moreover, the coalition of forces around Teng at the fifth plenum finally secured a majority on the Politburo. Four strong supporters of Hua—General Wang Tung-hsing, General Ch'en Hsi-lien, Wu Te, and Chi Teng-k'uei—were now removed from that body, and Wang was also removed from its Standing Committee. Hu Yao-pang and Chao Tzu-yang were elevated to the Standing Committee, where the Teng coalition could now muster four votes, the middle group had two with

Yeh and Li, and Hua was isolated as the only remaining advancer of the Cultural Revolution in the inner leadership core. Among the twenty-four remaining Politburo members, thirteen or fourteen supported Teng, only three were left with Hua, and seven or eight belonged to the forces around Yeh and Li. The group around Teng further strengthened its control over the Party machine by the official reestablishment of the Secretariat of the CC, which had been abolished in early 1967 and had gradually been being rebuilt since the third plenum, i.e., the first half of 1979. Headed by Hu Yao-pang in his capacity as secretary general, this body consisted, at that time, of ten secretaries, of whom seven were supporters of Teng, and three could be counted with the middle group. Hua had none of his genuine supporters in the new leading organ of the Party machine.

Hence, the triumph of Teng seemed almost complete. His main adversary of the period since 1976, Hua Kuo-feng, had been isolated. From 1977 to 1980, Teng had increased his voting strength on the Politburo from seven to thirteen or fourteen, while that of Hua had decreased from seven to three—or even two because Ch'en Yung-kuei no longer participated in Politburo activities. On the Standing Committee in 1977, there had been two advancers of the Cultural Revolution and two survival cadres, with Teng being the only rehabilitated purgee. After the third plenum, each of the major opinion and experience groups had had two members. Now, however, there were four purgees and two survivors, and Hua was alone as an advancer during the Cultural Revolution.

In terms of policies, the Teng coalition had thoroughly revised the CCP's rural policy, it had succeeded in introducing rather broad parameters of cultural competition, and it had started to push ahead a new concept of development, which will be analyzed in Part 4 of this book.[129] The reevaluation of Mao and the criticism of the Great Leap Forward and the Cultural Revolution were proceeding with rapid speed. Teng Hsiao-p'ing's offensive therefore seemed to have achieved almost all of its goals by the spring of 1980.

The triumph of Teng, however, probably appeared too absolute for many of the other elite veterans, in particular a number of PLA leaders. Teng may have made a mistake by denying the commander in chief of the Canton MAC, General Hsü Shih-yu—who had saved Teng in April 1976 and had been the main promoter of his second rehabilitation—the appointment as minister of national defense or chief of the General Staff. This action alienated Hsü from Teng and in addition to Hsü, his sworn brother; the director of the GPD, General Wei Kuo-ch'ing; as well as several other major figures of the Third FA loyalty group.

When almost the whole leadership assembled in Peking on May 17, 1980, for a memorial service in honor of Liu Shao-ch'i, Hsü was conspicuously absent. Absent, too, was an even more powerful elite figure, Marshal Yeh Chien-ying. On the very same day, Yeh acted as referee for a basketball match between the teams of two girls' secondary schools in his home *hsien* in Kuangtung, and he made sure that this fact was reported on the provincial radio[130]—a very strong gesture of defiance indeed. New alignments seemed to be shaping up, which could mean that new compromises would have to be sought in the process of the PRC's transition to new patterns of politics.

CHAPTER 11

The Demolition of a Successor and the Emergence of Compromise Politics, 1980–1983

The Fall of Chairman Hua

Although isolated in the inner leadership core, Hua Kuo-feng still kept his positions as chairman of the CCP/CC, prime minister of the State Council, and chairman of the CC's Military Commission after the fifth plenum. Within the elite, he was now increasingly supported by Yeh Chien-ying and Li Hsien-nien, who used him as a figurehead and a symbol for orthodox policies that they did not want to be too thoroughly revised. Thus, an emerging alliance of the survival cadres and the few advancers during the Cultural Revolution who had remained in the decision-making bodies tried to slow down the pace of reform, which Teng Hsiao-p'ing and Ch'en Yün with their respective followers wanted to speed up, particularly in the realm of economics.

Yet in spite of all orthodox opposition, the forces around Teng and Ch'en succeeded in initiating further policy changes. The most drastic ones again occurred in the field of rural societal policies as only a few weeks after the fifth plenum, in April 1980, the decollectivization of production began to take hold in the Chinese countryside. I shall discuss the new sweeping changes in the villages in Part 4 of this book,[131] but it should noted here that the speed and success of rural reform indicated the strength of the Teng/Ch'en alliance as long as those two leaders acted in unison.

The two did act in unison during most of 1980, gradually engineering the removal of Hua from his position as Mao's successor. As a first stroke, Teng managed to strengthen his forces in the state administrative machine. On April 16, a meeting of the NPC's Standing Committee decided to discharge General Ch'en Hsi-lien and Chi Teng-k'uei from their posts as vice-premiers. Instead, Chao Tzu-yang and Wan Li were appointed as new vice-premiers, thus bringing the number of leaders supporting Teng in the inner cabinet from seven to nine out of seventeen, i.e., a majority.[132]

As a next step, Teng wanted to induce Hua to resign as premier at the upcoming plenary session of the Fifth NPC, which was originally scheduled for early August. In order to achieve this goal, Teng started to promote the idea of a division of functions between the Party and the state administrative machine and offered his own resignation as vice-premier for that purpose. But strong opposition developed against this proposal, so the NPC session had to be postponed to early September, and an enlarged meeting of the Politburo convened from August 18 through 23, and again on August 31, in order to reach a decision on the new lineup of leaders on the State Council. The meeting was opened by Teng with a major speech in which he addressed all controversial points of the moment. For the first time, he officially aired his views on the problem of a new evaluation of Mao.

As a guideline for such an evaluation, Teng proposed three theses.

First, comrade Mao Tse-tung made, in his lifetime, indelible contributions to our Party, state, and people. His merits are primary, his mistakes secondary. Second, the mistakes and failures of the Cultural Revolution were the result of its—and also comrade Mao Tse-tung's—going against the scientific system of the Thought of Mao Tse-tung. Third, . . . the scientific system of the Thought of Mao Tse-tung has not only guided all the victories we have won in the past, but will also serve as our guiding thought . . . in the future.[133]

Thus Teng refrained from pressing for a full-fledged de-Maoization by attempting to create two Maos—a good one until the Great Leap or the Cultural Revolution and a bad one who worked against his own ideas in his late years. Teng also tried to redefine Maoism as a "scientific system," which, as we may recall, was now considered to be the crystallization of the collective wisdom of the CCP and could, therefore, be manipulated to suit the purposes of the current leaders. After this clarification, Teng went on to suggest thoroughgoing reforms in the political system: a separation of the functions of Party and state, the abolition of concurrent appointments in both subsystems, and a rejuvenation of the leadership. In regard to the last, he suggested that veteran Party leaders should retire into advisory positions and that age limits as well as limits on the tenure of office should be established in the Party statute, and also in a revised constitution of the PRC.

After long and obviously controversial discussions, Teng's suggestions were accepted by the Politburo on August 31, 1980, and implemented for the State Council at the third plenary session of the Fifth NPC on September 10. Hua Kuo-feng resigned as prime minister, and Teng's loyal follower Chao Tzu-yang assumed the leadership of the State Council. Teng, Li Hsien-nien, Marshal Hsü Hsiang-ch'ien, Ch'en Yün, General Wang Chen, and Wang Jen-chung also withdrew from their positions as vice-premiers, and Ch'en Yung-kuei was removed from that post, indicating the end of this particular Maoist's political career. Newly appointed as vice-premiers were Foreign Minister Huang Hua, General Chang Ai-p'ing, and the chairman of the Nationalities Affairs Commission, Yang Ching-jen.[134] Of the fourteen members of the cabinet after these changes, not a single person who had advanced during the Cultural Revolution was left; eight were former purgees, and six were cadres who had survived during that period.

Yet, although no longer premier, Hua still headed the Party and the Military Commission. His fall from these positions came only several months later, on December 5, 1980, after a series of intense meetings of the Politburo. For these meetings, which took place between November 10 and December 5, twenty-one full members and one alternate of the Politburo were present, as well as seven secretaries who did not belong to the Politburo. The official report of the meeting states that Marshals Liu Po-ch'eng and Nieh Jung-chen had taken leave because of illness and then declares, "Comrades Ch'en Yung-kuei and Saifudin were not invited to attend."[135]

In the Politburo, Hua Kuo-feng was placed under direct and full attack. Finally, he presented his self-criticism, admitting that he had pursued a "leftist leadership style," had long continued to "stick to the 'two whatevers,' " and had "taken a lukewarm attitude towards the rehabilitation of veteran revolutionary cadres." He also admitted that he had "tried to avoid or at least delay the rehabilitation of comrades Teng Hsiao-p'ing and Ch'en Yün, did not support the posthumous rehabilitation of comrade P'eng Te-huai, neither that of the April 5 movement," and had followed a "leftist style of a new 'Great Leap' " in economics.[136]

After Hua had thus disowned most of his past record in front of the major political leaders of the country, and shown "repentance," the Politburo passed a resolution that brought an end to Hua's political life, at least for the time being. Following are its central statements, which may be compared to what Yeh Chien-ying had said about Hua at the Eleventh Party Congress.

> Comrade Hua Kuo-feng eagerly produced and accepted a new cult of personality. He had himself called the wise leader, had his own pictures hung besides the pictures of comrade Mao Tse-tung, accepted poems and songs in his honor, and felt comfortable about this. This situation continued to exist until shortly before this year. To mismanage one's own relations with the Party and the people by elevating oneself is a severe problem of thought and a problem of Party character. . . .
>
> In the two years of 1977 and 1978, comrade Hua Kuo-feng promoted some "leftist" slogans in the realm of economic problems. The over-eagerness of these two years in economic work resulted in severe losses and calamities for the national economy. This is mainly a problem of too little experience, comrade Hua Kuo-feng is not alone responsible for it, but he has to assume an important part of the responsibility. . . .
>
> During the last four years, comrade Hua Kuo-feng has also done some successful work, but it is extremely clear that *he lacks the political and organizational ability to be the chairman of the Party. That he should never have been appointed chairman of the Military Commission, everybody knows.*

After this devastating declaration, the resolution of the Politburo stated:

> Comrade Hua Kuo-feng suggested that he should resign his posts, and that, even before the Sixth Plenum, he wanted no longer to lead the work of the Politburo, the Politburo's Standing Commission, and the Military Commission. The Politburo holds that *he indeed should concentrate his strength on deliberating his problems*, and therefore accepts his opinion that he no longer wants to lead the current work. But before the Sixth Plenum makes a final decision on this, he is still officially the chairman of the Party Center, and *he will have to receive foreign guests in the capacity of the Center's chairman.*[137]

Finally, the Politburo decided to "suggest to the Sixth Plenum" that Hu Yao-pang should become chairman of the CC and Teng Hsiao-p'ing, chairman of the Military Commission, and that both should assume the work of these positions immediately, "but not yet in formal name."

Although still remaining on the Standing Committee and the Politburo until the Twelfth Party Congress in September 1982, Hua had, only a little more than four years after succeeding Mao, for all practical purposes left the Chinese political scene. Mao Tse-tung's choice of his own successor was thus disavowed by the veteran cadres who now decided the political fate of the PRC. The first attempt to solve the problem of personal succession had proved a failure. Now, the remaining leaders set out to develop a new solution to the succession problem, first by enacting new policy changes that revised not only Mao's prescriptions but also many of Teng's policies since the spring of 1978.

Retrenching the Plan and Disciplining the Intellectuals: The Central Work Conference of December 1980 and Its Effects

Soon after the overthrow of Hua Kuo-feng, the Party leaders decided to convene a Central Work Conference of the members and alternates of the CC, PLA officers of high rank, and many officials of the PPCs in order to advance new policy prescriptions, which had been agreed upon chiefly by the groups around Teng Hsiao-p'ing and Ch'en Yün. The conference began on December 15, 1980. One day later, on December 16, its members listened to reports on the state of the economy given by Ch'en Yün and Chao Tzu-yang, which were then debated in detail. The conference concluded on December 25 with an address by Teng Hsiao-p'ing. This conference should be considered as another major turning point in the politics of the PRC, since the political line that was initiated at it has basically remained in force until today.

Ch'en Yün waged a scathing attack on the policy of deficit spending, which had been promoted by Hua and Li Hsien-nien from 1977 until the first half of 1979. He also reiterated a slogan to modify the slogan of the four modernizations: an Eight-Ideograph Directive: Readjustment, reform, correction, and improvement! (*T'iao-cheng, kai-ke, cheng-tun, t'i-kaol*).[138] In his speech, Chao Tzu-yang followed the new policy prescriptions set by Ch'en and went into details. Investment in heavy industry should be reduced by almost 30 percent in 1981, agriculture and the light and consumer goods industries should take priority over heavy industry, administrative and production personnel should be drastically reduced, national defense spending should be cut, and there should be a nationwide drive against waste and mismanagement.[139]

Thus, a new concept of development took shape, and it was based on more realistic estimates of the economic situation and brought about thoroughgoing retrenchments of the very ambitious plan of 1978, a plan that was no longer mentioned by the CCP media.[140] In his closing address at the Central Work Conference on December 25, 1980, Teng Hsiao-p'ing endorsed the retrenchment of the ambitious plan and the policies of austerity promoted by Ch'en Yün, but he was evidently more concerned about the establishment of discipline and the reassertion of the Party's leadership.[141]

We must steadfastly abide by the Four Basic Principles, we must absolutely not allow anybody to create disturbance, we must use the appropriate legal methods to deal with such disturbances. The very core of abiding by the Four Basic Principles is to abide by the Party's leadership. . . . If, in such a big country as China, there would not be the leadership by the Communist Party, it would fall apart, there would be no success at all.[142]

Teng then painted a rather bleak picture of the political situation in the country and called for strong disciplinary action.

Today, there are some regions where stability and unity are severely threatened . . . we experience covert support for youth disturbances, illegal organizations, open attacks on the Party and on socialism as a whole, activities of the remnants of "gang-of-four" supporters, arson, murder, manufacture of explosives, armed robbery, kidnapping, rape, organized prostitution, speculation, bribery and corruption, smuggling, drug trafficking, violation of state secrets, and unjustifiable payment of bonuses. . . . We must not take such a situation lightly. . . . Hence, we must strengthen the instruments of people's democratic dictatorship, we must resolutely wage a counterattack against all these influences which sabotage stability and unity![143]

What developments motivated Teng—who had encouraged the beginnings of the Human Rights and Democracy movement in November 1978 and who had, all through 1979 and 1980, time and again promoted the slogan that one should "liberate the thought" (*Chieh-fang ssu-hsiang*)—to emphasize again the repressive features of the political system? One may argue that this new turn was quite consistent with his attitude in the early 1950s, when he had followed Stalinist prescriptions in order to consolidate CCP rule in southwestern China, but he had been one of the last Party leaders to applaud the counterattack on the Hundred Flowers Campaign in the spring of 1957, and he had himself suffered from repression between 1967 and 1972, to which suffering many observers attributed the reformist, if not liberalizing, tendencies of Teng in 1978/1979. Hence, it appears more appropriate to argue that he had to compromise on a new disciplinary drive, a compromise that may have been relatively easy for him to make because of his deep belief in the necessity of Party control. If he indeed compromised, it was with tendencies that were increasingly rampant among the PLA leaders after the second half of 1980.

The PLA leaders were concerned about the drastic budget cuts, which had first been enacted during the third plenary session of the Fifth NPC in September, when defense expenditure was reduced by 15.2 percent,[144] and further aggravated by another reduction announced in March 1981, which lowered military funds by 24.4 percent from the original budget estimate for 1981.[145] Yet, even though a number of major PLA leaders had publicly aired their misgivings about the first round of cuts in September 1980, there were no reflections of military restiveness when the second round was announced in March 1981. Had the PLA lost its influence on political decision making and surrendered to the current political trend? Or were its leaders shifting their ability to influence policies to another front?

Even in the first days of 1981, it was obvious that the latter was the case when a strong group in the military elite chose the cultural and ideological front for a counterattack against the tendencies of 1978 and 1979. Even earlier, there had been clear indications that a number of PLA leaders were becoming increasingly uneasy about the relaxation of ideological discipline in literature and the arts, which had resulted in only thinly veiled attacks on Party and PLA cadres, sometimes ridiculing generals and always criticizing the special privileges of military personnel, e.g., "luxury shops, sumptuous dinners, and an excessive use of private cars."[146]

Beginning in January 1981, the PLA struck back. Its new political drive, obviously tolerated by Teng Hsiao-p'ing for compromise reasons, was mainly launched and sustained by the army newspaper, the *CFCP.* On January 4, this paper, for the first time in five years, mentioned positively a slogan coined by Lin Piao in 1969: First, do not fear bitterness; second, do not fear death! Following the lead of the *CFCP,* the *JMJP,* on February 22 and 24, began to revitalize the cult of Lei Feng, a model soldier who had been suggested for emulation by the public in March 1963 as a precursor of the Cultural Revolution. Lei had been the "shining example" of a positive attitudinal response during an era of most radical Maoism. On March 4, the *CFCP* followed up its thrust by calling for strict discipline, and it explained that the PRC type of democracy had to be understood as "democracy under the guidance of centralism."

In April 1981, the new political offensive by the orthodox circles of the PLA became even more blunt. On April 17, a *CFCP* editorial revitalized the term "strange talk and astonishing opinions" (*Ch'i-t'an kuai-lun*), which had last been used by the cultural revolutionary Left against the supporters of Teng in 1975/1976. On April 26, a major article in the *CFCP* stated that in order to "overcome the influence of wrong thoughts," one had also to turn against "rightist deviations"— which had not been attacked since October 1978.

During the last of April and early May 1981, several major PLA leaders took up this attack against—as it then was called—"both left and right deviations," and, hence, the *JMJP* deemed it necessary to define what was meant by these "deviations": It was the attitude toward the Four Basic Principles! "Leftist deviationists" argued that these principles "were meant to correct the Third Plenum," and "rightist deviationists" held that these principles "impede the implementation of the line of the Third Plenum." In fact, the *JMJP* proclaimed that the Four Basic Principles were "entirely coherent with the decisions of the Third Plenum."[147] Yet, although the *JMJP* argued, in a commentary published on April 24, that the "leftist deviation" was "the more pernicious," the *CFCP*, only two days later, stated that both deviations were equally dangerous—"left *and* right . . . or one can say right and left."[148]

About the same time, the orthodox forces in the PLA had found their personal target: Pai Hua, a member of the Cultural Work Group of the Wuhan MAC and the author of a realistic modern drama entitled *Bitter Love* (*K'u lien*). On April 20, the *CFCP* printed a vitriolic attack against the writer and his drama. However, at that time, the attack was reprinted only in the local newspapers of Peking and Chekiang, not in the *JMJP*. It was some time until the civilian Party leadership fully joined the drive to again discipline the intellectuals in the PRC.

By July 1981, the moves toward disciplinary action against the intellectuals had finally received the support of the official Party leadership. The *JMJP* joined the chorus of attacks against Pai Hua, sounding the clarion call for a nationwide purge of dissenting intellectuals. However, only very few people were directly persecuted, but the literary and arts scene, as far as it had official support—and that meant the permission to print or to exhibit—was thoroughly back to socialist realism by late 1981. Only traditional Chinese art, literature, and plays now fully coexist with the would-be "modern" cultural works promoted by the CCP.

Problems of De-Maoization: The Sixth Plenum, June 1981

Even though the communiqué of the fifth plenum, passed on February 29, 1980, by rehabilitating Liu Shao-ch'i, admitted that the CCP had committed grave errors during the period of the Cultural Revolution, it did not reveal that the plenum had also decided to set up an editorial group to draft an official Party resolution centering around a definite evaluation of the role of Mao. It appears that in a first draft, it was stated that although Mao had displayed great merit during the struggle of the CCP for power until 1949 and also during the first seven years of PRC history, he had committed mistakes (*ts'o-wu*) in 1957, severe mistakes (*yen-chung-te ts'o-wu*) during the Great Leap Forward 1958/ 1959 as well as in the early period of the Cultural Revolution, and even some crimes (*tsui-hsing*) during the last ten years of his life. A second draft, after the October 1980 conference, did not mention the word "crimes" any more, and "severe mistakes" were now confined to the Cultural Revolution.

At the Central Work Conference, Teng gave his new general directive concerning the evaluation of Mao, and it was much more cautious than one would expect from a leader who had been harshly persecuted by The Chairman.

> The evaluation of Party work since the establishment of the PRC should fully affirm the tremendous achievements made in the past thirty-one years. Of course, serious criticism should be conducted of shortcomings and mistakes, but we should not paint too gloomy a picture. Even the severe mistakes which were made during the "Cultural Revolution . . . should not be called counterrevolutionary." . . . We must in no way cast suspicion on or negate the fact that comrade Mao Tse-tung's merits are primary, and his mistakes secondary. When we emotionally describe his mistakes to the extreme, we can only tarnish the image of our Party and state, and undermine the prestige of the Party as well as of socialism. We can avoid confusion by differentiating between the Thought of Mao Tse-tung and his ideas in the later part of his life.[149]

During the spring of 1981, more positive evaluations of Mao increasingly dominated the CCP media, and on April 11, the Party's central organ reprinted the text of Huang K'e-ch'eng's speech of November 1980, which had been published by the *CFCP* one day earlier, on April 10, 1981. In that speech Huang repeated Teng's dictum that Mao had made severe mistakes during the latter part of his life, but that his merits were primary, and his mistakes secondary.

It should be noted that both Teng and Huang still spoke about "severe mistakes" committed by Mao during the last decade of his life, and Teng Li-ch'ün, in late March, continued to argue that the Great Leap Forward was "not only a mistake, but a disaster," although "the man who made the mistakes was a good man, and he had good intentions."[150] Such wording was further toned down in the final version of the Party resolution, which was unanimously passed at the sixth plenum of the Eleventh CC when it convened in Peking June 27–29, 1981.[151]

In the final version of the resolution, Mao's "mistakes" were confined to some decisions made during the Great Leap period and to the Cultural Revolution, and even for that latter period, the term "severe mistakes" is only very rarely applied. The document admits that the main cause of the Cultural Revolution lay in Mao's erroneous leadership, but his errors were those of a "great proletarian revolutionary." "While committing serious mistakes, he still thought that his theory and practice were Marxist and herein lies his tragedy."

In regard to Hua Kuo-feng, the resolution was much less understanding. It repeated the devastating evaluation of the Politburo's resolution of December 5, 1980, and the sixth plenum confirmed all the decisions of that body. Hua had to step down to seventh rank on the Standing Committee, Hu Yao-pang became the new chairman of the CC, and Teng was appointed chairman of the Military Commission.

The more positive evaluation of Mao, like many other decisions since the autumn of 1980, was obviously the result of a compromise between the forces around Teng and those around Ch'en Yün, and even more so with major survival cadres and PLA leaders. That Teng, in particular, had to compromise with major military figures is quite evident from the section in the document that deals with the Cultural Revolution. Although that movement, as a whole, is considered entirely wrong (*Wan-ch'üan ts'o-wu*), one aspect of it was—at that moment—entirely necessary (*Wan-ch'üan pi-yao-ti*), namely, the takeover of local and regional power by the PLA in early 1967, the so-called Three-Support, Two-Military Work, which General Ch'in Chi-wei—commander in chief of the Peking MAC and a supporter of Teng—had blamed for causing "great damage to the army" not quite three months earlier.[152]

But why this compromise? It was concluded because the patterns of group formation within the CCP ruling elite since the overthrow of the Maoist remnants around Hua Kuo-feng and Wang Tung-hsing in 1980—and, I would suggest, until now—have remained in the stage of differentiation, not of open factional confrontation. Hence, the scene is dominated, in terms of secondary group formation within the elite, by varying, issue-based coalitions of opinion groups. By the summer of 1981, at least three such groups had taken shape.

1. A revisionist group around Teng and Chao Tzu-yang, which could, then, command about eight votes on the Politburo
2. A centrist group around Ch'en Yün and P'eng Chen, joined by the career Bolshevik Hu Yao-pang, which could command about six to seven votes on the Politburo
3. An orthodox Stalinist group around Yeh Chien-ying and Li Hsien-nien, including the remaining people who had advanced during the Cultural Revolution (Hua Kuo-feng and Ni Chih-fu), which could command eight to nine votes on the Politburo

In this lineup of forces, the revisionists and the centrists agreed on expansions of the parameters of economic initiatives, particularly in the realm of agriculture, and on the introduction of limited elements of a market economy into the socialist system. The centrists and the orthodox Stalinists, in turn, agreed on strict discipline and on rather narrow limits for intellectual and art activities, as well as on a cautious evaluation of Mao's person and his role in CCP history.

Under these circumstances, the compromise, which had begun to develop at the December 1980 Central Work Conference and had been ratified by the sixth plenum, became recognizable.

1. The revisionists around Teng had to accept most of the orthodox— and in the case of the PLA, even Maoist loyalist—leaders' ideas concerning the evaluation of Mao.
2. The revisionists around Teng had to accept more restrictions on cultural life, a revival of Party doctrines, and an attempt to reimpose Stalinist discipline on the Chinese society.
3. The orthodox group had to accept limited and controlled tendencies toward economic liberalization.
4. The orthodox group had to accept the demotion of Hua Kuo-feng.

This and similar policy and personnel compromises have dominated domestic politics in the PRC since the end of 1980, and definitely since June 1981. They carry evident marks of the influence exerted by the orthodox Stalinist wing of the military elite and other survival cadres who want to return, not to the policies of cultural revolutionary mobilization and late Maoist doctrines, but to the repressive climate that characterized the PRC from 1951 to 1955, from 1962 to early 1965, and again in 1972/1973. These were not periods of Maoist radicalism, but of Stalinist dogmatism and Bolshevik one-party dictatorship. Compromises between the orthodox forces, the centrists, and the revisionists also determined the decisions of the Twelfth Party Congress, which, in September 1982, attempted to set the course for a transition to the stage of institutionalized rule.

The Twelfth Party Congress, September 1982

In February 1980, the fifth plenum had decided to convene the Twelfth Party Congress, which was to ratify the changes in the CCP line that had occurred since 1978 "ahead of time,"[153] and a tentative date seems to have been set for the early part of 1981. The debate over the reevaluation of Mao, however, delayed the opening of the congress, and so did a major effort toward administrative reform. The basic idea of this reform was to simplify the structures of the State Council and to rejuvenate its leadership. Three meetings of the NPC's Standing Committee in March, May, and August 1982 accomplished these tasks.[154]

The number of vice-premiers was reduced from thirteen to only two. Nine of the former vice-premiers were now appointed to the newly created position of state councillor (*Kuo-wu wei-yüan*),[155] and to them was added the chairman of the State Economic Commission, Chang Ching-fu, so that the inner cabinet, including the prime minister, was reduced from fourteen to thirteen members. In the realm of ministries and commissions, the reduction brought more sweeping results: Their number decreased from fifty-two to forty-three, and the number of institutions and organs under the direct leadership of the State Council was reduced from forty-one to fifteen. Overall, the reform led to a reduction in the number of State Council members from fifty-eight to forty-nine, i.e., by more than 15 percent, and the whole number of staff employed by the central organs of the state administrative machine declined from 49,000 to 32,000, i.e., almost 35 percent.

Most of the veteran leading cadres who lost their positions in the process of restructuring, however, took on the role of "adviser," keeping their salaries, houses, chauffer-driven cars, and other special privileges. Nevertheless, the reform of the State Council was a success for the revisionist group, which now seemed to be convinced that its concept for a sweeping reform of the Party structure could be implemented, too.

This concept was initially suggested in the first draft for a new Party statute, which had been circulated by the Party center in early April 1980.[156] Four more drafts followed, and from their thrust, it is possible to reconstruct the platform the revisionist group led by Teng Hsiao-p'ing—and in this case, Hu Yao-pang, too—approached the Twelfth Congress with.

1. A thoroughgoing rejuvenation (*Nien-ch'ing-hua*) of the central Party leadership. For this purpose, the drafts of the Party statute provided for age limits, average-age regulations, and limits on the period of office in the leading organs of the Party.
2. An incentive for elderly Party leaders to quit the "first line," i.e., the Politburo, by establishing a new advisory body, the CAC. This body, as well as the CDIC, was supposed to be on equal footing with the CC among the decision-making organs of the Party.
3. The abolition of the Politburo's Standing Committee and the takeover of all daily decision-making powers by the Secretariat of the CC.[157]
4. An official declaration in the Party statute that "large-scale class struggle in the form of turbulent mass movements are already a thing of the past," in order to ensure a stabilized and orderly transition to a new stage of Party rule.

These suggestions, however, met with stiff resistance from the orthodox forces, and apparently also from at least parts of the centrist group, so that Teng and his associates, once more, had to agree to a compromise that, this time, kept only a little of their original concept alive. This compromise was prepared at a Central Work Conference of the CC from July 30 through August 5, 1982, and it was ratified by the seventh plenum of the Eleventh CC, which met in Peking for one day, on August 6, to convoke the Twelfth Congress for September 1.

Just before the congress, the orthodox forces in the PLA made another attempt to turn the tide even more in the direction of their views than it had already been turned by the results of the preparatory meetings. On August 28, the CFCP, and also the Shanghai CFJP, published an article written by the Political Department of the PLA navy that launched a strong attack on the leaders around Teng. "Some responsible comrades," mainly those working in the fields of ideology, culture, and the media— so the article insinuated—had "supported bourgeois liberal points of view," and the leaders of the center had "failed to correct such erroneous tendencies early enough." Yet with this attack, the orthodox group had overplayed its hand. In late September, after the congress, the CFCP had to apologize for the article, and the director of the GPD, General Wei Kuo-ch'ing, and the commander in chief of the PLA Navy, Admiral Yeh Fei, were removed from their positions.

Four days after the article was published, the Twelfth Party Congress convened, on September 1, 1982, with 1,545 delegates. For the first time since the Eighth Party Congress in 1956, all proceedings were immediately reported by the CCP media, and the congress Secretariat even held regular information meetings for foreign correspondents.

The congress opened with an address by Teng and the "Political Report of the CC," read by Hu Yao-pang, which confirmed the compromise decisions on the reevaluation of Mao and also the decisions on economic problems that had been made at the Central Work Conference in December 1980.[158] On September 6, a second plenary meeting of the congress was held, and addresses were given by Yeh Chien-ying and Ch'en Yün, and the final vote on the new Party statute was taken.[159] In his speech, old Marshall Yeh praised the rejuvenation of the CC and declared that he himself had "several times expressed the wish to retire." Yet until the CC decided that he could retire, he would "concentrate all my strength and sacrifice my life for the Party," thus indicating that he was going to stay in the inner leadership core.

Ch'en Yün was much more outspoken concerning the task of rejuvenation. If this task were not solved now, he stated, "the cause of communism in our country will suffer setbacks." In order to avoid such a development, thousands of younger cadres should be promoted into leading positions on all levels "so that they may take over from the old comrades at a later date." But Ch'en set limits, too. Five categories of people, so he believed, "should never be promoted to leading positions."

> First, those who advanced in the "Cultural Revolution" by following the "gang-of-four" . . . ,
> second, those who are ridden with the spirit of factionalism,
> third, those who have beaten, smashed, and looted during the period of the "Cultural Revolution,"
> fourth, those who oppose the correct line of the Party's CC since its Third Plenum, and
> fifth, those who have gravely violated the laws and the discipline of the Party in economics and other sectors of the society.[160]

Thus, Ch'en wanted to exclude the cultural revolutionary generation of former Red Guards and, if possible, all those people who had advanced during the Cultural Revolution from the future ruling elite.

The orthodox Stalinists, however, managed to hold their own. In the final version of the new Party statute, age limits, average ages for positions in the leading organs of the Party, and limits on tenure in office were no longer mentioned. The CAC was established, but—contrary to the wishes of the revisionists—this body as well as the CDIC was clearly subordinate to the CC. The Politburo's Standing Committee remained in existence, and it became, for all practical purposes, the new collective leadership of the CCP while the Secretariat was responsible only for the daily work (*Jih-ch'ang kung'tso*) of the center "under the leadership of the Politburo and its Standing Committee."[161] The position of the chairman of the CC was abolished, the secretary general was to be responsible only for convoking the Politburo and its Standing Committee, and for "leading the work of the Secretariat." Finally, the statement that the times of "large-scale class struggle" were gone was not included in the statute.

The revisionist forces, therefore, had not been able to achieve the goals they had set themselves for the congress in terms of organizational reform. Yet they were slightly more successful when the congress, on September 10 and its closing day, September 11, elected the members and alternates of the new CC and the CAC and when, after a closing address given by Li Hsien-nien, the first plenum of the Twelfth CC assembled on September 12 and 13 to appoint the members of the Politburo and its Standing Committee.[162]

Of the 200 members of the Eleventh CC who were still alive on the eve of the Twelfth Congress, 97, or 48.5 percent, were reappointed to the Twelfth CC; 65, or 32.5 percent, were transferred to the CAC; and

38, or 19 percent, disappeared or were demoted to alternate CC status. Of the 210 new full members of the Twelfth CC, 98, or 46.7 percent, were entirely new, the 97 holdovers from the Eleventh CC made up 46.2 percent of the new body, and 15, or 7.1 percent, of the newly appointed full members had been alternates to the Eleventh CC.

For the first time since the Cultural Revolution, former purgees achieved a majority on the CC. Their number rose from 78 to 111, a share of 52.9 percent—an increase of the share by 36.3 percent as opposed to 1977. The number of survivors of the Cultural Revolution decreased from 87 to 62, for a share of 29.5 percent—marking a decrease of their share of 31.9 percent—and the number of advancers during the Cultural Revolution was cut in half from 32 to 16, so that their share was now only 7.6 percent—a decrease of 52.2 percent as opposed to 1977. The cultural revolutionary experiences of 21, or 10 percent, of the Twelfth CC are as yet unknown.

Ch'en Yung-kuei was now officially removed from the Politburo, and so were Hua Kuo-feng—who was now only a regular full member of the CC—P'eng Ch'ung, Keng Piao—who was transferred to the Standing Committee of the CAC—and General Hsü Shih-yu—who became a vice-chairman of the CAC. The old and ailing Marshal Liu Po-ch'eng retired totally. Of the two remaining Politburo alternates, Saifudin was also removed, and Mme. Ch'en Mu'hua kept her position. Seven new members joined the central decision-making body, five of whom—Hsi Chung-hsün, Hu Ch'iao-mu, Liao Ch'eng-chih, Wan Li, and Yang Shang-k'un—can be considered as belonging to the revisionist group, and two—Sung Jen-ch'iung and General Yang Te-chih—should rather be counted as centrists. The two newly appointed Politburo alternates, General Ch'in Chi-wei and Yao Yi-lin, are staunch supporters of Teng Hsiao-p'ing and seem to belong to the revisionist group, if one goes by their previous record.

The inner leadership core, the Standing Committee of the Politburo, remained unchanged except for the final removal of Hua Kuo-feng. On this committee, Teng Hsiao-p'ing and Chao Tzu-yang represent the revisionists; Hu Yao-pang and Ch'en Yün, the centrists; and Yeh Chien-ying and Li Hsien-nien, the orthodox Stalinists. Furthermore, Teng became chairman of the CAC and kept his position as chairman of the Military Commission.

The rejuvenation of the central leadership, however, had more or less failed. Although the average age of the full members of the CC, 64.4 years, was slightly lower than that of the Eleventh CC at the time of its appointment in August 1977, when the average was 64.6 years, the full members of the Politburo had an average age of 73.1 years as opposed to 71.6 on the eve of the congress, and the average age of the

Standing Committee, because of the removal of Hua, had risen from 72.6 to 74.5 years. A certain rejuvenation had taken place in the Secretariat, though, as its average age decreased from 68.9 to 66.6 years, or even 64.2 years if the two alternate members are included.

The attempt to rejuvenate the ruling elite was somewhat more successful in the thoroughgoing restructuring of the provincial Party leadership that was enacted between February and April 1983. It resulted in the appointment of new Party leaders in ten out of the twenty-nine administrative units and in a reduction of the number of full and alternate PPC secretaries from 283 to 147. By these measures, the average age of the first PPC secretaries was lowered from 68.5 to 65.6 years.

The decisions of the first plenary session of the Sixth NPC, which convened in the capital June 6–21, 1983, not only reestablished the position of an individual chief of state—which had been abolished officially in 1975—but it also resulted in further changes on the State Council. The number of vice-premiers was again increased to four, and the overall membership of that body rose from forty-nine to fifty-two. As a result, the average age of the ministers and other members of the State Council decreased from 64.9 to 63.7 years. This was not the case, however, with the newly established Central Military Commission of the state, the nine members of which, under the chairmanship of Teng Hsiao-p'ing, had an average age of slightly more than 77 years.

Policies of Enlightened Stalinism

With this account of the Twelfth Party Congress, the discussion of the political developments in the PRC since early 1975 comes to an end. The ensuing changes in the provincial Party leadership and the new PRC constitution, which was accepted by the fifth plenum of the Fifth NPC on December 4, 1982, together with the personnel decisions made by the first plenary session of the Sixth NPC in June 1983, have been presented in Part 2 of this book.[163] It is still too early to develop a reliable account of the developments that preceded and influenced the relevant decisions, so I therefore restrict myself, at this point, to a very brief overview of the lineup of political forces in the major central decision-making organs, as they presented themselves in the summer of 1983, and to an attempt to describe the major domestic policies enacted by the current CCP leadership.[164]

After the deaths of the secretary of the Secretariat, General Yang Yung, on January 6, 1983, and the Politburo member Liao Ch'eng-chih, on June 9, 1983,[165] the configuration of the major opinion groups seems to be as follows.

- The revisionists are represented by nine to ten full members and two alternates of the Politburo and by five out of nine members and probably one alternate of the Secretariat. On the Central Military Commission, they hold three out of nine seats.
- The centrists are represented by five to six full members and one alternate of the Politburo and by three members and one alternate of the Secretariat. Two of the members of the Central Military Commission can be counted with this group.
- The orthodox Stalinists are represented by eight or nine members of the Politburo and by four members of the Central Military Commission, but by only one member of the Secretariat.

In this context, it should also be pointed out that a new *t'ung-hang* structural group has appeared in the political decision-making bodies of the PRC: the former subordinates of Hu Yao-pang in the CYL during the time of his leadership of that mass organization between 1957 and 1966. Among the full members of the Twelfth CC, between twenty-five and thirty have a CYL background, including the new minister of foreign affairs, the new chairman of the State Council's Sports Commission, the new mayors of Peking and T'ienchien, the new director of the Foreign Liaison Department of the CC, and the new director of the General Office of the CC, to name only a few. This group will have to be closely observed during the years to come, because its influence on the Chinese political scene may well increase.

For the time being, the political compromise between revisionists, centrists, and orthodox Stalinists continues. All three of these groups seem to still agree that an intraelite conflict of the style and intensity that characterized the Cultural Revolution, the Lin Piao crisis, and the crisis over personal succession should not happen again as long as their leading figures—the members of the Politburo's Standing Committee—are alive. This could be the major consideration that has dominated their willingness to reach compromise solutions for all major policy problems since 1980, if not since March 1979. And for such compromise solutions, two possible coalitions are available.

1. A revisionist-oriented coalition in the field of economic policies and in the field of rural societal policies
2. An orthodox-oriented coalition in the area of policies regarding intellectuals and political dissent and in questions of Party discipline

The result of the compromise between these groups and between the opposing coalitions—among which the centrists hold the balance—can best be described as policies of "enlightened Stalinism." Yet if we use this term, we should be aware of its semantic meaning: "Stalinism" is the noun, and "enlightened," the adjective—in other words, the Stalinist or Bolshevik policy elements provide the basis, and the elements of enlightenment are supplementary.

These elements of enlightenment, or—if one wants to so describe it—the contribution of the revisionist group to current policies in the PRC, fall into five major areas.

1. The new rural societal policies, meaning a definite departure from traditional socialist prescriptions, although the new policies are limited to a decollectivization of production while the collective ownership of land is formally upheld
2. The continuing decentralization of industrial management and the introduction of free markets in the cities
3. The limited and controlled widening of the parameters for private initiative and small private enterprise, albeit within the framework of a planned economy
4. The attempts to establish a system of "socialist legality" by the promulgation of civil and criminal codes as well as regulations on civil and criminal court procedures in the summer of 1979, which have prompted an incipient, although still slow, development of a legal profession
5. The stress on factual knowledge and performance in education, which has led to a strengthening of the social position of intellectuals, in particular of the technological and scientific intelligentsia.

These elements, however, are limited and channeled by the continuing policies of Stalinism, i.e., policies that were originally developed in the USSR during the 1930s and 1940s. Here again, five points need to be mentioned.

1. The primary role for planning in economic policies, which is clearly expounded in the often-repeated statement that "the planned economy is the main factor, and the market economy auxiliary" (*Chi-hua ching-chi wei chu, shih-ch'ang ching-chi wei fu*)
2. The rather narrow limitations on private economic initiatives and the stress on socialism as the main factor in the economic system
3. The strict discipline to which literature and art are again subjected, combined with the persecution of all political and intellectual dissent
4. The continuing stress on Party discipline and on the indoctrination of the Party members as well as the masses with the ideas of

"Marxism-Leninism and the Thought of Mao Tse-tung" (the latter in its redefined meaning)

5. The insistence on the Four Basic Principles as the one and only guideline for all political and social action, among which the leadership by the CCP as the very essence of the political system appears to be the most important

None of these elements of enlightenment and Stalinism, however, can be called "Maoist" in the sense of the policy prescriptions and concepts developed by Mao Tse-tung after 1958. Although the attempts to stage a full critical evaluation of Mao's personal role failed in 1980/ 1981, and one, hence, cannot speak of person-related de-Maoization, the de-Maoization of policies enacted since the spring of 1978 has been almost complete.

The PRC in 1983 is no longer "Mao's China," but it is still a Marxist-Leninist one-party dictatorship, and even more so today than between 1978 and 1980. But has this totalistic one-party system already entered into the stage of institutionalized rule? Some of the developments brought about by the Twelfth Party Congress, and in the context of the Sixth NPC, could suggest that it has. But in spite of recognizable initial moves, the facts that not one single major decision-making body or leadership group has an average age below sixty years and the major centers of decision still have averages of over seventy mean that the problem of generational succession remains basically unsolved. And as long as this problem is not solved, the stage of transitional rule will continue, and future perspectives will be by no means unilinear but must be assessed in a differentiated way, presenting a number of alternative projections.

PART 4

Economics, the Society, and Political Perspectives, 1975–1983

CHAPTER 12

Economic Developments

A Political Recession, 1976/1977

As we saw in Parts 1 and 3, the concepts for economic development came under dispute during 1975.[1] Although actual economic decisions had been mainly directed by the concept of readjustment since the fall of Lin Piao in 1971, the cultural revolutionary Left, with the support of Mao himself, continued to press for a return to the Maoist developmental concept, at first during a campaign to criticize Lin Piao and Confucius in 1973/1974 and then, even more vigorously, after the spring and summer of 1975.

In August 1975, Teng Hsiao-p'ing, then substituting for the ailing Chou En-lai in the leadership of the state administrative machine, very clearly stated the major thrust of the developmental efforts under the readjustment concept by stressing that agriculture was to be the basis of the economy, while industry had to serve agriculture; that new technologies and new machinery had to be acquired by an expansion of foreign trade; that scientific research had to be strengthened in all enterprises; that order and responsibility had to be regained in the industries; and that distribution according to labor as well as material incentives should be considered as the basic principle of remuneration.[2] Such guidelines provoked the opposition of the Left within the CCP leadership, which, after the second purge of Teng in April 1976, once again tried to push the country on the road of development through mobilization, class struggle, and enthusiastic austerity.

At the same time, however, the majority of the provincial Party leaders tried to continue with the policies of the readjustment concept, sometimes neglecting, sometimes paying at least lip service to the mobilization initiatives that came out of the capital. Under these circumstances, the guidelines for the economy became ever more ambiguous. Moreover, leftist attempts to introduce an equalization of wages resulted in strong opposition from large parts of the industrial labor force, particularly from the better-paid skilled workers.

Fights between local factions became rampant in the factories, and working discipline, already shattered during the Cultural Revolution, broke down in many cities, so that a considerable number of industrial enterprises experienced absenteeism, go-slow strikes, and even the sabotage of equipment and transport facilities. This situation became aggravated during the winter of 1976/1977, when fights between supporters of the military-bureaucratic complex and those of the cultural revolutionary Left crippled industrial production in numerous places.[3]

Conflicting economic policies combined with labor unrest and a widespread breakdown of responsibility during the succession crisis produced a severe economic recession, a recession that was mainly politically motivated during most of 1976 and well into the spring of 1977. In his "Report of the Work of the Government" to the first session of the Fifth NPC on February 26, 1978, Hua Kuo-feng stated candidly: As a result of their [the so-called gang of four's] interference and sabotage, between 1974 and 1976, the nation lost about 100 billion yüan in gross value of industrial output, twenty-eight million tons of steel, and forty billion yüan of state revenues, and the whole economy was on the brink of collapse.[4] And indeed, the economic data for 1976 were discouraging. Although the official evaluation in early 1977 still spoke about "great strides of the economy" and an "overall favorable situation,"[5] the elite admitted only ten months later that, e.g., "the production of steel and non-ferrous metals, from 1974 to 1976, remained far below all expectations."[6]

There had been no growth of the GNP at all in 1976. In constant prices, it stood at the same amount as in 1975, which meant a per capita decline of the GNP by almost 1.4 percent. The production of coal grew only by 1 million tons, or 0.2 percent; that of electric energy, by less than 3.7 percent; and that of cement, by 6.1 percent. At the same time, the steel output decreased from 23.9 million tons in 1975 to 20.46 million tons in 1976, 14.4 percent; that of motor vehicles, by 3.4 percent; and that of sugar, by 0.9 percent while the production of chemical fertilizer, machine tools, paper, and a number of consumer goods showed only minimal or no increase at all.[7] The situation was further aggravated by the fact that owing to comparatively unfavorable— though not catastrophic—weather conditions in 1976, the grain production rose only by 0.4 percent over that of 1975,[8] which meant, given a population growth rate of 1.4 percent—an extremely conservative estimate—that the per capita grain production decreased from 309.9 kilograms to 306.7 kilograms, about 1 percent.

For a nation with an advanced industrialized economy, such figures would not be too alarming, if they just appeared once. But for an underdeveloped country like the PRC, they indicated a rather severe crisis, which had to be overcome as soon as possible if the development of the national economy were to advance again.

The new leadership of the CCP, which had seized control in the autumn of 1976—headed by Hua Kuo-feng, and in the realm of economics mainly represented by Li Hsien-nien and General Yü Ch'iu-li—succeeded in overcoming the recession during 1977. Between February and July of that year, industrial discipline was enforced in most enterprises, the transportation network was put into operation again, and thus, the existing capacities could be fully utilized during the second half of 1977. The results were convincing. In 1977, the GNP grew by 8.2 percent over 1976, mainly because of a 14.3 percent growth in industrial production. Agriculture, on the other hand, still continued to decline: The output of grain decreased from 286 million tons to 283 million tons, about 1 percent, which meant a per capita decrease of grain production from 306.7 kilograms to 299.4 kilograms, 2.4 percent. The impact of this decline, however, could be partially alleviated by an increase in grain imports from 2 million to 7 million tons, which contributed to an increase in the 1977 foreign trade turnover of 10.1 percent over 1976.

In late 1977, the CCP leadership could thus reasonably assume that the foundation for a new developmental thrust had at least quantitatively been created, and the leaders now prepared for such a thrust with a new concept. This new direction combined elements of the Stalinist concept of the 1950s with a desire for large-scale imports of Western technology.

Heyday of the Deficit Spenders:
The Great Leap Westward, 1978/1979

The new guidelines for economic development, which were promoted by the Hua-Li-Yü triumvirate but also, at least throughout 1978, supported by Teng Hsiao-p'ing and a number of his associates, in fact meant the introduction of a new concept of development to the PRC, the fourth to be followed since 1953. I propose to call it "the first modernization concept." The final goal of this concept was proclaimed by Hua Kuo-feng in his report to the first session of the Fifth NPC in February 1978: It was the achievement of the four modernizations—i.e., the overall modernization of agriculture, industry, national defense, and science and technology—so that the PRC would have been transformed by the year 2000 into a "modern, socialist, industrial great power" that would be able to "compete with the most advanced nations of the world."[9] As a general objective, the CCP media, in the spring of 1978, stated that the country should reach a per capita GNP of at least U.S. $2,000 by 2000 and that this figure would be achieved by a new Great Leap, which occasionally was even called a "flying leap" (*fei yüeh*).[10]

The new developmental concept with which these ambitious goals were to be reached can be characterized by four major principles.

1. In the order of developmental priorities, basic and heavy industries were to rank first, agriculture second, and light and consumer goods industries third.
2. Economic development should be strictly and centrally planned, and the plans would be as Yü Ch'iu-li put it in late 1977, "more comprehensive than before, and absolutely mandatory."[11]
3. The major motivation for developmental efforts should come from a strict application of highly differentiated wage scales and material incentives.
4. Capital investments should not be limited by the availability of state funds, and in order to promote a speedy modernization, the state should be willing to risk deficits and to accept domestic as well as foreign loans.

As we saw in Chapter 9,[12] Hua Kuo-feng set the targets for the initial stage of the new modernization drive rather high: an agricultural growth rate of 4–5 percent per year, industrial growth rates of more than 10 percent, an overall GNP growth of at least 8 percent annually, and a reduction of the population growth rate to less than 1 percent until 1985.

The PRC seemed to be at the threshold of almost unlimited growth. Hundreds of industrial projects were started or at least planned for during 1978, capital investments in the field of heavy industry increased rapidly, and Hua set the tune for the new Great Leap by using Maoist terminology to support a concept of development that, in fact, showed distinct Stalinist features.

The advanced industrialized nations of the West were to provide the technology for the PRC's modernization drive as the new leap was to be based upon a wide opening of the country to technology imports. Hence, the concept of 1978 was soon ironically called the Great Leap Westward (*Yang-yao-chin*) by some people in the PRC.[13] All through 1978 and well into 1979, even cool and hard-nosed European, U.S., and Japanese businessmen got starry looks in their eyes when talking about the almost unlimited opportunities of "the China market"— dreams that were reinforced by PRC delegations that started to swarm into Western Europe, the United States, and Japan in order to window-shop for modern technology.

During the first fifteen months after the proclamation of the first modernization concept by Hua at the first session of the Fifth NPC, the auspices appeared promising indeed. In 1978 and 1979, the PRC concluded trade agreements with Japan, the United States, and the European Community,[14] and by September 1978, more than 2,000 Chinese industrial enterprises had acquired hard-currency credits for the purchase of raw materials and technology in the West.[15] At the end of 1978, large-scale projects that were discussed with or initiated with the assistance of Western nations had reached an amount of U.S. $50 billion, and during 1979, government credit agreements were signed by the Bank of China with Great Britain, France, the Federal Republic of Germany, Italy, Sweden, Canada, and Japan.[16] The PRC had embarked on a large-scale attempt to secure the most modern technology for its modernization effort as quickly as possible.

The initial results of the Great Leap Westward appeared quite convincing, particularly in the realm of industry. In 1978, the GNP rose again, this time by 12.4 percent, and the foreign trade turnover increased by 39.5 percent. Industrial production grew by 13.5 percent, with very remarkable increases of 12.4 percent for coal, 14.8 percent for electric energy, a staggering 33.9 percent for steel, and 17.2 percent for cement. It seemed as if the first modernization concept was heading for success.

Yet, although the output of basic and heavy industries increased by 15.8 percent in 1978, light and consumer goods industries lagged somewhat behind with a growth rate of 10.8 percent. And although the grain production increased by 7.8 percent, or 6.3 percent per capita, more than 8.4 million tons of grain had to be imported.[17] Moreover, it soon became apparent that the increases in industrial output were merely quantitative. The quality of industrial products did not improve, and waste as well as unnecessary production rapidly became a widespread feature of an economic policy that followed a "ton ideology"—an emphasis on quantity rather than on quality. Furthermore, the gains in industrial production helped to increase the gap between the rural and the urban standards of living.

Most important, however, was the fact that the state ran into increasing debts and budgetary difficulties. In 1977, state revenues had amounted to JMP $87.45 billion and expenditures were JMP $84.35, for a revenue surplus of 3.5 percent, and in 1978, with revenues of JMP $112.11 billion and expenditures of JMP $111.10 billion, the revenue surplus had been 0.9 percent. But in 1979, when the ambitious plans of early 1978 fully influenced the state budget, revenues of JMP $110.3 billion stood against expenditures of JMP $127.4 billion, so that the deficit had reached JMP

$17.1 billion, or 15.5 percent of the revenue, the highest deficit ever encountered in the history of the PRC.[18] Foreign trade, too, had developed a deficit that amounted to U.S. $1,079 million in 1978—higher than the accumulated deficits of 1973, 1974, and 1975 (earlier deficit years were only 1951–1955, 1960, and 1970)—and in 1979, the deficit reached U.S. $2 billion, or 14.7 percent of the exports.

Thus, the implementation of the first modernization concept had rapidly created a quite severe financial crisis, which could be expected to become aggravated if the prescriptions of this concept were to be further followed without revisions. As elsewhere in the world, this crisis became the hour of "the fiscalists." Led by Ch'en Yün, Wan Li, and Yao Yi-lin, they started in May and June of 1979 to work for retrenchments in the ambitious plans of 1978, and during 1980, they increasingly advocated the implementation of yet another concept of development, under which the dreams of 1978 died away.

Incipient Retrenchment, 1979/1980

During 1979 and 1980, a number of personnel decisions in the realm of economic planning and management heralded the beginning of a move away from the high-flying plans and objectives proposed by Hua Kuo-feng and promoted by Li Hsien-nien, Yü Ch'iu-li, and other members of the petroleum clique[19] in 1978. Most important of these decisions was the establishment of a State Financial and Economic Commission (*Kuo-chia ts'ai-cheng ching-chi wei-yüan-hui*) as a supreme economic policymaking and coordinating body on July 1, 1979.[20] All thirteen members of this new organ were full members of the CC, and five of them were members of the Politburo. The position of chairman went to Ch'en Yün, who thus became the major leader on the PRC economic scene, replacing Li Hsien-nien in this position, who was only appointed vice chairman of the commission. Another critic of the first modernization concept and a close associate of Teng Hsiao-p'ing, Yao Yi-lin, took over the post of secretary general. Only three or four members of the commission could be counted as supporters of the Ten-Year Plan, which Hua had announced in February 1978, while nine were advocates of a slower, more balanced, and more controlled economic development— step by step—and opponents of the rhetoric of a new Great Leap.

The concurrent appointments of Ch'en Yün, Yao Yi-lin, and Po I-po as vice-premiers, announced on July 2, 1979, further strengthened the hand of those economic leaders who criticized deficit spending and increasingly advocated a turn toward fiscalist policies centering on a balanced state budget and a revision of developmental priorities.

The core group of these fiscalists now set out to squeeze the deficit spenders around Li Hsien-nien and Yü Ch'iu-li out of positions of responsibility for economic development. In February 1980, Po I-po was appointed chairman of a State Commission for Machine Building Industries, which was set up to coordinate the work of the nine ministries that were in charge of different sectors of machinery production, and on April 16, 1980, Chao Tzu-yang and Wan Li were made vice-premiers. As a result, five fiscalists opposed four deficit spenders in the inner cabinet. In August 1980, Yü Ch'iu-li was transferred from the chairmanship of the State Planning Commission to the much less influential chairmanship of a new State Energy Commission. Yao Yi-lin took over the leadership of the State Planning Commission, and at the same time, Wan Li was appointed chairman of the State Agricultural Commission. Finally, the triumph of the fiscalists was completed with the transfer of K'ang Shih-en from the chairmanship of the State Economic Commission to the Ministry of Petroleum Industry and the appointment of Yüan Pao-hua as chairman of the Economic Commission in March 1981.

In the spring of 1979, Ch'en Yün and his associates started to work for a drastic retrenchment of the plans of 1978, and they were soon able to score their first successes. As early as March, the CCP media began to speak about the necessity of introducing a period of "three years of consolidation" before the country could go ahead with more rapid modernization, and it was also indicated that a new order of developmental priorities was in the making.[21]

The move away from the new Great Leap that Hua had proclaimed in 1978 began in earnest with a Central Work Conference of the CC in April 1979, when, for the first time, the slogan of the four modernizations was supplemented by a new slogan, which was later to become more and more a substitute instead—the Eight-Ideograph Directive, named after the eight Chinese ideographs for four terms that now started to dominate economic policies: readjustment (t'iao-cheng), reform (kai-ke), correction (cheng-tun), and improvement (t'i-kao). The conference decided to postpone more than 100 development projects, mainly in heavy industry, that had been started in 1978.[22]

This tendency continued with drastic cuts in the Ten-Year Plan, which were announced at the second session of the Fifth NPC, convening in Peking from June 18 through July 1.[23] In his report on the work of the government, Hua Kuo-feng admitted that the growth of agricultural production was not keeping pace with that of industry, and hardly even with the growth of the population. The premier deplored that light and consumer goods industries were lagging behind, not able to overcome shortages, and producing goods of poor quality. Hence, a reorientation of investment priorities seemed to be necessary,[24] and it was immediately initiated by further cuts in the area of new heavy industrial development projects. More than 300 of them were now either postponed or entirely canceled. Through 1979, it was ordered that a total of 561 projects, mostly in basic and heavy industries, be stopped or delayed, and implementation of 330 of them really ceased.[25]

After these initial steps toward retrenchment by moving away from the rhetoric of the Great Leap, the economic performance of the PRC in 1980 was ambiguous. The real growth rate of the GNP, which had stood at 7.0 percent in 1979, declined to 5.2 percent,[26] but industrial growth remained comparatively high at 8.7 percent. The growth rate of basic and heavy industrial production, however, declined from almost 7.6 percent in 1979 to a little more than 1.3 percent in 1980 while the production of the light and consumer goods industries grew by 17.9 percent as opposed to 9.5 percent in 1979. Agriculture displayed a particularly poor performance, with the production of grain decreasing by 3.3 percent, which meant a decline in per capita grain production from 341.9 kilograms to 326.2 kilograms, i.e., a decline of 4.6 percent.

Yet the most severe threats to economic development arose from inflation and the continuing deficit of the state budget. In November 1979, the State Council had unfrozen the prices of more than 10,000 items of consumer goods, a move that, on the one hand, resulted in a sharp decrease of commercial activities but, on the other hand, spurred inflation, which, in 1980, according to official data, reached 11 percent for retail trade and 13.8 percent for food.[27]

After the large deficit of JMP $17.1 billion in 1979, state revenues continued to decline in 1980, this time by JMP $1.81 billion, so that, in spite of expenditure reductions of 4.8 percent as compared with 1979, the 1980 deficit still amounted to JMP $12.75 billion,[28] or 11.75 percent of revenue. Within two years, the policies of the deficit spenders and the aftereffects of those policies had thus resulted in an accumulated deficit of JMP $29.85 billion, the equivalent of more than U.S. $19.6 billion at the exchange rates of those years.

Faced with such figures, the fiscalists acted in late 1980 to implement more drastic changes in the developmental concept, which were characterized by a thoroughgoing reorientation of development priorities, further retrenchments in major investment projects, and across-the-board thrift. The new watershed of economic development was reached with the fall of Chairman Hua.

The Fiscalist Reaction, December 1980:
A New Shift of Line

Immediately after the removal of Hua had been decided upon by the Politburo on December 5, 1980,[29] the Central Work Conference was

Table 12.1.   Foreign trade of the PRC, 1975-1982 (billion U.S. $)[35]

Year	Turnover	Export	Import	Balance
1975	14.75	7.26	7.49	- 0.23
1976	13.44	6.86	6.58	+ 0.28
1977	14.80	7.59	7.21	+ 0.38
1978	20.64	9.75	10.89	- 1.14
1979	29.33	13.66	15.67	- 2.01
1980	37.82	18.27	19.55	- 1.28
1981	42.02	20.01	22.01	- 2.00
1982	40.09	22.14	17.95	+ 4.19
1983	43.44	22.14	21.30	+ 0.84

dominated by the fiscalists in general and by Ch'en Yün in particular, the latter pleading for a readjustment based on a policy of "standing solidly with both feet on the ground, and advancing in balanced steps."[30] Details of the policy changes were announced by Chao Tzu-yang. Investments in basic and heavy industries were reduced from JMP $24.1 billion in 1980 to JMP $17 billion in 1981, and those in shipping and communication facilities as well as transportation were reduced from JMP $50 billion to JMP $30 billion.[31] On December 7, the State Council had ordered a freeze on the price of all goods unfrozen in 1979[32] as a way of controlling inflation, and soon after the December 1980 work conference, deep budget cuts were introduced—expenditures in 1981 were 10.14 percent below those in 1980. With the help of these cuts, the 1981 deficit was reduced to JMP $2.54 billion, or 2.4 percent of revenue, and it remained in that range—JMP $3 billion each, or 2.71 and 2.44 percent of revenue respectively—for the budgets of 1982 and 1983.[33]

The first and foremost victims of the new emphasis on more thrift were some of the large heavy-industrial projects that had been greeted with great enthusiasm by business circles in Japan and Western Europe. In January 1981, seventeen large-scale projects, for some of which contracts had already been concluded with foreign firms, were canceled or postponed indefinitely, including the Paoshan steel complex near Shanghai; the petrochemical complexes in Nanking, Yenshan (Peking), and Shengli (Shantung); and the Tungfang chemical works in Peking. Japanese firms alone lost U.S. $1,541,400,000 in contracts—of which equipment worth U.S. $640,000,000 had already been delivered—and West German firms lost at least U.S. $919,000,000. All the cancellations and postponements affected contracts to the tune of U.S. $7 billion to $9 billion.[34]

By 1982, the new policies of thrift had started to affect the PRC's foreign trade, which had been expanding since 1978, as Table 12.1 indicates. A reduction in imports of 18.4 percent in 1982 compared with

1981 was the reason for the 4.6 percent decline of overall foreign trade in 1982.

But the cuts and retrenchments were only the beginning for a major change in the concept for development. When the trends that had evolved slowly since the spring of 1979, and had been put into full operation since the end of 1980, had taken their definite shape, another new developmental concept was dictating economic policies in the PRC. I propose to call it "the second modernization concept," and since it greatly varies from the first one, it can be considered the fifth concept to have been applied in the PRC since 1953. This new concept of development is characterized by five significant features.

1. In the order of developmental priorities, light and consumer goods industries rank first—for the first time in the history of the PRC— agriculture ranks second, and basic and heavy industries third.
2. Economic planning remains centralized, there is centralized management in basic industries but large experimental areas of decentralization on the level of the individual factory in manufacturing and light industries, and there is decentralized management of agriculture on the village level.
3. Material incentives and a highly differentiated wage scale are still the major motivating forces for developmental efforts, but they are supplemented by a limited and controlled acceptance of private initiative, particularly in agriculture and in the service sector.
4. The import of technology from the advanced industrial countries continues, but in a selective and controlled manner.
5. Budgetary policies are dictated by strict fiscalism, which has reduced deficits and is geared to eliminate them entirely.

Besides the new order of developmental priorities and strict fiscalism, the expansion of the decision-making powers of individual enterprises within the framework of centralized planning is the most essential part of the new concept. In the villages, such expansion has led to the introduction of the "responsibility system for agricultural production," which I shall discuss later.[36] In the realm of industry, first experiments with granting greater autonomy to the factories were started by Chao Tzu-yang in Ssuch'uan in October 1978. Six industrial enterprises were allowed to experiment with what was soon to be called "the eight rights": the right to retain part of the profits, the right to expand production with funds that the enterprise itself had accumulated, the right to retain 60 percent instead of 40 percent of the depreciation fund for fixed assets, the right to engage in production outside the state plan, the right of the enterprise to engage in the marketing of its products, the right to contract with foreign governments and firms to export its products, the right to issue bonuses to workers at the enterprise's own discretion, and the right to fire workers who neglected their work.[37]

In the spring of 1979, such experiments with greater enterprise autonomy were expanded into other areas of the country, and by the end of that year, the number of experimental plants had risen to 2,600. At the end of 1980, 6,600 factories out of 85,000 state-owned enterprises were experimenting with the eight rights, and they returned to the state JMP $29 billion in profits, which meant—according to official figures— almost 70 percent of all profits from state enterprises.[38] In 1982, the central authorities decided to grant similar autonomy to most industrial plants and to replace the turnover of profits to the state with a tax on the corporate income of all enterprises with managerial autonomy.

Moreover, elements of a market economy were increasingly introduced into commerce and the services, albeit under the principle of "planned economy as the main factor, market economy as a supplement" (*Chihua ching-shi wei chu, shih-ch'ang ching-chi wei fu*), which none other than the orthodox Stalinist Li Hsien-nien had proclaimed in January 1982.[39] In this context, private enterprises were again allowed to operate in the cities after late 1979, mainly in the services—such as small restaurants, barbershops, photographers, and street vendors—and in the sector of repair shops. In late 1981, the number of people working in such private small enterprises stood at 1.13 million,[40] and by late 1983, it had reached 7.36 million, or almost 7 percent of the urban work force.[41] In late 1982, there were in Shanghai alone 24,000 registered private enterprises, added to which there were at least 100,000 "unregistered, but openly tolerated" ones.[42]

Centralized planning, however, was by no means diminished under the second modernization concept. In December 1982, the goals of the Sixth Five-Year Plan, which covered the years from 1981 to 1985, were published.[43] This plan could be the first five-year plan since 1957 to have a fair chance for real implementation. The projections of the new plan appeared down-to-earth and quite realistic. It provided for an increase in the GNP from JMP $850 billion in 1980 to JMP $1,030 billion in 1985, i.e., by 21.2 percent, which means projected real growth rates of 4–5 percent per year. If these goals can be achieved, the per capita GNP of the PRC would reach about U.S $502 in 1985, which corresponds to the amount achieved in T'aiwan in 1965.

In 1981 and 1982, the new developmental concepts reaped impressive results. Although the GNP growth rate was rather small in 1981, 3 percent, it reached 7.4 percent in 1982. In 1981, the overall industrial production grew only by 4.1 percent, with a decline of 4.7 percent in heavy industry and an increase of 14.1 percent in light industry, but in 1982, the growth was more stabilized: 7.4 percent for industry as a whole, with 5.6 percent for light industry and 9.3 percent for heavy industry. The major success area in 1982, however, was agriculture, where, according to official CCP figures, a growth of 8.7 percent in grain production was achieved, after a growth of only 1.4 percent in 1981. Thus, the per capita grain production figure increased from 326.2 kilograms in 1981 to 348.2 kilograms in 1982, 6.7 percent.[44]

These figures look encouraging, and on their basis, we may project that the second modernization concept could turn out to be a reasonably successful one—if the CCP elite should decide to continue to implement the concept. But what about the overall economic performance in the thirty years from 1953 to 1982?

An Intermediate Economic Balance Sheet: 1953–1982

The three decades between the first year of the First Five-Year Plan, 1953, and the end of 1982 should be a long enough period to establish an intermediate balance sheet for the economic performance of the PRC under CCP rule. This performance has been most impressive in the realm of basic and heavy industries, not only until 1975 but during the period after the death of Mao as well, as the data presented in Table 12.2 show. Remarkable too, however, is the reduction in tractor and machine tools production since 1980, which is obviously due to changes in developmental priorities, which include the acceptance of importing higher-quality implements instead of manufacturing national products of insufficient quality. In the area of light and consumer goods industries, the performance was somewhat less dramatic, but there was a very impressive increase after 1980, again the result of a shift in developmental emphasis, as can be seen from Table 12.3.

In fact, the average annual growth rates of industrial production were somewhat lower in the period from 1976 to 1982 than in the twenty-three preceding years. Yet the emphasis changed drastically in favor of the light and consumer goods industries, as the data in Table 12.4 suggest. An average growth rate of 12.1 percent annually for a period of thirty years is indeed a reasonably good result. The PRC growth rate is not dramatically smaller than T'aiwan's 13.6 percent, yet it will take a number of more years of continuous growth to overcome the still rather remarkable gap between the growth of heavy industry and that of light industry.

In spite of the impressive results of 1982, overall agricultural production has continued to remain a severe problem since the death of Mao Tse-tung. The performance of the PRC, whether for the thirty-four years

Table 12.2. Production of basic and heavy industries in selected years
between 1953 and 1982[45]

Item[a]	1953	1975	1978	1980	1981	1982
Coal	69.68	482.0	618.0	620.0	622.0	666.0
Steel	1.774	23.9	31.78	37.12	35.6	37.16
Electricity						
(billion kwh)	9.20	195.8	256.6	300.6	309.3	327.7
Cement	3.88	46.26	65.24	79.86	84.0	95.2
Chemical						
Fertilizer	0.05	5.25	8.69	12.32	12.39	12.78
Tractors						
(1,000 units)		78.4	113.5	97.7	52.8	42.5
Machine tools						
(1,000 units)	20.5	174.9	183.2	134.0	103.0	100.5

[a]If not otherwise stated, in million tons.

Table 12.3. Production of light and consumer goods industries in
selected years between 1953 and 1982[46]

Item[a]	1953	1975	1978	1980	1981	1982
Cotton						
cloth						
(billion m)	4.685	9.4	11.03	13.47	14.27	15.12
Sugar						
(million t)	0.638	1.74	2.27	2.57	3.17	3.33
Paper						
(million t)	0.428	3.41	4.387	5.35	5.40	5.698
Radio						
receivers	25.0	9,356.0	11,677.0	30,038.0	40,572.0	17,036.0
TV sets						
Bicycles	165.0	6,232.0	8,540.0	13,024.0	17,540.0	25,133.0
Cameras			178.9	272.8	623.0	742.0
Sewing						
machines			4,865.0	7,678.0	10,390.0	12,793.0
Wrist-						
watches			13,511.0	22,155.0	28,780.0	33,243.0

[a]Unless otherwise stated, in 1,000 units.

Table 12.4. Average annual growth rates of industrial production
(in percent)[47]

Sector	1953-1975	1976-1979	1980-1982	1953-1982
Heavy industry	17.3	9.55	1.97	14.7
Light industry	10.2	9.25	12.5	10.3
Overall industrial				
production	13.3	9.4	6.7	12.1

Table 12.5. Development of agricultural production, 1949-1982[48]

Year	Food Grain Production (in million t)	Population (in millions)	Per capita Production (in kg)	Per capita Production Comparison in percent with 1931-1937	1949
1931-1937 average	171.00	485.00	352.6		
1949	150.00	540.00	277.8	-21.2	
1975	285.00	919.70	309.9	-12.2	+11.5
1978	304.75	958.09	317.8	- 9.9	+14.4
1980	320.52	982.55	326.2	- 7.5	+17.4
1981	325.02	996.22	326.2	- 7.5	+17.4
1982	353.43	1,015.00	348.2	- 1.2	+25.3
1983	387.28	1,025.00	377.8	+ 7.1	+36.0

Table 12.6. China's GNP and per capita GNP average annual growth rates, 1953-1982 (in percent)[51]

Period	Average Annual GNP Growth	Average Annual per capita GNP Growth
1953-1975	5.9	4.1
1976-1979	6.2	4.9
1980-1982	5.2	3.8
1953-1982	5.9	4.2

beginning in 1949 or for the seven years since 1975, has shown important limitations, although the great variations of earlier years seem to have subsided recently, as the data in Table 12.5 would indicate. The very good crop results of 1982 meant an increase in the per capita grain production of more than one-fourth over the last year of the civil war, but the status of the 1931–1937 per capita average had still not been reached again. That average was surpassed, for the first time since the establishment of the PRC, only in 1983, which means after half a century.

I shall turn to the problem of food in the PRC again later,[49] but at this point, I shall try to evaluate the overall economic performance of the PRC between 1953 and 1982, i.e., over thirty years, and to make some projections for the future prospects of the modernization program. Before the figures are presented, however, it is necessary to reiterate that it is difficult to obtain reliable data on the growth rates of the GNP before 1975.[50] The data in Table 12.6 again rely heavily on the work of Willy Kraus.

The average annual growth rates shown in the table were the result of remarkable fluctuations, which, although to a lesser degree, continued during the period after 1975, ranging between nil in 1976 and 12.4 percent in 1978. In only nine out of the thirty years were the growth rates in the range of normal variations for the PRC, between 4.4 and 7.4 percent; in twenty-one of the thirty years, the growth rate was either much higher or much lower than the average. After 1975, however, the growth rates remained within the regular variation range in four out of the seven years—1977, 1979, 1980, and 1982; those in 1976 and 1981 were much lower and that of 1978 was much higher than the average.

But how does this PRC performance compare with that of another Chinese society? In the thirty years from 1953 to 1982, the GNP of T'aiwan grew at an annual average of 8.7 percent, almost 47.5 percent more than that of the PRC, and T'aiwan's per capita GNP grew at an annual average of 6 percent, 42.9 percent more than in the PRC. Even during the period from 1976 to 1982—i.e., the post-Mao era—the average annual growth rate of T'aiwan's GNP was 8.7 percent as opposed to 5.7 percent in the PRC, and the average per capita GNP growth rate was 6.6 percent, or exactly 50 percent more than the PRC's 4.4 percent.

A comparison, however, should also be made with other East Asian and Southeast Asian countries. According to data available for the fifteen years from 1968 to 1982, the PRC's rather impressive GNP annual average growth rate of 6.9 percent was exactly as high as that of Thailand during the same period, higher than the Philippines' 5.6 percent, and lower than those of Singapore (10.8 percent), Malaysia and South Korea (7.8 percent), and Indonesia (7.5 percent). The overall average annual rate of growth in all of East Asia and Southeast Asia during this period was 7.2 percent, so the performance of the PRC must be evaluated as slightly below average in comparison with its Asian neighbors.[52]

I conclude this intermediate balance sheet with a question concerning the prospects for a successful conclusion of the PRC's modernization program adhered to by the current PRC ruling elite. Can the PRC be modernized within the foreseeable future? The answer to this question is first and foremost a matter of definition. When is a country "modernized"? i.e., under what circumstances can it, to again quote Hua Kuo-feng, "compete with the most advanced nations of the world"?

One possible answer to the question of definition could be derived from comparing the economies of an already modernized Chinese society and economy—i.e., that of the RoC on T'aiwan—and the PRC. In order to judge the differences between these two economics, Table 12.7 provides comparative data for the production of a number of industrial goods in the PRC and T'aiwan in 1983.

This comparison shows that the PRC still has a long way to go if the current state of T'aiwan's economy is used as an indicator for the achievement of the goal of modernization. This status could be achieved by the PRC—if it were to experience a long period of stability and sustained growth and if we make a comparatively optimistic estimate— at some time between 2025 and 2040, which also means that the PRC may be able to reach the current status of Japan toward the end of the next century.

Table 12.7. Relative production of industrial goods in the PRC and
T'aiwan, 1983[53]

Item	Unit	PRC	T'aiwan	PRC/T'aiwan Ratio
Coal	kg/person	697.5	119.4	5.84:1
Steel	kg/person	39.0	282.6	1:7.25
Electricity	kwh/person	342.8	2,429.8	1:7.09
Cement	kg/person	105.6	790.6	1:7.49
Chemical fertilizer	kg/hectare	131.3	1,607.3	1:12.24
Machine tools	persons/unit	8,452.0	20.7	1:412.66
Cotton	m/person	14.5	68.8	1:4.74
Sugar	kg/person	3.29	35.1	1:10.67
Paper	kg/person	6.4	24.9	1:3.89
Sewing machines	persons/ machine	94.3	7.1	1:13.28
TV sets	persons/set	150.0	3.6	1:41.67
Radio receivers	persons/set	51.27	2.21	1:23.20
Cameras	persons/item	1,107.0	7.94	1:139.42
Wristwatches	persons/item	29.55	1.12	1:26.38
Bicycles (PRC) Motorcycles (T'aiwan)	persons/unit	37.16	6.31	1:5.89

Yet by no means will the PRC achieve this definition of modernization
by the year 2000, a fact that is understood by the PRC elite. Even in
1979, the goal of achieving a per capita GNP of U.S. $2,000, proclaimed
in 1978, was abandoned. In January 1980, Teng Hsiao-p'ing still gave
a figure of U.S. $1,000, but that was readjusted again by Hu Yao-pang
in September 1982 when he projected that the PRC would reach the
goal of quadrupling its GNP by the year 2000 and achieving a per
capita GNP of U.S. $800. Hu's projections appear comparatively realistic.
If the PRC could, beginning in 1983, enter a period of a sustained GNP
growth of 6 percent per year, the result in 2000 would fall short of the
established overall GNP goal only by about 28 percent, and the projected
per capita GNP of U.S. $800 could indeed be achieved if there were a
sustained growth rate of the per capita GNP of 4.5 percent. Such an
achievement, however, would mean that by the year 2000, the PRC
would have arrived at the goal T'aiwan reached—in constant 1976
prices—in 1972, or twenty-eight years earlier. If these goals were reached,
the transition of the PRC to a modernized economy could begin. But
even such a modest achievement requires stability and order in the
society, and in this area, the PRC is still faced with severe problems.

CHAPTER 13

Social Developments and Problems

No Hunger in China?

For several hundred years, it has been a difficult task in China to secure adequate nutrition for the people, a problem that has been aggravated during the last three centuries by the fact that the area under agricultural cultivation has increased only one-fourth to one-fifth while the population has quadrupled. Thus, ever since the early nineteenth century, the country has time and again experienced regional famine. During the late 1870s, between 1907 and 1910, and also in the mid-1920s, such famines assumed nationwide proportions. But they were hardly an urban phenomenon—it was the peasants and not the city people who suffered from malnutrition and at times from even large-scale hunger.

Yet, with the exception of about eight to ten of the 150 years before 1949, such famines rarely hit the whole nation. In China, the problem of food supply was generally a problem of delivering grain from agricultural-surplus regions to agricultural-deficit regions in order to combat the regional famines that sprang up every few years, mainly in traditional problem areas. Such problem areas were the province of Kirin in Tungpei; southern Hopei; parts of Kiangsi; large parts of northwestern China, in particular Shensi and Kansu; and especially in Anhui and Kueichou. The situation improved remarkably during the 1930s, mostly because of the expansion of transport facilities and a stabilization of internal commerce. From 1935 until 1937—for the first time in more than 100 years—no provincewide famines were reported, although hunger still affected some regions within the traditionally undernourished provinces.

The twelve years of war from 1937 to 1949 again aggravated the food problem in the country, but its unification after the victory of the

CCP and the equalization of land ownership as a result of the land reform campaign during the early 1950s facilitated a remarkable improvement in the food exchanges between surplus and deficit regions. Under the impact of these improvements, which seem to have lasted—with some exceptions in 1955/1956—until the end of 1957, there developed in Western Europe and the United States the long-lasting myth that the CCP had managed to overcome its problems of malnutrition and famine. An almost never-ending file of occasional visitors to the PRC, from Simone de Beauvoir in 1958 to Dean Hewlett Johnson and Lord Montgomery in the early 1960s to Shirley Maclaine and John K. Galbraith in the early 1970s, insisted that there was "no hunger in China," and the world, in particular the world of the Western media, believed them. Even in 1972, the Australian writer Ross Terrill, writing about what he then perceived and presented as "the real China," stated that "the Chinese Revolution" had "in a magnificent way . . . fed the hungry."[54] "Chinese cuisine," so Terrill insisted, was "a daily joy to 800 million and *the* major factor in any calculation of bright and dark sides to the Chinese people's life in 1971."[55]

Yet beginning in the fall of 1959, ample evidence was available outside the PRC that China, from 1959 until the spring of 1962, was suffering from a nationwide famine of proportions that had not been reached since the late 1870s. During these "three bitter years," almost the whole country was affected by malnutrition, and starvation was by no means limited to the traditional problem areas. It occurred even in traditionally rich harvest regions, and it hit the cities, too. I have already indicated that official CCP sources, which hushed up the famine of the early 1960s for more than fifteen years, admitted in early 1981 that it had taken a toll of no fewer than 20 million lives.[56] Also in 1981, a study from Hunan revealed that although the average death rate for the years 1954 through 1958 was 1.19 percent, it rose to 1.45 percent in 1959, 2.54 percent in 1960, and 1.44 percent in 1961. The population increase rate, which had averaged 3.32 percent from 1954 through 1958, declined to 2.48 percent in 1959, 2.08 percent in 1960, and 1.81 percent in 1961, rising again to an average of 3.87 percent in 1962 through 1966. These figures would mean a death toll of at least 17.6 million during the three bitter years.[57] In fact, any figure between 15 million and 30 million deaths from starvation between 1959 and early 1962 would seem realistic.

Yet malnutrition and starvation were not restricted to the great national famine of those years. They continued—according to official CCP publications—all through the 1970s in the old problem areas of Anhui, Kueichou, Kirin, Kansu, and parts of Kiangsi as well as in parts of Kuangtung, Fukien, and even the traditionally rich province of Ssuch'uan.[58]

A decision passed by the third plenum of the Eleventh CC on December 22, 1978, admitted that "hundred and several tens of millions of people have not enough to eat" (*I yi chi ch'ien-wan jen liang-shih pu-tsu*),[59] and the pro-CCP Hongkong *Cheng-ming* stated in May 1979 that "200 million peasants suffer from hunger and are continuously undernourished."[60] The situation worsened during the winter of 1980/1981, when, according to a report by the United Nations Disaster Relief Organization (UNDRO), between 21 million and 23 million people in Hopei and Hupei were "on the brink of starvation," having existed on no more than 1,200 calories per day for more than a year.[61] In a very detailed and well-documented study, Rüdiger Machetzki arrived at the conclusion that in 1982, between 130 million and 150 million people lived in areas that had a food supply that was below the subsistence level.[62]

Since 1976, the CCP elite increasingly has tried to combat the problems of malnutrition with grain imports. Altogether, the PRC imported 155,484,000 tons of grain from 1961 to 1982 while it exported, during the same period, 31,538,000 tons, a net grain import of almost 124 million tons in twenty-two years, or an annual average of 5.6 million tons.[63] Still the problem of malnutrition has not yet been solved. Even in the agricultural surplus areas of the PRC, the supply of food is not abundant. A survey of 15,914 rural households, most of them in rather well-to-do regions, arrived at the following figures for food consumption per person per day: 1.55 pounds of grain, 12.2 ounces of vegetables, 0.24 ounce of edible oil, 0.75 ounce of meat, 0.1 ounce of fish, and 0.1 ounce of sugar, and one egg every twelve to fourteen days.[64]

From the data presented here, five conclusions can be drawn about the food supply in the PRC.

1. Although the difference between agricultural-surplus and agricultural-deficit areas decreased in the 1950s, the CCP elite has not been able to continue this trend since that time.
2. Under the CCP rule, the country experienced its most severe nationwide famine since the late 1870s, from 1959 to 1961.
3. Regional food supply crises and even starvation occurred again in at least 1974, 1976, 1978/1979, and 1981/1982.
4. Occasional famines and constant malnutrition were still affecting the traditional food problem areas in the early 1980s.
5. The notion that there has been and is no hunger in China under CCP rule is not supported by hard data and therefore cannot be sustained.

The current leaders of the PRC are aware of these facts. Since 1980, they have therefore embarked on policies that aim at an amelioration of the food supply situation through the widening of the parameters for private initiatives on the part of the individual peasant households, policies that have almost entirely eliminated collective production in agriculture. These policies have resulted in dramatic changes in the social conditions in the villages.

New Structures in the Countryside

The innovations that introduced social changes in the countryside began, on an experimental basis, in Ssuch'uan and Anhui under the leadership of Chao Tzu-yang and Wan Li, respectively. After the purge of the four major supporters of Hua Kuo-feng from the Politburo by the fifth plenum of the Eleventh CC on February 29, 1980, both Chao and Wan moved to the center to take up positions in the inner cabinet, and Wan was soon placed in charge of agriculture. These personnel developments precipitated the new turn in rural societal policies, which was first explained in a *JMJP* article on April 9, 1980.

All production teams were exhorted to establish a responsibility system for agricultural production (*Nung-yeh sheng-ch'an tse-jen-chih*). Under this system, the title deeds to land and the official ownership of large livestock, plow animals, and larger tools remain with the team, but the team can decide either to continue with collective production—and thus act as the major unit for production, accounting, and distribution—or to contract the means of agricultural production to working groups of between three and five families, and also to individual households. In the latter case, the production guarantee would be given by the household (*Pao-ch'an tao hu*). Thus, Teng Hsiao-p'ing's proposals of 1962, still refuted even by Chao and by Teng himself in the spring of 1979, were now acted upon.

Whenever the responsibility for production was contracted to the household—or in some cases, to individual persons—the family or person that signed the contract would guarantee to deliver a fixed amount of clearly defined products to the team, thus, in fact, becoming share-croppers. In such cases, the system of distribution according to work points (*Kung-fen*) became obsolete and was abolished, except for a small number of points for managerial work. Yet the *JMJP* article hastened to point out that the system of "responsibility to the household," or "to the individual person," would not mean "going it alone" (*Tan-kan*), or private ownership. The distinction, however, remained somewhat nebulous.

With the introduction of the responsibility system, the situation in the Chinese countryside diversified rapidly during the spring and summer of 1980, and a number of inconsistencies developed. In some areas, all of the arable land was divided among the individual peasant households, while in others, the local cadres took no action whatsoever to introduce the responsibility system. Practices in setting the amount of the *pao-ch'an* varied widely, and so did the powers that remained with the production team.

These developments made it necessary for the central authorities to formulate guidelines governing the introduction of the new system. In late September 1980, the CCP Party center did so by issuing an internal circular that first asserted that the "collective economy must not be tampered with" because "it is the basis of our country's agriculture."[65] Yet having said this, the circular then turned to the conditions for the introduction of the responsibility system. Little was said about those cases in which the *pao-ch'an* remained with the team or was to be given by the working group. The document concentrated on those cases in which the *pao-ch'an* was to be given by the individual household or person, thus indicating that *pao-ch'an tao hu* was, in fact, understood to be the core of the responsibility system. The decision to introduce this system was to be made by the team "with the advice of the brigade"—the people's commune obviously had no influence in this matter.

When the system of *pao-ch'an tao hu* was introduced, it meant the guarantee of work and production (*pao-kung pao-ch'an*). In this case, the circular explained, a peasant family, or—in rare cases—even an individual, guarantees for a period of one to three years delivery of a fixed amount of grain, cotton, vegetable, or industrial crop to the team on fixed dates. The team contracts to give the individual household or person land, seed grain, fertilizer, tools, and plow animals according to the number of agricultural workers. The remuneration is included in the production (*Lien-ch'an chi-ch'ou*), i.e., the peasant retains any surplus over the guaranteed amount to be delivered to the team, but he has to compensate the team if he fails to meet the *pao-ch'an*. Under these circumstances, the team no longer has the power of distribution. Its role as the basic accounting unit, for all practical purposes, has come to an end.

Yet in 1980, the document still restricted the introduction of *pao-ch'an tao hu* to poor, low-yield areas, "areas where the peasants are disappointed with collective economy," and those locations where it had been introduced before late September 1980. In such cases as the last, a return to unified management by the team was not deemed advisable. Richer areas and locations "where the collective economy is stabilized," however, were no longer allowed to transfer the *pao-ch'an* to the individual household.[66] Wherever the transfer was introduced, the document concluded, six conditions must be met.

1. The property rights of the collective must be secured.
2. For the land contracted to the peasant household, no title deeds should be issued, and the hiring of farmhands and the renting of arable land by the peasants were strictly prohibited.
3. The production team had to develop a system that absolutely guaranteed the livelihood of the families of soldiers, cadres, non-agricultural workers, and people who could not look out for themselves.
4. Collectively owned local factories and workshops must be preserved.
5. Collective tasks, such as public works and irrigation, must be fulfilled, and the teams must reserve the right to recruit labor for such tasks from the peasants.
6. The organization of the production team must continue to function.

If these conditions were met, the team could then, within the limitations set by the document, proceed with contracting land to individual households.

In spite of the somewhat restrictive note displayed by the Party center's circular, it was obviously read as an encouragement to turn to the introduction of *pao-ch'an tao hu*—increasingly during 1981, even in areas with high yields, which the circular still expressly exempted from the new system. In the spring of 1981, the Ssuch-uan leadership exhorted the teams to transfer the *pao-ch'an* to the household because this was "the type of responsibility system which the peasants preferred,"[67] and in the early autumn of that year, Kansu reported that 80.5 percent of the teams in that province had implemented the transfer of the *pao-ch'an* to the household, thus "greatly reducing the responsibilities of the teams, and also the administrative manpower."[68]

Moreover, during 1981, a tendency to eliminate the rural people's communes in terminology as well as to eliminate their functions became stronger. The Hsiangyang commune in Kuanghan *hsien*, Ssuch'uan, was abolished and replaced by a township people's government. The enterprises previously under commune management were reorganized into a united agricultural-industrial-commercial corporation, and the brigades were limited to strictly administrative tasks and renamed "administrative villages" (*Hsing-cheng-ts'un*). Only the teams continued to function as production units, but for them, the pre-1958 term "agricultural production cooperative" was now used again.[69] Similar provisions were suggested in a statement made by the secretary of the district (*ti-ch'ü*) PC of Hsingyang in Honan,[70] a move that seems particularly delicate because the district of Hsingyang includes Suip'ing *hsien*, where, in mid-April 1958, the first people's commune in China had been established. Such trends continued, and with the implementation of the December 4,

1982, constitution, the people's communes have lost their administrative functions entirely. All through 1983, communes in the country ceded these functions, and township people's governments were established.

During the winter of 1981/1982, another new type of responsibility system appeared, and it was rapidly substituted, in many places, for the *pao-ch'an tao hu* structure. This was the system of guaranteed management of affairs to the household (*Pao-kan tao hu*), often also called "the great management-of-affairs guarantee" (*Ta pao-kan*). Although under the *pao-ch'an* system, a specified crop output was still guaranteed by the peasants and the means of production guaranteed to them, under the *pao-kan* system, the production team only contracts arable land out to the individual peasant household, without specifying the crops, and the household pays a fixed, agreed-upon amount of money to the team, which seems to vary between 25 and 55 percent of the gross income from the contracted land. The peasant, then, decides what to grow and has to buy or rent seed grains, tools, and plow animals from the team. He retains all income from the land, except for the guaranteed sum and some 5–10 percent for social and reinvestment funds for the team. The *pao-kan* contracts seem to run usually for fifteen years, but in some cases they run even longer.

All through 1981 and 1982, the two guarantees (*Shuang pao*), which means both of the systems of *pao-ch'an* and *pao-kan*, became established in Chinese villages. Precise data on their prevalence are not easy to find, but in early 1983, the Ch'inghai media reported that "more than 95 percent" of the production teams had introduced the two guarantees, and in Fukien, it was reported that 98 percent of that province's 16,000 teams had established a responsibility system, with 91 percent of them choosing the *pao-kan* type, which would mean that 89.2 percent of all production teams in Fukien had chosen the *ta pao-kan*.[71] Somewhat similar data were reported from Kuangtung in the fall of 1983. For the whole country, the *JMJP* reported on August 1, 1983, that 99 percent of the teams had introduced a responsibility system, with the "two guarantees" types accounting for 93 percent. That would leave only 1 percent of all production teams in the PRC with the old system of collective production in teams and 6 percent with collective production in working groups. On a nationwide average, more than two-thirds of the 93 percent that had decollectivized agricultural production were most probably of the *pao-kan* type.

After the thoroughgoing reforms of 1980–1982, the new structures in the Chinese villages are as follows. The communes, which numbered 54,368 in 1981,[72] retain only very vaguely defined coordinating tasks and are still in charge of a number of local factories and some transport facilities. But they now resemble the communes of 1958, or even those of 1975, in name only. For all practical purposes, they have been abolished as units of the collective economy.

The brigades, 718,000 of them in 1981, have ceded or are ceding their administrative functions to the administrative villages, including the running of primary schools and health clinics, but they are still in charge of transportation and heavy agricultural machinery—whenever it is available—and they are responsible for public works that exceed the scope of a production team. Their coordinating functions in agricultural production, however, are no more clearly defined than those of the communes.

In spite of the introduction of the responsibility system, the production teams, 6,004,000 of them with an average membership of 136 people or about twenty-five families in 1981, seem to still be units of considerable importance. They have official ownership of the arable land, most agricultural tools, and the larger livestock; they distribute or sell seed grains and fertilizer; and they conclude the *pao-ch'an* or *pao-kan* contracts with the peasants. But only in that 1 percent of the teams that work according to the system of unified management by the team (*Sheng-ch'an-tui-te t'ung-yi kuan-li*) are they still in charge of the allocation of work points and, hence, of the distribution of profits to the member families. These functions have been transferred to the working groups in those 6 percent of the teams that practice the system of *pao-ch'an* to the group. Under both of the systems of *pao-ch'an* and *pao-kan* to the individual household—i.e., in 93 percent of all production teams in the country—collective production, and with it remuneration through work points and distribution, have virtually been abolished although collective ownership still persists. In fact, both of these systems mean the reintroduction of sharecropping and of a tenancy system to the Chinese countryside. The peasants in those 45–50 percent of the teams that practice the *pao-kan* system are, for all practical purposes, tenants of the production team, and they pay sometimes somewhat more, sometimes somewhat less, rent than the Chinese tenants before 1949.

The new structures have created a number of new problems in the villages. Under the *pao-ch'an* and *pao-kan* systems, the allocations of water, irrigation facilities, tools, animals, and other means of production have led to conflicts among the peasants. Further problems arise from the fact that under household contracting, the gap between rich and poor seems to be widening again in the countryside. In particular, soldiers' families suffer, for they lack at least one worker, and so do the families that consist mainly of old people and the infirm.

But in general, the decollectivization of agricultural production has resulted in a distinct improvement in the living conditions of the new tenants over those of the earlier collective farmhands. Between 1978 and 1981, the average peasant's per capita annual income increased from JMP $134 to JMP $223, or by 66.4 percent, while the average urban income rose only from JMP $614 to JMP $772,[73] or by 25.7 percent. Still, this figure amounted to a monthly income of only U.S. $9.70 per capita, or if one uses a depreciating factor of 2.8—which seems realistic— U.S. $27.16. Given an average family size of 5.54 persons in the villages,[74] the real rural family income would total about U.S. $150 per month.

Yet these low figures constitute a remarkable advance over the late 1970s. Hence, at least the more-well-to-do peasants in the comparatively wealthier agricultural areas have recently started purchasing television sets, bicycles, and some modern household equipment, and they have, on a large scale, started to build new houses, now quite often with bricks instead of clay. The introduction of the responsibility system has also promoted the modernization of agriculture, although in this area, the PRC has still a long way to go. In 1982, 26 percent of the arable land was engine-plowed by tractors or power tillers, and 37.6 percent was plowed mechanically with draft animals, which leaves 36.4 percent of the arable land still cultivated entirely by human labor. The use of electric energy in the villages had increased by 46.1 percent since 1978, although the amount used still amounted to only 43.1 kilowatt-hours per person annually. The number of tractors had gone up by 42.1 percent since 1978, to 792,032 or 1 for every 302 acres, and the number of power tillers had increased by 48.4 percent, to 2,037,000 or 1 for every 117 acres of arable land.[75]

Last, but by no means least, the new structures in the countryside have served as a strong incentive for enhanced production efforts by the peasants, and without any doubt, they have dissipated opposition in the villages, at least on the part of the more-well-to-do peasants. On the other hand, the new structures have resulted in a weakening of the control structures in the rural areas. If the current policy should be continued, both developments may contribute to a general stabilization of China's rural society and, hence, of the political system. The same cannot be said about the social developments and conditions in the cities.

The Cities: A Socialist Class Society

With a per capita income of almost JMP $420, or a little less than U.S. $219, in 1982[76]—which, in real terms, would mean an equivalent of about U.S. $650 after depreciation—the Chinese people in the PRC belong to the world's poor. Yet among them, the urban population, as a whole, is still remarkably better off than the peasants. According to a survey conducted by the authorities in 1980, the annual per capita income in cash and kind of the rural population amounted to 38.23 percent of that of the city dwellers.[77] Other official data published in the same source, however, indicate a rural per capita income of JMP $223 in 1981 as opposed to an urban per capita income of JMP $436, which would mean that the average rural income was only 51 percent of the urban one.[78] But these figures are open to considerable doubt, because the Sixth Five-Year Plan stated that the rural per capita income in 1980 was 24.7 percent of the urban income.[79] This figure seems to be closer to the truth, for data that I collected from PRC provincial broadcasts and interviews in the country between 1979 and 1982 indicate that the rural per capita income at that time was barely 30 percent of that in the cities. The gap in living conditions between the countryside and the cities is also obvious from data concerning the availability of durable goods in 1980. At that time, there were 21 people for every television set in the cities, but 486 per set in the villages, a city/village relation of 1:23. For radio sets, the ratio was 1:15; for sewing machines, 1:1.3; for bicycles, 1:3.4; and for wristwatches, 1:4.3.[80] Only in terms of living space are the peasants better off than the urban people, having 11.9 square meters available per person as opposed to 4.6 square meters in the cities.

There are indeed vast differences in income and living conditions. For the whole country, it was stated in 1981 that the poorest 40 percent of the populace earned 18.4 percent of the national income, and the richest 10 percent, 23.2 percent.[81] William Parish, in a very thorough study, arrives at a Gini coefficient of between 0.38 and 0.43 for the PRC, mostly based on data from 1977 and 1978,[82] and based on World Bank figures of 1981 and data collected from CCP provincial broadcasts between January 1981 and August 1983, I propose a Gini coefficient of between 0.41 and 0.42 for the PRC, as opposed to 0.45 for India and 0.28 for the RoC on T'aiwan. These figures are attributable not only to the rather large differential between rural and urban income, but also to differences among the people in the cities of China.

At the lowest end of the urban social spectrum, there are destitute peasants from rural disaster areas who have moved illegally into the cities as beggars or casual laborers doing odd jobs. In some cities, these people still sleep on the streets, in drainage pipes, or even in public toilets; in others, such as Wuhsi and Canton, they live in straw-hut or bidonville slums.[83] Every once in a while they are driven away by police, but they return after a few days or weeks.

The lower income group also includes the unemployed, many of the illegally returned rusticated youths, temporary workers, and workers in the lower grades of the wage scale. In 1980, the official CCP media admitted that 21.4 percent of all rural people were living under "relatively difficult conditions" and that 2.1 percent had to "cope with great difficulties."[84] At the same time, "more than 20 percent" of the urban population was living in "dangerously delapidated slums."[85] Since 1975, because of the impact of inflationary tendencies, full-time workers in grade 1 and also some of those in grade 2 of the eight-grade wage scale have obviously moved down from the lower middle to the lower income group.

But the overwhelming majority of the full-time workers, together with engineers and the lower-level administrative cadres, are still in the middle income group, with wage grades 4 or 5 generally marking the border line between the lower and upper middle income brackets. New members of the middle income group include people who have started private small operations in the service and repair sectors and many of the workers they hire. The mainstays of the middle group are definitely the workers and employees. In 1977, their average monthly wage was JMP $58. Wage raises in October 1977 and November 1979 were supposed to have increased this amount to JMP $67.10, or 15.7 percent, but official data from 1981 indicate an average wage of only JMP $63.16, ranging from JMP $77.98 for construction workers, JMP $73.99 for transport workers, and JMP $68.64 for industrial workers to JMP $51.93 for workers in collective enterprises, mostly craftsmen.[86] If these data are correct, it would mean that since 1977, the average wage has increased by only 8.9 percent.

But even if the average wage had increased 15.7 percent, most of the gains would have been eaten up by inflation, which amounted to at least 14.3 percent between 1978 and 1982[87] and possibly as much as 16 percent. In the spring and summer of 1983, inflation began to escalate further, so that, beginning on July 7 and continuing through at least the end of August, provincial broadcasts I collected from twenty-two out of the twenty-nine administrative areas called for increased efforts to "combat inflation," which, in some places, seemed to have reached 8–10 percent for consumer goods.

Nevertheless, the industrial, construction, and transport workers are members of a privileged class, at least in terms of their social prestige, as they make up the proletariat that is supposed to rule the country. Yet attempts to make them assume at least an important share in the running of the factories through the establishment of clerks and workers' representative assemblies (*Chih-kung tai-piao ta-hui*) have been thwarted.[88] Addressing a national congress of the labor unions on October 11, 1978, Teng Hsiao-p'ing himself had called for the establishment of such bodies in all state-owned enterprises, with the authority even to "appeal to the higher organs and ask for the punishment and removal" of managerial personnel who were "in serious default or . . . indulged in wicked behavior."[89] Although this concept of workers' participation was mentioned now and then in the CCP media, not much happened until the late summer of 1980 when such institutions were established on an experimental basis in a number of factories. In the future, it was then proclaimed, these organs which were elected by the employees, should make the major decisions concerning the enterprise and even elect the factory director.[90]

But when the Party center finally promulgated temporary regulations for these assemblies on June 15, 1981, and had them published in the *JMJP* on July 20 of that year, the provisions were so restrictive that the role of the new organs hardly differs from that of the so-called labor unions in most other socialist countries. In order to clarify the trend that the policies of enlightened Stalinism take concerning workers' participation, the *JMJP* commented on these regulations on August 17, 1981, as follows: "Naturally the means of production do not belong to the workers, but to the whole people, represented by the state. Therefore, the workers in the enterprise cannot deal with the means of production as they wish, following their own interests."

Although the workers thus far have not profited very much from the policies of the post-Mao leadership—neither in their economic well-being nor in their role in the enterprises, although they have at least held their own—the intellectuals in general and the scientific and technological intelligentsia in particular definitely have. The cultural revolutionary persecutions have ended, most scholars and specialists who were purged during the Cultural Revolution have returned to their positions, and many of them even have gotten their dwellings back, although the intellectuals in the humanities often have to share their dwellings with other people. Natural scientists and technicians with higher qualifications now make up a highly privileged group. Many of them are exempt from the duty to attend political meetings, they usually earn more than JMP $160 per month, and their salaries can range, in some special cases, up to JMP $1,300 per month, or twenty times the average wage of employees and workers.

Hence, the scientific and technological intelligentsia, and also those artists and writers who abide by the rules of the newly proclaimed "socialist realism," can now again, as before the Cultural Revolution, be counted as part of the new upper income group—or rather, upper class—the mainstays of which are, without doubt, the 80,000 leading cadres. With an average monthly salary of about JMP $198,[91] a bit more than three average workers' wages, these cadres are not even highly paid. Their status, therefore, is not defined principally by their official income but by their special privileges. These include private cars with drivers; free lodging in individual houses or bungalows, often with swimming pools; household personnel—maids, cooks, gardeners, and handymen—paid by the state or by the Party; free access to reserved resorts; and the right to shop in special department stores or in "friendship stores," which are otherwise reserved for foreign nationals. When these cadres eat out, special compartments are reserved for them in the restaurants, and special clubs show movies and stage vaudeville shows that are restricted to them and their children, "the high-cadres' kids" (*Kao-kan tzu-ti*).[92]

Among the cadres, corruption is rampant. In fact, taking bribes and embezzling funds were rather common even as early as the 1960s and 1970s, all earlier reports to the contrary notwithstanding, and since early 1981, in a drive to combat cadre corruption that continues until today, such acts have been admitted by the PRC media.[93] From January 1980 to August 1983, I collected 987 reports about cadre corruption from provincial broadcasts. Between January 1 and July 31, 1982, alone, there were 527 such reports from twenty-six administrative areas, involving bribes and embezzled public funds that ranged from JMP $1,300 to JMP $1.4 million. In spite of such campaigns to combat corruption, it does not seem to have reduced, and it may even be on the increase.

The urban society in the PRC, therefore, is a class society, perhaps one of the most uncompromising in the world. The tendencies toward the stabilization of this class society, which had once been shaken during the crisis of the Cultural Revolution, have become ever stronger since 1975, and it appears that this trend will continue.

Unemployment, Crime, and the Problems of the Young Generation

According to Marxist-Leninist doctrine, one of the major features of a socialist system is that the problem of unemployment has been solved. In a socialist society, it is claimed, everybody has a job, and nobody has to fear that he or she may lose it. In most socialist countries, therefore, unemployment is hidden by overstaffing enterprises and by keeping more people in agriculture than is necessary, a situation that results in very low or even nonexistent unemployment rates but also in a very low rate of labor productivity. This situation seems to have been the case in the PRC until the Cultural Revolution. Then, more than 12 million youngsters were sent down from the cities to the countryside and to border areas, a measure that spurred opposition among the youth but also helped to temporarily relieve the population pressure, at least in some of the major cities. During the period of social turmoil in 1975, and again in 1976/1977, however, many of these youngsters returned illegally to their home cities, living there without working permits. Although the working-age population increased between 1976 and 1983 at annual rates of about 2 percent, new jobs could only be sluggishly created because of the overstaffing of all enterprises and offices. Furthermore, because of the economic reforms since 1979/ 1980, a number of unprofitable plants have been closed, and all of these factors together have resulted in a dramatic increase in urban unemployment.

After more than a decade of insisting that there were no unemployed people in China, the CCP media, by mid-1978, began to speak about grave employment problems,[94] although the term "unemployed" (*Shih-yeh*) is usually not used, "waiting for employment" (*Teng ch'iu-yeh*) being used instead. In 1980, PRC officials admitted that there were 900,000 unemployed young people ranging in age from fifteen to thirty in greater Shanghai alone, which would have meant an unemployment rate of at least 30 percent in that age bracket for that city,[95] and in early 1982, the official media gave a figure of 26 million urban people waiting for employment,[96] which would have meant an urban unemployment rate of 23.6 percent. Other data suggest figures between 17.5 and 23.1 percent, but it is safe to assume that by now, one-fifth of the urban work force in the PRC is unemployed, a figure that is a little higher than the 18 percent reported for India in 1981.

Since 1979, the ruling elite has taken a number of steps to counter this development. First, between 1979 and 1982, approximately 12.5 million new jobs were created or passed on to younger people after the retirement of their former holders.[97] Yet even a conservative estimate would lead to the conclusion that if this figure is correct, the number of urban unemployed must have increased by about 3 million during those four years. If we follow official PRC data, we arrive at a figure of 10.86 million newly employed between 1980 and 1982,[98] 1.13 million of whom went into private operations. This is the second measure the elite has taken in order to fight unemployment: People waiting for employment are encouraged to start their own businesses, either individually or in small collectives, mainly in repairs and in the service sector. A third measure is to induce older workers to retire before they have reached retirement age. If they do so, they receive a bonus in addition to their old-age pay, and their sons or daughters can take over their former jobs. Karl Marx probably had more than this method in mind when he talked about a "labor aristocracy," but the inherited job has become a rather common feature in Chinese factories.

All of these measures, however, have so far managed only to keep the unemployment rate around 20 percent. They have not reduced it significantly, and the number of people who reach working age will increase until 1988/1989, when the large groups born from 1968 until 1973—years with population increase rates between 2.75 and 2.09 percent—reach employment age.

Unemployment in the cities has been one of the two major reasons for an upsurge in crime, which the country has experienced since 1977. The other reason for this upsurge can be found in the aftereffects of the breakdown of public order and discipline during the Cultural Revolution and again during the turbulent times of 1976/1977. During these crises, many Chinese lost their fear of the CCP authorities, and others, in particular young people, learned that violence could bring immaterial as well as material profits. Beginning in mid-1978, and increasingly since the spring of 1981, the CCP media, especially the provincial radio broadcasts, day after day revealed the occurrence of crimes in the internationally accepted sense of the word—thefts, robberies, bank and train robberies, murders, which are often crimes of passion, rape, and gang rape—as well as crimes in the sense of Communist ideas—mainly smuggling, black marketeering, and counterrevolutionary activities such as listening to foreign broadcasts, distributing oppositional leaflets, and armed resistance against cadres and police.

This crime wave has also taken hold in the countryside, but there mostly in the form of the reappearance of traditional forms of behavior, e.g., gambling on a large scale[99] and the selling of girls as brides.[100] In January 1983, the provincial leadership of Fukien complained that "the selling of girls and arranged marriages happens continuously in the whole province and has developed into a very serious situation."[101]

An even worse traditional habit has made its reappearance in the Chinese countryside during the recent years, one that is directly connected with CCP policies: the killing of infant girls. This trend is a result of the rigorous birth control campaign that the CCP elite first enacted in 1977 in the cities and since 1979, has tried to expand to the villages. In the context of this campaign, the authorities tried first to encourage two-child families, and since late 1980, they have advocated one-child families.[102] The methods used are the denial of registration for any third child—later in some areas, any second child—fines for three or more children, forced abortions—including cesareans for women in their seventh or eighth month of pregnancy[103]—and forced tubal ligations. Since 1979/1980, these measures seem to have had remarkable success in the cities, but the countryside still has not accepted them on a large scale. Yet even when the one-child family is strictly encouraged and sometimes even enforced in villages in which the control structures are still intact, the peasants want male children. This preference is because, according to traditional Chinese folk religion, only a son can officiate at offerings to the ancestors and also because, according to rural tradition, the daughter-in-law lives with the parents of her husband, thus guaranteeing them care in their old age. Hence, there is a tendency to kill newly born girls in order to still have a chance to get a boy under the one-child system. Between early May and early July 1983 alone, the CCP media reported the killing of infant girls—in some cases several hundreds—in Liaoning, Hunan, Hupei, Ssuch'uan, Kirin, Anhui, and Kansu.[104]

In order to cope with the upsurge in crime, the CCP elite, beginning in 1978 and increasingly since early 1980, has turned to strict persecution and severe punishment. On June 7, 1983, Chiang Hua, then president of the Supreme People's Court, reported to the first session of the Sixth NPC that in the five years from 1978 to 1982, regional courts on all levels had handled 939,000 cases of "counterrevolutionary criminals and criminals who disturbed the social order or committed serious crimes," handing down, among other punishments, 2,944 death sentences, an annual average of almost 589 executions.[105] In mid-July 1983, a new nationwide campaign against rampant crime began, but it was also directed against what the elite calls "loafing, economic crimes, and counterrevolutionary activities." In the context of this new campaign, I collected reports about 347 immediately executed death sentences from seventeen administrative units during the period from July 16 to September 14, 1983, alone.

Such stern measures may eventually stem the tide of the crime wave, but they will not solve the problem of the spiritual and moral crisis that, since the repression of the Human Rights and Democracy movement in 1979, has spread among the urban youth in general and the intellectual youth in particular.[106] It seems that by 1983, urban people between fifteen and thirty years of age could be divided into three major groups.

1. The last remnants of the cultural revolutionary generation, now between twenty-eight and thirty years of age. These people lost their faith in the Party at an early age, and because of their experiences as young children in 1967/1968, they tend to engage in active resistance, and often in criminal acts as well.
2. Those who are between twenty-three and twenty-seven years of age and therefore had most of their secondary schooling in an extremely low-quality educational system until 1977. This group is outwardly thoroughly disciplined, but its members care only about the late acquisition of factual knowledge in order to have hope for a reasonably good career and are totally cynical about the Party and the demands of the elite.
3. Those who are now between fifteen and twenty-two years of age and, hence, had a chance to get a somewhat better secondary

education. These people, too, are mainly interested in factual knowledge and a career, but among them—according to many reports—admiration for Western civilization, pop music, and "things foreign" is rampant. As a rule, they are not easy to mobilize politically, but they may have positive responses toward elite demands in order to not invite trouble (*chao ma-fan*).

None of these three groups seems to be willing to render active support for the Party's policies or to believe in the official doctrines of the ruling elite. The CCP media have reported that many young people believe that "socialism cannot match capitalism";[107] that they ask, Can socialism really save China? The fatherland is so backward, how can one love it?; and that they tend to point toward their own experience, stating, "It is not that I don't love my fatherland, it's the fatherland that doesn't love me."[108]

Since the spring of 1981, the authorities have tried to counter such attitudes with an increase in political indoctrination in the schools and with large-scale propaganda campaigns stressing patriotism and good behavior. These campaigns are conducted under the slogan of Five-Speak, Four-Beauty, Three Warm Loves (*Wu-chiang, ssu-mei, san je-ai*), exhorting the young generation to speak about civilization, speak about politeness, speak about public order, speak about health, speak about virtue; have beauty in the heart, have beauty in the speech, have beauty in the environment, have beauty in the behavior; warm love for the Party, warm love for socialism, warm love for the fatherland.

The success of such endeavors, however, is still in doubt. Since 1981, the month of March has been especially dedicated to this campaign under the name of "civilization-and-politeness month" (*Wen-ming li-mao yüeh*). An overseas Chinese from Europe who ceded his seat on a Peking bus in April 1983 to an ailing lower-level cadre was criticized by a young man: "You are a stupid fool! This is April; the civilization-and-politeness month is already over!" (*Ni shih-ke sha-kua! Hsien-tsai ssu-yüeh-fen, wen-ming li mao yüeh i-ching kuo-ch'ü-le!*). This example leads us, finally, to some more general questions about attitudinal responses of the populace to elite stimuli.

Attitudinal Responses: A Second Political Society?

After seizing power in 1949, the CCP, under the leadership of Mao Tse-tung, set out to create—by education, indoctrination, and coercion— a "new man" for the "new society," which was supposed to be in the making. The ideal type of this new man was a person who dedicated his whole life to the service of the goals that the ruling elite formulated.

He was supposed to work wholeheartedly for the collective, to sacrifice his freedom of personal choice, and to not ask for many material rewards as long as his most basic physical needs were met. His dress was to be plain, his dwellings simple, his food frugal. He was supposed to refrain from amusement and to find all his pleasure in working for the common good. Relations between the sexes were to serve the preservation of the Chinese nation within the limits set at any given time by the changing population policies of the elite. Moreover, these relations could support the exchange of working experiences and mutual education, but their aim was not individual delight. Thus, constant readiness to serve, unselfishness, sacrifice for the collective, the renunciation of personal amenities, and a glowing dedication to Marxist-Leninist visions of the future were the basic characteristics of this new man. Until the Cultural Revolution, his model was the civilian cadre; between 1967 and 1972/ 1973, it was the soldier; and since then, it has been the cadre again, recently supplemented by the engineer who burns midnight oil to acquire foreign technology.

Yet with the revelations about cadre corruption and special privileges during the Cultural Revolution, the ensuing revelations about military greed for power and privilege during the Lin Piao crisis, and the social unrest of the 1970s, it had become evident that the attempt to create a new man has ended in dismal failure. Since 1975, it has become obvious, that the society of the PRC is what it always was, and most probably will continue to be: an assembly of people who, as most people everywhere in the world, are first and foremost interested in their own and their family's well-being, in improvements in their living conditions, however modest, and in the small pleasures of individual life.

The post-Mao leaders have taken a somewhat more realistic attitude toward these facts of Chinese life than The Chairman did. Although still proclaiming frugality, dedication, service to the collective, and personal discipline as required attitudes, the current political leaders take the universal quest for improvements in individual life into account. Hence, they have made material rewards and deprivations the major motivating forces of their drive for the modernization of China, and they have even, as we have already seen, granted some limited and controlled leeway for private initiatives as additional incentives to work toward the goal of achieving "socialist industrial great power" status, if not by the year 2000, then at least within the next century.

Yet, as the Four Basic Principles[109] clearly show, the leaders continue to be pledged to the visions and methods of Marxism-Leninism. On the Chinese mainland, a positive attitudinal response of the populace to elite stimuli therefore means the acceptance of the Marxist-Leninist authorizing myth of historical materialism, the Marxist-Leninist world view, and, at any given period, the current line of the Marxist-Leninist party. It also means to abide by the ruling elite's orders and to internalize the patterns of behavior that it advocates.

In this respect, the situation in the PRC after thirty-four years of CCP rule, and three years of policies dictated by enlightened Stalinism, is ambiguous at best. Old and middle-aged intellectuals in the humanities have mostly lost their ideals. No longer severely persecuted, they seem to be content that they have, as a rule, regained their pre–cultural revolutionary living conditions, and many of them appear to support the current ruling elite, albeit without much enthusiasm, as long as it guarantees that there will be no return to the Cultural Revolution. The same holds true for the majority of the scientific and technological intelligentsia, who enjoy substantial privileges under the conditions of the socialist class society. Yet younger intellectuals in the humanities, many artists and writers, and remnants of the Red Guard generation among the urban youth have turned toward active or at least passive dissent, and even resistance.

The majority of the urban youths care only about a career and about enjoying life as much as their still extremely limited means allow. Many young people in the cities, and apparently an increasing number in the richer village areas as well, have adopted an attitude of total cynicism toward the demands of the elite, but there is rarely any indication that they may soon turn toward active opposition or resistance.

The leading cadres, in particular those who suffered severe persecution during the later stages of the Maoist era, form the hard core of active support for the current ruling elite. Supportive behavior is also displayed by those mid-level cadres who were victims of the Cultural Revolution, while others on that level resent the widening of the economic parameters that the current leadership has enacted. Such an attitude is rather common among many of the basic-level cadres, who are particularly dissatisfied with the new rural societal policies, which have put limits on their authority[110] and tend to impede their opportunity to enrich themselves by selling favors to collective farmhands.

Engineers and highly skilled workers in wage grade 8 and possibly 7 profit from the policies of the second modernization concept. Hence, they can be counted as comparatively strong supporters of the current leaders, not because of their advanced proletarian consciousness, but because of material improvements in their living conditions. Workers in the middle and lower wage grades, 1–6, on the other hand, developed very high expectations during the initial stages of the policies of modernization, and many of them have been gravely disappointed. Hence, this group has ceased to support the current CCP line, and it has, since the autumn of 1980, displayed an increasing propensity toward dissent. The same statement can be made about the urban poor—the temporary workers, contract workers, handymen, and beggars—although they cannot take time for active resistance from their daily ordeal to secure the most basic necessities of life.

With the introduction of the responsibility system, the resistance of the peasantry against elite policies has ended. Those peasants who profit from the new rural societal policies can be expected to support them, although only for the sake of their personal interest and under the condition that these policies are not changed. Yet such support is mostly not expressed in political activities but in making the utmost use of all chances for an improvement of individual living conditions. Since 1982, there have been increasing indications that these peasant groups, which may constitute about two-thirds of the rural population, are beginning to pressure for even more elite concessions, with the ultimate goal of a total decollectivization of agriculture, including property rights for the arable land. Since the elite is not willing to give into such demands, new tensions may be expected in the future, but currently, the central leadership is not facing large-scale rural dissent. On the other hand, a strong minority of the peasants—in particular the families of soldiers, families with less-than-average manpower, and the underachievers in agricultural production—oppose the lowering of the levels of collectivization and tend to call for a return to Maoist rural policies.

We can, with reasonable safety, conclude that the policies of the current elite are supported by a social coalition of leading cadres, a sizable group of the middle-level cadres, the older intellectuals in the humanities, the majority of the scientific and technological intelligentsia, engineers, and the best-paid industrial workers. Younger intellectuals in the humanities, large portions—if not the majority—of industrial labor, and some elements of the urban poor form a social coalition that pressures for a further widening of the parameters of political competition and economic activities. A third social coalition, consisting of the majority of the basic-level cadres, a second sizable group of the mid-level cadres, and the lower income group among the peasantry, stands ready to support a return to the platform of late Maoism, or at least a strengthening of the orthodox Stalinist traits in elite policies.

All three of these social coalitions, however, are minorities. If those peasants who profit from the new rural societal policies make up about two-thirds of the rural population—and this seems to be a fairly reasonable estimate—they would represent between 49 and 54 percent, or almost exactly half, of the Chinese people in the PRC. As long as they tolerate the current ruling elite because of its rural policies, the trend toward a stabilization of Party rule that has become recognizable since 1981 will most probably not be thwarted. Yet the rural majority is not an active part of the official political society of concentric circles described in Chapter 4.[111] Does it, then, constitute an alternative, a second political society?

The answer is no. There is no center that could move this rural majority into political action, there is not even a nucleus for an organization that could aggregate and articulate peasant interests on a level higher than that of the village. The Chinese countryside—despite more than three decades of campaigns, mobilization efforts, passive and even active resistance—is still divided into millions of uncoordinated societies with almost pure parochial political cultures. These minuscule political societies have successfully resisted all attempts to introduce a nationwide culture, but they have as yet not been able to generate the momentum to unite for a nationwide drive toward systemic change.

The nucleus of a second political society can, however, be detected in a number of small urban circles that combine the remnants of Red Guard organizations of the late 1960s with those forces of the Human Rights and Democracy movement of 1978/1979 that went underground when the movement was repressed in 1979/1980. These circles actively oppose the policies of the ruling elite with a general platform calling for the introduction of elements of a participatory political culture to the subject culture of the official political society. They exist outside the parameters of the official political society, forming numerous small cores that have supporters, mostly among workers and other elements of the urban population. But these circles have, as yet, no national organization, and they have so far not succeeded in forging links with the splintered peasantry. If they should be able to develop links, they would be a formidable danger for the totalistic single-party system. But as long as the CCP is the only nationally organized political force and as long as there is no viable alternative to the official political society, which is dominated by its ruling elite through the structure of concentric circles, the Party will rule, if only by default of its active opponents. This seems to be the vista for the foreseeable future. We have now to ask which projections can be envisaged for further economic, social, and political developments if this situation continues.

CHAPTER 14

Whither China?
Alternative Projections

Economic Perspectives

Social scientists are no prophets, and when they have posed as such, they have usually come out with very poor records. In the following discussion of future perspectives for the PRC, I can therefore not advance clear-cut and unilinear predictions, but only suggest alternative projections of the future, or rather of two different futures: the immediate and the intermediate. I define immediate future as the period until the last years of this decade, i.e., until 1988/1989, and intermediate future as the period from 1989/1990 until the end of this century or into the early years of the twenty-first century. First, I discuss how the economy of the PRC might develop during these two periods; second, I discuss the social perspectives, and third, I turn toward the perspectives for the political system.

The last year of the Sixth Five-Year Plan is to be 1985, and this plan has been entirely dictated by the second modernization concept. The success or failure of this plan will most probably strongly influence the setting of the goals for the Seventh Five-Year Plan, scheduled for 1986–1990, and hence, economic policies for the second half of the 1980s. If the sixth plan achieves its rather modest goals, which is highly probable given the cautious and realistic nature of its projections, the second modernization concept will continue to be implemented, possibly with slightly but not significantly higher goals, for the following five years. In this case, the current policies of decollectivized production in agriculture; a broadening of the parameters for enterprise autonomy within the framework of a planned economy; limited and controlled leeway for private initiative in the commercial, services, and repair sectors; as well as selective cooperation with and technology imports from Western countries will continue. These policies could well mean success for the seventh plan, too.

However, with increased consumption and the continued presence of Western personnel working on industrial cooperation projects, the patterns of urban life-styles in China are bound to undergo escalating changes. With further improvements in agricultural production, rural pressure for even more decollectivization will probably mount. Both of these developments will weaken the political and social control structures the Party has at its command, and that could lead toward increasing resentment among the cadres, which, in turn, would tend to promote at least an orthodox Stalinist backlash against the current economic development policies.

Such a backlash would definitely occur if the goals of the Sixth Five-Year Plan should not be achieved. In this case, a return to the policies of the first modernization concept could hardly be avoided. That would mean that the Seventh Five-Year Plan would give priority to the basic and heavy industries, reduce enterprise autonomy, and greatly reduce the goal projections for consumer goods. Such measures would be accompanied by attempts to recollectivize agricultural production, at least to abolish the *ta pao-kan* system wherever it has been introduced. A new economic crisis of proportions similar to that of 1979/1980 would follow, and the seventh plan would most probably end in failure.

But an all too dramatic overfulfillment of the goals of the sixth plan could also lead to an unfavorable development of the economy during the five years of the seventh plan. If the sixth should greatly exceed its goals, the new goal projections for the seventh would most probably be set so high that the performance in 1986–1990 would necessarily fall short of the elite's expectations In this case, the developments that could be expected for 1985 if the sixth plan did not achieve its goals would unfold by 1990, and the return to the first modernization concept could lead to misappropriations and dislocations during the early 1990s. In both cases, critical economic conditions would probably lead to social crises and new political confrontations.

On the basis of those perspectives for the immediate future, four alternative projections can be advanced for the intermediate future, i.e., for the 1990s and the early 2000s.

1. There would be a continuation of the policies of the second modernization concept with an increased elite responsiveness to demands from the society. Such a continuation would mean a further strengthening of the elements of a market economy: more enterprise autonomy, more decision-making power for scientific and technological personnel, more cooperation with Western countries, and significantly less political in-

terference in the economy. It could also mean a decollectivization of rural property rights, i.e., an all-out return to private farming. If this development should occur, the goals that were set in 1980/1981 for the year 2000—quadrupling the 1980 GNP, and achieving a per capita GNP of U.S. $800—may be almost or fully reached. But such a policy development means that the elite would have to enact sweeping revisions of its Four Basic Principles, and it is highly doubtful that the political generations that follow the one in control of the Party center now will be ready for such revisions.

2. There would be a continuation of the policies of the second modernization concept within the framework of a rigid adherence to the Four Basic Principles. This possibility would mean freezing the parameters for enterprise autonomy, decollectivized agricultural production, and individual initiatives on the level of 1983. Demands to widen them would be refused by the elite, and in order to sustain this refusal, the bureaucratic elements of the economy would have to be reasserted. As a consequence, social tensions could mount, and producers as well as consumers would try to turn toward a rapidly growing "second economy," which, in turn, would result either in a belated surrender of the elite to the demands from the society or in a new strengthening of the repressive features of the economic and the political systems.

3. There would be a return to the policies of the first modernization concept combined with a return of orthodox Stalinists to the economic command positions. This development would mean that the economy of the PRC would move in the same direction the economies of the USSR, Romania, East Germany, and Czechoslovakia have taken since the early 1970s: mandatory piece planning, a centralization of economic management, tight control of private markets, a recollectivization of agricultural production, and the reestablishment of basic and heavy industrial priority over the light and consumer goods industries. According to all previous experience, the result would be a stagnation of economic development after some great strides in heavy industrial production, restriction on imports from Western countries, aggravating shortages of consumer goods, and ensuing social unrest. Under such conditions, not even the comparatively modest, recently proclaimed goals for the year 2000 could be reached.

4. There would be a leftist backlash against the policies of the second modernization concept, which would produce either a return to the Maoist concept of development or a new developmental concept with strong Maoist overtones. Such a backlash would mean a move away from material to immaterial incentives, attempts to reintroduce a high level of rural collectivization, severe restrictions on all interchanges with

Western countries, mass movements, and the promotion of rigid austerity. In this case, a severe economic crisis, possibly even of the proportions of 1960, could hardly be avoided. The economy of the PRC, again, would be thrown back by at least ten years, and the political system would be gravely destabilized.

To date, it is not easy to allocate probability ratings to these four alternative projections, but given the characteristics of the political system and the trends among the ruling elite, the second and the third projections appear more likely to develop than the first and the fourth. If this assumption should prove correct, the economic perspectives of the PRC for the year 2000 would appear somewhat more pessimistic than optimistic, though not without any hope.

Social Perspectives

Although it seems legitimate to expect economic cycles of approximately five years in developing economies, social developments appear to take more time. If we discuss the perspectives for the society in the PRC, it seems therefore appropriate to concentrate on the intermediate future. Indeed, we should not expect significant social changes in the immediate future, i.e., until 1988/1989. Even if we look at the features the society could display toward the end of this century, the changes that will have occurred by then will most probably still not be dramatic.

First and foremost, the society on the mainland of China will continue to be a predominantly rural one, at least until the late 1990s and probably well beyond that time. Even by the year 2000, one would have to expect that between 75 and 80 percent of the populace will still live in hamlets, villages, and small towns and that about 70 percent, but at least two-thirds, of the inhabitants of the PRC will still work in agriculture.

Hence, the social conditions in the countryside will continue to be the most important aspect of the Chinese society by the end of this century. If the current economic policies of the second modernization concept should be continued until then, the gap in living conditions between the countryside and the cities may have narrowed somewhat. As we have seen, the Sixth Five-Year Plan projects a 1985 rural per capita income of about 26 percent of that in the cities. A linear continuation of such a development would mean that the rural income may have reached 31 percent of the city average by the year 2000, and I would even estimate a possible 35 percent. Yet a continuation of the present developmental policies would also mean that the trend toward larger income differentials *within* the villages could continue. Differences between the richer and the poorer groups of the peasant population, in this case, will increase, and a general improvement of the standard of living in the countryside will be accompanied by a widening of social gaps, i.e., richer agricultural areas will develop faster than the poorer ones, and the standard of living of the more-well-to-do peasants will increase significantly faster than that of the rural lower income groups.

In the cities, the urban work force will most probably grow to approximately 180 million to 200 million people by the late 1990s, with at least 50 million, or between 25 and 28 percent, unemployed. Only if the industrial and service sectors of the economy should expand far beyond all current expectation would the unemployment rate fall below 20 percent by the end of this century, but there seems to be little hope that, even under such favorable conditions, it could reach a figure below 15 percent.

These projections mean that urban crime and public order problems in general and urban youth problems in particular will persist until the end of the century, although they may possibly not increase if no political turmoil instigates more social disturbances, as happened during the Cultural Revolution. Again given a continuation of the policies enacted between 1980 and 1983, the major changes to be expected in the urban society until the year 2000 would be a significant increase in the intellectual standards of the cadres and an increase in the population of the cities in general. In this context, a reduction of the current deficit of trained technical and scientific personnel by about half could be considered a realistic projection, although even by the end of this century, the demand for such personnel would still be far greater than the supply.

But what about the relations between the political elite and the populace and what about the possible development of social coalitions in the 1990s? In order to answer these questions, we again have to consider alternative projections. At least three different scenarios can be envisaged for the last decade of this century.

1. A continuation and gradual intensification of the policies advanced under the second modernization concept would continue to receive the support of a social coalition of scientists, leading cadres, and people privately engaged in the urban economy. This coalition could then, on a long-range basis, gradually be joined by the majority of the peasants and by large portions of industrial laborers in the higher wage grades. This coalition, which might later be enlarged by intellectuals in the humanities and urban youth, would make up a majority and could effectively isolate the basic cadres, the village poor, and the leftist mid-level cadres. In this case, a stabilization of the political system could be expected. Yet such a development would require far-reaching ideo-logical and political concessions by the ruling elite, at least similar to

those that have been made in Hungary, and it appears doubtful that the elite would be willing to grant such concessions.

2. The ruling elite, supported by a coalition of mid-level cadres, military officers, the majority of the basic cadres, and part of the scientific and technical intelligentsia, would successfully impose strict political and economic discipline on the cities and refuse any further broadening of the parameters for private initiative in the countryside. Such a development would most probably provoke the formation of an oppositional social coalition of intellectuals in the humanities, industrial workers, urban youth, and people privately engaged in the urban economy. The more-well-to-do majority of the peasants would, in this case, turn toward passive opposition, but the ruling elite, if it develops a minimum consensus to consolidate its power, could prevent a linkup between an active urban and a passive and divided rural opposition by means of police repression. This situation would result in the evolution of a bureaucratically administered society in the PRC for a number of decades, in other words, a social Sovietization of the Chinese mainland.

3. A social coalition of basic cadres, a majority of the mid-level cadres, a minority of workers in the lowest wage grades, and some of the village poor would support a turn of the then-ruling elite toward the developmental concepts and policies of Maoist social mobilization and class struggle. In this case, events similar to those between 1974 and 1976 could be expected. In opposition to such policies, intellectuals, the majority of the urban youth, the workers in the higher wage grades, people who have begun to become privately engaged in the urban economy, and the majority of the peasantry would form a social coalition that, in this case, would be a majority one waiting for a leadership core. If such a core should evolve, it would mean another defeat for the leftist forces, at least of proportions similar to those in 1976/1977. If such a core did not evolve, however, uncoordinated social unrest, massive manifestations of passive resistance, and major political turmoil would result in a dangerous crisis for the political system.

Today, it appears impossible to allocate probability ratings to these three scenarios. Any of them could determine the situation of the society in the PRC during the last years of this century, but in 1983, there is, in fact, no certainty about any of these projections. Which factors will decide the outcome? Karl Marx's assumption that the socioeconomic base determines the political and ideological superstructure notwithstanding, past experiences in the PRC suggest strongly that the economic and social perspectives of the country depend upon the political perspectives.

Political Perspectives

In order to project future perspectives for the political system of the PRC, one has to start from the fact that despite all efforts by some of the current leaders to enact policies of elite rejuvenation, the ruling elite is still highly over-aged. As we have discussed previously, the average age of the Politburo's Standing Committee at the end of 1983 was 75.5 years, that of the whole Politburo was 73.8 (including the alternate members, 73.0), that of the Secretariat was 66.5 (including the alternate secretaries, 64.1), that of the whole CC was 65.4, that of the Presidium of the NPC was 75, that of the State Council's inner circle was 65.4, that of the State Council as a whole was 63.7, that of the Central Military Commission was 76.8, that of the military area commanders in chief was 67.9, and that of the provincial Party leaders was 65.2 years. Altogether, the 222 leading cadres of these organs and leadership groups had an average age of 65.7 years and an average Party membership period of 49.2 years.

A composite personal profile of this elite would therefore result in a person born in 1917/1918 who joined the CCP about 1934, the year the Long March started. Hence, the current leadership group is not yet a postrevolutionary one but one of civil war veterans. This fact is even more obvious when we look at the current decision combine, which has an average age of 71.2 and an average Party membership of 54 years. This ruling elite is bound to leave the political scene because of biological reasons, in the foreseeable future and most probably in fast sequence. The average life expectancy of a Politburo member, computed from the ages of those members of that body who have died in office since 1956, is 75.5 years. By the end of 1983, fourteen out of twenty-four current Politburo members had already passed that point, and by 1988, twenty will have done so. By then, fourteen of them will be 80 years old or older.

From these data, we can draw two reasonably safe conclusions. First, although the problem of personal succession to Mao Tse-tung was temporarily solved first in 1976/1977 and a second time, with the demise of Hua Kuo-feng, in 1980/1981, the problem of generational succession remains as yet unsolved. Second, the problem of generational succession will have to be solved toward the end of the 1980s.

Until such a solution does come about, it appears very likely that the policies of enlightened Stalinism, as they have been developed through revisionist-Stalinist compromises since late 1980, will continue, though not without being disputed by revisionist as well as by orthodox Stalinist forces. Yet all such possible challenges notwithstanding, the current leaders seem to agree that intraelite conflict must not escalate into open confrontation and that, to make sure such escalation does not occur, the consensus on procedures must be preserved. It seems therefore appropriate to project continuous policy disputes until the late 1980s, but these disputes will most probably be settled by consecutive short-lived compromises rather than by open conflict, because the secondary group-formation within the ruling elite will tend to remain confined to varying issue-based coalitions, which means to opinion groups rather than to factions.

But what will happen after 1988/1989? This question could only be answered with a reasonable degree of precision if we knew how the ruling elite in general, and the decision combine in particular, would be composed. But at the end of 1983, only a few possible successors were in sight. Of the twenty-five full members of the CC who will be younger than sixty by 1988, five were women, two belonged to national minorities, and six of seven were model peasants or labor heroes. Therefore, half of the younger CC members in 1983 belonged to groups that have, at least so far, scarcely been represented in the decision combine. Of the remaining eleven to twelve younger CC members, seven had a long service record in the CYL at a time when it was led by Hu Yao-pang, and three had made their career in the security establishment. These people may be part of the leadership generation to come, but the sample is too small to provide sufficient indications about the overall composition of the successors.

In more general terms, four future leadership reserves can be distinguished.

1. The approximately 1,500 combat heroes (*Chan-tou ying-hsiung*) of the last stage of the civil war and the Korean War who will most probably be the succeeding generation in the PLA leadership; most of them are now around fifty years of age.
2. The more than 10,000 former students who have returned from technical, scientific, managerial, organizational, and secret police studies in the Soviet Union and East European countries during the 1950s and early 1960s; they, too, are now mostly about fifty years old.
3. An unknown, but surely rather large, number of rural mobilization cadres of the Great Leap Forward with comparatively low formal educational standards; they range now between forty-five and fifty-five years old.
4. Between 30,000 and 150,000 leaders and activists of the Red Guard and revolutionary rebel organizations during the Cultural Revolution; now mostly between thirty-two and forty years of age, they are currently excluded from advancing within the system, but they may still wait for a possible future chance.

The biographical backgrounds and past political experiences of these four groups differ widely indeed. For this reason, it appears doubtful that the PRC, during the 1990s, will be ruled by an elite capable of arriving at more than a superficial consensus, if at any at all.

Thus, we cannot project the development of the political system in the PRC after 1988 in unambiguous terms. Here, too, we have to consider alternative projections, of which I can envisage at least three.

1. There might be a long-lasting, sustained victory for the revisionist platform now promoted by Teng Hsiao-p'ing and Chao Tzu-yang. This victory might then result in a stabilization of CCP rule combined with gradual, slow, but steady economic and social development under the auspices of the second modernization concept.

2. There could be an evolution of full-fledged orthodox Stalinist policies, with cautious attempts at a recollectivization of agricultural production, full emphasis on the development of heavy industry, more centralized industrial planning and management, and even more severe repression in the areas of education and culture than since early 1981. If such policies should prevail, the result, during the 1990s, would be that the transition to institutionalized and, hence, stabilized rule could be completed, but with a high degree of bureaucratization, and therefore there would be further delays in economic and social development.

3. There might be a return of the mobilization developmental policies and the doctrines of Maoism, with a renewed emphasis on class struggle, violent purges of anti-Party elements, enthusiastic austerity, and immaterial incentives as the major motivating force for development. This projection would most probably mean another protracted period of political and social crises, followed by crises of the national economy, which might even lead to a breakdown of the current political system of totalistic single-party rule.

Today, it is impossible to allocate probability ratings to these three projections. Which of them will finally prevail depends on a large number of determinants, of which the attitude of the PLA, the political outlook of the mid-level cadres, the intensity of group formation, the coherence of intraelite groups, and the intellectual and spiritual condition of the youth could be crucial. Under such premises, the second projection, which, in fact, would mean a Sovietization of the political system in the PRC, is not necessarily the least probable of the three.

However, so much does seem to be almost sure. The PRC will experience more policy disputes, more political benchmarks, and possibly even several more major political crises during the last decade of this century. Only if the first or the second projection should have materialized by the end of the 1990s, could the transition to institutionalized rule, which has so far just begun, have run most of its course. Yet until the transition has been almost completed, the political perspectives of the PRC will remain uncertain, and such uncertainty will characterize not only the further development of the political system but, in its wake, the perspectives for the position of the PRC in international politics as well.

The PRC in International Politics: Strategies and Perspectives

Although this book deals with the political system and the domestic politics of the PRC, it seems appropriate to add some thoughts on the role of the country in international politics and on the perspectives for future developments in this area. Fascinated by the sheer weight of China's territory and population, a considerable number of West European people as well as a number of European occasional observers of the Chinese scene—but only a very few China specialists—talk about the PRC as a "third great power" beside the Soviet Union and the United States. This term, insufficiently defined and used without much reflection, finds its corollary in the United States in repeated assumptions that there is a "power triangle" consisting of the Soviet Union, the United States, and the PRC, from which the decisive impulses for the development of world politics emanate. Ever since the early 1970s, such evaluations have been refuted by almost all major spokesmen for the ruling elite of the PRC, which seems to take a very realistic approach toward the actual potential of China's role in international affairs.

Indeed, the term "great power," or "world power"—which I consider to be a synonym—needs a precise definition if it is to be used in an analysis of international relations. In the world of the late twentieth century, a great power should be defined as a country that

- is entirely self-sufficient in the production of weapons, including modern high-technology systems;
- leads a group of allies that rely on its protection and support;
- is physically able to establish its military presence in any place on the globe whenever its leadership deems such a presence politically necessary; and
- can field a credible nuclear second-strike capability.

Until today, and most probably for at least several decades to come, none of these characteristics suits the realities of the PRC. If one calls it a "great power," one goes beyond the current economic and political realities.

As of now, the PRC is, without any doubt, a major regional power in East Asia, militarily stronger but economically incomparably weaker than Japan. It is in East Asia where the direct political interests of the country—as defined by the ruling elite—are at stake. The PRC's leaders constantly express opinions about international conflicts and world political events beyond East Asia, but they lack the potential to influence them, although they may occasionally have some nuisance value, particularly on developments in South and West Asia, Africa, and the Pacific.

East Asia is therefore the major operational area for the PRC's international strategies. In this region, the country's major counterparts are Japan, the ASEAN countries (Indonesia, Malaysia, the Philippines, Singapore, Thailand, and Brunei), Vietnam, to a certain extent the United States—which, because of its geographic situation and power reserves, is incomparably more important to the PRC than the PRC is to it—and first and foremost, its northern neighbor, the Soviet Union.

A further concern of the PRC in East Asia—in international politics, the term "PRC" has to be defined more precisely as the Politburo of the CCP—is the existence of the Nationalist Chinese elite in the RoC on T'aiwan. The PRC would refute the notion that its relations with T'aiwan are part of international politics, but in fact, they are, and they influence its relations with other countries. Compared with East Asia— including Southeast Asia—all other regions or subjects of international relations—including the underdeveloped countries, international organizations such as the United Nations, and Europe—constitute only a secondary operational area for the foreign policy of the PRC.

Despite all the intraelite conflicts and domestic political convulsions, the PRC's foreign policy, since the beginning of the 1970s, has been fairly consistent and apparently not very controversial among the Chinese leadership, at least until the fall of 1982 when important changes and significant disputes seem to be beginning to develop. Two major goals are pursued in the international strategies of the PRC, but in a very clear order of priority: first, to ensure the national security of the country against any foreign threat perceived by the ruling elite, and second, because this elite consists of Marxist-Lenists, to promote the spreading of Communist totalistic single-party systems over as many countries as possible, as long as such promotion does not adversely affect the PRC's national security.

In one respect, these two goals have been in conflict since the early 1960s: in the Peking decision-making circles, the Soviet Union, a Communist-ruled country, has been perceived as one of the major threats to the security of the PRC (until the autumn of 1982, even the most dangerous one). At its very core a conflict over problems of leadership and international strategies, the dispute between the Soviet Union and the PRC—or rather, Communist Party of the Soviet Union (CPSU) and the CCP—has assumed the features of ideological, organizational, and even territorial conflict. Thus, the development of Sino-Soviet relations has become the most important determining factor of the PRC's foreign policy. China's relations with the United States, Japan, Western Europe, and the underdeveloped regions of Asia, Africa, and Latin America are mainly aspects of its relations with the Soviet Union. After these relations deteriorated to the brink of military confrontation in 1968/1969, the ruling elite of the PRC has, albeit in ever-changing composition, designed three successive strategies to cope with the perceived Soviet threat.

1. From the end of the Cultural Revolution to the purge of Lin Piao in 1971, the PRC followed a strategy of seeking allies in the so-called Third World—mainly among the Communist and related radical revolutionary movements in Asia and the African and Arabian countries—for a simultaneous conflict with both the Soviet Union and the United States, attacking them as social-imperialist and imperialist respectively.

2. From the fall of 1971 until the later part of 1978, there was a strategy of constructing a network of international cooperation with Third World countries *and* the minor non-Communist powers of Western Europe and Japan to contain the perceived Soviet expansionism. Under this strategy, one or two superpowers were considered as enemies, but one could partially and in a limited way cooperate with the less-dangerous, minor enemy, the United States, against the major one, the Soviet Union.

3. From the second half of 1978 until 1981/1982, the PRC developed the strategy of an antihegemonist (meaning anti-Soviet) united front made up of the PRC, the United States, Japan, and Western Europe, which was supposed to contain Soviet expansionism—with the major containing tasks being reserved for the United States.

These three strategies, however, have failed. Except for a few countries and some guerrilla movements of different strengths, of which only two—the Khmer Rouge in Cambodia and the forces of Robert Mugabe in Zimbabwe—have been partially or temporarily successful, the Third World refused to accept the PRC as its leader, and those countries were not willing to turn against the Soviet Union. Neither were the countries of what the CCP media called the Second World, mainly Western Europe and Japan, whose national security depends on their ties to the United States rather than on a fictitious alliance with the PRC. Since 1981, the

United States and its Western European allies have been mainly concerned about containing Soviet advances in Latin America, Africa, and West Asia and about achieving a satisfactory agreement with the Soviet Union on strategic and European theater nuclear arms reductions. Thus, the PRC had to realize that its proposed allies were not willing to join an antihegemonist united front of which the PRC was a part.

Strategically speaking, the foreign policy of the PRC since the end of the Cultural Revolution has been a series of failures, but it has been very successful in other respects. The PRC has definitely overcome its international isolation. In 1971, its fight for membership in the United Nations was finally won resoundingly. Between 1970 and 1977, most West European, Asian, African, and many Latin American countries established diplomatic relations with Peking, dropping their recognition of the RoC on T'aiwan if they had been represented there. Japan did the same in 1972, and finally, on December 15, 1978, the administration of President James Earl Carter gave the ruling elite of the PRC its ultimate success: U.S. diplomatic recognition in almost complete compliance with the terms stipulated by the Peking leadership. By the end of 1982, the PRC had established diplomatic relations with 132 countries while only 23 maintained formal ties with the RoC on T'aiwan. The competing Chinese political system appeared almost entirely isolated.

Yet even this successful drive for international recognition was bound to reach its limits. After establishing these diplomatic relations, the problem of making them work for the goals of the PRC has, so far, only partially been solved. The KMT leadership on T'aiwan has not given in to several consecutive offers from Peking for a peaceful reunification of the motherland. Keeping in mind the experiences of Tibet with similar offers made in 1950/1951—as they became obvious in 1959—the RoC has, so far, even refrained from any initial talks or official contacts. Although diplomatically isolated, T'aiwan has workable economic and cultural ties with more than 100 countries, and 58 maintain paradiplomatic establishments under various different names in T'aipei. In most countries of Europe, it is still easier to travel with an RoC passport than with one from the PRC.

On balance, the ruling elite of the PRC has been extremely successful in establishing and conducting bilateral relations with most countries in the world since 1971, and it has won a respectable position in the councils of the United Nations. But its major world political strategies to counter the perceived Soviet threat have failed. How about its record in the region where the PRC has the leverage of a major power, East and Southeast Asia?

Relations with Japan have developed very fruitfully for both countries in the field of economics. The Japanese government perceives that the

Soviet Union as a threat is much more dangerous than the PRC and seems, at the moment, only concerned about a possible Sino-Soviet rapprochement. But for security, Japan relies on the United States rather than on its ties with the Peking elite. North Korea has consistently maintained close ties with the PRC. Relations between the two countries are very friendly, but the authorities in Pyongyang meticulously try to balance this relationship with at least workable, if not friendly, relations with the Soviet Union.

After North Vietnam won the second Vietnam War, the PRC's relations with this Communist-ruled neighbor gradually deteriorated until, on July 3, 1978, the PRC terminated all its aid to the reunified Vietnam, which had concluded a treaty of friendship with the Soviet Union. On February 17, 1979, the PLA attacked Vietnam, losing much of its previous fighting prestige in the ambiguous to unsuccessful outcome of the seventeen days of the third Vietnam War. Since then, the two largest all-Asian Communist-ruled countries live in hostile coexistence, and neither excludes the possibility of a new military confrontation in the future. The major objective of the PRC in the Third Vietnam War, the withdrawal of the Vietnamese army from Cambodia—where it had driven Pol Pot, the close ally of the CCP, into the jungles—could not be achieved.

However, the attack on Vietnam helped to improve the relations of the PRC with Thailand, which perceived that the Vietnamese threat was more imminent than the one from China. On the other hand, the unwillingness of the current Chinese leadership to terminate its support of Communist guerrilla and underground movements in a number of Southeast Asian countries has hurt the development of friendly and politically feasible relations with Malaysia, Singapore, and Indonesia. Hence, the ASEAN countries are split in their attitude toward the PRC, with Thailand taking a friendly, Malaysia, Singapore, and Indonesia a more hostile, and the Philippines a neutral stand.

Sino-Indian relations are still overshadowed by an unsettled border dispute, by CCP policies of genocide in Tibet—resumed in August 1983—and by the PLA attack on India in the fall of 1962. In 1978, there were indications of an incipient rapprochement, but this tendency was again interrupted when the Chinese attacked Vietnam, which led to increased common interests between India and the Soviet Union.

In its own region, the PRC has mostly operated with diplomatic skill, and it enjoys a comparatively positive stand. But it has also alienated some of the ASEAN countries, Vietnam, and India, so that, by the autumn of 1983, the overall balance was still ambiguous—although some renewed signs of a Sino-Indian rapprochment seem to have developed since then.

Since 1980, the most dramatic changes have occurred in the crucial realm of the PRC's foreign policy, Sino-Soviet relations. The conflict between the Communist-ruled great power and the Communist-ruled major East Asian regional power seemed to have reached its apex when the PRC government notified the Soviet government on April 4, 1979, of its intention to not prolong the Sino-Soviet treaty of alliance, which had been concluded thirty years earlier in 1950. Thus, since April 1980, the two countries have no longer been allies according to the formal terms of a treaty. Yet, at the same time, the Peking elite agreed to start negotiations with the Moscow elite about a new arrangement between the two countries. Paradoxically, the termination of the formal alliance may have become the starting point for a rapprochement, which could eventually lead to the solution of the conflict between the two countries.

In November 1979, the CCP media ceased to use the epithet "revisionist" in referring to the Soviet Union. Talks on the vice-ministerial level started, only to be interrupted by Peking after the Soviet Union's intervention in Afghanistan. But in two major speeches during 1982, in Tashkent in the spring and in Baku in September, Leonid Brezhnev offered to resume the negotiations, and the Chinese side finally agreed in the fall of 1982. For these negotiations, the PRC ruling elite advanced four conditions.

1. A reduction of Soviet forces along the Chinese border and a mutual retreat from the immediate border to rear positions in order to reduce tensions
2. The withdrawal of Soviet forces from Outer Mongolia
3. The termination of Soviet support for Vietnam as long as Vietnamese troops continue to occupy Cambodia
4. The withdrawal of Soviet troops from Afghanistan

It appears highly doubtful that the Soviet Union will agree to these conditions. There are currently no indications that the Moscow elite would be willing to withdraw its support of Vietnam as the Soviet Union has a long tradition of standing by its allies. But in the long run, the outcome of the Sino-Soviet negotiations will be decided, not by the Soviet Union's acceptance or—much more likely—refusal of China's conditions, but by the amount and intensity of common interests between the two governments and parties.

The Soviet Union and the PRC have conflicting positions on Indochina, Afghanistan, and on the solution of their border disputes. These are strong conflicts of interest indeed, but in regard to both Cambodia and Afghanistan, they at least agree that Marxist-Leninist single-party rule must be continued. On the other hand, the major differences between the CCP and the CPSU in the realm of Party doctrine or ideology have almost entirely disappeared. In economic policies, the PRC elite now takes a more moderate stand than the CPSU elite, and in regard to the general aspects of the political system, I have suggested earlier that a trend toward Sovietization is at least one of the probable alternative projections for China's future. Thus, major aspects of the Sino-Soviet conflict of yore have already been dissipated, or may be dissipated in the future.

In other questions of world politics, the two countries have an increasing number of common interests. Their positions on West Asian, or Near East, politics have always been at least similar, if not in accord. In May 1983, in a dramatic move, Prime Minister Chao Tzu-yang withdrew Chinese support from the National Liberation Front guerrilla movement of Holden Roberto in Angola and officially recognized the Soviet-supported government of that country, thus accepting Soviet interests in regard to the most important point of Sino-Soviet disagreement in Africa. In early October 1983, the CCP, which only a year before was still calling for a strengthening of the defense capabilities of NATO in Europe, started to support the peace movement in the Federal Republic of Germany.

Since 1978, Sino-Soviet trade has been increasing, albeit very slowly. In the spring of 1983, the first Soviet students in seventeen years arrived in Peking to study Chinese, and the first Chinese students in sixteen years took up their studies in the Soviet Union and some East European countries. East European tourists have also reappeared in the PRC. All of these indications do not necessarily mean that a Sino-Soviet rapprochement, and a major reorientation of the PRC in international politics, are bound to occur, but they make it impossible to consider the Sino-Soviet conflict as an unchangeable factor.

The future perspectives for the role of the PRC in international politics are, therefore, as ambiguous and equivocal as those for the development of the economy and the society. Similarly, they also depend upon the political perspectives of the country. Closely connected with these political perspectives, I would suggest three possible alternative projections for the future of Sino-Soviet relations, which, in turn, would influence the PRC's general position in the world because it appears reasonably safe to assume that, at least until the end of this century, the PRC's international policies will continue to be determined by its relations with the Soviet Union.

1. A return to the Maoist policy of simultaneous conflict with both the Soviet Union and the United States, backed up by a full-

fledged revival of "people's war" doctrines and a new closing of
the country to contacts with the Western world

2. The gradual development of a détente on a state-to-state basis
   between the PRC and the Soviet Union, which would result in a
   policy of friendly equidistance toward the governments in Moscow
   and Washington, combined with a continuation of efforts to contain
   the Soviet Union in East Asia

3. A Sino-Soviet rapprochement that would directly continue to the
   stage of a renewal of Party-to-Party relations and a resumption
   of an all-out and worldwide strategic cooperation between the
   two Communist-ruled countries

Those, however, are projections for the 1990s. Prior to that time, the
alternatives will be either a continuation of the conflict, which still has
not ended, in the forms that characterized Soviet-U.S. relations during
the period of the Cold War from 1947 to 1962, or a fast development
toward state-to-state détente. Only after the generational succession has
taken place in the PRC could a resumption of strategic cooperation
between the PRC and the Soviet Union come about.

Economic, social, and political perspectives for the PRC all indicate
that the large East Asian country will not complete the transition to
institutionalized rule, and hence, to more long-range policy projections,
before the mid- or late 1990s. Until then, the PRC will remain a variable
factor in world politics. Once institutionalized rule does finally come
about, it may very well be accompanied by a new Sino-Soviet strategic
alliance. Such an alliance might be deemed vital by both Communist
single-party systems in order to safeguard Party rule, which as far as
the PRC is concerned, will most probably continue until the end of this
century. However, that system may also be threatened with a definite
breakdown because of economic and social developments during the
first decades of the twenty-first century.

Conclusion: Transition to Institutionalized Rule in Totalistic Single-party Systems

Sixty-six years after the Russian revolution, available historical materials allow us to make an effort to systematize the development that totalistic single-party systems of Communist persuasion appear to undergo. Max Weber first drew the attention of social scientists to the fact that charismatically legitimized rule usually develops toward a transition to institutionalization and, hence, to rational rule legitimation, a process he called "the routinization of charisma" (*Veralltäglichung des Charismas*). The experiences of the Soviet Union since the October revolution of 1917 indicate that securing the transition from charisma to institution can be a severe problem for totalistic single-party systems that were established, not by foreign military intervention, but by an indigenous revolution. These experiences, as well as my observation of political developments in the PRC since 1958, lead me to suggest that Communist single-party systems seem to run their historical course through three stages of development.

1. Charismatic rule, as in the Soviet Union under Lenin and in the PRC under the leadership of Mao Tse-tung until the late 1950s
2. Transitional rule, which assumed the form of monocracy in the Soviet Union under Stalin and which, in an entirely different manner, has characterized the political system of the PRC ever since late 1958
3. Institutionalized rule, which the Soviet political system reached in the mid-1950s

The stage of charismatic rule is characterized by the dominating role of the leader who led the Party to its revolutionary victory. The most significant organizational feature of this stage is the undisputed control the Party, as a political body rather than as a bureaucratic machine, exerts over all other subsystems, e.g., the administrative machine, the armed forces, the institutions of economic management, and the social groups. During this stage, intraelite conflicts are manifested by terminological divergencies and removals, but very rarely by expulsions from the Party. As a rule, only opponents outside the Party are physically exterminated—the only exceptions to this rule are the death of Camilo Cienfuegos in Cuba and the executions of Stalinists in Yugoslavia in 1948. Secondary intraelite group formation remains confined to opinion groups.

Political developments in the PRC have shown that the stage of transitional rule must not necessarily assume the form of monocracy, as it did under Stalin in the Soviet Union. In the PRC, the series of cyclical intraelite conflicts and crises since 1958 has taught us that there is also a second form of transitional rule, the transitional crisis system.

In a monocracy, the political decision-making process is dominated by the people who are close to the leader, which balances the bureaucratic competition of different subsystems; in the transitional crisis system, it is characterized by the confrontation between majorities and minorities *within* the different subsystems. In a monocracy, conflict signals are removals, expulsion from the Party, and first and foremost, large-scale purges involving physical extermination; in the transitional crisis system, conflicts are mostly signaled by terminological divergencies, removals, expulsions, and occasionally an open rift within the Party. Physical extermination, albeit there are a number of significant exceptions, has usually been limited to Party members who rank below the ruling elite.

In a monocracy, opinion groups are mostly destroyed in their formative stage. They cannot condense into factions because the paranoia of the monocrat means that he perceives evolving opinion groups as coherent circles with alternative platforms and has them immediately liquidated. The transitional crisis system, on the other hand, is virtually based upon the interplay between the formation of opinion groups and their condensation into factions, one of which comes out as the victor in each intraelite conflict, only to split up again as a new crisis cycle begins. As the former charismatic leader retires more and more to—or is pushed into—the role of a legitimizer, and several leaders compete on an equal footing after his death, political initiatives are questioned, divided, and—with regard to long-term decisions—paralyzed.

The stage of institutionalized rule results in competition among bureaucratic machines, which is time and again stabilized by interorganizational compromise. The characteristics of this stage have been defined by Graham Allison as the elements of bureaucratic politics: government through negotiation and compromise between the function-oriented interests, perceptions, and political goals of the different machines.[1]

The signals of conflict are now limited to terminological divergencies and removals. Occasionally, there may still be isolated expulsions from the Party, but physical extermination of Party members has definitely ended. The balance-by-compromise among bureaucratic subsystems frequently has to be restored. A minority group that has lost out at one point may be needed again for a new coalition at another and, hence, must not be entirely liquidated. In terms of intraelite group formation, primary and protosecondary groups take priority over secondary groups, among which, if they appear at all, opinion groups are now more important than factions (the compromise nature of the political decision-making process makes the condensation of opinion groups into factions a very rare phenomenon).

In the stage of institutionalized rule, the character and content of intraelite conflict change fundamentally. The great confrontations over power positions and political platforms, as they developed during the transitional stage, have become a matter of the past. Their place is taken by bureaucratic rivalries among the machines. Very early in the discussion on the organizational theory of the Communist movement, in 1903, Leon Trotsky opposed Lenin's idea of the Party as a group of professional revolutionary cadres by warning, "These methods lead, as we shall experience, to the following: the Party organization takes the place of the Party, the Central Committee takes the place of the Party organization, and finally, the dictator takes the place of the Central Committee!" Yet this prophecy has only materialized in intermediate terms: In the third stage of Communist single-party rule, the bureaucratic machines take the place of the dictator.

Under these conditions in the stage of institutionalized rule, the content of intraelite conflict is less and less determined by the quest for political, economic, or social change and more and more determined by the interests of autonomous machines to alter the weights in the scales of the bureaucratic balance of interests. Corresponding to this depoliticization of the content of conflict is a depersonalization of the conflicting forces.

These characteristics make it inevitable that in the stage of institutionalized rule, a change of leadership in totalistic single-party systems, in which the instrument of elections is unknown, can be brought about in only two ways: either by a succession of generations of administering rather than politically leading bureaucrats or by a new revolution.

In the mid-1950s, the Soviet Union reached the stage of institutionalized rule. The same holds true, though in some cases only in the early 1960s, for Outer Mongolia and most East European countries where there has never been a stage of charismatic rule. Here, institutionalized rule succeeded a special form of transitional rule, derived monocracy, which was totally dependent upon the monocrat of the Soviet Union and was restricted to mere executive functions within the framework of Stalin's policy decisions.

But what about the PRC? With the overthrow of the cultural revolutionary Left in October 1976 and the ensuing stabilization at the Eleventh CCP Party Congress, it appeared, for some time, that the PRC had also embarked on the path toward institutionalized rule. Yet the new intraelite conflict over power positions and political platforms since the spring of 1978 has made it obvious that the political system of the PRC remained a transitional crisis system at least until late 1980 or mid-1981.

The question of whether it is now, after the Twelfth Party Congress in September 1982 and the first session of the Sixth NPC in June 1983, moving toward institutionalization can be answered only if we use a catalog of criteria for the transition to institutionalized rule. Such a catalog can be developed from the Soviet Union and East European experiences and would include at least five indicators, all of which have to be present in a system that has reached the stage of institutionalized rule.

1. The leaders of the Party and the state administrative machine serve their statutory terms of office, and the leading organs meet at statutory intervals.
2. Party decisions concerning the constitutional powers of the state administrative machine are regularly ratified by ensuing decisions of the leading state organs.
3. Promotion within the leading organs of the Party is preceded by promotion in the subsystems of the state administrative machine, the armed forces, or the mass organizations; e.g., a person becomes first a minister and then, at the next possible date and *because* of this promotion, a full member of the CC.
4. The subsystems develop their own channels of elite recruitment and career patterns, albeit under the control of the Party center.
5. A generation that joined the Party *after* the establishment of Communist rule—the postrevolutionary generation—has taken over the majority of positions in the decision combine, as well as within the ruling elite in general.

If we apply these criteria to the PRC in the fall of 1983, we arrive at the conclusion that the first and second indicators were already clearly recognizable. But the third, the fourth, and—most important—the fifth, generational succession, had not yet evolved.

The political system of the PRC, therefore, may have begun its movement toward the stage of institutionalized rule, but it has not yet arrived at that stage. Therefore, there can be only a partially affirmative answer to the last of the questions that I asked in the Introduction to this book, the question of whether the Chinese experience since the death of Mao can provide clues for a typology of transition under Communist rule. The political developments in the PRC between 1975 and 1983 have resulted in a great deal of data that confirm the theory of the transitional crisis system, but only a little that tend to verify the indicators for the transition to institutionalized rule.

The continuing omnipresence of the generation of revolutionary and civil war veterans, as well as the fact that a Maoist backlash against the policies of enlightened Stalinism is one of at least three equally viable alternative projections for the intermediate future of China, means that the political system of the PRC is still transitional crisis system, even though the tendencies toward institutionalized rule appear to be increasing. If institutionalized rule should finally develop in the PRC during the 1990s, the incipient political advance of people who have been trained by and started their careers in the Bolshevik machines of the civilian Party apparat and the CYL, the return of the Party statute and the state constitution to structures similar to those modeled after Soviet examples in the 1950s, and the reorganization of the security establishment according to Soviet models strongly suggest that the political and organizational present of the Soviet Union may well be the future of the PRC. Socialism, probably in its bureaucratic prototype, would then be the most likely future perspective for politics, economics, and the society in the PRC, at least for the intermediate future, until the early years of the next century.

It is exactly in this projection that China's most severe developmental problem can be found. For following is the historical experience the world has witnessed since the Russian October revolution of 1917 and the system that it created: Between socialism on the one hand and modernity and social progress on the other there exists—to put it into Marxist-Leninist terms—an antagonistic contradiction. They are incompatible.

Postscript

The draft manuscript for this book was completed in early November 1983, and the revision of the manuscript by June 1984. During the period between the completion of the manuscript and the beginning of the final stage of its production in January 1985, significant developments have occurred on the domestic political scene in the PRC. The revisionist forces around Teng Hsiao-p'ing were able to strengthen their position so that the politics of compromise, which appear to continue, seem to display a comparatively stronger share of revisionist content than in 1982-1983.

In rural societal policies, the responsibility system has been further consolidated. According to numerous statements of the CCP media in the spring and summer of 1984, the *pao-kan tao-hu* concept of production contracting now extends to more than 95 percent of the production teams in the country, and the contracts under which arable land is— for all practical purposes—rented to the peasants for individual production have been extended to a duration of fifteen years, thus making investments by the farming families more worthwhile than under the earlier contracts, which were concluded for three to five years.

Of even greater significance could be the developments in the urban and industrial economy and society, which were introduced by the opening of seventeen coastal and lower Yangtzu cities for foreign investment and the settlement of foreign firms and increased by the decisions of the third plenum of the Twelfth CCP/CC, which convened in Peking in October 1984. On October 20, this meeting passed a draft resolution on the reform of the economic system, introducing sweeping changes in the management and planning structures. The resolution summarizes the different experimental reforms that had been enacted in a great number of enterprises, and in the largest cities, since 1979-1980 and extends them over the whole country.

Starting from the beginning of 1985, all industrial enterprises have to implement a "responsibility system," which is to be based on the individual leadership and responsibility of the plant manager. With the exception of the sector of basic industries—mining, steel, and energy production—all industrial enterprises will be responsible for their own supplies of raw materials, the setting of their detailed production targets, their sales, and the marketing of their products. In regard to profits, they will have to pay taxes only to the state organs and will be able to make their own decisions on the allocations of investments and bonuses to their workers. On the other hand, the state organs will no longer bail out enterprises that have losses, and if such losses continue for a long period, they will be closed down, and their workers will be laid off.

Prices of basic foodstuffs, and some basic industrial products such as energy, steel, and heavy machinery, will continue to be controlled by the central economic authorities, but the prices of most agricultural products—in particular for vegetables, fruits, fowl, fish, and industrial crops—and of most consumer goods, services, and repairs are going to be decontrolled and allowed to develop according to the market laws of supply and demand. In the areas of services and repairs, individual enterprises are now fully legitimized. In addition, private clinics and private law firms can be established, with a license to engage up to five employees and subject to taxation only by the state.

Piece planning is going to be replaced by a framework of so-called guidance plans, which will give general directives to rather than set detailed and explicit production targets for the enterprises. The resolution of the third plenum, however, still stresses that the PRC will continue to implement a basically planned economic system, in which the market forces are now accepted in an auxiliary role.

Still, the economic decisions of October 1984 indicate that the PRC intends further departures from the centralized system of economic planning and management as it is practiced in the USSR and was practiced in China between 1953 and 1957 and again between 1972 and 1979-1980. Instead, the PRC will move toward experimenting with a "socialist market economy," which has been comparatively successful in Hungary yet much less so in Yugoslavia and East Germany.

In order to provide a theoretical base for the reforms of the economic system, the ruling CCP elite decided in late 1984, to prepare for a new move toward a revision of Party doctrines. In an editorial published on December 7, 1984, the *JMJP* stated that some of the teachings of Marx and Lenin would no longer fit the necessities of the late twentieth century and that Marxism-Leninism must be "applied creatively, taking the realities of the 1980s into consideration." This article has been interpreted by many foreign observers as the beginning of a departure of the CCP from communism, and even from Marxism. In my view, this is an overinterpretation. In fact, the article does no more than suggest basic approaches that Mao Tse-tung had already proposed in 1940, 1942, 1945, and 1956, this time as a lever to promote the policies of economic reform. Variations in the application of Marxist concepts according to the actual situation of China and the world—at least within the limits of the angle from which the CCP leaders decided to see them—have always been a part of official CCP doctrine. Nevertheless, the revisionist thrust in the article indicates that at the end of 1984, the revisionist and enlightened Stalinist forces within the ruling elite of the PRC were—for the time being—definitely stronger than the orthodox Stalinist wing of the CCP.

How do these recent developments relate to the economic perspectives suggested in the first part of Chapter 14? For the immediate future, the suggestions that the second modernization concept will continue to be implemented and that the current policies of decollectivized production in agriculture and a broadening of the parameters for enterprise autonomy within the framework of a planned economy will continue to be confirmed. The intermediate future, however, remains shrouded in uncertainties, so that it is still necessary to present alternative projections. The current reforms could eventually strengthen the probability of the second economic projection—continuation of the policies of 1983-1984 within the framework of a rigid adherence to the Four Basic Principles—over the third, viz., a return to the first modernization concept. I would even suggest that if the economic reform should prove a success until about 1990, the probability of first projection—increasing elite responsiveness to the demands of society—could increase.

Yet I caution against overenthusiasm. Even the resolution of October 20, 1984, reiterates with strong words the Four Basic Principles, particularly the leadership by the Party. If the policies of a "socialist market economy" should be continued until the end of this century, the forces they are bound to unleash in the urban society will sooner or later demand first a revision and then possibly even an abolition of the Four Basic Principles, which, for all practical purposes, would mean the abolition of the totalistic single-party system. By then, however, the major promoters of the current reform, who are now between sixty-five and eighty-two years of age, will mostly have left the political scene, and the youngest of them will be in their early or mid-seventies. There is not the slightest indication that the succeeding elite will be as dedicated to the revisionist program as they are, and many indications seem to suggest that it will be much less so.

Hence, the possibility of a return to a Soviet-type system of centralized planning and a reduction of private initiatives has, in my view, not significantly decreased during 1984, all economic reforms and theoretical revisionism notwithstanding. Even if elements of the market economy are being strengthened, socialism—characterized mainly by state and collective ownership of the means of production—continues to be the major aspect of the PRC's economic system, combined with unrestricted Party dictatorship. Unless these two features of the situation in the PRC are abolished, the future remains uncertain. Whether they will be abolished one day, nobody can tell, but there is room for very strong doubt, since, in that case, the CCP would commit political suicide, and that can hardly be expected.

Jürgen Domes
Saarbrücken, January 14, 1985

Acronyms

AFP	Agence France Presse
APCs	armored personnel carriers
APD	Association for the Promotion of Democracy
ASEAN	Association of Southeast Asian Nations
CAC	Central Advisory Commission
CC	Central Committee
CCP	Chinese Communist Party
CDIC	Central Disciplinary Investigation Commission
CFCP	*Chieh-fang-chün pao*
CFJP	*Chieh-fang jih-pao*
CKYC	*Chung-kung yen-chiu*
CKT	*Chih-kung tang*
CM	*Cheng-ming*
CMC	Central Military Commission
CNA	*China News Analysis*
CPPCC	Chinese People's Political Consultative Conference
CPSU	Communist Party of the Soviet Union
CQ	*China Quarterly*
CYL	Communist Youth League
DL	Democratic League
DPWP	Democratic Peasants' and Workers' Party
FA	field army
FEER	*Far Eastern Economic Review*
GNP	gross national product
GPD	General Political Department
GRSD	General Rear Services Department
HC	*Hung-ch'i*
HHYPP	*Hsüeh-hsi yü p'i-p'an*
ICBM	intercontinental ballistic missile
IRBM	intermediate-range ballistic missile

JMP	*Jen Men Pi* (Chinese People's Bank Dollar)
JMJP	*Jen-min jih-pao*
KCJP	*Kuangchou jih-pao*
KJJP	*Kung-jen jih-pao*
KMJP	*Kuang-ming jih-pao*
KMT	National People's party (*Kuo-min tang*)
KMTRC	KMT Revolutionary Committee
LDT	League for the Democratic Self-Government of T'aiwan
LW	*Liao-wang*
MAC	military area command
MRBM	medium-range ballistic missile
NATO	North Atlantic Treaty Organization
NCNA	New China News Agency
NDCA	National Democratic Construction Association
NFJP	*Nan-fang jih-pao*
9-3	September 3 Society
NPC	National People's Congress
PBS	people's broadcasting station
PC	people's congress
PLA	People's Liberation Army
PPC	provincial Party committee
PRC	People's Republic of China
RC	Revolutionary Committee
RoC	Republic of China
TKP	*Ta-kung-pao*
UNDRO	United Nations Disaster Relief Organization
WHP	*Wen-hui-pao*

Wade-Giles/Hanyu Pinyin Romanization Conversion Table

Amoy / Xiamen
Anhui / Anhui
An P'ing-sheng / An
  Pingsheng
Anshan-Fushun-Penhsi /
  Anshan-Fushun-Benxi

Canton / Guangzhou
Ch'ang-an / Changan
Chang Ai-p'ing / Zhang
  Aiping
Chang An-p'ing / Zhang
  Anping
Ch'ang-cheng / Changzheng
Chang Chih-hsiu / Zhang
  Zhixiu
Chang Chih-tung / Zhang
  Zhidong
Chang Ching-fu / Zhang
  Jingfu
Ch'angch'un / Changchun
Chang Ch'un-ch'iao / Zhang
  Chunqiao
Chang P'ing-hua / Zhang
  Pinghua
Ch'angsha / Changsha
Chang T'ing-fa / Zhang Tingfa
Chan-kuo / Zhanguo

Chan-tou ying-hsiung /
  Zhandou yingxiung
Chao Hai-feng / Zhao Haifeng
Chao Hsing-ch'u / Zhao
  Xingchu
Chao ma-fan / Zhao mafan
Chao Tzu-yang / Zhao Ziyang
Chaowuta / Zhaowuda
Chekiang / Zhejiang
Chen / Zhen
Chenchiang / Zhenjiang
Cheng-chih-chü / Zhengzhiju
Cheng-chi-chü chang-wu wei-
  yüan-hui / zhengzhiju
  changwu weiyuanhui
Chengchou / Zhengzhou
Ch'engtu / Chengdu
cheng-tun / zhengdun
Cheng Wei-shan / Zheng
  Weishan
Ch'eng Yüeh / Cheng Yue
Ch'en Hsi-lien / Chen Xilian
Ch'en Kuo-tung / Chen
  Guodong
Ch'en Mu'hua / Chen Muhua
Ch'en P'i-hsien / Chen Pixian
Ch'en Tsai-tao / Chen Zaidao
Ch'en Tu-hsiu / Chen Duxiu

Ch'en Wei-ta / Chen Weida
Ch'en Yi / Chen Yi
Ch'en Yün / Chen Yun
Ch'en Yung-kuei / Chen
  Yonggui
Ch'i / Qi
Chia Ch'i-yün / Jia Qiyun
Chia-ju wo shih chen-te /
  Jiaru wo shi zhende
Chiang Ch'ing / Jiang Qing
Ch'iang Hsiao-ch'u / Qiang
  Xiaochu
Chiang Hua / Jiang Hua
Chiang Kai-shek / Jiang Jieshi
Chiang Wei-ch'ing / Jiang
  Weiqing
Chiang Yung-hui / Jiang
  Yonghui
Ch'iao Hsiao-kuang / Qiao
  Xiaoguang
Ch'iao Kuan-hua / Qiao
  Guanhua
Ch'iao Shih / Qiao Shi
Chieh-fang / Jiefang
Chieh-fang-chün pao /
  Jiefangjun bao
Chieh-fang jih-pao / Jiefang
  ribao
Chieh-fang ssu-hsiang /
  Jiefang sixiang
chien-ch'ih / Jianchi
Chih-hsia-shih / Zhixiashi
Chih-kung tai-piao ta-hui /
  Zhigong daibiao dahui
Chih-kung tang / Zhigong
  dang
Ch'ih Pi-ch'ing / Chi Biqing
Chi-lü chien-ch'a wei-yüan-
  hui / Jilu jiancha weiyuanhui
Ch'in / Qin
Chinan / Jinan
Ch'in Chi-wei / Qin Jiwei
Chinchou / Jinzhou

Ch'ing / Qing
Ch'inghai / Qinghai
Chingkangshan / Jinggangshan
Ch'inghua (University) /
  Qinghua (University)
Ch'ing-jen / Qingren
Ch'ing-ming / Qingming
Ch'ingtao / Qingdao
Ch'ingt'ien / Qingtian
Chinmen (Quemoy) / Jinmen
Chinshan / Jinshan
Ch'in Shi-huang / Qin
  Shihuang
Ch'i-t'an Kuai-lun / Qitan
  Guailun
Ch'iu-shih-pao / Qiushi bao
Chin-t'ien / Jintian
Chi P'eng-fei / Ji Pengfei
Chi Teng-k'uei / Ji Dengkui
Chi-ts'eng tsu-chih / Jiceng
  zuzhi
Chiuchiang / Jinjiang
Chiu-san hsüeh-hui / Chiusan
  xuehui
Cho Lin / Zhuo Lin
Chou / Zhou
Chou En-lai / Zhou Enlai
Chou Hui / Zhou Hui
Chou Jung-hsin / Zhou
  Rongxin
Chou Ku-ch'eng / Zhou
  Gucheng
Chou Shih-chung / Zhou
  Shizhong
Chou Yang / Zhou Yang
Chua-kang chih-kuo /
  Zhuangang zhiguo
Chiang Tse-tung / Jiang
  Zedong
Ch'ü / Qu
Ch'üan-chün cheng-chih kung-
  tso hui-yi / Quanjun
  zhengzhi gongzuo huiyi

Chuang / Zhuang
Ch'üan-kuo jen-mn tai-piao ta-hui ch'ang-wu wei-yüan-hui / Quanguo renmin daibiao dahui changwu weiyuanhui
Ch'üan-kuo min-chu chien-kuo-hui / Quanguo minzhu jianguohui
Ch'üan-kuo tai-piao ta-hui / Quanguo daibiao dahui
Chu-hsi / Zhuxi
Chu Hsüeh-fan / Zhu Xuefan
Chu Hung-hsia / Zhu Hongxia
Chu-jen / Zhuren
Chukiang / Zhujiang
Ch'un-ch'iu / Chunqiu
Chün-chung / Zhunzhong
Ch'ün-chung ts'an-k'ao hsiao-hsi / Junzhong cankao xiaoxi
Chün-fa / Junfa
Chung-fa / Zhongfa
Chung-hua / Zhonghua
Chung-hua jen-min kung-he-kuo chu-hsi / Zhonghua renmin gongheguo zhuxi
Chung-hua min-kuo / Zhonghua minguo
Chungking / Zhongqing
Chung-Kung chung-yang chün-shi wei-yüan-hui / Zhonggong zhongyang junshi weiyüanhui
Chung-kuo / Zhongguo
Chung-kuo-jen / Zhongguoren
Chung-kuo jen-ch'üan / Zhongguo renquan
Chung-kuo kung-nung hung-chün / Zhongguo gongnong hongjun
Chung-kuo jen-min cheng-chih hsieh-shang hui-yi /

Zhongguo renmin zhengzhi xieshang huiyi
Chung-kuo kuo-min-tang ke-ming wei-yüan-hui / Zhongguo guomindang geming weiyuanhui
Chung-kuo min-chu ts'u-chin-hui / Zhongguo minzhu cujinhui
Chung-kuo min-chu t'ung-meng / Zhongguo minzhu tongmeng
Chung-kuo nung-kung min-chu-tang / Zhongguo nonggong minzhu dang
Chung-nan / Zhongnan
Chung-yang chi-lü chien-ch'a wei-yuan-hui / Zhongyang jilü jiancha weiyuanhui
Chung-yang chün-shih wei-yuan-hui / Zhongyang junshi weiyuanhui
Chung-yang fa-pu / Zhongyang fabu
Chung-yang pan-kung-t'ing / Zhongyang bangongting
Chung-yao chih-shih / Zhongyao zhishi
Chu Te / Zhu De
Chu Yüan-chang / Zhu Yuanzhang

Fan-chi yu-ch'ing fan-an feng / Fanji youqing fananfeng
Fa-chia / Fajia
Fang Yi / Fang Yi
Fan-shih p'ai / Fanshi pai
fei yüeh / fei yue
Foshan / Foshan
fu'ch'iang / fuqiang
Fuchou / Fuzhou
Fukien / Fujian
Fu Yüeh-hua / Fu Yuehua

Haik'ou / Haikou
Hainan / Hainan
Han / Han
Han Fei / Han Fei
Hangchou / Hangzhou
Han Hsien-chu / Han Xianchu
Han P'ei-hsin / Han Peixin
Hank'ou / Hankou
Han-jen / Hanren
Hao Chien-hsin / Hao Jianxin
Harbin / Haerbin
Heilungkiang / Heilongqiang
Hei Po-li / Hei Boli
Hofei / Hefei
Ho Lung / He Lung
Honan / Henan
Hongkong / Xianggang
Hopei / Hebei
Hsia-fang / Xiafang
Hsian / Xi'an
Hsiang / Xiang
Hsiang Nan / Xiang Nan
Hsiang Shou-chih / Xiang
Shouzhi
Hsiangt'an / Xiangtan
Hsiao Ch'üan-fu / Xiao Quanfu
Hsiao Hua / Xiao Hua
Hsiao-k'ang / Xiaokang
Hsiao-p'ing / Xiaoping
Hsi Chung-hsün / Xi
Zhongxun
Hsieh Cheng-yi (Ms) / Xie
Zhengyi
Hsien / Xian
Hsien Heng-han / Xian
Henghan
Hsienyang / Xianyang
Hsin / Xin
Hsin Chün-chieh / Xin Junjie
Hsingyang / Xingyang
Hsin-ssu-chün / Xinsijun
Hsinan / Xinan

Hsing-cheng-ch'ü / Xingzhengqu
Hsing-cheng-ts'un / Xingzhengcun
Hsipei / Xibei
Hsiu-cheng / Xiuzheng
Hsiu-cheng chu-yi / Xiuzheng zhuyi
Hsiu-yang sheng-hsi / Xiuyang shengxi
Hsü Chia-t'un / Xu Jiatun
Hsü Ching-hsien / Xu Jingxian
Hsü Hai-tung / Xu Haidong
Hsü Hsiang-ch'ien / Xu Xiangqian
Hsü Shih-yu / Xu Shiyou
Hsü Te-heng / Xu Deheng
Hsüeh Mu-ch'iao / Xue Muqiao
Hsüeh-hsi wen-chien / Xuexi wenjian
Hu Ch'i-li / Hu Qili
Hu Ch'iao-mu / Hu Qiaomu
Hu Chüeh-wen / Hu Juewen
Hu Yao-pang / Hu Yaobang
Hu Yü-chih / Hu Yuzhi
Hua-hua / Huahua
Hua Kuo-feng / Hua Guofeng
Huangan / Huang'an
Huanghe / Huanghe
Huang Hua / Huang Hua
Huang Huang / Huang Huang
Huang Huo-ch'ing / Huang Huoqing
Huang K'ê-ch'eng / Huang Kecheng
Huang-ti / Huangdi
Huapei / Huabei
Huatung / Huadong
Hui / Hui
Hui-fu / Huifu
Hunan / Hunan
Hung-ch'i / Hongqi

Hung Hsüeh-chih / Hong
  Xuezhi
Huo Shih-lien / Huo Shilian
Hupei / Hubei

I chia i chu / Yi jia yi zhu
I-chih / Yizhi
I-erh pu kou, i-wu tsui shao /
  Yier bu gou, yiwu zui shao
I jen i chu / Yi ren yi zhu
Ishak Bey Saifudin / Ishak
  Seypidin
I-yüan-hua / Yiyuanhua

Jao Shou-k'un / Rao Shoukun
Jao Shu-shih / Rao Shushi
Jen-ch'üan yün-tung /
  Renquan yundong
Jen Chung-yi / Ren Zhongyi
Jenhe / Renhe
Jen-min cheng-fu / Renmin
  Zhengfu
Jen-min cheng-fu chu-hsi /
  Renmin zhengfu zhuxi
Jen-min cheng-fu wei-yüan-
  hui / Renmin zhengfu
  weiyuanhui
Jen-min chieh-fang-chün /
  Renmin jiefangjun
Jen-min chih sheng /
  Renminzhisheng
Jen-min jih-pao / Renmin
  ribao
Jen-min kung-she / Renmin
  gongshe
Jen-min tai-biao ta-hui /
  Renmin daibiao dahui
Jen Wan-ting / Ren Wanding
Jih-ch'ang kung-tso / Richang
  gongzuo
Jung Yi-jen / Rong Yiren

K'aifeng / Kaifeng

Kai-ke / gaige
Kang / Gang
K'ang Chien-min / Kang
  Jianmin
K'ang Sheng / Kang Sheng
K'ang Shih-en / Kang Shi'en
K'ang Yu-wei / Kang Youwei
Kan-pu / Ganbu
Kansu / Gansu
Kao-kan tzu-ti / Gaogan zidi
Kao Yang / Gao Yang
K'e-hsüeh min-chu fa-chih /
  Kexue minzhu fazhi
Ke-ming / Geming
Ke-ming san-chieh-he /
  Geming sanjiehe
Ke-ming wei-yüan-hui /
  Geming weiyuanhui
Keng Piao / Geng Biao
Kiangsi / Jiangxi
Kiangsu / Jiangsu
Kirin / Jilin
Kowloon / Jiulong
Kwangchouwan /
  Guangzhouwan
Kuang-hsü / Guangxu
Kuang-ming jih-pao /
  Guangming ribao
Kuangsi / Guangxi
Kuangtung / Guangdong
Kuan Kuang-fu / Guan
  Guangfu
Kueichou / Guizhou
Kueilin / Guilin
K'u lien / Ku lian
Ku Mu / Gu Mu
Kung / Gong
Kung-ch'an-chu-yi ch'ing-nian-
  t'uan / Gongchanzhuyi
  qingniantuan
Kung-fen / Gongfen
Kung-jen jih-pao / Gongren
  ribao

K'ung-tzu / Kongzi
Kuningt'ou / Guningtou
K'unming / Kunming
Kuo / Guo
Kuo-chia an-ch'üan pu-tui /
    Guojia anquan budui
Kuo-chia ts'ai-cheng ching-chi
    wei-yüan-hui / Guojia
    caizheng zhingji weiyuanhui
Kuo Feng / Guo Feng
Kuo-min ke-ming chün /
    Guomin gemingjun
Kuo-min tang / Guomindang
Kuo-wu wei-yüan / Guowu
    weiyuan
Kuo-wu-yüan / Guowuyuan
Kuo-wu-yüan ch'ang-wu hui-
    yi / Guowuyuan changwu
    huiyi
Kuo-wu-yüan tsung-li /
    Guowuyuan zongli
Kuoyang / Guoyang
Ku-wen wei-yüan-hui /
    Guwen weiyuanhui

Lanchou / Lanzhou
Lao-tung kai-tsao / Laodong
    gaizao
Lao-tzu / Laozi
Lei Feng / Lei Feng
Li Ching-ch'üan / Li Jingquan
Li Fu-ch'un / Li Fuchun
Li Hsien-nien / Li Xiannian
Li Hsüeh-chih / Li Xuezhi
Li Hung-chang / Li
    Hongzhang
Li-I-che (Pseudonym) / Li
    Yizhe
Li Kuang-t'ao / Li Guangtao
Li Li-an / Li Li'an
Li Li-kung / Li Ligong
Li P'eng / Li Peng
Li Ssu-ch'eng / Li Sicheng

Li Te-sheng / Li Desheng
Li Tzu-ch'i / Li Ziqi
Li Wei-han / Li Weihan
Liang Ch'i-ch'ao / Liang
    Qichao
liang-hsin / liangxin
liang-shih / liangshi
Liao Ch'eng-chih / Liao
    Chengzhi
Liao Chih-kao / Liao Zhigao
Liao Han-sheng / Liao
    Hansheng
Liaoning / Liaoning
Liao-wang / Liaowang
Lien-ch'an chi-ch'ou /
    Lianchan jichou
Lin Hu-chia / Lin Hujia
Lin Piao / Lin Biao
ling-tao / lingdao
Ling-tao kan-pu / Lingdao
    ganbu
Liu Chieh / Liu Jie
Liu Hua-ch'ing / Liu Huaqing
Liu Hsiang-p'ing (Ms) / Liu
    Xiangping
Liu Hsing-yüan / Liu
    Xingyuan
Liu Kuang-t'ao / Liu
    Guangdao
Liu P'ing / Liu Ping
Liu Po-ch'eng / Liu Bocheng
Liu Shao-ch'i / Liu Shaoqi
Liu-shi kung-ren / Liushi
    gongren
Lo Jung-huan / Luo Ronghuan
Loyang / Luoyang
Lüshun / Lushun
Lung-shan / Longshan
Lung Yü-lan (Ms) / Long
    Yulan
Lushan / Lushan
Lu Ting-i / Lu Dingyi

Mach'eng / Macheng
Ma Li / Ma Li
Ma T'ien-shui / Ma Tianshui
Ma Wen-jui / Ma Wenrui
Mao Chih-yung / Mao
Zhiyong
Mao Tse-tung / Mao Zedong
Mao Yüan-hsin / Mao Yuanxin
Matsu / Mazu
Meng / Meng
Meng K'e / Meng Ke
Min-chu ch'iang /
Minzhuqiang
Min-chu tang-p'ai / Minzhu
dangpai
Min-chu yün-tung / Minzhu
yundong
Min-chu yü shih-tai / Minzhu
yu shidai
Ming / Ming
Moanshan / Mo'anshan
Mo-tzu / Mozi

Nanch'ang / Nanchang
Nanchung / Nanzhong
Nan-fang / Nanfang
Nanking / Nanjing
Nansha (Spratleys) / Nansha
Ni Chih-fu / Ni Zhifu
Nieh Feng-chih / Nie Fengzhi
Nieh Jung-chen / Nie
Rongzhen
Nien-ch'ing-hua / Nianqinghua
Ninghsia / Ningxia
Nung / Nong
Nung-fu-p'in shih-ch'ang /
Nongfupin shichang
Nung-ts'un chi-shih /
Nongcun jishi
Nung-yeh sheng-ch'an tse-jen-
chih / Nongye shengchan
zirenzhi

Pai Hua / Bai Hua
Pai hua yün-tung / Baihua
yundong
Pai Tung-ts'ai / Bai Dongcai
Pa-lu-chün / Balujun
Paoan / Bao'an
Pao-ch'an / Baochan
Pao-ch'an tao hu / Baochan
daohu
Pao-ch'an tao tsu / Baochan
daozu
Pao-kan tao-hu / Baogan
daohu
Pao-kung pao-ch'an / Baogong
baoch'an
Paot'ou / Baotou
Pei-fang / Beifang
Peking / Beijing
Peking chih-ch'un / Beijing zhi
chun
P'eng Chen / Peng Zhen
P'eng Ch'ung / Peng Chong
P'enghu (Pescadores) / Penghu
P'eng Te-huai / Peng Dehuai
P'ingchiang / Pingjiang
P'ing-chung / Bingzhong
P'i Teng / Pi Deng
Po I-po / Bo Yibo
Pu / Bu
Pu-p'ing-teng t'iao-yüeh /
Bupingdeng tiaoyue

San-chih liang-chün kung-tso
/ Sanzhiliangjun gongzuo
San hsiang chih-shih / San
xiang zhishi
Sanchih / Sanzhi
San k'u-nien / San kunian
San kuo / Sanguo
Sha Yeh-hsin / Sha Yexin
Shamien / Shamian
Shang / Shang
Shanghai / Shanghai

Shansi / Shanxi
Shantung / Shandong
She-lun / Shelun
Sheng / Sheng
Sheng-ch'an ta-tui /
Shengchan dadui
Sheng-ch'an-tui /
Shengchandui
Sheng-huo / Shenghuo
Shengli / Shengli
Shensi / Shanxi
Shenyang / Shenyang
Shih / Shi
Shih-chang / Shizhang
Shih Huang-ti / Shi Huangdi
Shih Liang (Ms) / Shi Liang
Shih-shih ch'iu shih / Shishi
qiushi
Shih-tai / Shidai
Shih-yeh / Shiye
Shih-yu chi-t'uan / Shiyou
jituan
Shou-pei pu-tui / Shoubei
budui
Shu-chi / Shuji
Shu-chi ch'u / Shujichu
Shui-hu chuan / Shuihuzhuan
Sian or Hsian / Xi'an
Sinkiang / Xinjiang
So-lieh-hsi-te ch'ün-chung /
Suoliexide chunzhong
Ssuch'uan / Sichuan
Ssu-hsiang chi-pen yüan-tse /
Sixiang jiben yuanze
Ssu-jen-pang / Sirenbang
ssu-hua lun-t'an / Sihua
luntan
Ssu-ke hsien-tai-hua / Sige
xiandaihua
Ssu-wu lun-t'an / Siwu luntan
Su Chen-hua / Su Zhenhua
Su Yi-jan / Su Yiran

Su-fan yün-tung / Sufan
yundong
Sui / Sui
Suip'ing / Suiping
Sun Ching-wen / Sun Jingwen
Sun Yat-sen / Sun Yixian
Sung Cheng-ming / Song
Zhengming
Sung Chiang / Song Jiang
Sung Jen-ch'iung / Song
Renqiong
Sung P'ei-chang / Song
Peichang
Sung P'ing / Song Ping
Su-wei-ai ch'ü / Suweiaichu

Tachai / Dazhai
Ta chih / Da zhi
Tach'ing / Daqing
T'aipei / Taibei
T'aip'ing / Taiping
T'aiwan / Taiwan
T'aiwan min-chu tzu-chih hui
/ Taiwan minzhu zizhihui
T'aiyüan / Taiyuan
Talien / Dalien
Ta luan / Da luan
Ta ming, ta fang, ta pien-lun,
ta-tzu-pao / Daming, dafang,
dabianlun dazibao
T'an Chen-lin / Tan Zhenlin
T'an Ch'i-lung / Tan Qilong
T'ang / Tang
Tang-hsing / dangxing
T'ang K'e / Tang Ke
Tang-nei he-tso / Dangnei
hezuo
Tang-te chih-pu / Dangde
zhibu
Tang-tsu / Dangzu
Tang-wai he-tso / Dangwai
hezuo
T'angshan / Tangshan

Tan-kan / Dangan
T'an-suo / Tansuo
T'ao Chu / Tao Zhu
Tapiehshan / Dabieshan
Ta yao-chin / Dayaojin
Teng Ch'iu-yeh / Deng Qiuye
Teng Hsiao-p'ing / Deng
    Xiaoping
Teng Li-ch'ün / Deng Liqun
Teng Ying-ch'ao / Deng
    Yingchao
T'iao-cheng / Tiaozheng
T'iao-cheng, kai-ke, cheng-tun,
    t'i-kao / Tiaozheng, gaige,
    zhengdun tigao
Ti-ch'ü / Dichu
T'ieh Ying / Tie Ying
T'ien / Tian
T'ienanmen / Tiananmen
T'ienchin / Tianjin
T'ien Chi-yün / Tian Jiyun
T'ien-hsia / Tianxia
T'ien-ming / Tianming
T'ien-tzu / Tianzi
Ti-fang pu-tui / Difang budui
Ti-i shu-chi / Diyi shuji
Ting Sheng / Ding Sheng
Tseng Kuo-fan / Zeng Guofan
ts'o-wu / cuowu
Tso-yeh-tsu / Zuoyezu
tsui-hsing / zuixing
Tsui-kao jen-min chien-ch'a-
    yüan / Zuigao renmin
    jianchayuan
Tsung-chih-pu / Zongzhibu
Ts'unghua / Conghua
Tsung-shu-chi / Zongshuji
Tsunyi / Zunyi
Tuan Chün-yi / Duan Junyi
T'ung-chih / Tongzhi
Tungfang / Dongfang
T'ung-hang / Tonghang
T'ung-hsiang / Tongxiang

T'ung-hsüeh / Tongxue
T'ung-meng-hui /
    Tongmenghui
Tungpei / Dongbei
Tung Pi-wu / Dong Biwu
Tungsha (Pratas) / Dongsha
Tungyin / Dongyin
Tzu-chih-ch'i / Zizhiqi
Tzu-chih-chou / Zizhizhou
Tzu-chih-ch'ü / Zizhichu
Tzu-chih-hsien / Zizhixian
Tzu-liu-ti / Ziliudi
Tsui-kao jen-min fa-yüan /
    Zuigao renmin fayuan
Tz'u Hsi / Ci Xi

Ulanfu / Ulanhu
Ürümchi / Urumchi

Wai-kuo-jen / Waiguoren
Wan-ch'üan ts'o-wu /
    Wanquan cuowu
Wan-ch'üan pi-yao-ti /
    Wanquan biyaodi
Wan Li / Wan Li
Wang Cheng / Wang Zheng
Wang Ch'eng-han / Wang
    Chenghan
Wang Ch'ien / Wang Qian
Wang En-mao / Wang Enmao
Wang Fang / Wang Fang
Wang Feng / Wang Feng
Wang Hê-shou / Wang Heshou
Wang Hsiu-chen / Wang
    Xiuzhen
Wang Huai-hsiang / Wang
    Huaixiang
Wang Hung-wen / Wang
    Hongwen
Wang Jen-chung / Wang
    Renzhong
Wang Kuang-mei (Ms) / Wang
    Guangmei

Wang Ping-ch'ien / Wang
Bingqian
Wang Tung-hsing / Wang
Dongxing
Wei Ching-sheng / Wei
Jingsheng
Weihaiwei / Weihaiwei
Wei Ch'un-shu / Wei Chunshu
Wei Kuo-ch'ing / Wei Guoqing
Wen-chang / Wenzhang
Wenchou / Wenzhou
Wen-hui pao / Wenhuibao
Wen-ming li-mao yüeh /
Wenming limaoyue
Wu Chiang / Wu Jiang
Wu Hsüeh-ch'ien / Wu
Xueqian
Wu K'e-hua / Wu Kehua
Wu Kuei-hsien (Ms) / Wu
Guixian
Wu Leng-hsi / Wu Lengxi
Wu Te / Wu De
Wu-chiang, ssu-mei, san je-ai
/ Wujiang simei sanreai
Wuchiu / Wujiu
Wu-fan yün-tung / Wufan
yundong
Wuhan / Wuhan
Wuhsi / Wuxi

Yang Ching-jen / Yang Jingren
Yangchou / Yangzhou
Yang Ju-tai / Yang Rudai
Yang Shang-k'un / Yang
Shangkun
Yang-shao / Yangshao

Yang Te-chih / Yang Dezhi
Yangtzu / Yangzi
Yang-yao-chin / Yangyaojin
Yang Yung / Yang Yong
Yang Yi-ch'en / Yang Yichen
Yao Ming-te / Yao Mingde
Yao Wen-yüan / Yao Wenyuan
Yao Yi-lin / Yao Yilin
Yeh-chan-chün / Yezhanjun
Yeh-chan pu-tui / Yezhan
budui
Yeh Chien-ying / Ye Jianying
Yeh Fei / Ye Fei
Yeh T'ing / Ye Ting
Yen Chi-tz'u / Yan Jici
yen-chung-te ts'o-wu /
Yanzhongde cuowu
Yennan / Yan'an
Yenshan / Yanshan
Yi kang wei kang / Yi gang
wei gang
Yi liang wei kang / Yi liang
wei gang
Yin Fa-t'ang / Yin Fatang
Ying-ming ling-hsiu /
Yingming lingxiu
Yu T'ai-chung / You Taizhong
Yu-ch'ing fan-an feng /
Youqing fan'anfeng
Yüan / Yuan
Yüan Pao-hua / Yuan Baohua
Yüan Shih-k'ai / Yuan Shikai
Yü Ch'iu-li / Yu Qiuli
Yü Hui-yung / Yu Huiyong
Yümen / Yumen
Yünnan / Yunnan

Notes

NOTES TO INTRODUCTION

1. The census taken in the PRC on June 30, 1982, resulted in an officially announced population figure of 1,008,175,288. The world population figure was estimated at approximately 4,590 million people in 1982. Hence, according to these figures, the population of the PRC accounted for 21.96 percent of that of the world.

2. For my accounts of political developments from 1949 to 1974 see Jürgen Domes, *The Internal Politics of China, 1949–1972* (London: C. Hurst and Company, 1973), and Jürgen Domes, *China After the Cultural Revolution: Politics Between Two Party Congresses* (London: C. Hurst and Company, 1976).

3. For example: "One of the major crimes of the Gang of Four, in their stereotyped scribblings, was to tell lies. They were dishonest in words and deeds, they issued false reports, they trumped up falsified typical cases, they handed out false experiences, fabricated false stories. . . . They circulated rumors based on nothing than thin air, and fabricated facts. . . . They exaggerated, played up sham models, and bragged to their whim" (*Chieh-fang-chün pao* [Liberation Army daily], Peking [hereafter, *CFCP*], October 18, 1977).

4. Christian Graf von Krockow, "Vorwort" [Preface], in Harald Fischer, Christian Graf von Krockow, and Hermann Schubnell, *China: Das neue Selbstbewusstsein* [China: The new self-consciousness] (Munich and Zurich: Piper and Company, 1978), p. 7.

5. Out of a great number of books, at least the following should be mentioned as examples here: John M. Lindbeck, ed., *China: The Management of a Revolutionary Society* (Seattle and London: University of Washington Press, 1971); A. Doak Barnett, ed., *Chinese Communist Politics in Action* (Seattle and London: University of Washington Press, 1969); Robert A. Scalapino, ed., *Elites in the People's Republic of China* (Seattle and London: University of Washington Press, 1972); Richard H. Solomon, *Mao's Revolution and the Chinese Political Culture* (Berkeley: University of California Press, 1967); Lucian W. Pye, *The Spirit of Chinese Politics* (Cambridge, Mass.: M.I.T. Press, 1968); Benjamin Schwartz, *Communism and China: Ideology in Flux* (Cambridge, Mass.: Harvard University Press, 1968); Harold C. Hinton, *An Introduction to Chinese Politics* (New York: Praeger, 1973);

William W. Whitson and Chen-hsia Huang, *The Chinese High Command: Communist Military Politics, 1927–1971* (New York: Praeger, 1973); William L. Parish and Martin K. Whyte, *Village and Family in Contemporary China* (Chicago and London: University of Chicago Press, 1978); B. Michael Frolic, *Mao's People* (Cambridge, Mass.: Harvard University Press, 1980); and James R. Townsend, *Politics in China*, 2d ed. (Boston: Little, Brown and Company, 1980).

6. *China News Analysis* (hereafter, *CNA*), Hongkong, no. 1248 (December 17, 1982), p. 3.

7. This list is a slightly revised version of my priority catalog of sources presented in Domes, *China After the Cultural Revolution*, p. 2.

NOTES TO PART 1

Chapter 1

1. Data on physical geography are mostly taken from Theodore Shabad, *China's Changing Map: National and Regional Development, 1949–1971*, 2d ed. (New York: Praeger, 1972), pp. 4–23 and 56–91.

2. Rüdiger Machetzki, "VR China: Zustand einer Wirtschaft, Grenzen einer Reform" [PRC: State of an economy, limitations to a reform] (Paper given at the Institut für Asienkunde, Hamburg, November 1982), p. 2.

3. Ibid.

4. See Chapter 3.

5. New China News Agency (hereafter, NCNA), Peking, October 27, 1982.

6. NCNA, Peking, August 25, 1980. The figure of 11 million registering for the preliminary examinations was computed from the 1.9 million who registered in seven administrative units, of whom 570,000 qualified for the final entrance examination (NCNA, Peking, July 4, 1980).

7. NCNA, Peking, April 28, 1983.

8. *Jen-min jih-pao* [People's daily], Peking (hereafter, *JMJP*), December 13, 1982.

9. Ibid.

10. *Chiao-yü p'ing-lun* [Educational review], Wuhan, no. 3 (September 1982), p. 6. In T'aiwan, however, the number of illiterates decreased by 77.1 percent over the same period (*T'aiwan Statistical Data Book 1982* [T'aipei: CEPD, Executive Yüan, 1982]), p. 7.

11. See George Moseley, *The Party and the National Question in China* (Cambridge, Mass.: Harvard University Press, 1966); June Teufel Dreyer, "China's Minority Nationalities in the Cultural Revolution," *China Quarterly* (hereafter, *CQ*), London, no. 35 (July-September 1968), pp. 96–109; and June Teufel Dreyer, "Traditional Minorities' Elites and the CPR Elite Engaged in Nationalities Work," in Robert A. Scalapino, ed., *Elites in the People's Republic of China* (Seattle and London: University of Washington Press, 1972), pp. 416–450.

12. Full text in *JMJP*, December 5, 1982.

13. My personal observations.

Chapter 2

14. One of the most succinct descriptions of the origins of the Han can be found in Wolfram Eberhard, *A History of China*, 4th rev. ed. (Berkeley: University of California Press, 1967), pp. 4–12.

15. Ibid., pp. 24–35.

16. See Frederick W. Mote, *Intellectual Foundations of China* (T'aipei: Rainbow Bridge Book Company, 1971), pp. 29–92.

17. S. Wells Williams, *The Middle Kingdom*, vol. 1 (New York: Charles Scribner's Sons, 1883), p. 4.

18. See Marie-Luise Näth, *Chinas Weg in die Weltpolitik* [China moves into world politics] (Berlin: De Gruyter, 1976), pp. 26–29, and Yang Lien-sheng, "Historical Notes on the Chinese World Order," in John K. Fairbank, ed., *The Chinese World Order: Traditional China's Foreign Relations* (Cambridge, Mass.: Harvard University Press, 1968), pp. 20–33.

19. Joseph R. Levenson, *Confucian China and Its Modern Fate*, Vol. 1, *The Problem of Intellectual Continuity* (Berkeley: University of California Press, 1965), p. 101–102 (my italics).

20. See Mote, *Intellectual Foundations*, pp. 116–123, Eberhard, *History of China*, pp. 60–65.

21. For the classical examination system, see Chang Chung-li, *The Chinese Gentry: Studies on Their Role in Nineteenth-Century China* (Seattle and London: University of Washington Press, 1955), pp. 165–209.

22. Ibid., pp. 116f. Chang gives, for the time before the T'aip'ing Rebellion, a figure of 30,000 and for the time after it, 80,000 officials altogether. As a whole, he estimates the number of family elders at 1.1–1.4 million (pp. 111f.).

23. See earlier in this chapter.

24. One should, however, not overlook the fact that extrajurisdiction was first introduced to China at the request of the Manchu court because Chinese officials and judges did not want to be bothered by conflicts among the barbarians and therefore asked them to settle their legal disputes among themselves.

25. *Min-kuo erh-shih-liu nien Chung-hua min-kuo chiao-yü t'ung-chi* [1937 educational statistics of the Republic of China] (Nanking: Ministry of Education, 1937), p. 11.

26. Chi Hwa Chen (Ch'en Chih-hua), "Verkehrsentwicklung und Verkehrsplanung in China und ihre Auswirkungen auf die Volkswirtschaft" [Transportation development and transportation planning in China and their implications for the economy] (Ph.D. dissertation, University of Vienna, 1941), pp. 90 and 104.

27. *Min-kuo erh-shih-liu nien ch'i yüeh chiao-t'ung-pu kung-tso pao-kao* [July 1937 working report of the Ministry of Communications] (Nanking: Ministry of Communications, 1937), p. 8. See Hollington K. Tong, *Chiang Kai-shek*, 2d ed. (T'aipei: China Publishing Company, 1953), p. 204.

Chapter 3

28. Data taken from Willy Kraus, *Economic Development and Social Change in the People's Republic of China* (New York: Springer, 1982), table A-14 on p. 347.

29. Kuo Hung-t'ao, vice-chairman of the State Economic Commission, in *JMJP*, July 28, 1982; quoted in *CNA* no. 1247 (December 3, 1982).

30. Kraus, *Economic Development and Social Change*, table A-15 on pp. 348–349.

31. *1981 Chung-kuo t'ung-chi nien-chien* [1981 Chinese statistical yearbook] (Peking: National Statistical Bureau, 1982) (hereafter, *1981 Statistics*), p. 269, and *JMJP*, September 8, 1981.

32. *1981 Statistics*, p. 270.

33. *1981 Chung-kuo pai-k'e nien-chien* [1981 Chinese encyclopedic yearbook] (Peking: Encyclopedic Publishers, 1981), p. 318.

34. *Kung-jen jih-pao* [Workers' daily], Peking (hereafter, *KJJP*), October 16, 1982.

35. *KJJP*, May 27, 1982.

36. Chao I-neng, "Industries," in Union Research Institute, ed., *Communist China 1949–1959*, vol. 2 (Hongkong: Union Research Institute, 1961), p. 157.

37. Mikhail Kapitsa, "An Important Date in the Life of Two Nations," *Kraznaia sviesda* [Red star], Moscow, February 14, 1964.

38. The data in this table are taken from Kraus, *Economic Development and Social Change*, Table A-8 on pp. 338–340.

39. Source of data, ibid.

40. Source of data, ibid.

41. The official PRC journal *Ching-chi kuan-li* [Economic management] no. 3 (March 1981), p. 3, says 20 million people died from famine between 1959 and 1962. Roderick MacFarquhar, *The Origins of the Cultural Revolution*, Vol. 2, *The Great Leap Forward, 1958–1960* (London and Kuala Lumpur: Oxford University Press, 1983), p. 335, gives a range of 16.5 million to 29.4 million deaths.

42. According to the minister of agriculture, General Sha Feng, in November 1975 in Revolutionary Committee of Juch'eng *hsien*, PRC, Hunan Province, ed., *Hunan nan-pu nung-yeh kan-pu hui-yi-te pao-kao* [Report on the agricultural cadres' conference of southern Hunan] (Juch'eng, ca., 1975), p. 3.

43. Production data according to official PRC figures, mainly, *Hung-ch'i* [Red flag], Peking (hereafter, *HC*), no. 10 (1979), p. 64, no. 4 (1980), p. 28, and no. 5 (1980), pp. 28f.; population figures for 1958, 1960, 1962, 1965, and 1971: estimates by the author; 1931–1937, 1949, 1951, and 1957: official PRC figures; production and population figures for 1975: Kraus, *Economic Development and Social Change*, p. 327 and 335.

44. Kraus, *Economic Development and Social Change*, Table A-10 on p. 342.

45. Subramaniam Swamy, "China's Economic Growth," *China Report* (New Delhi) 9:6 (November/December 1973), pp. 28f.; Alexander Eckstein, "Economic Growth and Changes in China," *CQ* no. 54 (April–June 1973), pp. 235f.; Arthur G. Ashbrook, Jr., "China: Economic Policy and Economic Results," in U.S. Congress, Joint Economic Committee, *People's Republic of China: An Economic Assessment* (Washington, D.C.: Government Printing Office, 1972), pp. 3–31; Wei Wou, "Communist China's Trade with Southeast Asia: An Empirical Estimation," in Ts'ai Wei-p'ing, ed., *Proceedings of the Fifth Sino-American Conference on Mainland China* (T'aipei: Institute of International Relations, 1976), p. 589;

and Werner Klatt, "China's Economy: A Statistical Balance Sheet," in Lien Chan, ed., *Proceedings of the Third Sino-American Conference on Mainland China* (T'aipei: Institute of International Relations, 1974), p. 751.

46. Data computed from Kraus, *Economic Development and Social Change*, table A-1 on pp. 326–327.

47. This figure was suggested by Liu Ta-chung and Yeh Kung-chia in a very detailed and well documented study in 1959. Kraus would arrive at 6.9 percent for this period, but that figure seems too high.

48. RoC, Commission of Economic Planning and Development, Executive Yüan, *Taiwan Statistical Data Book 1982* (T'aipei, 1982), pp. 24 and 26.

49. Kraus, *Economic Development and Social Change*, table A-1 on pp. 326–327. If one applies the same method to an evaluation of growth in T'aiwan, the variance for normal growth would be between 7.2 and 10.2 percent, and growth rates fell within this range for twelve out of the twenty-three years. Extremes ranged between 1.1 and 13.5 percent, i.e., 12.4 percentage points as opposed to 39.9 percentage points in the PRC.

Chapter 4

50. Hsüeh Mu-ch'iao, ed., *Chung-kuo ching-chi nien-chien (1982)* [Almanac of China's economy (1982)] (Peking: Economic Management Publishing Corporation, 1982), part 8, pp. 6–7.

51. Sha Feng in Revolutionary Committee of Juch'eng *hsien, Hunan nan-pu*, p. 1.

52. Computed from a number of official PRC sources by Ts'ai Ming-ch'in, "A Study of the Unemployment Problem on the Chinese Mainland," *Chung-kung yen-chiu* [Studies on Chinese communism], T'aipei (hereafter, CKYC), 17:3 (March 1983), p. 32.

53. For details, see Jürgen Domes, *Socialism in the Chinese Countryside: Rural Societal Policies in the PRC, 1949–1979* (London: C. Hurst and Company, 1980), pp. 4f.

54. See Kim [pseud.], "La réforme agraire en Chine," *Quatrième internationale* (Paris) no. 6 (October 1953), pp. 30f., and Henry J. Lethbridge, *The Peasant and the Communes* (Hongkong: Dragonfly Press, 1963), p. 198.

55. Chang Tsung-tung, *Die Entwicklung der festlandchinesischen Landwirtschaft aus der Sicht der chinesischen Regierung* [Development of mainland Chinese agriculture from the point of view of the Chinese government], Research reports of the State of Nordrhein-Westfalen, no. 936 (Cologne and Opladen, 1961), p. 91.

56. *JMJP*, November 15, 1958.

57. *1980 Chung-kuo pai-k'e nien-chien* [1980 Chinese encyclopedic yearbook] (Peking: Encyclopedic Publishers, 1980), p. 293.

58. See John Gardner, "The Wu-fan Campaign in Shanghai: A Study in the Consolidation of Urban Control," in A. Doak Barnett, ed., *Chinese Communist Politics in Action* (Seattle and London: University of Washington Press, 1969), pp. 477–593.

59. *Chieh-fang jih-pao* [Liberation daily news], Shanghai (hereafter, *CFJP*), January 7, 1956, and *Ta-kung-pao* [The Impartial], T'ienchin (hereafter, *TKP*), September 13, 1956.

60. Ch'en Chien-jen, *Die Lohnstruktur in der Volksrepublik China* [Wage structure in the PRC] (Bern: SOI Publishers, 1972), pp. 48f. and 58–89.

61. *JMJP*, March 23 and July 18, 1957.

62. Computed from reports in *JMJP*, *TKP*, *Kuang-ming jih-pao* [Light daily], Peking (hereafter, *KMJP*), *Wen-hui-pao* [Literary daily], Shanghai (hereafter, *WHP*), and Hongkong newspapers from July 15 through November 30, 1957; also *Chekiang jih-pao* [Chekiang daily], October 25, 1957; *Ch'inghai jih-pao* [Ch'inghai daily], December 12, 1957; *Kansu jih-pao* [Kansu daily], February 4, 1958; *Shensi jih-pao* [Shensi daily], March 11, 1958; *JMJP*, December 5, 1957, and March 7, 1958; *KMJP*, May 24, 1958; and *CFJP*, February 16, March 11 and 14, 1958. See also Douwe W. Fokkema, *Literary Dissent in China and the Soviet Influence, 1956–60* (The Hague, London, and Paris: Brill, 1965), p. 147.

63. I computed this figure from PRC provincial broadcasts out of twenty-four administrative units between July 1, 1978, and December 31, 1979.

64. These figures are the average values computed on the basis of seventy-three interviews with refugees in Hongkong in April 1962.

65. NCNA, Peking, December 22, 1975.

66. See Chapters 8 and 13.

67. *T'ung-chi kung-tso* [Statistical work], Peking (November 1981), pp. 12f.

68. Computed upon the basis of a population share of 40 percent between the age of zero and fifteen years (i.e., about 403 million people) and approximately 45 million people between their sixteenth and eighteenth year, i.e., altogether 448 million people, which means—for mid-1982—560 million people in the age bracket of eighteen and older.

69. NCNA, Peking, August 7, 1982.

70. See Pt. 1 note 50.

71. This figure can be detected from data on internal Party documents, particularly *Chung-fa* circulars, which have found their way outside the PRC. It was confirmed during interviews I conducted with two cadres who had fled to Hongkong in June 1970 and August 1975. For the *Chung-fa* documents, see Kenneth Lieberthal, James Tong, and Yeung Sai-cheung, *Central Documents and Politburo Politics in China* (Ann Arbor: Center for Chinese Studies, University of Michigan, 1978).

72. This figure was given by Teng Li-ch'ün, then vice-president of the Chinese Academy of Social Sciences, in *KJJP*, March 27, 1981.

73. For a detailed analysis of the political elite up to 1978, see Jürgen Domes, *Politische Soziologie der Volksrepublik China* [Political sociology of the PRC] (Wiesbaden: Akademische Verlagsgesellschaft, 1980), pp. 164–186.

74. Data base: All 97 members of the Eighth, 118 of 170 members of the Ninth, 137 of 195 members of the Tenth, 163 of 201 members of the Eleventh, and 189 of 210 members of the Twelfth CC. The relevant date is always December 31 of the year the CC was appointed, with the exception of the Ninth for which December 31, 1968, is the date used.

75. Data base: All 97 members of the Eighth, 151 of 170 members of the Ninth, 169 of 195 members of the Tenth, 181 of 201 members of the Eleventh, and 169 of 210 members of the Twelfth CC.

76. Data base: All 97 members of the Eighth, 126 of 170 members of the Ninth, 145 of 195 members of the Tenth, 163 of 201 members of the Eleventh, and 149 of 210 members of the Twelfth CC.

77. Data base: All 97 members of the Eighth, 143 of 170 members of the Ninth, 182 of 195 members of the Tenth, all 201 members of the Eleventh (data available for 195), and 189 of 210 members of the Twelfth CC.

78. Data base: All members of the Eighth, Ninth (data available for 168 of 170), Eleventh (data available for 199 of 201), and Twelfth (data available for 207 of 210); 190 of 195 members of the Tenth CC. Persons who were given a military rank in 1955 are counted as PLA.

79. Data base: All members of the Eighth and Eleventh (data available for 200 of 201), 162 of 170 members of the Ninth, 189 of 195 members of the Tenth, and 189 of 210 members of the Twelfth CC.

80. See Robert J. Birrell, "The Centralized Control of the Communes in the Post-'Great-Leap' Period," in Barnett, *Chinese Communist Policies in Action*, pp. 409f.

81. In an interview, a young refugee in Hongkong gave me a figure of 15,000 illegally returned youths for the city of Canton alone on August 17, 1977.

82. The participation of illegally returned youths in criminal acts is confirmed by two documents: a "Proclamation of the Public Security Office of Canton," dated March 27, 1976, and a "Proclamation by the People's Court of Wuchou," dated April 25, 1976 (both documents in my possession). Concerning prostitution, see the interviews conducted by Ivan and Miriam London in *CNA* no. 1046 (July 9, 1976).

83. This figure was given to me by British authorities in Hongkong in August 1975.

84. Peking Central People's Broadcasting Station (hereafter, PBS), December 3, 1975; Chekiang PBS, October 6 and 9, 1975; Anhui PBS, August 23, 1975; Liaoning PBS, November 6, 1975; NCNA, Ch'angch'un, October 9, 1975; NCNA, Lanchou, August 24, 1975; *T'uan-chieh pao* [Unite daily], K'unming, February 15, 1975; *Huiyang pao* [Huiyang daily], August 27, 1975; and *Chekiang jih-pao*, October 8, 1975.

NOTES TO PART 2

Chapter 5

1. The Chinese text of this currently used CCP Party statute was first published in *JMJP*, September 9, 1982; English in *Beijing Review*, September 21, 1982 (hereafter, *1982 Statute*).

2. Although July 1 is celebrated as the founding date of the CCP, the establishment of the Party in fact took place sometime between June 20 and 30, 1921 [see exchange of letters between C. Martin Wilbur and Kuo Hua-lun in *Issues and Studies* (T'aipei) 19:2 (February 1983), pp. 70f.].

3. C. Martin Wilbur and Julie L. How, eds., *Documents on Communism, Nationalism and Soviet Advisers in China* (New York: Columbia University Press, 1959), pp. 90 and 495. See also Teng Chung-hsia, *Chung-kuo chih-kung yün-tung chien shih* [Short history of the Chinese labor movement] (Yenan: New China Publishing House, 1943), pp. 211–217, and J. Heller, "The Labour Movement in China," *Communist International* (Moscow) no. 17 (November 1925), pp. 2–5.

4. Conrad Brandt, *Stalin's Failure in China* (Cambridge, Mass.: Harvard University Press, 1958), pp. 100–104, and Benjamin I. Schwartz, *Chinese Communism and the Rise of Mao* (Cambridge, Mass.: Harvard University Press, 1958), p. 73.

5. Mao Tse-tung, "On Coalition Government," *Chieh-fang jih-pao* [Liberation daily], Yenan, May 2, 1945.

6. Sources of data, 1949–1961: Franz Schurmann, *Ideology and Organization in Communist China*, 2d rev. ed. (Berkeley: University of California Press, 1968), pp. 129f.; 1969: *JMJP*, April 28, 1969; 1973: NCNA, Peking, August 29, 1973; 1977: *JMJP*, August 19, 1977.

7. *1982 Statute.*

8. Ibid., Art. 10(1).

9. Ibid., Art. 3.

10. Ibid., Art. 3(4).

11. Ibid., Art. 1.

12. Ibid., Arts. 5–7.

13. *JMJP*, July 1 and November 17, 1961.

14. *1982 Statute*, Art. 30.

15. *JMJP*, September 28, 1959, and information provided to me by cadres of the CCP Secretariat in September 1982.

16. *1982 Statute*, Arts. 24–29.

17. Ibid., Arts. 18 and 19.

18. Ibid., Art. 20.

19. For the sociopolitical structure of these CC, see Chapter 4.

20. *JMJP*, February 29 and March 1, 1980.

21. *1982 Statute*, Art. 21.

22. In alphabetical order, which comes closest to the order by the number of strokes in the ideograph of the family name, now often used in the PRC. One secretary, General Yang Yung, died on January 6, 1983.

23. The current director is Ch'iao Shih.

24. Current directors are Teng Li-ch'ün, Ch'en Yeh-p'ing, Yang Ching-jen, Ch'ien Li-jen, and Lo Ch'ing-ch'ang, respectively.

25. *JMJP*, December 23, 1979.

26. Han Kuang, Han T'ien-shih, Li Ch'ang, Ma Kuo-jui, and Wang Ts'ung-wu.

27. *1982 Statute*, Art. 22.

28. Teng Hsiao-p'ing.

29. In alphabetical order with the exception of the Standing Committee, see Pt. 2 note 22.

30. The Mongolian Ulanfu and the Chuang Wei Kuo-ch'ing.

31. The dispute over the Great Leap Forward and its results (1959–1962), the Cultural Revolution (1965/1966–1969), the Lin Piao crisis (1970/1971), the succession crisis (1974/1975–1977), and the conflict over the concept of modernization (1978–1982).

32. A very succinct and thorough study that argues this point has been presented by Lucian W. Pye, *The Dynamics of Chinese Politics* (Cambridge, Mass.: Oelgeschlager, Gunn and Hain, 1981), in particular, pp. 1–75 and 127–182.

33. Nieh Jung-chen, Mme. Teng Ying-ch'ao, and Wan Li.

34. See Chapter 7.

35. K'ang Shih-en, T'ang K'e, Sun Ching-wen, and Sung Cheng-ming, respectively.

36. These three were Ch'en Yi, Ch'en Yün, and Li Fu-ch'un, who had been purged in 1967 but were already partially rehabilitated by the latter part of 1968.

Chapter 6

37. For the history and structure of the non-Communist united front parties, see Lyman P. VanSlyke, *Enemies and Friends: The United Front in Chinese Communist History* (Stanford Calif.: Stanford University Press, 1967), pp. 208–219.

38. *KMJP*, May 1, 1950.

39. "Statute of the CPPCC," December 11, 1982, *JMJP*, December 12, 1982.

40. *Chung-hua jen-min kung-he-kuo hsien-fa* [Constitution of the PRC] (Peking: People's Publishing House, 1954).

41. *KMJP*, April 28, 1966.

42. The minister of agriculture and forestry, General Sha Feng.

43. "Constitution of the PRC," January 17, 1975, in *Chung-hua jen-min kung-he-kuo ti-ssu-chieh ch'üan-kuo jen-min tai-piao ta-hui ti-i-tz'u hui-yi wen-chien hui-pien* [Collection of documents of the first session of the Fourth NPC of the PRC] (Hongkong: San Lien Bookstore, 1975), pp. 31–42.

44. "Constitution of the PRC," March 5, 1978, in *Chung-hua jen-min kung-he-kuo ti-wu-chieh ch'üan-kuo jen-min tai-piao ta-hui ti-i-tz'u hui-yi wen-chien* [Documents of the first session of the Fifth NPC of the PRC] (Hongkong: San Lien Bookstore, 1978), pp. 3–24.

45. "Constitution of the PRC," December 4, 1982, in *JMJP*, December 5, 1982.

46. See Chapter 10.

47. P'eng Ch'ung, "Report on the Credentials of the Delegates to the Sixth NPC," *JMJP*, May 10, 1983.

48. *JMJP*, June 8, 1983.

49. *JMJP*, June 19, 1983. In this source, the year of birth for Li Hsien-nien is given as 1909, although he himself told Edgar Snow that it was 1905. For Wang Jen-chung, 1917 is given, although 1907 is reliably established. There are several other cases of this type of "rejuvenation" by lowering the year of birth.

The years of birth given in this book follow the official data unless there is more reliable information available.

50. *JMJP*, June 20, 1983.

51. "Organizational Law for the People's Congresses and the People's Governments of All Levels," July 4, 1979, *JMJP*, July 5, 1979.

52. Data according to *CKYC* Editorial Board, ed., *Chung-kung nien-pao* [Yearbook on Chinese Communism 1980] (T'aipei: Institute for the Study of Chinese Communist Problems, 1980), chap. 1, pp. 24 and 26.

53. Ibid., p. 26.

54. See first section of this chapter.

Chapter 7

55. This section relies mostly on William W. Whitson and Chen-hsia Huang, *The Chinese High Command: Communist Military Policies, 1927–1971* (New York: Praeger, 1973).

56. See Jacques Guillermaz, "The Nanchang Uprising," *CQ* no. 11 (July-September 1962), pp. 161–168, and C. Martin Wilbur, "The Ashes of Defeat," *CQ* no. 18 (April-June 1964), pp. 3–55.

57. See Roy Hofheinz, "The Autumn Harvest Uprising," *CQ* no. 32 (October-December 1967), pp. 37–88.

58. See Whitson and Huang, *Chinese High Command*, pp. 125f.

59. Ibid., p. 32.

60. See Chapter 5.

61. For the commissar system, see Whitson and Huang, *Chinese High Command*, pp. 436–457.

62. See ibid., pp. 70f.

63. See Jürgen Domes, *The Internal Politics of China, 1949–1972* (London: C. Hurst and Company, 1973), pp. 130–134.

64. NCNA, Peking, May 24, 1965.

65. Reuters, Peking, August 1, 1983.

66. Computed on the basis of 104 major military leaders in 1965, 87 in 1970, 91 in 1977, and 88 in 1983.

67. NCNA, Peking, October 27, 1982.

68. Gerhard Albrecht, ed., *Weyers Flottentaschenbuch/Warships of the World 1984/85* (Koblenz: Bernard and Graefe, 1984), pp. 34–41 and 684.

69. *JMJP*, June 26 and 29, 1984.

70. Data collected by T'aiwan intelligence and presented on tables at an exhibition in T'aipei in September 1984. All data on military strength except for the navy and overall manpower are taken from this source.

71. "Constitution of the PRC," December 4, 1982, *JMJP*, December 5, 1982, Art. 93.

72. Ibid., Art. 62, no. 6.

73. *JMJP*, June 21, 1983. Concerning the Cultural Revolution status, it should be noted that "survived" for a PLA cadre does not necessarily have the same meaning as for a civilian. More PLA cadres survived the Cultural Revolution in office than civilians did.

74. Generals Yang Te-chih (PB member) and Hsiao K'e (CAC member).
75. Generals Yang Ch'eng-wu (CC member), Chang Chen (CC), Wu Hsiu-ch'üan (CAC member), Wang Shang-jung (CAC), Ho Cheng-wen, Ch'ih Hao-t'ien, Hsü Hsin (CC alternate), and Adm. Liu Hua-ch'ing (CC).
76. Generals Liang Pi-yeh (CC), Chu Yün-ch'ien (CC), Fu Chung (CAC), Kan Wei-han (CAC), Huang Yü-k'un, Yen Chin-sheng, Shih Chin-ch'ien, and Hua Nan.
77. Generals Chang Ling-pin (CAC), Ho Piao (CAC), Ho Ch'eng, Jao Cheng-hsi, Chang Hsien-yüeh, Li Yüan, Chang Ju-kuang, Fan Tzu-yü, Sun Hung-chen, Hsü Kuang-yi, and Wang Cheng-chu.
78. Generals Sung Ch'eng-chih (Artillery), Ho Chin-heng (Second Artillery, CC), Huang Hsin-t'ing (Armored Forces, CC), T'an Shan-he (Pioneers, CC), and Ch'en Tsai-tao (Railway Troops, CAC).
79. Ralph Powell, "The Party, the Government, and the Gun," *Asian Survey* 10:6 (June 1970), p. 471.

NOTES TO PART 3

Chapter 8

1. See Jürgen Domes, *The Internal Politics of China, 1949–1972* (London: C. Hurst and Company, 1973), pp. 221f., and Jürgen Domes, *China After the Cultural Revolution: Politics Between Two Party Congresses* (London: C. Hurst and Company, 1976), pp. 201f.
2. *JMJP*, September 8, 1975.
3. See Domes, *China*, pp. 184–203.
4. Shanghai, Peking, T'ienchin, Liaoning, Hopei, Anhui, and probably Tibet.
5. See *Chung-hua jen-min kung-he-kuo ti-ssu-chieh ch'üan-kuo jen-min tai-piao ta-hui ti-i-tz'u hui-yi wen-chien hui-pien* [Collection of documents of the first session of the Fourth NPC of the PRC] (Hongkong: San Lien Bookstore, 1975).
6. Ibid., p. 35.
7. Ibid., p. 12 (my italics).
8. Chang Ch'un-ch'iao, Chi Teng-k'uei, Hua Kuo-feng, Ch'en Yung-kuei, Mme. Wu Kuei-hsien, and Sun Chien.
9. Reuters, Peking, January 27, 1975. Chang's appointment was officially confirmed by the NCNA, Peking, on October 9, 1975; that of Teng, however, only by the resolution of the third plenum of the Tenth CC on July 23, 1977, which "reinstated" him, inter alia, as chief of the General Staff.
10. NCNA, Peking, January 16, 1975.
11. *JMJP*, February 9 and 22, 1975.
12. Yao Wen-yüan, "On the Social Basis of the Lin Piao Clique," *HC* no. 3 (March 1975), pp. 20–29, and Chang Ch'un-ch'iao, "On Exercising Dictatorship over the Bourgeoisie," *HC* no. 4 (April 1975), pp. 3–12.
13. *JMJP*, December 19, 1976; see also *CNA* no. 1169 (February 11, 1977).
14. The Chinese text of the Li I-che wall poster can be found in Hsüan Mou, ed., *Li I-che ta-tzu-pao lun-chi* [Collected essays on the wall poster of Li I-che] (T'aipei: CKYC Publishers, 1976), pp. 155–208.

15. *Chung-fa* document no. 9 (1975). The full text of this document is not yet available outside the PRC, but it is mentioned in PRC, Yünnan Province, Yünnan Provincial Higher People's Court, Public Security Bureau, RC of the K'unming Railway Bureau, "Circular Note," April 14, 1975 (unpublished document, copy in my possession).

16. *Chekiang jih-pao* [Chekiang daily], July 13 and August 24, 1975; Chekiang PBS, July 22 and 25, August 8, 10, 17, 19, 20, 23, 25, and 26, 1975; NCNA, Hangchou, August 2, 1975; Heilungkiang PBS, August 18, 1975; Hunan PBS, August 23 and 26, 1975; and Hopei PBS, September 12 and 14, 1975.

17. NCNA, Lanchou, August 24, 1975; *Chekiang jih-pao*, October 8 and 24, 1975; Chekiang PBS, October 9 and 22, November 16, 1975; Kiangsu PBS, November 7, 1975; Kiangsi PBS, November 11, 1975; Liaoning PBS, November 6, 1975; and Peking Central PBS, December 3, 1975.

18. NCNA, Shanghai, May 5, 1976.

19. For a comprehensive analysis of personnel politics in 1975, see Li Ming-hua, "The Chinese Communist Leadership Reorganization," *Issues and Studies* 12:3 (March 1976), pp. 37–56.

20. Excerpts in *Hsüeh-hsi yü p'i-p'an* [Studies and criticism], Shanghai (hereafter, HHYPP), no. 32 (April 1976), pp. 20–27.

21. Excerpts in ibid., pp. 28–35. Teng's speech introducing this document to the State Council can be found in *Teng Hsiao-p'ing wen-hsüan* [Selected writings of Teng Hsiao-p'ing] (Peking: People's Publishing House, 1983), pp. 28–31.

22. The formulation of these slogans provides an instructive example for the process of political communication in the PRC. Their first available mention, to my knowledge, is in the internal document from Yünnan dated April 14, 1975, and cited in Part 3, note 15, above. The term "three directives" is first found in *JMJP*, October 1, 1975. HHYPP, pp. 11–19, alleges that Teng Hsiao-p'ing first used the formula "Three directives as the link" (*San hsiang chih-shih wei kang*) in a circular on October 7, 1975. An article of the PLA's GPD in *JMJP*, November 2, 1975, had it in this version: "With Chairman Mao's directives . . . as the link."

23. *JMJP*, September 16 and 19, October 10, 14, 16, 20, 21, and 23, 1975. See also *CNA* no. 1019 (November 7, 1975), no. 1022 (December 5, 1975), and no. 1027 (January 16, 1976).

24. Among others, Li Chang [pseud.], "Teng Hsiao-p'ing Has Opposed Marxism in Every Respect," *HC* no. 5 (May 1976), pp. 35–40. For unknown reasons, Teng's address at the first Tachai conference is not included in *Teng Hsiao-p'ing wen-hsüan*.

25. *Chung-yao ti-ch'ing hui-pao* [Important reports on the enemy's situation], T'aipei, no. 183 (December 10, 1975), pp. 12–14.

26. *JMJP*, January 1, 1976.

27. *JMJP*, January 16, 1976 (my italics).

28. E.g., *JMJP*, February 17, 1976.

29. Mao Tse-tung, Wang Hung-wen, Chang Ch'un'ch'iao, Ch'en Yung-kuei, Chi Teng-k'uei, Chiang Ch'ing, Hua Kuo-feng, Wang Tung-hsing, and Yao Wen-yüan (full members); Ni Chih-fu and Mme. Wu Kuei-hsien (alternates).

30. Ch'en Hsi-lien, Li Te-sheng, and Wu Te (full members); Saifudin (alternate).
31. Teng Hsiao-p'ing, Yeh Chien-ying, Chu Te, Hsü Shih-yu, Li Hsien-nien, Liu Po-ch'eng, and Wei Kuo-ch'ing (full members); Su Chen-hua (alternate).
32. *Yomiuri Shimbun* (Tokyo), February 29, 1976.
33. *JMJP*, March 10, 1976.
34. *JMJP*, March 28, 1976.
35. Peking Central PBS, April 7, 1976.
36. This was revealed to me by a PRC diplomatic-military official, a former subordinate of Hsü Shih-yu, in September 1979.
37. *JMJP*, August 29, 1977.
38. For contemporary official PRC reports on the T'ienanmen demonstrations, see *JMJP*, April 8, 10, 18, 25, and 27, 1976; NCNA, Peking, April 7, 10, 11, 12, and 23, 1976; Peking Central PBS, April 7 and 16, 1976; and *HC* no. 5 (May 1976), pp. 7–34. For a later official evaluation, see *JMJP* correspondent, "The Real Picture of the T'ienanmen Incident," *KMJP*, November 21 and 22, 1978.
39. *KMJP*, November 22, 1978.
40. *WHP*, Shanghai, November 21, 1978.
41. Honan PBS and Peking Central PBS, April 12, 1976; Fukien PBS, April 9, 1976; Kiangsi PBS, May 3, 1976; Chaowuta League PBS, May 18 and 28, 1976; *Hainan jih-pao* [Hainan daily], Haik'ou, April 11, 1976; and Yünnan PBS, April 22, 1976.
42. Agence France Presse (AFP), Peking, April 30, 1976.
43. Kuangsi and Ssuch'uan PBS, May 8, 1976.
44. *JMJP*, December 24, 1976.
45. Peking Central PBS, April 16 and 20, 1976.
46. NCNA, Shanghai, May 5, 1976; Peking Central PBS, May 21, 1976; and *JMJP*, May 29, 1976, respectively.
47. NCNA, Peking, May 3 and July 19, 1976.
48. Shensi PBS, May 26, 1976; Anhui PBS, August 2, 1976; Hopei PBS, August 3, 1976; and NCNA, Harbin, August 11, 1976.
49. NCNA, K'unming, June 1, 1976.
50. *South China Morning Post* (Hongkong), January 5, 1977.
51. *JMJP*, July 30, 1976.
52. *JMJP*, August 8 and 23, and September 7, 1976.
53. For a detailed discussion of the positions and attitudes of Hua, see Jürgen Domes, "The 'Gang of Four' and Hua Kuo-feng: Analysis of Political Events in 1975–76," *CQ* no. 71 (September 1977), pp. 487f.
54. The Central Condolence Mission, which Hua Kuo-feng led to T'angshan on August 4, consisted of two representatives of the mass organization Left but also four veteran cadres and seven PLA leaders (NCNA, Peking, August 4, 1976).
55. *JMJP*, October 1, 1976.
56. *Ming-pao* [Clearness daily], Hongkong, October 11, 1976.
57. *JMJP*, October 25, 1976.

Chapter 9

58. Information provided to me by a vice-chairman of the Chinese People's Association for Friendship with Foreign Countries in Peking, September 1980.

59. Amnesty International, ed., *Political Imprisonment in the People's Republic of China* (London: Amnesty International, 1978), pp. 26f. and 65–69.

60. Kiangsi PBS, June 9, 1977.

61. *JMJP*, October 20, 1977.

62. *JMJP*, November 30, 1976.

63. *JMJP*, December 28, 1976.

64. *JMJP*, February 7, 1977.

65. See Chapter 11.

66. *Kuangchou jih-pao* [Canton daily] (hereafter, *KCJP*), November 24, 1976.

67. Hunan PBS, January 4, 1977.

68. Hunan PBS, June 12, 1977.

69. A copy of this letter—an internal document of the CCP's Kuangtung PPC—is available in the archives in T'aiwan, although it was not published there. A German translation can be found in *Der Spiegel* (Hamburg) 31:17 (April 1977), pp. 161–164.

70. Statement by a member of the Chinese Academy of Social Sciences in an interview with me in Peking, September 1980.

71. *JMJP*, July 23, 1977 (my italics).

72. *JMJP*, August 1, 1977.

73. Hua Kuo-feng, "Political Report at the Eleventh Congress of the CCP," in *Chung-kuo kung-ch'an-tang ti-shih-i-tz'u ch'üan-kuo tai-piao ta-hui wen-chien hui-pien* [Collection of documents of the Eleventh CCP Party Congress] (Peking: People's Publishing House, 1977), pp. 4f.

74. Ibid., p. 30.

75. Ibid., pp. 84f.

76. Ibid., pp. 112f.

77. Names listed in *Chung-hua jen-min kung-he-kuo ti-wu-chieh ch'üan-kuo jen-min tai-piao ta-hui ti-i-tz'u hui-yi wen-chien* [Documents of the first session of the Fifth NPC of the PRC] (hereafter, *Documents Fifth NPC*) (Hongkong: San Lien Bookstore, 1978), pp. 154–197.

78. "Constitution of the PRC," March 5, 1978, in ibid., pp. 76–104.

79. Ibid., Art. 43.

80. Hua Kuo-feng, "Unite and Strive to Build a Modern, Powerful Socialist Country!: Report on the work of the Government Delivered at the First Session of the Fifth NPC," February 26, 1978, *Documents Fifth NPC*, pp. 3–70.

81. Ibid., pp. 24f.

82. Ibid., p. 32.

Chapter 10

83. *JMJP*, May 30, 1978.

84. *KMJP*, May 11, 1978.

85. *JMJP,* June 4 and 5, 1978, respectively.
86. *JMJP,* June 6, 1978. The speech can also be found, in a slightly edited version, in *Teng Hsiao-p'ing wen-hsüan* [Selected writings of Teng Hsiao-p'ing] (Peking: People's Publishing House, 1983), pp. 108–120.
87. Hu Chi-wei, "The Struggle in the Higher Circles of the Party," *Cheng-ming* [Debate], Hongkong (hereafter, *CM*), no. 34 (August 1980), p. 51. This is a reprint of a speech by the then-editor of *JMJP* at the Central Party School on September 13, 1979, which was not published inside the PRC.
88. *JMJP,* June 24, 1978. See also *CNA* no. 1134 (September 22, 1978).
89. Kuangsi PBS, August 9; Heilungkiang PBS, August 12; Anhui PBS, August 18; Yünnan PBS, August 25; Sinkiang PBS, August 27; Honan PBS, August 28; Hupei PBS, September 4; Huhehot PBS, September 7; *JMJP,* September 11; and Kuangtung PBS, September 17, 1978, respectively.
90. AFP, Peking, October, 11, 1978.
91. *KMJP,* November 16, 1978 (my italics).
92. *KMJP,* November 17, 1978.
93. A very lively account of the early days of the Human Rights and Democracy movement by a Canadian correspondent in Peking can be found in John Fraser, *The Chinese: Portrait of a People* (New York: Summit Books, 1980), pp. 199–271. See also Fox Butterfield, *China: Alive in the Bitter Sea* (New York: Times Books, 1982), pp. 406–434. The most comprehensive collection of journals and other materials of the movement is Institute for the Study of Chinese Communist Problems, T'aipei, ed., *Ta-lu ti-hsia k'an-wu hui-pien* [Collection of mainland underground publications], 15 vol. thus far (T'aipei: CKYC Publishers, 1980–). Of a considerable number of materials from that period in English translation, the three most useful are Lin Yi-tang, ed., *What They Say: A Collection of Current Chinese Underground Publications* (T'aipei: Institute of Current China Studies, 1980); James D. Seymour, ed., *The Fifth Modernization: China's Human Rights Movement, 1978–1979* (Stanfordville, N.Y.: Coleman, 1980); and David S.G. Goodman, *Beijing Street Voices: The Poetry and Politics of China's Democracy Movement* (London: Marion Boyars, 1981).
94. *Kuan-ch'a-chia* [The Observer], Hongkong, February 1979, pp. 37f.
95. Chin Sheng (Wei Ching-sheng), "Human Rights, Equality, and Democracy," *T'an-suo* [Exploration], March 1979; here quoted from Seymour, *Fifth Modernization,* p. 141.
96. "Manifesto of the Thaw Society," March 8, 1979, wall poster in Peking (photograph in my possession).
97. Peking Central PBS, February 8 and 12; WHP, Shanghai, February 9; and Shanghai PBS, February 12, 1979.
98. *Peking jih-pao* [Peking daily], March 31, 1979 (my italics). The Four Basic Principles were formulated in their definite form in a speech by Teng Hsiao-p'ing at a Party conference on theoretical work on March 30, 1979; the full text can be found in *Teng Hsiao-p'ing wen-hsüan,* pp. 144–170.
99. NCNA, Peking, October 16, 1979.
100. *JMJP,* December 1, 1979.
101. *JMJP,* December 26, 1979.

102. *JMJP*, December 23, 1978.

103. See the next section of this chapter.

104. "Constitution of the PRC," March 5, 1978, in *Chung-hua jen-min kung-he-kuo ti-wu-chieh ch'üan-kuo jen-min tai-piao ta-hui ti-i-tz'u hui-yi wen-chien* [Documents of the first session of the Fifth NPC of the PRC] (Hongkong: San Lien Bookstore, 1978), Art. 7.

105. *KMJP*, May 22, 1978.

106. *JMJP*, December 23, 1978.

107. "Working Regulations for Rural People's Communes: Draft for Experimental Introduction," in *Hsüeh-hsi wen-chien* [Documents for study], Peking, February 1979.

108. Ssuch'uan PBS, January 22, and *JMJP*, January 31, 1979.

109. Hunan PBS, March 14 and 17; Kiangsi PBS, March 21; and Kueichou PBS, March 25, 1979.

110. *CNA* no. 1192 (October 28, 1980).

111. "Announcement Concerning the Opening of Trade in Collective Markets," RC of the Wa Autonomous *hsien* of Ts'angyüan, Yünnan, February 10, 1979 (leaflet, copy in my possession), and "Announcement Concerning the Regulations for Agricultural Supplementary Goods' Markets," RC of Peking City, April 30, 1979 (poster, photograph in my possession).

112. My personal observations in July 1979.

113. Ssuch'uan PBS, January 17, 1979.

114. Information given me by officials of the National Economic Commission of the PRC in September 1980.

115. Chao Tzu-yang, "Speech at the Central Ssuch'uan Rural Work Cadres' Conference," September 16, 1979 (internal Party document, copy in my possession).

116. *JMJP*, January 4, 1980.

117. Kueichou PBS, July 21, 1980, and *JMJP*, September 6, 1980, respectively.

118. Hupei PBS, September 16, 1980, and Hunan PBS, October 25, 1980.

119. Shansi PBS, October 8 and 11, 1979.

120. Shansi PBS, December 22 and 24, 1980.

121. *KMJP*, February 2, 1980. See also *CNA* no. 1192 (October 28, 1980).

122. *CFCP*, March 26, 1979.

123. Lu Chung-chien, "The Victory of the Pragmatists as Seen From the NPC Plenary Session," *CM* no. 21 (July 1979), pp. 5f.

124. *JMJP*, May 22, 1979.

125. *JMJP*, July 3, 1979.

126. *JMJP*, September 29, 1979.

127. NCNA, Peking, September 30, 1979 (my italics).

128. *JMJP*, March 1, 1980.

129. See Chapter 12.

130. Kuangtung PBS, May 17, 1980.

Chapter 11

131. See Chapter 13.

132. *JMJP*, April 17, 1980.

133. The Chinese text of Teng's speech was first circulated in the internal Party document *Chung-fa* (1980) no. 66, September 11, 1980, and published in *CKYC* 15:7 (July 1981), pp. 106–140. An English translation was published even earlier in *Issues and Studies* 12:3 (March 1981), pp. 79–103. A slightly edited version can now be found in *Teng Hsiao-p'ing wen-hsüan* [Selected writings of Teng Hsiao-p'ing] (Peking: People's Publishing House, 1983), pp. 280–302.

134. *JMJP*, September 11, 1980.

135. "Notice of the Meeting of the Politburo of the CCP/CC," December 5, 1980 (internal Party document), *CKYC* 17:4 (April 1983), pp. 82f.

136. Lo Ping, "A Record of the Reorganization of the CCP Core Group," *CM* no. 40 (February 1981), pp. 7–9.

137. "Notice of the Meeting of the Politburo," pp. 82f. (my italics).

138. Ch'en Yün, "The Economic Situation and the Lessons of Economic Experience: Speech at the Central Work Conference," December 16, 1980, *CKYC* 17:4 (April 1983), pp. 85–86.

139. Chao Tzu-yang, "On Several Problems Concerning the Readjustment of the National Economy: Speech at the Central Work Conference," *CKYC* 17:4 (April 1983), pp. 86–95.

140. See Chapter 9.

141. Teng Hsiao-p'ing, "Go Through with the Method of Readjustment, Guarantee Stability and Unity: Speech at the Central Work Conference," December 25, 1980 (hereafter, Teng, *Speech*), *CKYC* 17:4 (April 1983), pp. 95–104 (now also published in *Teng Hsiao-p'ing wen-hsüan*, pp. 313–333).

142. Ibid., p. 97.

143. Ibid., pp. 102f.

144. *JMJP*, September 13, 1980.

145. *JMJP*, March 8, 1981.

146. *JMJP*, November 11, 1980.

147. *JMJP*, April 24, 1981. See also *CNA* no. 1207 (May 22, 1981).

148. *CFCP*, April 26, 1981 (my italics).

149. Teng, *Speech*, pp. 100f.

150. *KJJP*, March 27, 1981.

151. "Resolution on Several Problems of Party History Since the Establishment of the PRC, Unanimously Approved by the Sixth Plenum of the Eleventh CCP/CC," June 27, 1981, *HC* no. 13 (July 1981), pp. 3–27.

152. *JMJP*, April 4, 1981.

153. *JMJP*, March 2, 1980.

154. *JMJP*, March 9, May 5, and August 24, 1982. A very instructive account of the administrative reforms can be found in *China Directory 1983* (Tokyo: Radiopress, 1982), pp. 79–100.

155. General Yü Ch'iu-li, Keng Piao, Fang Yi, Ku Mu, K'ang Shih-en, Mme. Ch'en Mu-hua, Po I-po, Chi P'eng-fei, and Huang Hua.

156. Document *Chung-fa* (1980) no. 29, April 4, 1980; reprinted in *Fei-ch'ing yüeh-pao* [Rebel situation monthly], T'aipei, no. 9 (1980), pp. 74–83 and 97. A very concise description of the debates on the Party statute that preceded the Twelfth Party Congress is given by Peter Schier, "Die Vorgeschichte des XII. Parteitages" [Antecedents of the Twelfth Party Congress] *China aktuell* (Hamburg), December 1982, pp. 724–732.

157. This suggestion was indicated by Hu Yao-pang in an interview with the director of *AFP*, Henri Pigeat (*AFP*, Peking, August 23, 1982; Chinese in *TKP*, Hongkong, August 26, 1982).

158. *JMJP*, September 2, 1982.

159. *JMJP*, September 7, 1982.

160. Ibid.

161. Art. 21. The Chinese text of the 1982 statute was first published in *JMJP*, September 9, 1982; English in *Beijing Review*, September 21, 1982.

162. NCNA, Peking, September 10, 11, and 12, 1982.

163. See Chapter 6.

164. For a more detailed account of policy developments between 1976 and 1982, see Jürgen Domes, "1976–82: Evolution of a New CCP Line?" *Issues and Studies* 18:7 (July 1982), pp. 40–65.

165. *JMJP*, January 7, 1983, and NCNA, Peking, June 10, 1983, respectively.

NOTES TO PART 4

Chapter 12

1. See Chapters 3 and 8.

2. Teng Hsiao-p'ing, "Some Points of View on the Development of Industry," August 18, 1975, in *Teng Hsiao-p'ing wen-hsüan* [Selected writings of Teng Hsiao-p'ing] (Peking: People's Publishing House, 1983), pp. 28–31.

3. See Chapter 9.

4. *Chung-hua jen-min kung-he-kuo ti-wu-chieh ch'üan-kuo jen-min tai-piao ta-hui ti-i-tz'u hui-yi wen-chien* [Documents of the first session of the Fifth NPC of the PRC] (Hongkong: San Lien Bookstore, 1978), p. 10.

5. *JMJP*, January 1, 1977.

6. NCNA, Peking, November 2, 1977.

7. Data taken from Willy Kraus, *Economic Development and Social Change in the People's Republic of China* (New York: Springer, 1982), table A-1 on pp. 326–327 and table A-8 on pp. 338–339.

8. Ibid., p. 285. For a somewhat different treatment of the economic development of the PRC, although with not very different results, see Shigeru Ishikawa, "China's Economic Growth Since 1949—An Assessment," *CQ* no. 94 (June 1983), pp. 242–281.

9. See Chapter 9.

10. For example, *JMJP*, March 7, 1978.

11. *Peking Review*, March 10, 1978, pp. 22f.

12. See Chapter 9.

13. This term was used by leading economic officials in Peking in conversations with me in September 1980.

14. See Kraus, *Economic Development and Social Change*, pp. 288f.

15. NCNA, Peking, September 15, 1978.

16. Kraus, *Economic Development and Social Change*, p. 289.

17. See Part 4 note 7.

18. Ibid., table A-2 on p. 328, and Hsüeh Mu-ch'iao, ed., *Chung-kuo ching-chi nien-chien (1982)* [Almanac of China's economy (1982)] (hereafter, *1982 Almanac*) (Peking: Economic Management Publishing Corporation, 1982), part 8, p. 4.

19. See Chapter 9.

20. *JMJP*, July 2, 1979.

21. *Beijing Review*, March 9, 1979, p. 5.

22. Kraus, *Economic Development and Social Change*, pp. 293f., and Wu Yüan-li, "Planners and Entrepreneurs in the PRC," *Asian Affairs* (September/October 1981), p. 33.

23. See Yü Ch'iu-li's report on the plan to the second session of the Fifth NPC, *JMJP*, June 22, 1979.

24. Kraus, *Economic Development and Social Change*, p. 301.

25. Lowell Dittmer, "China in 1980: Modernization and Its Discontents," *Asian Survey* 21:1 (January 1981), p. 33.

26. United States, Directorate of Intelligence, ed., *Handbook of Economic Statistics, 1983* (Washington, D.C.: National Foreign Assessment Center, 1983) (hereafter, *Statistics 1983*), table 13 on p. 35.

27. *JMJP*, January 1, 1981.

28. *1982 Almanac*, part 8, p. 4.

29. See Chapter 11.

30. Ch'en Yün, "The Economic Situation and the Lessons of Experience: Speech at the Central Work Conference," December 16, 1980, *CKYC* 17:4 (April 1983), pp. 83–86.

31. Chao Tzu-yang, "On Some Problems of the Readjustment of the National Economy: Speech at the Central Work Conference," December 16, 1980, *CKYC* 17:4 (April 1983), p. 89.

32. Ch'en Yün, "Economic Situations," p. 85, and *JMJP*, December 8, 1980.

33. *1982 Almanac*, part 8, p. 4.

34. Kraus, *Economic Development and Social Change*, p. 311, and *Far Eastern Economic Review (FEER)*, February 20–26, 1981, p. 47.

35. Data from *1982 Almanac*, part 8, p. 32. For 1982, see NCNA, Peking, May 8, 1983. For 1983, see *JMJP*, April 30, 1984.

36. See Chapter 13.

37. *Beijing Review*, April 6, 1981, pp. 23f.

38. NCNA, Peking, March 6, 1981. See also Kraus, *Economic Development and Social Change*, pp. 304f.

39. *JMJP*, January 25, 1982. See also *CNA* no. 1227 (February 26, 1982).

40. *1982 Almanac*, part 8, p. 6.

41. *CFJP,* March 7, 1984.
42. Marlene R. Wittman, "Shanghai in Transition: Implications of the Capitalist Intrusion," *Issues and Studies* 19:6 (June 1983), p. 69.
43. *JMJP,* December 13, 1982.
44. Ch'ien Yüan-heng, "Comment on the Situation of the Chinese Communist Industry in Recent Years," *CKYC* 17:3 (March 1983), p. 65, and NCNA, Peking, May 8, 1983.
45. Data sources, 1953 and 1975: Kraus, *Economic Development and Social Change,* table A-8 on pp. 338f.; 1978–1981: *1982 Almanac,* part 8, pp. 5 and 16f.; 1982: *Chung-kuo ching-chi hsin-wen* [Chinese economic news] (Peking) no. 4 (January 14, 1983) and NCNA, Peking, May 8, 1983.
46. Data sources, ibid.
47. Data sources, ibid., and Ch'ien Yüan-heng "Comment on the Situation."
48. Data sources, ibid. and *JMJP,* April 30, 1984. The population figure of 1,015 million for the end of 1982 is my own estimate.
49. See Chapter 3.
50. See Chapter 13.
51. Data sources, 1976–1977: Kraus, *Economic Change and Social Development,* table A-1 on pp. 326–327; 1978–1982: *Statistics 1983,* pp. 35f.
52. Data computed from *FEER,* December 10–16, 1982, p. 68.
53. Data sources, PRC: *JMJP,* April 30, 1984; T'aiwan: *Industry of Free China* (T'aipei) 62:3 (September 1984), pp. 92–115.

Chapter 13

54. Ross Terrill, *800,000,000: The Real China* (Boston and Toronto: Little, Brown and Company, 1982), p. 9.
55. Ibid., p. 14.
56. See Chapter 3.
57. Authors' collective, *Jen-k'ou li-lun kai-shuo* [A general introduction to population theory] (Ch'angsha: Hunan People's Publishing House, 1981), p. 81.
58. For documentary evidence, see Jürgen Domes, *Misinformation and Misconceptions about China in Western Political Science in the 1970s,* Tamkang Chair Lecture Series no. 45 (T'aipei: Tamkang University, 1983), pp. 8f., and Horst F. Vetter, *China's neue Wirklichkeit* [China's new reality] (Hamburg and New York: Campus, 1983), pp. 120–122.
59. *Hsüeh-hsi wen-chien* [Documents for study], Peking, February 1979, p. 2.
60. *CM* no. 19 (May 1979), p. 86.
61. *FEER,* February 13–19, 1981, p. 7; *FEER,* May 15–21, 1981, p. 96; and *AFP,* Peking, February 7, 1981.
62. Rüdiger Machetzki, "VR China: Zustand einer Wirtschaft, Grenzen einer Reform [PRC: State of an economy, limitations to a reform] (Paper given at the Institut für Asienkunde, November 1982), p. 26.
63. Hsüeh Mu-ch'iao, ed., *Chung-kuo ching-chi nien-chien (1982)* [Almanac of China's economy (1982)] (Peking: Economic Management Publishing Corporation, 1982) (hereafter, *1982 Almanac*), part 8, pp. 47 and 59.

64. Computed from ibid., pp. 29f.

65. Party document *Chung-fa* (1980) no. 75, September 27, 1980; facsimile in *CKYC* 15:3 (March 1981), pp. 111–118, here, pp. 1f. of the document.

66. Ibid., p. 6. For a very informative treatment of the new rural structures, see David Zweig, "Opposition to Change in Rural China: The System of Responsibility and People's Communes," *Asian Survey* 23:7 (July 1983), pp. 879–900.

67. Ssuch'uan PBS, March 8, 1981.

68. Kansu PBS, September 20, 1981.

69. See an article by Lin Cheng and Ch'en Wu-yüan in *Ching-chi kuan-li* [Economic management] no. 4 (April 1981), pp. 37–41.

70. NCNA, Chengchou, August 25, 1981.

71. Ch'inghai PBS, January 4, 1983, and Fukien PBS, January 27, 1983, respectively.

72. *1982 Almanac*, part 8, p. 9. This is also the source for the following figures for brigades and production teams.

73. Ibid., p. 61.

74. Ibid., pp. 29f.

75. Computed from ibid., p. 13, on the basis of 97 million hectares of arable land.

76. Computed from NCNA, Peking, May 8, 1983.

77. Computed from *1982 Almanac*, part 8, pp. 28f.

78. Computed from ibid., p. 61.

79. *JMJP*, December 13, 1982.

80. Computed from *TKP*, Hongkong, January 15, 1981.

81. World Bank, ed., *China: Socialist Economic Development Report*, no. 3391, CNA, June 1, 1981, p. 64, and *Economist* (London), June 20, 1981, pp. 34f., as quoted by Vetter, *China's neue Wirklichkeit*, p. 127.

82. William L. Parish, "Egalitarianism in Chinese Society," *Problems of Communism* (Washington, D.C.) 30:1 (January/February 1981), p. 41. The Gini coefficient is a measurement for the income distribution in a given society. Theoretically, a coefficient of 0 means total equality, and a coefficient of 1, total inequality. In reality, coefficients vary from 0.19 (most equal) to 0.63 (most unequal).

83. Vetter, *China's neue Wirklichkeit*, p. 126.

84. NCNA, Peking, December 30, 1980.

85. *JMJP*, August 5, 1980.

86. Computed from *1982 Almanac*, part 8, pp. 6f.

87. United States, Directorate of Intelligence, ed., *Handbook of Economic Statistics, 1983* (Washington, D.C.: National Foreign Assessment Center, 1983), table 29 on p. 51.

88. *CNA* no. 1229 (March 26, 1982).

89. *JMJP*, October 12, 1978.

90. *CFJP*, October 24, 1980.

91. Teng Li-ch'ün in *KJJP*, March 27, 1981.

92. See Vetter, *China's neue Wirklichkeit*, pp. 111–117.

93. The first official reports known to me were broadcast on Fukien PBS, January 4, and Ssuch'uan PBS, January 5, 1981.

94. Among others, Honan PBS, June 8, 1978; Anhui PBS, June 10, 1978; and Hopei PBS, November 11, 1978.

95. Statement by a Shanghai city government official to me on September 12, 1980.

96. *KJJP,* January 14, 1982.

97. *KJJP,* March 7, 1983.

98. *T'ung-chi kung-tso* [Statistical work], Peking (November 1981), pp. 12–13, *1982 Almanac,* part 8, pp. 6–7.

99. First mentioned by Kiangsi PBS, January 19, 1980, and since then, continuously until the present.

100. First mentioned by Kiangsi PBS, June 26, 1980.

101. Fukien PBS, January 10, 1983.

102. For a detailed and succinct report on the birth control campaign in a rural area of Kuangtung, see Steven W. Mosher, *Broken Earth: The Rural Chinese* (New York: Free Press, 1983), pp. 224–261.

103. Ibid., pp. 254f.

104. Liaoning PBS, May 3; Hunan PBS, May 5; Hupei PBS, May 10; Ssuch'uan PBS, May 22; Kirin PBS, June 25; Anhui PBS, June 25; and Kansu PBS, July 2, 1983, respectively.

105. *Chung-hua jen-min kung-he-kuo ti-liu-chieh jen-min tai-piao ta-hui ti-i-tz'u hui-yi wen-chien* [Documents of the first session of the Sixth NPC of the PRC] (Hongkong: San Lien Bookstore, 1983), p. 94.

106. For a very thorough discussion of the problems of youth in the PRC, see Thomas B. Gold, "China's Youth: Problems and Programs," in Chang Ching-yü, ed., *The Emerging Teng System: Orientation, Policies, and Implications* (T'aipei: Institute of International Relations, 1983), part IV-2, pp. 1–24.

107. Ssuch'uan PBS, March 2, 1980.

108. *JMJP,* March 19, 1981.

109. See Chapter 10.

110. See, e.g., Zweig, "Opposition to Change," pp. 887f. and 889f.

111. See Chapter 4.

NOTES TO CONCLUSION

1. Graham T. Allison, *Essence of Decision: Explaining the Cuban Missile Crisis* (Boston: Little, Brown & Co., 1971).

Suggested Further Reading

Chapter 1

Shabad, Theodore. *China's Changing Map: National and Regional Development, 1949–1971*. 2d ed. New York: Praeger, 1972.

Chapter 2

Bianco, Lucien. *Origins of the Chinese Revolution*. Stanford: Stanford University Press, 1971.

Chang Chung-li. *The Chinese Gentry: Studies on Their Role in Nineteenth-Century China*. Seattle and London: University of Washington Press, 1955.

Eberhard, Wolfram. *A History of China*. 4th rev. ed. Berkeley: University of California Press, 1967.

Fairbank, John K., ed. *The Chinese World Order: Traditional China's Foreign Relations*. Cambridge, Mass.: Harvard University Press, 1968.

Latourette, Kenneth S. *The Chinese: Their History and Culture*. 2d rev. ed. New York: Columbia University Press, 1943.

Levenson, Joseph R. *Confucian China and Its Modern Fate*. 2 vols. Berkeley: University of California Press, 1965.

Mote, Frederick W. *Intellectual Foundations of China*. T'aipei: Rainbow Bridge Book Company, 1971.

Thornton, Richard C. *China: A Political History, 1917–1980*. Boulder, Colo.: Westview Press, 1982.

Williams, S. Wells. *The Middle Kingdom*. 2 vols. New York: Charles Scribner's Sons, 1883.

Chapter 3

Baum, Richard, ed. *China's Four Modernizations: The New Tehcnological Revolution*. Boulder, Colo.: Westview Press, 1980.

Chen Nai-Ruenn. *China's Economic Revolution*. Cambridge, Mass.: Harvard University Press, 1977.

Chen Nai-Ruenn, and Galenson, Walter. *The Chinese Economy Under Communism.* Edinburgh: University of Edinburgh Press, 1969.
Eckstein, Alexander. *Communist China's Economic Growth and Foreign Trade— Implications for U.S. Policy.* New York: Praeger, 1966.
Field, Robert M.; Lardy, Nicholas R.; and Emerson, John P. "Industrial Output by Province in China, 1949–73." *China Quarterly* 63 (July-September 1975), pp. 409–434.
Howe, Christopher. *Employment and Economic Growth in Urban China, 1949– 1957.* Cambridge: Cambridge University Press, 1971.
Kraus, Willy. *Economic Development and Social Change in the People's Republic of China.* New York: Springer, 1982.
Prybyla, Jan S. *The Chinese Economy.* New York: Columbia University Press, 1978.
Wu, Yuan-li. *The Economy of Communist China.* New York: Praeger, 1965.

Chapter 4

Domes, Jürgen. *Socialism in the Chinese Countryside: Rural Societal Policies in the PRC, 1949–1979.* London: C. Hurst and Company, 1980.
Eberhard, Wolfram. *Social Mobility in Traditional China.* Leiden: Brill, 1962.
Lewis, John, ed. *The City in Communist China.* Stanford: Stanford University Press, 1971.
Parish, William L., and Whyte, Martin King. *Village and Family in Contemporary China.* Chicago and London: Chicago University Press, 1978.
Perkins, D. H. *Agricultural Development in China, 1368–1968.* Edinburgh: University of Edinburgh Press, 1969.
Scalapino, Robert A., ed. *Elites in the People's Republic of China.* Seattle: University of Washington Press, 1972.
Schram, Stuart R. *Authority, Participation, and Cultural Change in China.* Cambridge: Cambridge University Press, 1973.

Chapter 5

Barnett, Doak A. *Cadres, Bureaucracy, and Political Power in Communist China.* New York: Columbia University Press, 1967.
Domes, Jürgen. *China After the Cultural Revolution: Politics Between Two Party Congresses.* London: C. Hurst and Company, 1976.
——. *The Internal Politics of China, 1949–1972.* London: C. Hurst and Company, 1973.
Guillermaz, Jacques. *The Chinese Communist Party in Power, 1949–1976.* Boulder, Colo.: Westview Press, 1976.
——. *A History of the Chinese Communist Party, 1921–1949.* London: Methuen; New York: Random House, 1972.
Harrison, James P. *The Long March to Power.* New York: Praeger, 1972.
Lewis, John W., ed. *Party Leadership and Revolutionary Power in China.* Ithaca, N.Y.: Cornell University Press, 1970.

Pye, Lucian W. *The Dynamics of Chinese Politics*. Cambridge, Mass.: Oelgeschlager, Gunn and Hain, 1981.

──────. *The Spirit of Chinese Politics*. Cambridge, Mass.: M.I.T. Press, 1968.

Schwartz, Benjamin I. *Chinese Communism and the Rise of Mao*. Cambridge, Mass.: Harvard University Press, 1958.

Solomon, Richard H. *Mao's Revolution and the Chinese Political Culture*. Berkeley: University of California Press, 1971.

Chapter 6

Barnett, Doak A., ed. *Chinese Communist Politics in Action*. Seattle and London: University of Washington Press, 1969.

Johnson, Chalmers, ed. *Ideology and Politics in Contemporary China*. Seattle: University of Washington Press, 1974.

Lindbeck, J., ed. *China: Management of a Revolutionary Society*. Seattle: University of Washington Press, 1971.

Saich, Tony. *Politics and Government in the People's Republic of China*. London and Basingstoke: Macmillan, 1981.

Schurmann, Franz. *Ideology and Organization in Communist China*. 3d rev. ed. Berkeley: University of California Press, 1981.

Tang, Peter S.H., and Maloney, Joan. *Communist China: The Domestic Scene, 1949–1967*. South Orange, N.J.: Seton Hall University Press, 1967.

Tung, William L. *The Political Institutions of Modern China*. The Hague: Brill, 1964.

Waller, Derek J. *The Government and Politics of the People's Republic of China*. 3d ed. New York: New York University Press, 1982.

Chapter 7

Gittings, John. *The Role of the Chinese Army*. London: Oxford University Press, 1967.

Griffith, Samuel B. *The Chinese People's Liberation Army*. New York: Praeger, 1968.

Huck, Arthur. *The Security of China*. New York and London: Columbia University Press, 1970.

Joffe, Ellis. *Party and Army: Professionalism and Political Control in the Chinese Officer Corps, 1949–1964*. Cambridge, Mass.: Harvard University Press, 1965.

Rhoads, Edward J.M. *The Chinese Red Army, 1927–1963: Annotated Bibliography*. Cambridge, Mass.: Harvard University Press, 1964.

Robinson, Thomas W. "Chinese Military Modernization in the 1980's." *China Quarterly* 90 (April-June 1982), pp. 231–250.

Whitson, William W., and Huang, Chen-hsia. *The Chinese High Command: A History of Communist Military Politics, 1927–1971*. New York: Praeger, 1973.

Chapters 8–11

Barnett, Doak A. *Uncertain Passage.* Washington, D.C.: Brookings Institution, 1974.

Chang Ching-yü, ed. *The Emerging Teng System: Orientation, Policies, and Implications.* T'aipei: Institute of International Relations, 1983.

Ching, Frank. "The Current Political Scene in China." *China Quarterly* 80 (October-December 1979), pp. 691–715.

Domes, Jürgen. "The 'Gang of Four' and Hua Kuo-feng: Analysis of Political Events in 1975–76." *China Quarterly* 71 (September 1977), pp. 473–497.

Fraser, John. *The Chinese: Portrait of a People.* New York: Summit Books, 1980.

Friedman, Edward. "The Politics of Local Models: Social Transformation and State Power Struggles in the People's Republic of China: Tachai and Teng Hsiao-p'ing." *China Quarterly* 76 (October-December 1978), pp. 873–890.

Gardner, John. *Chinese Politics and the Succession to Mao.* London and Basingstoke: Macmillan, 1982.

Goodman, David S.G. *Beijing Street Voices: The Poetry and Politics of China's Democracy Movement.* London: Marion Boyars, 1981.

Onate, Andres D. "Hua Kuo-feng and the Arrest of the 'Gang of Four.'" *China Quarterly* 75 (July-September 1978), pp. 540–565.

Seymour, James D., ed. *The Fifth Modernization: China's Human Rights Movement, 1978–1979.* Stanfordville, N.Y.: Coleman, 1980.

Chapter 12

Cheng, Chu-yuan. *China's Economic Development: Growth and Structural Change.* Boulder, Colo.: Westview Press, 1982.

Ishikawa, Shigeru. "China's Economic Growth Since 1949—An Assessment." *China Quarterly* 94 (June 1983), pp. 242–281.

Kraus, Willy. *Economic Development and Social Change in the People's Republic of China.* New York: Springer, 1982.

Liu, Cyril C. "The Reinstatement of Economics in China Today." *China Quarterly* 85 (March 1981), pp. 1–48.

Nickum, James E., and Schatz, David C. "Living Standards and Economic Development in Shanghai and Taiwan." *China Quarterly* 77 (January-March 1979), pp. 25–49.

Prybyla, Jan S. *The Chinese Economy.* New York: Columbia University Press, 1978.

Chapter 13

Bernstein, Richard. *From the Center of the Earth: The Search for the Truth About China.* Boston: Little, Brown, 1982.

Bonavia, David. *The Chinese.* New York: Lippincott and Crowell, 1980.

Butterfield, Fox. *China: Alive in the Bitter Sea.* New York: Times Books, 1982.

Frazer, John. *The Chinese: Portrait of a People.* New York: Summit Books, 1980.

Mosher, Stephen W. *Broken Earth: The Rural Chinese.* New York: Free Press, 1983.

Chapter 14

Hsüeh Chun-tu, ed. *China's Foreign Relations: New Perspectives.* New York: Praeger, 1982.

Pollack, Jonathan D. "Chinese Global Strategy and Soviet Power." *Problems of Communism* (January-February 1982), pp. 54–69.

Yahuda, Michael. *China's Role in World Affairs.* London: Croom Helm, 1978.

Yin Ch'ing-yao. "Peiping's Foreign Policy After the 12th CCP National Congress: Its Continuity and Changes." *Issues and Studies* 19:1 (January 1983), pp. 31–51.

Other Titles of Interest from Westview Press

†*China and the World: Chinese Foreign Policy in the Post-Mao Era,* edited by Samuel S. Kim

Perspectives on Development in the PRC, edited by King-yuh Chang

The Chinese Mosaic: The Peoples and Provinces of China, Leo J. Moser

Aging in Post-Mao China: The Politics of Veneration, Ada Elizabeth Sher

Three Visions of Chinese Socialism, edited by Dorothy J. Solinger

China: The 80s Era, edited by Norton Ginsburg and Bernard A. Lalor

The Making of a Premier: Zhao Ziyang's Provincial Career, David L. Shambaugh

†*China's Cultural Heritage: The Ch'ing Dynasty, 1644–1912,* Richard J. Smith

China as a Maritime Power, David G. Muller, Jr.

The Chinese Defense Establishment: Continuity and Change in the 1980s, edited by Paul H.B. Godwin

The China Quandary: Domestic Determinants of U.S. China Policy, 1972–1982, Robert G. Sutter

The Limits of Reform in China, edited by Ronald A. Morse

†*China Briefing, 1982,* editied by Richard C. Bush

†*China in World Affairs: The Foreign Policy of the PRC Since 1970,* G. W. Choudhury

†*Huadong: The Story of a Chinese People's Commune,* Gordon Bennett

†Available in hardcover and paperback.

About the Book and Author

The Government and Politics of the PRC:
A Time of Transition
Jürgen Domes

Since 1975, the People's Republic of China has experienced crises in political succession, as well as major economic and social realignments. This book provides an introduction to the government and politics of the PRC with special emphasis on the impact of the events since 1975.

After a brief description of the basic geographic, economic, social, and historical conditions that influence political decision making in China, Dr. Domes discusses in detail the political developments of the post-Mao era. He thoroughly explores the period in which Hua Kuo-feng led the Party—an era of transition, dominated by the emerging conflict between Hua's traditionalist forces and a revisionist coalition headed by Teng Hsiao-p'ing—then explains Teng's victory and Hua's forced resignation (in 1981) from Party leadership.

Emphasizing the close and complex interrelationships among social, economic, and political factors, Dr. Domes assesses the fate of the Chinese economy since 1957 and the changes that are occurring now in Chinese society. He examines, for example, the heyday of the deficit spenders, "the Great Leap Westward," unemployment, crime, new structures in the communes, and the response of youth to current issues. He then develops alternative projections for the future of the political system in the People's Republic of China.

In the final section of the book, China's experiences from 1975 through 1983 are put into a comparative context. Dr. Domes presents a typology of transition in single-party systems, concluding that the transition from charismatic to institutionalized rule has not yet been accomplished in China and that the future of the political system, in the long term, remains uncertain. Despite the difficulty of forecasting, however, certain trends appear most likely to shape China's future. For China watchers, Dr. Domes's predictions are on the "must read" list.

Jürgen Domes is professor and chairman of the Political Science Section and director of the Research Unit on Chinese and East Asian Politics at the Saar University in Saarbrucken, West Germany. He is also a member of the editorial board of *Asian Survey* and convener of the Standing Group on China and East Asia of the European Consortium for Political Research.

Index